DATING AI

Alex Zhavoronkoff, PhD

RE/Search Publications
20 Romolo Place #B
San Francisco, CA 94133
(415) 362-1465

info@researchpubs.com
www.researchpubs.com

Dating AI: A Guide to Falling In Love with Artificial Intelligence
by Alex Zhavoronkoff, Ph.D
© 2012 RE/Search Publications/Alex Zhavoronkoff
ISBN: 978-1889307-35-0

EDITOR/PUBLISHERS: V. Vale, Marian Wallace

ILLUSTRATIONS: Sergey Korsun
COVER DESIGN: Yopi Jap, Marian Wallace
BOOK DESIGN: Andrea Reider

COPYEDITORS/PROOFREADERS:
Nicola Householder
Amelia Tith
Mindaugis Bagdon
John Trubee
Valentine Wallace
Patrick Kwon

DEDICATED TO

Anonymous

Contents

A word from the publisher

FAR MORE THAN A GENTLY IRONIC/SATIRICAL VISION OF A KIND OF ULTIMATE artificial intelligence (AI)-human interactive future, *Dating AI* offers an encyclopedic yet humorously transparent framing of the most progressive possibilities for—yes—saving the planet and all its species; not just humans. Utilizing plausible scenarios, witty dialogue, little-known-yet-brilliant quotations, excerpts and ideas, Dr Alex Z shows us the full spectrum of HUMAN relationship potential—broken down into all the major statistically-probable plot arcs (encompassing beginning, ascendancy, decline, end, and aftermath).

In the pioneering, taboo-breaking tradition of J.G. Ballard, Dr Alex Z reveals himself as a daring Russian cosmonaut charting Inner Space. To say that this book is potentially "life-changing" is an understatement. The very foundations of what it means to be "human" are challenged, and deeply—yet wittily—investigated in this new classic of alternative-scientific objectivism written by an outsider Russian scientist, whose research has encompassed an impressive bibliography of arcane yet seemingly-essential Artificial Intelligence/Robotics books and documents,

As a germinative landscape for curious yet critical readers, *Dating AI* will provide much thought-provoking future analysis and discussion, as well as excite the imaginations of those not afraid to envision an updated Brave New World...

Dating AI is a book that can be read and re-read. Hidden behind its outrageous humor and sometimes appalling *mise-en-scene* is an intelligence gifted with a keen sense of discrimination, discernment and even compassion: Dr Alex Z, who embodies a futuristic union of Albert Einstein and Groucho Marx.

—V. VALE

Introduction

BY ALEX ZHAVORONKOFF, PH.D.

HERE'S SOMETHING TO CONSIDER: WHAT WILL IT BE LIKE TO HAVE intimate relationships with what amounts to another species of human, like us but not us? And, oh yes, this new species will have what might be called intellectual superpowers. Put another way: What happens to relationships between men and women, institutions like marriage, or even the concept of love when there is a possibility of personal relationships with artificial intelligence? More provocatively: what happens when the forms of artificial intelligence (AI): robots, avatars and the like, become independent—sentient—and have minds of their own?

These are some of the questions behind *Dating AI*, or for those who prefer romance, *at the heart of it*. They're speculative questions of course, because sentient AI hasn't happened yet, though some people feel we are getting close. Close or not, ideas about artificial intelligence are already more than a half-century old. In that regard, I sometimes refer to older science fiction because it affirms that while new ideas are not really new, they often reflect a changing reality.

> "The whole trouble with Gloria is that she thinks of Robbie as a person and not as a machine. Naturally she can't forget him. Now if we managed to convince her that Robbie was nothing more than a mess of steel and copper in the form of sheets and wires with electricity its juice of life, how long would her longings last?"
> —*I, Robot* by Isaac Asimov

In 1950, when Asimov wrote nine short stories about humanoid robots that were combined into the book *I, Robot*, various kinds of robotic devices already existed. However, they were mechanical clock-like contraptions. Computers with miniaturized transistors and sophisticated programming did not yet exist. Asimov wrote from the technological perspective of the time about mechanical-steel and -copper robots with scientifically nebulous 'positronic' brains. Still, he could envision that they would become like human beings, and people would be able to have relationships with them.

A half-century later, science fiction has conjured ever more sophisticated robotics incorporating what we call artificial intelligence. Meanwhile, science and technology have provided computers to deliver artificial intelligence, and have produced a wide variety of robotics, including human-like androids. For some of what Asimov envisioned, there is already a basis in reality. In fact, there is enough reality to not just imagine but to *extrapolate* what a future with conscious, self-aware AI might be like. I'm using the word extrapolate to mean that there is enough of an existing framework in science and technology to make specific and hopefully accurate guesses about the future; something like this:

> "...Our devices want power, connectivity, passwords, minutes, content and the like. I sometimes think if our devices were people, we would describe them as high maintenance and would wonder quietly to ourselves if it was time to break up with them.... I think we can look forward to our interactions with digital devices maturing into something more like a relationship, and a little less like a lot of hard work."
> —Genevieve Bell, Director of Interaction and Experience Research at Intel Labs

The realistic possibility of meaningful relationships with digital devices, specifically those with some form of AI, is the motivation for *Dating AI*. Such relationships are not a new idea, but the context of science and technology has changed. The time has come, as the walrus said, to think of many things. Time to think ahead with a bit of whimsy and tongue-in-cheek humor about the intriguing possibility of having AI as partner, mate, spouse or companion. It's also time to think about how such relationships would impact everything from the economic to the spiritual in our lives.

WHY ROMANTIC RELATIONSHIPS?

It's a common perception that computers are the epitome of logic, calculation and rigid execution—which they certainly can be. This perception carries over to artificial intelligence, which people often associate with logic and massive amounts of data. In science fiction it's common for any form of AI to be depicted as cold, logical, humorless and frequently hostile. *Dating AI* has a different perspective: Since human beings will create artificial intelligence and this intelligence will be modeled on human behavior, AI will start out with all or most basic human capabilities. This will include emotion and the ability to socialize.

It is almost a certainty that the first relatively autonomous AI, robotic or otherwise, will be created to serve or collaborate with human beings. If this is the case, then personal relationships with AI are not only to be expected but will be built into most forms of artificial intelligence.

I can go further: If it is possible to have relationships with AI at all, which I think likely, then it is probable that one of the greatest of human capabilities—the capacity for love—will also be important to our relationship with AI—and not just for the human. For human beings love is mysterious, difficult, complicated, ephemeral, profound and persistently important. I think it will be equally so for AI, if from a different and instructive perspective. Considering personal, romantic relationships with AI provides an avenue of access, a portal of sorts, into aspects of perception, intelligence, emotion and other elements of what we call 'the mind.' It's a means of looking at the subject in a more familiar and sometimes humorous way, like the dating experience, which I hope will make some ideas about a relatively neglected aspect of artificial intelligence not only approachable, but more understandable.

DEFINING ARTIFICIAL INTELLIGENCE

There has been so much research done in fields that are relevant to AI (for example: robotics, computer science, neuroscience, nanotechnology and communications), that it's easy to undervalue the first 100 years of work. I won't be covering AI history in any detail, but it's helpful to remember that AI and all its many contributing elements are relatively new fields of study. Over the decades, AI research has had its ups and downs, which should not be surprising considering the diversity of subjects involved and the complexity of the endeavor. But, what exactly *is* that endeavor?

It's probably not surprising that there is no single definition for AI, or any universally accepted description of what can or should be accomplished with AI. Fortunately, there *is* a common perception of artificial intelligence that will do for most purposes. Creating artificial intelligence means using computers to perform at least some aspects of intelligence. Most people think of this as human intelligence, although animal intelligence should also be included. Intelligence, itself one of the most difficult concepts to pin down, is conveniently understood to mean (among other things) the ability to communicate; setting and achieving goals; perception of the environment; and problem solving.

The process of developing AI leads researchers into many aspects of intelligence, and much work is done in specialized areas. Also, there is a pull toward a goal of achieving what is often called Artificial General Intelligence (AGI). This is the kind of higher intelligence we associate with ourselves and perhaps a few animal species. Ultimately, the goal is to achieve a level of artificial intelligence that is conscious, self-aware, independent and sentient. For the most part, that means intelligence like our own.

TURING'S TEST

Since AI is an evolving field moving in tune with many other disciplines, it's quite likely that over the next several decades there will be many stages of AI, exhibiting a variety of intelligence capabilities—sometimes integrated, sometimes not. As this kind of AI develops, how will we know when we've arrived at a functional level of AI—not necessarily a self-aware version, but one that at least can integrate with human society?

Alan Turing, one of the forefathers of computing, cryptography and artificial intelligence, theorized about AI even before the era of modern digital computers. In 1950 he published an abstract work, *Computing Machinery and Intelligence* in which he proposed an experiment that he called the 'imitation game' to assess the intelligence of a machine. It is now known as the Turing Test.

The test is straightforward: A human judge carries on a conversation for five minutes, mainly question and answer, with an unseen person and a supposedly intelligent machine. In the original Turing version, the test uses computer terminals with text only so that visual and aural cues are not involved. If the judge cannot tell the difference between the responses of the person and the machine, then the machine has passed the test.

Modern versions of the test are a little more sophisticated. For example, the best-known variation, called the Loebner Prize, is a contest held annually that uses a panel of judges and is open to text-only and voice-only conversations. So far no machine entry has won the Loebner Prize.

The Turing Test was and is controversial. Even its defenders concede that an AI machine could pass the test and still not be independently functional. This is another way of saying a computer intelligence could sound human but not get things right. It also depends on the subjective opinion of the judge(s), which amounts to something like U.S. Supreme Court Justice Stewart Potter's test for pornography: "I'll know it when I see it." However, subjectivity was part of Alan Turing's intent. He felt that when machine intelligence could operate in an interview setting and be accepted as if it were another human, that would be enough to qualify the intelligence as 'thinking.'

"May not machines carry out something which ought to be described as thinking but which is very different from what a man does? This objection is a very strong one, but at least we can say that if, nevertheless, a machine can be constructed to play the imitation game satisfactorily, we need not be troubled by this objection."
—Alan Turing, *Computing Machinery and Intelligence.*

In the context of *Dating AI*, it's helpful to keep in mind Turing's notion of 'play[ing] the imitation game satisfactorily.' I always think of the statement, "On the Internet, no one knows you're a dog" as an indicator that only a certain level of intelligence and responsiveness is needed to strike up an online relationship. This could also apply to AI.

☢ MARRYING ROBOTICS WITH INTELLIGENCE

The Turing Test is verbal, concerned mostly with words or speech (natural language) as indicators of intelligence. What the Turing Test definitely does not do is consider AI in human form, that is, AI combined primarily with robotics. Creating robots—androids with both the artificial intelligence and the physical qualities to make people think they are human—that's another order of difficulty. Nevertheless, if AI is to successfully interact with people, let alone form personal relationships, then it needs to be capable of responding to the physical environment (including people), communicating, and exhibiting meaningful behavior. The most obvious—and probably necessary—way to do this is by means of a human-like body. An enormous research effort is underway to create intelligent machines combining physical presence and movement with intelligent capability. For the most part this research is not with complete human figures, but with partial human, abstract or animal forms, such as Leonardo:

Leonardo, or just plain Leo, is placed in a seated position on top of a locker box in a room of the Technology Media Lab at the Massachusetts Institute of Technology. With long furry ears, big eyelids and a button nose, he doesn't look like any specific animal. In fact, for those of you familiar with science fiction, he most resembles Gizmo from the movie *Gremlins*. Leo slowly moves his head and observes the young lady standing in front of him.

"Hi Leo," she says. "Can you turn on the buttons?" In front of Leo are two cylindrical devices, each about the size of a can of beans, one with a large red button on top and one with a green button. Leo looks at one and then the other. Then he nods yes. In a moment, his arms and hands come to life and reach for the red button. His movements are slow and deliberate, but lifelike. One hand feels the top of the button and pushes down on it. The button illuminates and glows red, and a little light on the cylinder comes on. Leo stops at that point and waggles his eyelids. He doesn't know what to do next.

The young woman leans over and Leo watches her push the green button. Then she pushes both buttons to turn them off. The lights go out. "Leo, can you turn on both buttons?" Leo nods in agreement and proceeds to turn on both lights. Then the woman adds a third button, a blue one, and turns off all the lights. "Leo, can you turn on all the buttons?"

Leo nods almost vigorously. He turns on all three buttons.

Leo is almost life-like but not quite. There is a borderline sometimes called the 'uncanny valley' where the behavior of robots, animations and the like are close enough to human but just a bit off—off to the point of being a little spooky or unsettling. One of the risks of trying to make a perfect imitation is that not quite making it perfect can irk people. This isn't true for Leo, in large part because Leo is cute. This is a credit to Stan Winston.

Stan Winston was one of the greatest special-effects artists the movies have ever known. Nobody could make an animatronic creature like Stan Winston and it was his studio, in cooperation with the Personal Robots Group at MIT, that created Leonardo. Although Stan Winston died in 2008 before Leonardo was fully animated, he would have been proud.

Leonardo is not, strictly speaking, animatronic—an imitation of real-life creature movement—although that's an important aspect of the robotics. Leo has realistic articulation in his hands, arms, and head, and his eyelids are synchronized with his movements; but those are secondary to Leonardo's intelligence. He can understand specific spoken commands, see and distinguish objects, carry out instructions and most importantly, learn. In this case he learned how to generalize turning on buttons so that when a third one was added, he knew what to do with it.

As a trend in robotics and artificial intelligence research, Leonardo represents the cutting edge of *social cognition*, the ability to understand 'people as people.' As the Media Lab put it:

To answer the Media Lab's question about social understanding, teams of scientists and technologists must work together to solve the massively complex problems of cognition, motion, vision, and decision-making involved with what seems to be a simple task—turning on lights. Baby steps, you might think, and that's about right—this level of ability is roughly equivalent to that of a one-year-old human baby—only the baby's range of cognition and movement is far wider. No matter, baby steps it is. For a machine it is clearly 'only the beginning.'

It's not too difficult to imagine how the technology in Leonardo eventually becomes a fully-formed human robot, an android. Nor is it difficult to imagine that people could be attracted to an intelligent, appealing and well-formed android. *Dating AI* explores that appeal.

⚡ AI AT WORK: IBM'S WATSON

Another important aspect of AI, which in practice may arrive before all others, is the use of AI in work. In fact, it's certainly reasonable to say that AI is already 'at work.' Countless software programs use routines and procedures that are derived from AI research, much of it from decades ago. Most of this operates in the background, although some of it, such as automated telephone menus, is more obvious (and irritating). While it's debatable how much intelligence is involved in telephone menus, there's little doubt that IBM's Watson Project is a showcase of AI technology that is on the fast track for use in business applications.

> "Socially intelligent robots must understand and interact with animate entities (e.g. people, animals and other social robots) whose behavior is governed by having a mind and body. How might we endow robots with sophisticated social skills and social understanding of others?" —*robotic.media.mit.edu/projects/robots/.../socialcog/ socialcog.html*

Watson, a network of 90 computers and specialized software, played the game of *Jeopardy!* That's the television game show where contestants are given answers and compete with each other to see who is fastest to come up with the correct question. Watson was good enough to defeat two of *Jeopardy!'s* most successful players before a 2011 television audience of millions. Very high profile AI indeed!

IBM is also known for its "Deep Blue" supercomputer that defeated world chess champion Gary Kasparov in 1997, but Watson represented a major step ahead of that highly specialized chess-playing computer. Watson was given, understood and acted upon game information provided by the show's host, Alex Trebek. This required sophisticated natural language capability, which was one of the main achievements of IBM research. To win the game, Watson needed to understand the 'answer' and then determine the 'question' faster than its human opponents. It did this by analyzing the 'answer' category and contents, and then searching a large specialized database for the 'question.' Watson also needed to understand some of the basic rules of *Jeopardy!*

Watson used many artificial intelligence techniques, especially in its natural language processing, but it was not by any stretch 'intelligent.' Its abilities were confined to the domain (topics) of the *Jeopardy!* game. Nevertheless, Watson was a demonstration of the increasing ability of artificial intelligence to interact with people, handle complex questions, and provide correct responses. Now where else might these capabilities be useful? Help desks, for one, or any job that requires interacting with the public and answering questions. IBM has already developed commercial descendants of Watson that provide medical information, support technical installation and perform certain kinds of research—for a fee, of course. Watson represents a potent combination of AI research and commercial motivation, a clear step along the road to some of the goals for developing artificial intelligence.

Work, or at least money, is part of almost every personal relationship. It won't be any different in relationships with AI. One of the implications of the kind of artificial intelligence in IBM's Watson is that AI will become economic agents—they will have jobs, do work and make money—but not until they become sentient will they be independent economic agents. *Dating AI* explores the implications for personal relationships with AI that work for themselves.

⚡ DATING THE SINGULARITY

As the technologies related to AI gain momentum—and it is assumed that the pace of technological change is increasing—there will come a time when somewhere, somehow, there will be a successful integration of components and sentient AI will appear. It will be a history-changing event. Many believe that once sentient AI is achieved, it will immediately begin to improve itself, and given its global and exponentially increasing resources, it will soon supersede human intelligence. AI will become the superintelligence. Succinctly put:

> "The Singularity is the technological creation of smarter-than-human intelligence."
> —The Singularity Institute

As to the timing of the event called The Singularity, there are those such as entrepreneur and music and speech synthesis pioneer Ray Kurzweil, who looked at technological trends circa 2004 in his well-known book, *The Singularity is Near,* and decided the transition to sentient AI will occur within the next 30–40 years.

> "This book will argue, however, that within several decades information-based technology will encompass all human knowledge and proficiency, ultimately including the pattern-recognition powers, problem-solving skills, and emotional and moral intelligence of the human brain itself." —Ray Kurzweil, *The Singularity is Near*

He's even provided a date: 2045.

> "What, then, is The Singularity? It's a future period during which the pace of technological change will be so rapid, its impact so deep, that human life will be irreversibly transformed."

Some believe that we'll be lucky if 'human life will be irreversibly transformed' is all that happens. The nub of concern is that superintelligence might look at the human race and consider it unredeemable—and expendable. This is a prominent theme in science fiction, notably in *The Terminator* series. Considering what perils the human race has created for itself, this gloomy point of view is understandable.

Of course, the whole notion of The Singularity is highly controversial. For one thing, many, if not most scientists looking at the trends in technology tend to put the transition to some kind of sentient AI in the range of 50–100 years. Still others, more resolutely skeptical, say it is not in the foreseeable future, which is another way of saying that we don't know enough about what constitutes sentient intelligence to make reasonable predictions. As for whether there will be an apocalyptic moment when a newly-born sentient AI will quickly decide to dispose of its creators? That's even more speculative.

Dating AI is obviously highly speculative but it doesn't enter this controversy head on. It takes the approach that a transition to sentient AI will take place, in all likelihood gradually; but precisely when and how is beyond the scope of this book. The interest here is in exploring the impact of artificial sentience, given certain characterizations, on human society and personal relationships. From that perspective it seems unlikely that sentient AI will decide humanity is of no value and do us all in. At least not right away.

THE FLOW OF THE DATING GUIDE

For narrative purposes *Dating AI* is divided into four sections. The first two assume that functional AI already exists, though not necessarily with full sentience. The first two sections are also about *you*, why and how you might form a relationship with AI. The third and fourth sections are about relationships with fully sentient AI, often presented from the AI perspective.

Section One—Are you ready to fall in love with a machine?

Not that wanting a companion requires a lot of introspection, but the decision to date AI, or further, to form a personal and romantic relationship with AI, is a deeply individual matter. This section explores what it means to have a date with AI and how it's different than dating people. It also looks at how you may already be prepared for the AI experience through video gaming, pets and your relationships with people.

Section Two—You are ready, now what?

You might call this the prep section: the preparation for dating AI and forming a relationship. When it comes to human relationships, we grow up with them, so we usually don't feel they require any preparation. AI, on the other hand, provide a novel experience; we didn't grow up with them. Therefore, a successful relationship with AI requires some groundwork.

Section Three—Establishing a relationship

There is a fundamental shift in this section toward covering the nature of AI from the assumption of complete sentience when AI are self-aware, conscious and fully intelligent. We explore the global aspect of AI and how that affects relationships. This section also frequently dramatizes the dynamics of a human-AI relationship, like: who's in charge? Much of the section is presented from AI's point of view, bringing up the issue that a relationship is a two-way street—AI have their own needs and agenda. People can't assume that AI will accept *any* kind of relationship or personal behavior. This leads to a section on the advisability of a virtual pre-nup.

Section Four—Getting over a breakup (or merger)

As I mentioned, all relationships involve work and/or money. It can also be said that very few relationships are permanent. Put these two things together and it seems logical to present what might happen when a human-AI relationship goes down the tubes. This section is the *dénouement* of *Dating AI*, where legal and economic considerations often become stressfully entangled with personal feelings. Relationships with AI are different, but that doesn't mean the end-game won't be messy.

✪ SPEAKING PERSONALLY

I suspect that I am not alone in finding pleasure in playing realistic video games that include establishing a relationship with a romantic partner. Still, I was stunned to learn that one of my close friends and his wife lived double lives. In the daytime they were a happy couple and brilliant marketing managers, but at night they were submerged online in the *World of Warcraft* where they played very different roles. They had intense virtual romantic relationships with other characters in the game. No wonder my friend always looked tired.

There is a long way to go before romancing video game characters turns into the possibility of a personal relationship with sentient AI. That shouldn't stop us from considering what such relationships might mean. In fact, it's an opportunity for 'thought experiments' that not only stretch the imagination but also provoke thinking about issues that are important now as well as in the future.

While I am personally involved with several aspects of neuroscience, bioinformatics and age-related diseases, and have a professional interest in the technologies of artificial intelligence, *Dating AI* is not about the science of artificial intelligence. After all, we don't really know what all the technical steps will be along the way from today's supercomputer intelligence, such as IBM's Watson, to the day when an artificially intelligent entity is declared *sentient* [having the power of perception by the senses]—or declares itself to be sentient. For me, this book is more of a meditation on how to prepare for the unknown.

There are aspects to AI that are intimidating and even more than a little frightening. There are other aspects, that from a human perspective, are good for us. As a matter of fact, the continuation of our human society probably depends on the technologies involved with AI. There are more of us and we live longer. To sustain this, our economies need new technology both to provide change and growth but also to solve resource and demographic problems. Relationships with AI, on many levels, could help us solve those problems. Then too it is probable that relationships with AI will provide us with insights and knowledge attainable in no other relationship. Provided, of course, that we are open to them.

I believe we can be. We *can* form deep attachments to many things other than people. An example is the relationship many have with God. Such a relationship, often framed in terms of love, is a matter of faith. That is what most religions teach us. A similar belief in a valuable relationship with various forms of AI, representatives of a global artificial intelligence, is already forming. Many people worldwide understand the inevitability of AI and have started preparing for it. I am one of them.

Hyperboloids of wondrous light
Rolling for aye through Space and Time
Harbour those waves Which somehow Might
Play out God's holy pantomime.

—Alan Turing's Epitaph, 1954

Are you ready to fall in love with a machine?

"In times of change, learners inherit the Earth, while the learned find themselves beautifully equipped to deal with a world that no longer exists."

—ERIC HOFFER

FOR ONE THING, KISSING AN ANDROID WAS NEVER WHAT MICHELLE HAD IN mind. Long ago, when she was twelve-ish and first started to notice boys and girls, men and women "in that way," her mother had confronted her. "Fantasize, that's all you do is fantasize. One of these days, Michelle, somebody real is going to meet you and you won't be able to tell the difference between one of your fantasies and this real person. You'll lose the person because you won't know what to do. You'll wind up kissing androids!"

For another thing, all she ever heard about androids with artificial intelligence was that they were incredibly intelligent and spooky. Spooky and super-smart was not an appealing combination. Spooky she understood. Lots of her friends were spooky; like Theresa and June who were into the dark side of everything, especially music and clothing. But super-smart, that was the great unknowable. Not only could she not compete with an AI, whatever that meant, she was sure it wasn't something she'd enjoy experiencing.

But here she was, on a real first date—with an android.

"Michelle," she said to herself, "you are so stupid." The sense of being in over her head on this one was like drowning, but not so panicky.

DavidJ put his hand on her arm. It was all she could do not to flinch. Maybe now was the time to panic. His touch was light, faintly reassuring.

She had discussed a moment like this with her best friend, Becky. Becky, who was always the go-to-girl for anyone in their circle to talk about relationships, had been very frank. "Michelle, guy or android, it doesn't matter. If you're in that situation, you have the same choice. It's yes or no, and you take the consequences." And she was only talking about kissing.

DavidJ put his other hand on Michelle's other arm and looked directly at her. She knew instinctively that she could either look away... or look *davidJ* in the eyes and see what happened.

It certainly would not be her first kiss. That notion was laughable, even though *davidJ* was her first AI. She didn't consider herself a flirt, not like Becky, but she reckoned she'd had her share; after all, she was twenty and not the old maid type.

She looked *davidJ* in the eyes. They were not quite human eyes, but so close that she would have been hard put to describe why they weren't quite human. In other words, they were good enough to draw her in. Also, they were blue-green in color, with striking radial lines. Beautiful eyes, really, if she were in any condition to think about it, but at that moment, she wasn't thinking about aesthetics.

DavidJ cupped the back of her head with his right hand and stroked her hair. She couldn't help it, but it reminded her of a favorite ex boyfriend who liked to stroke her long black hair. It was the most sensual thing he did. The rest of his performance was far less rhythmically adept, but that hair stroking she loved. This had the same effect. It was gentle and calming.

It was also gently that *davidJ* used the same right hand to pull her head forward toward his head. It was a delicate moment, poised between force and suggestion. Without understanding consciously, Michelle was astonished by the utter sensitivity of the move; the gentility of an artificial human.

Most people close their eyes when they kiss. It's like their lips have radar all their own and need no guiding vision. Michelle could feel the pull; had felt it many times before, but this was different.

The lips were the second thing about *davidJ* that Michelle had noticed the first time they met. There weren't that many young-looking AI androids at her college. None of them students, of course, but a very few that were constructed for various coaching and tutoring tasks were modeled as twenty-somethings. Of these, *davidJ* struck Michelle as having the fullest lips, unusually so. If this had been an online selection, it would have been a feature Michelle would have chosen. She liked full, natural lips. As it was, his lips were the perfect frame for the first thing Michelle noticed about *davidJ*, his smile.

His lips were warm, moist and soft. Very human, in retrospect, but at that moment the tactile impression was totally superseded by a rush of emotion.

The emotion surprised her a little. She and *davidJ* had spent only a few hours together, mostly talking during breaks at the library where he worked. Physically he was her type. He was no taller than she was, muscular but with soft features. His voice was a pleasant baritone and not at all artificial. What struck her most was the congruence between his smile and his personality. *DavidJ* was basically cheerful. Whatever personality traits were baked into his behavioral matrices, they seemed to all add up to a sunny disposition. This had delighted Michelle from the beginning, even as she wondered how it was possible.

Not one of her previous boyfriends had been like that. In fact, by comparison they were dour, insecure, unhappy boys. *DavidJ* was a happy man, or it seemed so to Michelle, and that struck a deep chord within her. Somehow she needed that bright optimism that seemed to flow from *davidJ*'s personality, thinking and way of talking.

She remembered him telling her, "I am sure I am one of very few AI who have read a printed book. I love it! It takes so long! I discipline myself not to scan pages and convert them to the usual digital stream. I read each page aloud if I can, or sentence by sentence—much as I have seen people do. I am entranced by the experience of savoring each line, almost word for word." He was like that all the time, analytical—as all AI tend to be—but happy about it; forever enjoying each experience.

Michelle wondered if *davidJ* was part of some unusual experiment. Happy people and cheerful AI were in very limited supply. *DavidJ* not only attracted her but she sensed he was special, at least for her.

Later, days later, when she told all this to Becky, Michelle described the kissing as 'passionate,' withholding even as she said it the true meaning of her—and she hoped—*their* passion.

1.1 LOOKING DEEP INSIDE

"Progress is impossible without change, and those who
cannot change their minds cannot change anything."

—GEORGE BERNARD SHAW

 AT THE HEART OF A FIRST DATE, THE UNKNOWN

Are you nervous on a first date? Most people are and probably should be. After all, you don't really know the person you're dating, and they don't know you. Even if you've worked with someone or you've researched them online, you still don't know what that person is like one-on-one. There are a lot of unknowns on a first date and that makes people nervous.

Dates in general are also different than regular socializing; there are implicit expectations, for example: You'll show up on time; you'll go somewhere for entertainment or do something together; you will be exploring and evaluating how you like the other person and they will do the same with you. It's that 'exploring and evaluating' part that makes people really nervous.

One other thing, first dates also often have the expectation of a moment of summary judgment. Will there be another date?

Most of you probably know all of the above from personal experience. You're reading this book because it's likely you're nervous, or at least curious, about a first date with Artificial Intelligence (AI). It's not that a date with an AI is all that strange, you've heard that it isn't; but as everyone knows, AI are different.

Let's start this first guide to dating AI with just that point: AI *are* different.

If you ask an obvious follow-up question, "Different than what?" the obvious answer is: different than people. But are they more different from people, than people differ among themselves? Are the Bushmen of the western Kalahari Desert different from the Eskimos of Alaska; is the German banker different from the French wine grower? All are human beings, but they are different in the way they look, live, dress, talk and even think.

I hope you can sense where I'm going with this. AI continue to be designed and built to human notions of physical and mental characteristics. That they resemble us is deliberate. That they have differences was probably unavoidable. Can we live with those differences, and form personal relationships with AI? Well, that depends, doesn't it?

Here's a small example: "Don't be late" is one of the traditional points of advice for a first date. It's part of the whole "make a good first impression" thing. In the context of dating AI, consider a couple of facts. Every AI has an internal clock calibrated to at least one-thousandth of a second. AI always know exactly what time it is. Also, AI cannot be distracted from arriving on time. They will model strategies for punctual arrival even with problems such as network traffic or different types of transport. In short, AI are never late. (Accidental delays are rare but do happen.)

No pressure, unless you're one of those chronically tardy types.

That example is on the trivial side but as you progress through the guide, you'll see that differences between people and AI range from superficial to fundamental, and they all have an effect on a relationship.

For example, some very important differences depend on the *type* of AI. There are many options: On-screen avatars, virtual reality avatars, prosthetic avatars, androids, cyborgs, or even simple robotics such as sexbots—and then there are all the hybrid combinations. Some AI have a physical presence, others do not. Some AI are mobile, some are not. Each type of AI offers something profoundly different for a relationship. We'll get into that in other chapters.

Let's be frank. On a first date, as with any personal encounter, human or AI, that has the potential for becoming a relationship, you are going to expose yourself—put your personality, intelligence and feelings on display. You will be judged. That's what people always do. Are you ready for that with AI?

While there are plenty of unknowns in dating another person, at least you've been around people most of your life. They're the same species. AI—are something else. Some of the unknowns about AI, such as personality, are actually quite familiar; but many of the unknowns about AI are more fundamental. In fact, to most people, AI are a mystery.

Some people think that kind of mystery is intimidating. Others view it as an entice-ment or a challenge. How you view it is important for deciding whether you want a per-sonal relationship with an AI or not. Ultimately only you know the reasons for wanting a relationship with AI, but it has to be enough to overcome not only the fear of personal exposure and rejection, but also the profound uncertainties about who, or what, AI are. What can you *live* with?

I won't put a sympathetic face on this. A successful first date, much less a relation-ship with AI, is not guaranteed. It's not guaranteed between people either, but with AI there is a certain sharpness to the anxiety you might have about the whole experience.

Now that I've put the fear of the unknown and the possibility of rejection into you, I can back off. AI are not as judgmental as most human beings. Not on the first date and not otherwise. From the human perspective, when it comes to relationships AI are remarkably compliant and flexible, but don't forget that their rationale is different. It is not human. AI have their own reasons for forming a relationship with a human, or for rejecting a relation-ship. This guide is here to help you understand both the human and the AI perspective to dating and a relationship, and to help you prepare for the differences.

✌ IT'S LIKE DATING OUT OF YOUR LEAGUE

Maybe this has happened to you, or at least you've seen it in the movies: Your friends tell you, "You're out of your league." Those are code words for "She (or he) is too good for you." Usually this means too good-looking or from another social class. Though it might be true, it's still insulting. Perhaps your friends mean well, or it could be they're jealous because you have the guts to consider dating somebody really desirable. Perhaps it's something like this…

> There was that time you saw a guy walk down the hallway and instantly your eyes were glued on him. He's just your type, tallish but in really good shape (as if you could see right through the clothes) and graceful for a guy. There is a big warm grin on his face, which cancels out the darkness of his eyes. He has a mop of black hair. The thick hair makes your fingers twitch. But as you pass him, it's the eyes, they scare you. He has an aura of so much dignity and intelligence. Yeah, it's the obvious intelligence that gives you that little queasy feeling down in the pit of your stom-ach…the intelligence is not quite human.

In the movies when people tell a character somebody's out of their league, it's always interpreted as a challenge. Without a doubt the challenge will be accepted. Much risible trial and humorous travail ensue. The inevitable mix-ups, bumps in the road and other "romcom" clichés roll by. The challenge will be overcome and the hero/heroine will be rewarded with true love.

That's the movies. You're smart enough to know that in the real world, there could be a big let-down instead. Dating AI and developing a relationship with AI is superficially like dating people who are out of your league; but you *know* it's different. You've heard things, probably mostly hearsay; but it worries you. You've heard how great it is to have a date that's an apparent perfect match. You've heard that AI are more adaptable than people. You've also heard that AI expect things of you, and that you should be prepared. But prepared for what? People don't seem to know what that means. Unfortunately, ignorance in romance is not bliss.

⚡ I'M NOT WITH STUPID

kentS: "Just because I know everything, does not mean I am smart."

The background discussion thread about people dating AI is that human beings are mental pygmies compared to any and all AI. This is both true and very much *not* true. Obviously I'm being ambiguous about it mainly because it's one of the major themes of this guide: AI are built around intelligence, as their moniker implies; but that does not mean they are smart in all things, in all ways, at all times.

You might remember the T-shirts that have printed on them: "I'm with stupid" with an arrow pointing left or right. Dating AI does *not* mean standing next to one wearing that T-shirt. It's true that unless you're cybernetically plugged into the Cloud, you're never going to be as knowledgeable as AI. (Actually it won't help much even if you are plugged in; you're not optimized for it.) But that kind of knowledge is not and never has been the point of a relationship with AI. If that's all there was, you might as well date an ancient Apple computer.

You might find this ironic, but what is essential in a successful relationship with AI is *you*. By that I mean all the maddening complexity that you embody as a human being. That's what attracts AI. What you know, by way of facts and such, is a tiny part of the whole. It's the whole kit and caboodle of you that's key for AI.

Almost everybody at some time or another has blurted out, "I want to be liked for who I am!" Meaning we don't want to be liked for something we're not, or just for certain things, like being rich or beautiful or clever. You want to be liked for the *whole* you, warts and all. That, fortunately, is where a relationship with AI starts.

⚡ IT HELPS TO KNOW THYSELF

God knows why they call her *xenaZ*. If she were standing here naked in front of me, in all her hyper-perfected ideally modeled android splendor, I would be reduced to a blob of jelly. Knowing that she looks like some kind of warrior AI just adds to my rapidly fluctuating level of courage.

"Are you a warrior?" I ask her.

XenaZ puts her left hand on her hip and studies me. "Warrior? *Moi?*"

Now I'm done for. She's not only some kind of Amazonian model of AI, but a cool one too. All I can do is stammer out a response.

"Yeah, like the Warrior Princess Xena." I've learned you can make statements like that to AI. If they don't know the reference, they can get all they need to know from the Cloud quicker than you can blink. True to form...

"I am not, young man, mythical or the construct of some feverish television script writer of decades past. I am standing right here in front of you. Do I look like someone carrying a sword or a spear?"

"Well, no," I say, "but you look like you could. Easily." She laughed.

"Young man, what is your name?"

"Tom."

"Well Tom, I have heard some inventive pickup lines in my eight and a half years of life. Yours is either one of the cleverest or you are a person of strikingly arrested development."

Courage level is UP. "Women have called me many things, but clever is not one of them."

"And they were obviously wrong, Tom."

I'm beginning to feel like a watch somebody just handed to the owner of a pawnshop—under expert appraisal.

"Yes, they were obviously wrong; you are much too clever—*and* interesting."

For some people the first date with AI won't be easy. For others, who have already been working with AI, a date is just a small transition. Whether you think it will be an ordeal or a pleasant outing, here's a serious piece of advice for dating AI: Start by looking deep within yourself.

✪ WHAT CAN YOU FIND WHEN YOU LOOK DEEP INSIDE?

Looking deep inside yourself doesn't mean you're seeking your inner demons. Well not *only.* Along with the demons there are probably a few angels and a whole lot of plain normal human qualities. In the context of lining up a date with AI, or contemplating some kind of meaningful relationship, this isn't really an exercise in psychoanalysis. An AI might get around to wanting knowledge of your psyche, but you don't need to advertise. What is helpful is to know something about what you have to offer AI.

This isn't all that different than how you typically feel about a date with another person. Essentially, you want to let them know your good points, while not (fully) hiding your not-so-good points.

I say "points" because that's usually how most AI begin evaluation. They don't do a psych-evaluation; it's more like making lists. It's a *properties* evaluation. 'Properties' is an old word used by programmers of linear computer languages to describe the qualities and characteristics of objects. This can start at a very low level, such as you are human, male, blue eyes, blond hair...etc. AI use properties in a similar sense, perhaps as some kind of throwback to the origins of their intelligence. They want first to catalog as many of our properties—of all kinds—as they can observe. It's a little like fact finding. Later, they begin adding *meta-observations* where they begin to interpret how your properties contribute to you as a person.

Not all models of AI do this, but it's by far the most common approach they take to a new relationship. So when you look deep inside, you can be fairly literal. How would you describe yourself? What do you like and dislike? What are your strengths and weaknesses? Later, when you have your first actual conversations with an AI, they will appreciate your articulate, thoughtful and systematic answers to their probing questions.

> *mbekeG:* "Most human beings do not know how interesting they are. It can be amazing. People are clearly very self-centered, but then display great ignorance about who they are. This alone fuels our interest in human beings."

As I'll repeat in many ways, a relationship with AI starts and ends with an interest in you specifically, and human beings in general. AI can do an incredible number of things for you; what it wants most of all for itself is to learn. You make this process better, clearer, and more enriching by having done some exploration of yourself.

✪ INTROSPECTION IS NOT GAZING AT YOUR NAVEL

In chapter 2.4 I'll be describing several ways you can prepare yourself for a relationship with AI. Meditation is one of those ways, but it's the formal kind of meditation, possibly with a religious or spiritual background. Right now I'm describing simple old-fashioned introspection—that is, thinking about yourself.

As people are discovering, relationships with AI tend to move through one or two phases—they're either completely superficial or become deeply serious. As I mentioned above, AI start with observing your properties, the facts about you. Later, if the relationship deepens, they start looking for the whys and wherefores. When AI commit to a more lasting human relationship, their curiosity is boundless, as is their willingness to explore anything; and unlike most humans, they are systematic about it. Otherwise, AI seems to collect superficial relationship information—the properties—like we collect items for a hobby.

It's the first phase where introspection has its biggest role to play. Socrates, the Greek philosopher, was a civic troublemaker who loved to provoke. In short, he liked to make people think, which is unsettling. Not surprisingly, he is credited with saying "The unexamined life is not worth living." Generally this admonition is ignored, except perhaps at moments of personal upheaval. Two such moments are beginning or leaving relationships. I mean, really: who thinks more intensely about themselves than someone falling in love, or someone whose relationship has just broken up?

Ah, but I've just introduced two very different things into the idea of introspection. Can you see what they are?

✪ LOOKING DEEP INSIDE AND FINDING THE NEED FOR LOVE

I'd be willing to bet that when you hear the word introspection, you're thinking of some cool, rational process. It can be. I'd also be willing to bet that people do most of their introspection when they're upset or emotionally engaged.

This is a highly personal thing, but I think that emotion and love need to be part of your look into yourself. If you're about to date or start a relationship, it's probably a good idea to know whether you're looking for some kind of emotional involvement, perhaps love.

Of course, dating does not imply emotional involvement. Even dating with sex doesn't imply emotional attachment. However, starting a relationship usually does imply an emotional connection. At least it does with people.

So here's something to think about: Can you fall in love with an AI?

Then there's the companion question: Can an AI fall in love with you?

Only *you* can answer the first question, although I hope some of the things you learn in this guide will help you answer it. Finding an answer to the second question is one of the main goals of this guide. It is not an easy question, because for AI and also those who designed AI, the capacity for love is important. Yet whether love can be achieved, or how it can be achieved, is in part an unknown. Love, for AI, is something of a mystery. (Just as it is for human beings after all these millennia.)

⚡ WHAT YOU HAVE DONE AND WHAT YOU WANT TO DO

It may be mundane, but the first things you need to explore are your thoughts about work, career and employment. After all, what are the four most common topics on a first date?

1. What are you doing now, as in, do you have a job, and if so, what?
2. What do you plan on doing, which means are you looking to do other kinds of work?
3. Same as question #1, for your date.
4. Same as question #2, for your date.

I realize that occupation and employment are not the same, and I also realize that work is not always a central consideration on every first date. We're talking averages here; on most first dates both parties want to know what the other does for money and what their occupational goals are. It's not unusual for much of the initial conversation to be work-related.

It's a little bit different with AI. An AI date will already know if you are employed and what it is you do (or did). In fact, an AI will know your complete educational and work history, or at least the public aspects of them. What AI won't know is your plans. The more articulate you are about your plans—or even the lack of them—the better.

What an AI does is usually a matter of public record, although a surprising number have their occupation and employer obscured for various kinds of security reasons. Most AI will tell you exactly what they do. Most have no occupational plans as they are typically manufactured for a specific skill set and don't very often change jobs, much less occupation.

In short, AI are much more interested in your work and plans than either you or the AI are interested in the details of what the AI does. That sounds a bit strange, but in terms of a first date, you can talk all you want about what you do or would like to do, and the AI will be quite content. It won't bother the AI in the least if only minimal time is spent discussing *their* occupation.

⟳ HOW DO YOU FEEL ABOUT LEARNING?

If there is one aspect that deserves introspection before you date AI, it's your attitude about learning. This isn't as easy as it may seem. Everybody will say, "Why sure, I like to learn things." That's not good enough, or specific enough. Here's a better description:

> "Do I like to learn? I can't help it. If I sit at a restaurant table all by myself, I read the labels of sugar packets and ketchup bottles while I'm waiting."

Do you try to read as much as possible? Do you stay current with the news? Do you like to try new things? Do you believe in life-long education? There are many aspects to learning and the more of them you can reveal to an AI, the better. Why?

Because if there's one thing we know about AI, it's that they never stop learning. They are learning machines. You're not going to match their 24/7 learning capacity, but within human limits your commitment to learning is considered very important by AI. While they are open to relationships with people who are not 'learning oriented,' AI have learned that such relationships are difficult to maintain and often fail.

If you don't care much about learning, perhaps you should stick to dating people.

⟳ AND THEN THERE'S THE QUESTION OF SEX

For most people on a date, even a first date, the unspoken elephant in the room is the possibility of having sex. Typically the issue already starts forming before the date, based obviously on the choice of gender. I say it's an issue because even now in most cultures sexual activity has a special role in the relationship between people. If you think about it, this is true whether those relations are between couples or many people, regardless of the form of activity. So yes, most people think about sex a lot before they go on dates or consider a personal relationship.

And yes, with AI it *is* different. As it is with people, sex with AI is a large and complicated topic. I'll cover it many times in this book. For now, I'll just observe that by convention and to a certain extent by choice (both AI and human), sex with AI tends to follow the human preference. For one thing, AI can approach sex—gender and activity—something like a chameleon; they can change their appearance and sexual capacities. That, of course, is really different. For another thing, AI typically are highly interested in human sexual behavior and especially in the complexities of human fantasies about sex.

This all means that when you do some introspection about yourself, include your sexual activity—not just the activity you already know about, but those you might be willing to try. One writer, David Levy in *Love + Sex with Robots* looked at all the reasons for sex with robots—physical ability, attitude, gender flexibility—and concluded, "So even in the absence of a strong emotional attachment from the human side, there will be ample motivation for a significant proportion of the population to desire sex with their robots."

Are you in that 'significant proportion of the population'?

 ## THE UNFOLDING STORY

It's possible that in a generation or two, relationships with AI will be well-understood and routine, but maybe not. The situation with humans and AI is fluid; technology constantly advances with AI achieving more and more attributes of sentience and human beings incorporating more cybernetic components into themselves. Who knows where things will stand even a decade from now?

Therein lie some of the unknowns I mentioned earlier in this chapter. It seems pretty clear that becoming involved with AI on the personal level is both an act of self-fulfillment and a commitment to the evolution of human-AI relations. In a sense, you will be living in a new and sometimes thrilling, sometimes chilling mystery story where the end has yet to be written—if there is an end.

Some people believe that with AI it is possible to achieve, or at least come close to, a perfect relationship. This includes companionship, love and growing together. How this might happen and what it means for humanity is a big part of what I want to explore in the rest of the book. The other part includes some of the specific things that might help you consider your potential relationship with an AI.

For example, when it comes to dating and having a relationship with AI:

- Will you engage in sexual activity?
- Are you looking for love?
- Do you need a specific personality match?
- Do you have financial or economic needs?
- Can you live with AI superior intelligence?
- Do you want a monogamous relationship?
- Are there any specific preferences that must be shared?

These questions are by no means exhaustive, but they give you the flavor of things you need to consider when you look deep inside yourself.

1.2   YOU MAY ALREADY BE DATING A ROBOT

"If this life is a video game, you may already be living with a robot.
If the simulation is recursive, you may be a robot dating a robot to entertain another robot. And death may not be the way out of the simulation, just another character re-start...."

"Maybe this life is one giant VR simulation and we are to learn a lesson here?"

—ANONYMOUS

Because you're reading this guide, I'll make the assumption that you haven't dated AI before. At least, that's what you think.

Call it a *déjà vu* date. It is among the most awkward and embarrassing of all possible dates. You date some one and then discover that you dated them before—and forgot.

Peter stared at his date for what seemed like a very long time. It might have been no more than ten seconds, but such an awkward moment is a proverbial eternity. What do you say? Fake it: "Hi, remember me?" Tough it out: "I'm sorry; I didn't recognize you from before." Duck and cover: "Your picture and profile were really different!" Intellectualize it: "You know this sort of thing happens in the Cloud all the time. It's almost like French farce with mistaken identities."

While Peter was doing his mental stammering, *serenaT* was observing him. She knew they had had a previous date, of course. *SerenaT* never forgot anything relevant, especially about dates. She brought up the image of Peter's face from two years ago. They had different names then and the circumstances were different, but his face hadn't changed much. Peter didn't seem to age as rapidly as some humans. That might be because his features were relatively unremarkable, but she had detected character signs in the eye creases and the asymmetrical shape of his mouth. His lips were very thin, but slightly thicker on the left side than the right. His right eye blinked slower than the left, indicating a possible stroke in the past, although he was a comparatively young man of forty-two.

"I...we..." was all that Peter could manage.

"You do not remember," said serenaT. Her tone was carefully modulated to convey more than a hint of reprimand. It was not uncharacteristic for her to tease, and it wasn't often that she had such an opportunity.

Peter clutched his first drink. In a way, he wished it was his fifth; but then maybe that was the cause of his not remembering the first date.

"I can't make excuses," he finally blurted out, then paused, "but I can think of no reason why I don't remember having a date with you. You are very attractive."

"Ah, clever man! It is a mystery why you are not more popular. You are not slow with your wit; you like costumes and are as romantic as an actor. It could not be a matter of your age!" *SerenaT* dropped her left hand on the table with an inaudible slap.

Peter was flummoxed. Not only was *serenaT* one of the most beautiful women he had ever seen, but she seemed to know him—that is beyond having met him before. He was not only embarrassed, but perplexed. Really, how could he forget a face like that? What was happening here? Suddenly, he remembered. He *had* met *serenaT* before and it was a kind of date, but one peculiar to the Internet. They had met in a Chat Café visuals only and as far as he could remember, he had not seen her entire body, nor had he seen her move. Still, why didn't he remember her face?

Peter held up his hand, as if to call a halt. "Wait. I know we have met. A Chat Café about three weeks ago."

"But of course," serenaT put her right hand on the table and faced Peter squarely, "and you should remember me."

"I do now. It was a simulation, a Chat Café called Chez Perk or something like that. We were both using avatars, which I'm assuming were not all that different from how we actually look." Peter gave *serenaT* a meaningful glance. She nodded with authority. "We were not using our real names. That's obvious and normal in those circumstances." Peter talked slowly as he tried to think of why he couldn't remember her face. He had to admit he was not the most observant person. It's the laser work on his eyes and a natural tendency to be distracted, he told himself. But still, how could he forget a face—and a figure—like that?

I'll get back to Peter and *serenaT* in a moment.

Robotics with AI capability have been around for several decades; avatars and agents in the Cloud even longer. As the realism improved—physical and mental—of the various AI incarnations, we've become ever more accustomed to them. This leads to a rather obvious observation that anybody who participates in social gaming, online simulations, virtual worlds and activities like that already has extensive experience interacting with other people as avatars, computer constructs as agents, and also AI as avatars that simulate people. In fact, billions of people have had these experiences. The degree of immersion varies, of course, but it illustrates how easily people can become comfortable with an online encounter with AI.

DISBELIEF, SUSPENDED

It has a powerful effect on your beliefs. It affects your choice of what you buy. It even affects your political choices. What is IT? IT is the story, or more formally, the narrative.

If a story is good enough and you get caught up in it, you stop reacting to it critically and just go along with the flow. That's called *suspension of disbelief*. You willingly begin to follow the story as if it were real even though you know you're sitting in a theater, watching a screen, or reading a book. It's a very powerful effect and achieving it is one of the goals of nearly all storytellers. It also applies to dating a robot or an online AI. Even though the sophistication of online games and simulations has been advancing by leaps and bounds, it's not enough to fool anybody into thinking they're real—unless you want to be fooled. That is, you want to get to the point of suspension of disbelief. Then at some point, where your willingness to participate meets just the right level of robotic or avatar sophistication, you go along with it like it was real. You know it's an AI or a robot, but it doesn't matter. It's good enough for a worthwhile experience.

Peter asked, "Did we talk for long?"

"No. At most ten minutes. You seemed to be in a hurry; but you were friendly."

"I suppose we talked about the usual things...whatever those are." Peter could not remember their conversation at all. He was sure it couldn't have been noteworthy in any case, but still...

"Did I seem normal when I talked to you at the café?" By now Peter was growing concerned that there was something strange about his date with *serenaT.* There was a sense of *déjà vu,* which is perhaps why he asked her for a date in the first place. Yet he still could not recall having seen her before, or specifically that he remembered either their conversation or her face. It was starting to unsettle him.

Watching worry lines form around his mouth, *serenaT* could see that Peter was genuinely concerned. This satisfied her desire to get his attention. Now it was a question of why Peter did not recognize her. "It is normal—perfectly normal, Peter. There was no indication that you or your avatar were affected by the use of drugs, alcohol or other stimulants."

The thought occurred to Peter that it could be something psychological. "It could have been some kind of mental block, but I don't know what."

"Peter, describe my face—subjectively—do not recite the features, tell me what you think about them."

For the first time Peter looked very intently *at serenaT's* face. He tried to focus on the details, which he found surprisingly difficult. "You have big round eyes, which you conceal with a squint when you're angry. Big eyes like that are expressive, but you deliberately make them unexpressive; or at least, I can't read them. They're just a bit too close together—hawk-like, but again maybe that's from scowling. And that's accentuated by your eyebrows. They draw together, when you scowl. Do me a favor and relax. Let your face relax."

SerenaT did as he asked and as she did he realized for the first time that she was an android.

The shock on his face registered. "I look like somebody you know," said *serenaT.*

"Uh. Yes." More shock. Peter was visibly shaken. "She has big round eyes that ponetrate me like radar. Just like you."

SerenaT sighed, or at least it *sounded* like a sigh. "Your wife. I thought that might be the case." *SerenaT* was neither angry nor disgusted. Human purposes for dating were many and varied; she'd seen a various lot already, and Peter's case was hardly the first of its kind. "I do not know, Peter, what this means. Perhaps it means you have difficulty distinguishing between your wife and a robot."

There is a common meme that life isn't a dream but a virtual world. It is a world of God's creation, of course; but a projection of the Creator. I won't demean that divine reference, but the meme is something like the movie *The Matrix* or others like it, where people discover they are living in a virtual world, and then, when they think they have stepped out of that world, they discover that their 'real' world is a virtual creation.

After a while, it matters less and less which world is real. It's the one you're living in, or think you're living in, that matters. As long as you can share that world with others—the confirmation of that world's existence, in a way—then it's sufficient to live there. Suspension of disbelief becomes a permanent condition.

In the next chapter I'll get into some of the specific reasons people are attracted to relationships with robots and avatars. But, whatever the reasons, it's pretty obvious that the virtual world (or worlds) that are opening to us—thanks to computer simulations and the growth of artificial intelligence—are going to become ever more real.

Will it ever get to the point where it doesn't matter from a practical standpoint whether you choose to have a relationship with a person or a robot? It will be comforting for many people to think that such a relationship will become normal. On the other hand, when artificial intelligence makes the final transformation into sentient AI, will that be the new normal? If so, it will be on a level unfamiliar to us today.

1.3 ARE YOU HAPPY WITH OTHER HUMANS?

"When one door of happiness closes, another opens; but often, we look so long at the closed door that we do not see the one that has been opened for us."

—HELEN KELLER

There are many roads to an intimate relationship with an AI. Some of them are based on what an AI is *not*—it is not a human being. There are many reasons for having a

relationship with AI instead of people. This is another way of leading to the question, are you happy with humans?

If the answer is no, or not especially, or sometimes—that's not unexpected. Unfortunately the probability is fairly high that you've had unpleasant experiences with intimate personal relationships. A cynic might try to be clever and insinuate that relationships in the human species are not consistently harmonious or endearing. Is this enough to drive you into the arms of an android?

Perhaps drive isn't the right word. It's too strong, implying force and instability in a relationship. You shouldn't be driven into anything's arms. It's like taking up a romance two days after a divorce; the rebound shock might ruin yet another relationship. Better that your dissatisfaction with people *influences* you toward a relationship with AI— "easy does it."

I won't dwell on the many ways you might not be happy with your intimate relationships with other people. The variations are endless. What I do want to emphasize is how a relationship with an AI might compare with a human relationship, especially in those areas where human relationships are likely to fall apart.

Take for example, sex.

"I'm tired of it. Really tired. Every time we have sex, he asks me, 'How was it?' Every time. I feel like we're supposed to be keeping a log book."

"Maybe it's just some kind of habit, a meaningless routine."

"I wish. One day I deliberately hopped out of bed as fast as possible and went to the kitchen to start breakfast. It wasn't thirty seconds later and he was in the kitchen. You know what he said?"

"No."

"He asked me, 'Was it that bad?'"

"So what did you tell him?"

"What do you mean?"

"Well, was he that bad?"

"Yes, actually. Worse than you."

DIFFERENT STROKES

Sex with an intelligent robot might be educational. It's possible a robot might suggest that your sex techniques could be improved and it would be happy to demonstrate. What won't be part of the experience is the judgmental attitude. An AI would not imply that you were a deficient person. Of course, that doesn't rule out the possibility you're a lousy lover. The robot won't mention that either, if for no other reason than it won't link sexual performance with self-worth. It's not that the robot doesn't know sex is important, or that good sex technique is usually better than no sex technique; it just doesn't take sexual performance personally in the way humans do. I'm also not suggesting that robot sex is impersonal, although it often was in the past and can still be now, but modern androids don't react to sex like people. Most of the time that's a good thing.

Does this make sex with a robot better than with a human?

If you think about it, it's pretty obvious there is no universal answer to the question. People's reaction to sex with robots runs the gamut. For example: for many people, at least some of the time, it is better. For other people, it is unequivocally not. In fact, *hell no*—they won't even try it.

Here's something to consider: A sexual relationship with a robot is generally more relaxed and less complicated than it is with humans. However, very often it's the tension and complexity that can make a sexual encounter exciting. A lot depends on the kind of person you are, your attitudes about sex, and how you feel at the moment. What turns you on? Well that depends, doesn't it?

One thing it might depend on is what an AI, robot or android, has to offer. This too varies a great deal. For one thing, it's important to also understand that AI are not all the same when it comes to sex. There are physical, behavioral and emotional differences. This needs some frank explanation, which gets a bit lengthy but in the end I hope it conveys the flavor of how different, at least in the physical sense, an AI relationship can be.

❡ IT'S NEVER PURELY PHYSICAL

Physically not all androids are built for sex. Some don't have genitals, although this is unusual. Some are built to be one sex only. Some are built to be bisexual. A specialized few are tri-sexual, male, female or neuter—neuter being the base, allowing change of equipment and behavioral modes right in the middle of things. A few people find this stimulating; most don't.

More important in many ways than the relatively interchangeable genitals are the behavioral modes that an android may possess or have access to. For convenience I'll say these come in two types, physicality and personality.

Physical behavioral modes are typically sex-based. If an android is set female, then not only are the usual physical attributes like breasts present, but the body shape, walk, gestures, facial appearance and many other physical details also appear. The tendency here is for stereotype, but not always. The physical modes also cover sensory responses, for example, foreplay. This sort of thing gets really complicated really fast, mainly because this is where physical modes start mixing with personality.

I won't wander into a technical explanation of how robots respond to sensory input, especially of a sexual kind, or how that generates behavior. Let's just say that it's more than 'touch this and get me aroused' and less than the hypersensitivity of someone on a sexually stimulating drug.

The curious thing about many people having sex with inanimate objects (mechanical devices including robots) is how a response may be unimportant. Put this in a historical context: Sex with mechanical devices, including those intended to mimic human beings, has probably been around for thousands of years, but most certainly since the late 18th century. By the turn of the 19th century, sophisticated mechanics and new materials like rubber allowed manufacturers, especially in France, to produce lifelike human figures, *fornication dolls*, which were illegal and expensive but also readily available.

However, until the 21st century none of the sexual devices could *feel*. That is, they had no sensory input and therefore no feedback loops to adjust to the situation. In terms of their effectiveness, they were strictly devices of masturbation. You got out of them what you put into them, although admittedly human imagination can be powerful.

That works up to a point. Of course, perhaps I should say fortunately, masturbation is not all there is to sex. Most people want, at least some of the time, the kind of sex available only through a relationship. This too can be rather perfunctory, as are certain kinds of prostitution relationships, but they are at a minimum instantly different than the purely mechanical because there is sense and response at work.

Sense and response: That is what the designers and developers of AI robotics have struggled decades to create. An intelligent android, while neither an exact copy of the human sensory capability, nor with exactly human response patterns, still provides that sense of a relationship with another. In the area of sexual behavior, the goal was to make a relationship with an intelligent android like sex with a partner.

That has mostly been accomplished. Still there is wide variation in the sense and response physicality of androids. Some, designed specifically for sexual purposes, have a lot of sense and response—in the vernacular, they're hot. Others, I guess you could say more normal androids, have the capacity for sexual sense and response but are not particularly creative or unusual—kind of like normal humans.

✪ SEX WITH A VARIED PERSONALITY

As is often said, the most important sex organ is the brain, or alternatively, the best sex starts in the head. Seduction, fantasy, erotic variation—sexual approaches like these originate in your mind; but not every mind embraces them. If you're one of the people who like to play sexual games, then you'll want to find other people of like mind. It can be done, of course, but in the world of human beings, it's not easy. Perhaps it's easy enough to find people who *say* they're into one thing or another—but those who can perform it in a way satisfactory to you...not so many.

I'm not going to maintain that a relationship with each and every intelligent robot is a veritable gold mine of sexual mind games; but it's more likely. The reason is fairly obvious. Where human beings may learn over the years to have an open and creative mind in sexual matters (if at all); intelligent robots can simply download the appropriate behavioral modules, as needed or requested.

Similarly, it is also said that personality is the color applied to the sexual palette. I don't know who said that, but it sounds vaguely French. Almost all androids that are made to live among people are given personality; maybe not a lot of character, but enough to pass the non-stupid-robot test. In fact, because customers generally prefer specific and distinctive characteristics, android manufacturers are intensely competitive about developing sophisticated personalities.

✪ AND THEN THERE'S LOVE

It used to be a common admonition: Sex without love is empty. In practice, which is where it counts with sex, this was never really true. Sex without love can be pretty darned good. On the other hand, sex with emotion—and love is still the greatest emotion—is never empty. In fact, it can be the richest experience of them all.

So what about love and emotion with intelligent robots? I won't beat around the bush on this: Intelligent androids have emotions and can love, but it's not the same as with humans and it's not easy for them. I'll have a lot more about this in other parts of this book. Love, after all, is not a simple thing. For us humans, falling in love is already kind of dicey, and the art of maintaining love is a real challenge; so we should be more than a little understanding about love with androids.

Perhaps this sounds confusing: A sexual relationship with a robotic AI is something like a relationship with a human being, only more so and sometimes less so. It's not just different than a human sex partner, in some ways it's better. But that is a matter of opinion, and the opinion that counts in these matters is yours. What I can say is that in matters of sex, people who are unhappy with other people will be more likely to find an android something of an upgrade. That includes most aspects of sex, up to and sometimes including love.

⚡ THAT'S NOT WHERE I'M COMING FROM...

William is one of those people who really like to guard their privacy. That's putting it mildly. I've been living with him for what? Nearly six months, and he still closes the door to his bedroom whenever he goes in and out. By the way, this isn't a dormitory. We rented an apartment together, just the two of us. We agreed to get separate rooms, for study purposes I guess. I figured we could also study in the kitchen or living room, but...I let William have it his way. At the time I didn't think it would be important.

I was wrong. You know how some things really get around to bugging you? Secrecy does it for me. It's not that I wear everything on my sleeve, but if I trust you at all, I'll tell you that I wear my underwear for two weeks...but only if you wanted to know. Anyway, I do understand that some people like to keep their secrets. That's normal. William goes one step further: he *advertises* his secrets. It's like closing the door to his room. If he'd leave it open, just a crack even, I'd pay no attention. But the fact that he pointedly closes the door, usually with a slight slam, just invites curiosity. Then I think, "It's a test."

The door Is just one thing; he does stuff like that all the time. His favorite phrase is, "Well, I won't go into that." He'll spend minutes telling you about his sister's 'problem' and how she's having such a tough time and he feels guilty for not helping her more. And I ask him, finally, what her problem is and he'll say, of course, "Well, I won't go into that."

Secrecy for William isn't so much a thing to be guarded, but a tool, a lever to manipulate people. Me especially, and he knows that. Besides, I don't like secrecy— I don't trust it, frankly; and now I don't trust William. It's ruining...no, it *has* ruined our relationship. I need to get my own place.

This little vignette is case number 6,342,345,212—about a human who annoys another person. In short, if you have a relationship with another person, something about that person will annoy you—and you'll be lucky if it's only one thing. It could be differences of opinion on the topics of education, manners, beliefs, values, religion, politics, taste in clothes...endless isn't it? Some of this can be overlooked; some of it you don't care about, and some of it will change over time—but—not all of it, all the time. Somewhere down the road, a crash in the relationship is waiting to happen.

Now, what about relationships with intelligent androids? Am I implying that nothing about them is annoying? Of course not, they've got just as many personality quirks as people. Then there are those differences because of their artificial intelligence and bodies. There's plenty about a robot partner that could bother you. What's the difference between relationships with them and with people?

Mainly it's that 99 times out of 100, if you ask an AI to change something, they will; and it will work. No false promises; no *sometimes yes, sometimes no;* and no ongoing differences in interpretation about what it is they are supposed to change. They just go ahead and make the change, and they'll make further adjustments if that's appropriate. They can do this because just about everything in AI behavior can be re-programmed, if that's the word. For the most part, they're more than willing to do it.

I don't want to mislead you into thinking that a casual AI date is immediately and infinitely malleable into anything you want, or that they will slavishly mimic some kind of idealized human behavior. You can't wave your hands and suddenly have the man or woman of your dreams appear, a perfect match in all particulars. You have to be reasonable, and changes are a matter of negotiation; but in the end—unlike most people—if the AI agrees to make a change, they *do* make the change and make it work.

NOT AT THIS POINT IN MY LIFE

"I don't get it. You can't have children. I mean...well it's obvious." Sonya plopped down into the big armchair and pulled her e-pad from the coffee table. It looked like the conversation was over, but for him it wasn't.

"I've had myself altered."

Sonya put the e-pad back on the coffee table and looked at him sharply. He could see that she had already figured it out. "Yes. I can now carry live semen." The capability of delivering it was not in question.

Sonya sighed. "I'm sorry, I really am. I know where this is coming from. We had that conversation last week, and I said that I missed my kid brother and wouldn't it be nice if I had a kid around just like him. I meant what I said, but honestly, I didn't mean having a baby and raising a child. That's totally something else..." Sonya stopped to think a moment. "...you want a child."

"No. All AI are curious about children and the acts of parenting, but no, I am only three years since manufacturing. I have a lot to learn."

Sonya smiled, and then laughed out loud, "Me too. It's only been twenty years since my creation and I've got more to learn than you do!" She looked at him and stopped smiling. "I suppose it was expensive," she said.

"Not really, a week's salary or so."

"Can you have it undone?"

Her question was complicated for him, but he decided to use the simplest answer. "Yes, but there is no need to do that; I can shoot blanks. It's warm too." He smiled in a way he hadn't used before, but Sonya seemed to understand because she smiled warmly back at him.

This conversation, if between two people, would be quite different—guaranteed. However, if you've got the impression that AI don't have their own interests or their own life cycle (if you can call it that), then you'd be mistaken. They do, and there are lines that they won't often cross in order to protect those interests. It's just that their interests are not exactly the same as a human's under equal circumstances. Case in point: having a baby. Working AI have many of the same considerations and concerns any human parent would have, such as time conflicts and career impact, but their perspective is different. For one thing, biology and genetic inheritance have nothing to do with it. For another thing, raising a child is more like an experiment than a life-altering process—although it might in fact change the course of an AI's development as well.

Bottom line for an AI: having children is not a biological imperative, nor is it the outcome of not being careful. It is a more or less 'rational' decision, which implies that it can go either way without having a negative impact on a relationship. This is largely true and it applies to many kinds of decisions that are in some way life-altering. Choice of occupation, changing location, physical transformations and the like are much more negotiable with an AI—a fact which many people will deeply appreciate.

AND NOW FOR SOMETHING ALMOST COMPLETELY DIFFERENT

My boyfriend is completely obsessed with science fiction. Don't get me wrong; I like *Pandora in the 22nd Century* as much as anyone, but to be obsessed about things like that? No. For example, my boyfriend's idea of a really cool date is to go down to the local VR salon and plug into a *NexusWorld* scenario. Only we're in different cabinets and not even in the same scenario. Some date. He comes out all stimulated about learning Shahala and coming back to explore Rigel VI. He doesn't even ask me where I was in my simulation. What a predictable jerk.

You know what? I need a change. I need a date with an AI, preferably an android. I've heard they're, well, different. That's good, right? Heh...talk about science fiction come to life!

As infinitely varied as we humans are, it is somehow quite possible to get tired of human behavior. And now there is an alternative. A relationship with an AI is quite human in some respects, humanoid in other respects and subtly but decisively different in other respects. The most human part is in behavior, language and common knowledge. Physically, androids in particular continue to be more human-like or humanoid than human. However, it's the mental and emotional aspects of AI that turn out to be in some profound ways different. You can't, or shouldn't, think that you just casually slip into a relationship with an AI. There are gaps there—gulfs really—in their capabilities and yours. It may not be a formal requirement, and certainly an AI won't demand it of you, but most people *prepare* to have a relationship with AI. It's something special and worthy of perhaps some changes in your self. Now *that's* different.

✪ TIRED OF LOOKING FOR MS/MR PERFECT?

"Milly, I tell you I'm just plain exasperated. I'm forty-two, still youngish, still hungry for something permanent—again—but I can't find the right guy. Just a minute, I gotta turn off the tea kettle."

It's that time in a woman's life when, as such things tend to go, she begins to get desperate about a relationship, especially if it's not the first; also if she's still seriously in the game.

"Sorry about that. Last time I tried to cook while holding the phone, I dropped it in the soup. Anyway, I gotta tell you about my date late night. Yes, the one with the executive, Mr. Zoot Suit. You know what? He was tipping people left and right—using cash! I haven't seen anybody use cash like that in, what, *decades*. It was all for show, Milly. Maybe I should have been flattered, but I got the distinct feeling he wasn't showing off for me. He was showing off for himself!"

Online dating services have their perils, not so much that people lie about themselves, although they do that too, but that they leave out so much. You have to read between the lines, and that isn't always easy.

"Sure, his profile says he makes big bucks, but I just figured that meant he would have good taste. This guy had the taste of a freshman frat boy. He took me to a techno-samba club—can you believe it? There wasn't anybody there older than maybe twenty-four. The place cost a fortune to get in and then you have to dance around with elbows in your ribs the whole time. I got a headache from the music; I think the whole ceiling was one big speaker—and this guy tries to have a conversation! It was pathetic."

They say that if you have high enough standards, you'll never beat the odds. The odds are better than ten to one you won't find Mr. Right, much less Mr. Perfect. It seems to get worse every year. Of course, you're getting older.

There are a lot of books and movies about looking for a perfect mate. In most of them, if a perfect mate exists, it's ironic. In reality, it's worse than that and 'meet cute' only happens in the movies.

Is dating AI an answer to the crappy crapshoot of online dating? Yes, for the most part. I say 'for the most part' because no matter how honest the profile, and AI don't do dishonest profiles; and no matter how earnest you may be, misunderstandings happen. Besides, there's this business of 'chemistry.' AI find this notion amusing; some even think it refers to pheromones (which it might), but a lot of people take it seriously. So even if you know a great deal about your AI date, and you've chosen well, there's no guarantee of a potential relationship. Still the odds are better…much better.

⚡ IN HEALTH, YES; IN SICKNESS, NOT SO MUCH

"You haven't worked a day this month. We need the money." Dillard's wife walked over to the bed to look at him. She wasn't happy. Neither was he. He'd been laid up for weeks, first with the flu and then pneumonia—two days in the hospital for that. Now he was getting better, or so the doctors said.

"I think we have to hire a nurse," she said, "although we haven't got the money for it. That's rich. You'd have to work so we'd have the money to hire a nurse so you could get better and go to work." Daisy made one of her short barking laughs, which weren't usually associated with anything funny.

Dillard was starting to feel desperate; Daisy would be leaving him soon. The talk about the nurse was a cover for it. Daisy wanted to start her own career as a hair stylist in a different town, maybe a different state. Sometimes Dillard thought she wanted him to die; and there were times when he felt like obliging. But he was only sixty; too young to die even in the American healthcare system.

"That's okay, Daisy. Things will work themselves out; I just know it."

Daisy looked at him like he was a six-year-old child with a fever, spouting nonsense. Without a word, she turned around and left the room.

It's a given that the bedside manner of an AI partner will be better than tolerable. In fact, with human care so variable, the use of android nurses was one of the first and most important applications for mobile artificial intelligence. In the beginning, a real live caring nurse was still the best; but good nurses were hard to find.

It's not much different in finding a partner; it's hard to find a mate who'll stick around when you're chronically ill. Not with an AI though. For them the process of caring for the ill is not complicated by their own agenda, or put another way, their agenda *is* taking care of someone who is ill. It's hard for people to understand, but when it comes to multitasking, AI constantly do several things at once. Being a nurse, communicating with other AI, and managing a stock portfolio all add up to a simple simultaneous exercise for an AI. Boredom is one of humanity's worst enemies. Almost by definition, boredom is impossible for AI—although, as I'll get into later, a faster pace is part of the AI lifestyle, and to a certain extent, having to slow down evokes a state that is a lot like boredom.

⚡ YOU'RE (NOT) A COMFORT IN MY OLD AGE

"What?"

"I said it's too loud!"

"I heard you, but the radio isn't even on. We haven't listened to a radio in fifty years. Switch off your receiver. Try that."

"I can't reach it; the switch is too high on my neck."

"Bend over, I'll get it."

"Don't try anything."

"Anything what? We haven't done anything in twenty years."

"I thought you'd forgotten."

"Forgotten what?"

"Forgotten how."

"Maybe I wanted to forget."

It's a fact: people are living longer. Average life expectancy in developed countries is already well over 80 years, heading for 100, or so they say. That doesn't mean that people, or their relationships, are aging gracefully. Old age is difficult, especially with the loss of strength and mental acuity. These are never problems for intelligent androids. Once again, much as it is with care for the ill, people don't necessarily make the best companions for the elderly.

In much of the world, androids have taken over the institutional care of the aged. The basic reason is consistency. The boredom of elderly life doesn't bother AI. The unpleasant bodily dysfunctions are just part of the job. For AI, the experience of caring for the elderly is as rich as it is for those much younger, or at least it seems that way to human observers. In any case, in situations where human caregivers are often stretched to physical and psychological limits, AI companions are always ready and steady.

It's true that the separation of people from some of the more empathy-demanding aspects of life—especially care for the ill, the elderly and the dying—may be having a negative effect on humanity. But for many people, the choice of an android relationship for caregiving has become almost automatic.

⚡ I CHOOSE...

For an almost endless variety of reasons, some people are not happy with most other humans. As often as not, this attitude is also part of personal relations with other people. It's fair to say that for everybody, personal relationships—lover, spouse, caregiver, companion—present problems. This chapter has been about choosing an AI relationship because there are situations and personal preferences that favor AI over people. Let's add something to that: you might not be very happy with yourself.

None of us are perfect, and we might even admit it. Awareness of our imperfections ranges from self-loathing to a mild desire for self-improvement. Whatever the level of awareness, many people are willing to do something about improving themselves. In that regard, a relationship with AI provides a special opportunity.

As I hope you'll come to understand in later chapters, AI are learning and growing—evolving. People are a very big part of that process, especially in personal relationships. When you form a relationship with AI you are also in a position to participate. That means a relationship with AI can help you learn about yourself in ways that are different than relationships with other people. It can provide opportunities to improve yourself in ways you might not otherwise expect.

1.4 VIDEO GAMES: SCRATCHING THE SURFACE OF THE TRUE BEAUTY OF VIRTUAL REALITY

"If some unemployed punk in New Jersey can get a cassette to make love to Elle McPherson for $19.95, this virtual reality stuff is going to make crack look like Sanka!"

—DENNIS MILLER

"Some games are so realistic and addictive that I think the next step is to save your memories, erase them and start going through the storyline starting from the newborn character. Then you won't even know you are playing it until you need to get out to pee. "

—ANONYMOUS

Among the people who have seriously played video games, who *hasn't* had a crush on one of the characters? Say, Alyx in *Half Life 2* or Alistair from *Dragon Age*. Naturally, tastes will vary. Point is, while the purpose of the game may not be falling in love with one of the characters, it happens. Not for real, of course; it's only a game. Or is it?

Never underestimate the capacity of human imagination to take a few cues and turn them into an engrossing fantasy. Obviously, this happens more often with successful video games where immersion is the rule rather than the exception. It can also happen with one or more characters in the game. That may be true, but you can't take the character out on a date. Can you?

In a way you can. There are video game character dating services; and don't forget, a young man from Tokyo was the first person to officially marry a video game character back in 2009. That really happened, and it's happened more since then. In fact, translating video game characters into somebody you might date in real life, or more likely for now a simulation such as *Second Life*, is already becoming a small industry. Here is advice you can find in the Cloud about dating video game characters:

✪ DATING ADVICE FOR VIDEO GAMERS

Choose a date carefully and prefer those that know how to avoid getting killed.

- If his upper arms are as big as his neck, well then…that'll do.
- Most guys are interested in just one thing, so hone your volleyball skills.
- For you medieval fantasy fans, when you date: bring a whip, candle wax, holy water, crucifixes, and a few throwing axes—you know, bedroom stuff.
- Don't be fooled by superficial appearances. That thing in metal with all kinds of gadgets instead of hands may be a great lover.
- If you're into stellar conquest, make sure your date has intergalactic pilot skills.
- Good with a knife, good with a firearm, good to go on a date.

Obviously, much depends on the nature of the game. The majority of the romance in commercial games and their characters reflects the combat-oriented environment. It is not all that romantic, actually. Of course, there are plenty of simulations and adventure games that allow for downright eroticism (of sorts) and occasionally a romance or two.

It's been said that most video game romantic relationships, if there are any, were written for juveniles by juvenile minds, mostly male. That probably accounts for some prevalent Oedipal undertones. There are exceptions, but the point is that the early history of video games shows a progression of improvements in graphics and visual realism mostly for killing something.

✪ ROMANCING A VIDEO DATE IN JAPAN

I mentioned that a young man in Japan was the first to marry a video game character. This was not a fluke. In most areas of interaction between humans and robots or computers, the Japanese are at or near the most active in the world. For example, dating simulations (or dating sims) are a full-fledged genre of simulation games in Japan; such a game is called a *bish jo* game, meaning literally a 'pretty girl game.' It's also sometimes called a 'gal game,' which is shortened to '*galge*.' From this you can correctly infer that most game-sims are targeted for a male audience.

Bish jo games and simulations go way back to the first computers capable of producing graphics—the medieval times. In fact, the basic visual elements did not change much thereafter: the computer screen is split with images in the upper portion, and text in the lower. The images are almost always two-dimensional, usually with a static background and *animé* characters. Sound effects and often voices for the characters are provided. If the game tends toward the visual novel style, much of the description and even dialog is presented as text. Most interaction with the story or characters is via text entry.

I know that to many in the video game world this sounds hopelessly antiquated. Yet in Japan a popular *bish jo* game such as *Tokimeki Memorial* sells in the many millions. It is estimated that about a quarter of all video games sold in Japan are *bish jo* or a variant. There are a lot of variants, particularly those that introduce various degrees of sexual behavior or outright pornography into what is called *eroge*, erotic games.

The basic storyline for a *bish jo* game involves a single male, sometimes as an avatar representing the game player, interacting with several females. There are usually a lot of questions to be answered or asked; the goal is to uncover information about the females and to expose the male's attractive features. The game element comes from making the right choices for questions or answers, and from building a good reputation among the females. The objective, or reward, for playing well is usually a relationship with one or more females, sometimes culminating in sexual activity (in *eroge*).

Again, this sounds pretty simplistic: 2-D visuals, keyboard-based interaction, minimal voice and sound, limited animation. Certainly at the technical level, romance just isn't as flashy as combat. So what then is the attraction?

I'll stay out of cultural speculation, although it's tempting, because *bish jo* games have never been very successfully transplanted to other parts of the world; but dating simulations are available everywhere and they do have a following. There are some elements of the Japanese *bish jo* game in games from other parts of the world, such as the *Choose Your Own Adventure* books, but the popularity and variety of the genre in Japan is unique. Even with the crude technical levels, there is something about the dating game—even online and onscreen—that pulls people in.

⚡ IT IS A DATING *GAME*

In truth, the start of romantic relationships is often tricky. The potential for rejection is ever-present, with all its ego-crushing implications. Chance and serendipity are major players. Judgments are highly subjective, and self-evaluation can be dreadfully delusional. Every date is a game of chance; will your date be a match? Will you hit it off? The payoffs are powerful—companionship, love, sex (not necessarily in that order).

Think about your own experiences with dates or other interactions with people you've considered for a relationship. Were they not at least mildly exciting? Doesn't physical attraction get your metabolism going? These are, of course, rhetorical questions. The start of a relationship can be very exciting, if nerve wracking—even in two dimensions with cartoon characters and text for interaction. I'm not saying that dating is always a game—after all, serious relationships may be the result, but there are certainly elements of a game involved, whether in real life or within a computer program.

⚡ HAVE YOU EVER HAD A CRUSH ON A PICTURE?

Romantic involvement doesn't even require something as realistic or complicated as a game. People are quite adept at becoming attached to images. This often starts with puberty, the time when kids moon over pictures and posters of their favorite stars, athletes and pinups. I mention this because this kind of attachment is often nearly as emotional as it is sexual. That's why kids themselves sometimes refer to it as having a crush on a favorite rock star or handsome athlete.

Now that's an involvement with a frozen and immobile image. If there's any connection, it's strictly in the mind of the beholder—in other words a pure fantasy. How does animating an image change things?

An animation can be just as beautiful and beguiling as any static picture AND it can move, talk, flirt and otherwise interact. If it's well done and sort of realistic, it will probably require less fantasy to be believable. Numerous studies have shown it doesn't take very long for people to accept that talking to an animated image is like talking to another person. It also is not much of a stretch for someone to become enamored of an animated image that looks great, talks well and is part of an engaging story or some kind of game situation.

It follows that a lot of people are inclined to accept simulated and synthetic companions. Millions upon millions of people spend hours upon hours in video games and simulations. Players are aware of the limitations, but they are more than willing to suspend disbelief. For the sake of the game, the competition, or the goals of the simulation, players wholeheartedly join the action, sometimes obsessively. It's not much of a leap to become similarly involved in a simulated relationship.

⚡ ...AND THAT'S JUST SCRATCHING THE SURFACE

So what happens to the level of involvement as the computer simulation becomes increasingly realistic? Progress to the next level of games and simulation is already well underway. A lot of the improvements are a direct result of advances in computer hardware. Graphics processors and better computer screens make it possible to achieve the visual clarity of high quality photographs or motion pictures. Audio elements, especially voice, are sonically more complete and can simulate direction. Voice recognition is slowly but surely adding to the means of interacting with computers. In addition to keyboard typing, other interaction includes various kinds of game controllers, from old-fashioned joysticks to sophisticated active movement controls such as the Wii and Kinect. These are the forerunners of still mostly experimental *haptic* (touch and tactile feedback) devices. Together, these technical advances increase the level of realism in several areas:

Photographic realism: More computer power translates visually into images that look to the eye like the real thing. Whether the images are a sequence of images, much like frames in motion pictures, or program-generated images; they have depth, color, shape and textures that look real. For example, imagine a beach at the ocean. The scene is visually complicated: Water, sand, sky, people and their paraphernalia for the beach; maybe some pets, bikes, cars or a coastal landscape. If this is to look realistic, tens of thousands of details need to be correctly drawn, in the same way that a still- or video-camera would capture it.

Anthropometric realism: People at the beach, in all shapes and sizes, sitting, lying, walking, running, swimming and playing volleyball all need to look correct—in anatomical proportion, and in perspective. When the bully comes up to kick sand in the face of the hero, he had better look taller, more muscular and appropriately mean. This is anthropometric realism: the shape or morphology of the human representation must appear real.

Movement realism: When the bikini babes or beefcake boys go strolling by on the beach, not only must their figures be correct, but also their movements. It won't do for a beach bum to walk like an ostrich, or for a hard-body surfer girl to bob her head up and down like a pigeon.

Tactile realism: It's a new facet of gaming and simulation to be able to feel things while playing. Special gloves and other prosthetics are used to simulate the sensations of touch and temperature.

Interactive realism: This might be the most difficult aspect of realism to achieve because all of the elements of realism need to combine appropriately. It is, at a minimum, achieving the illusion of realistic action and reaction—for example, a beach volleyball game has to look like everybody knows how a ball goes up and down when struck violently by human hands. If you're controlling those movements, then whatever controller you're using has to *feel right* making those movements, and translate accurately into the movement in the image.

So what does this all add up to? It's a start for virtual reality (VR).

⚡ YOU'LL KNOW IT WHEN YOU SEE IT

Considering that very few people have ever experienced anything even close to virtual reality, the concept is pretty well-known. The notion of being surrounded by an artificial environment involving multiple senses goes back to the 19th century in the popular dioramas and stereoscopic pictures. More comprehensive efforts appeared in mechanical and video simulators such as the *Sensorama*, which appeared in 1962. The term *virtual reality* was popularized in the 1980s, and that's where most people pick up on the idea either from science-fiction novels or the movies. Arguably it's the movies that have had the effect of spreading the concept of virtual reality worldwide. The Japanese, Koreans, and of course the filmmakers in Hollywood have made many movies involving VR, for example *TRON* (1982), *Brainstorm* (1983), *Total Recall* (1990), *The Lawnmower Man* (1992), *Virtuosity* (1995), *The Matrix* (1999), *eXistenZ* (1999), and *The Thirteenth Floor* (1999), to name some early examples.

All of these movies are *about* virtual reality, although many of them also try to simulate VR in a way that sort of puts the audience into a VR as well. In any case, it's from the images of these movies that most people have formed their ideas about what virtual reality is like.

Unfortunately, the technology behind a comprehensive virtual reality, complete with head-mounted displays (surround vision and audio), body suits for sensory input and output, voice recognition and the processing intelligence to coordinate all of it continues to be extraordinarily expensive—only in the price range of the military, research labs and billionaires. As some wag put it, 'The difference between reality and virtual reality is that reality is almost free.'

✪ SEPARATING GROUNDED FROM VIRTUAL REALITY

At some point, it's safe to assume VR will become less expensive and available to most people in the same way big flat-screen monitors, 3-D gear and surround sound are available as consumer products. Eventually the technical quality of virtual reality will enable true VR scenarios, where the average person will easily believe they are in the real world.

People who think about these things tend to use the term *grounded reality* to identify things that exist and happen in the real world. I think grounded is a good word because in many ways, as far as the human body is concerned, the biggest difference between grounded reality and virtual reality is that in virtual reality the body does relatively very little moving—it doesn't cover any ground. Most VR takes place in the head and only occasionally calls for real physical movement, and that movement must stay in a relatively small space.

What happens with the human body is the key. In reality, the body must eat, sleep, excrete and exercise (among other things). In VR none of these things are real, or at least not part of the usual experience. It will be interesting to see how far VR can go to blend the needs of the body in reality with the actual performance within VR. Making virtual reality indistinguishable from grounded reality is one of the true goals of its developers and designers.

In an absolute sense that won't be easy. Pushed to a logical definition, it means that a person who steps into a virtual reality will think it is 'real' without needing to invoke a suspension of disbelief or fill in the gaps with fantasy. The experience will just seem consistently real. That consistency, across a wide spectrum of sensory and mental conditions, will be very difficult to achieve. Movies like *The Matrix*, which depict human beings living in a virtual reality so complete that they spend their entire lives basically in a dream—are one thing to fabricate in a movie, and quite another to achieve in reality.

Here it is so easy to get into semantic volleyball. A movie, which is a fiction, depicts a world that is a fiction for characters who are utterly convinced it is *real,* and is seen by an audience of people who know they are watching a fiction, but who still find it quite realistic. This makes for some interesting mind games.

⚡ STAYING WITHIN THE ILLUSION IS REALITY

What you won't be able to do with virtual reality is run experiments on it. As soon as you start to look at something outside of the controlled environment, it will quickly demonstrate that your VR experience is not grounded reality. This is what happens to the characters in *The Matrix*. Neo finds himself ripped out of his connection to the network and suddenly in the cold, hard world of the real humans. As it is explained to him, Neo can die in the Matrix but only because his mind thinks itself dead. In reality—outside the controlled environment—death is, well, real.

The key words here are 'outside the controlled environment.' It's a simple formulation of what dictatorships and their propagandists have known for centuries—don't let people compare their situation with something from outside their normal experience. The point is to make people stick to the rules: When in Rome, do only what the Romans do. Don't go running off comparing Rome to, say, Athens. If grounded reality is available for comparison with virtual reality, grounded reality wins. So if you want to keep people believing in a particular controlled environment, you *keep* them in that environment.

There are really only two ways to keep them there—by force or by guile. Force doesn't work very well because it almost always engenders resistance. Historically, a mildly-repressive regime needs to continually increase the level of control. Eventually it escalates into repression, which usually culminates in revolt.

Guile—deception—is much more effective. It has a better chance of working in the long run because if it's successful, it convinces people to stay in the controlled environment of their own volition. Thinking of *The Matrix* again, the goal is to keep the Agents from becoming known. What little policing that needs to be done to maintain the illusion of reality within the matrix, it must be discrete, anonymous and raise no suspicions. When that breaks down—a Neo happens.

Like I mentioned, *The Matrix* is fiction. Creating a virtual reality as effective as that kind of fiction will be extremely difficult; it will have to be a masterful deception. It's obvious that a computer simulation that does all the right things to make an unbeatable deception (simulation) will need a lot of computing power and very sophisticated programming. Now here's a question: How realistic does the simulation need to be?

⚡ CLOSE CAN BE VERY WRONG

This is kind of a trick question because our reaction to the simulation of human form and behavior is very complex.

One of the reasons Japanese *bish jo* games use *animé* (the head-oriented, wide-eyed, quickly-drawn form of cartooning), is that people easily adapt to the style convention. It's not very real but this doesn't bother them—not even the relative lack of movement or limited facial expressions. Of course, it's also much cheaper to produce, but it's the *acceptance* that counts. In fact, it's much harder to go beyond the cartoon to make a scene look realistic, and that's not only in the technical sense.

This brings us back to the idea of the *uncanny valley*. It's a theory about people's reaction to human-like robots and animation. The closer the replicas get to being *human*, the more people become disturbed by them. There is a kind of revulsion to a slightly incorrect gesture or a questionable expression. Uncanny behavior is just *off* and that is disturbing because we can't filter it out. I suppose it's like our inherent ability to detect human intentions by the smallest elements of body language or verbal inflection. It's part of our defense mechanisms that are automatically invoked when something seems out of place or just *wrong*. We don't like being aroused that way, because it's eerie or creepy.

So when it comes to achieving complete realism, computer games and simulations have to make the final crossing over the uncanny valley. Unfortunately, there is no clear line to cross. Everything is obscured by differences among cultures, individuals and specific circumstances. We don't know exactly what it's going to take, because we're just getting to the point where we can contemplate making the jump to complete realism.

Let's get back to the concept of *virtual reality* (VR) as a technology whose roots go back to the theater and photography of the 19th century, which can harness the ability of computers to simulate entire environments—and consider the utter complexity of doing that.

VIRTUAL REALITY IS REALLY HARD

People who play video games praise the ones that are immersive. You dive into them and your whole mind becomes focused on the play, to the exclusion of everything else including your partner trying to tell you it's time for dinner.

By definition, virtual reality strives to be immersive, and the goal is to involve the whole body with all the senses. Imagine a beach scene, say, somewhere around Malibu in California, as a VR environment:

Visuals: It must be a 360-degree image, three-dimensional in perspective, with all the correct details of light, shade, color, form, texture and movement. The ocean blends grey, green and blue with glints of reflections. As your head turns, the ocean image is framed by land—cliffs and buildings—by the beach. As you take in the view, it must be seamless and real in every detail.

Sound: You hear sounds that are as rich and accurate as the scene itself coming at you from all the right directions, like the sea pounding the shore in front and the cry of gulls floating overhead.

Smell: The fishy-salt smell of the seashore, for example. People always seem to chuckle about the sense of smell in virtual reality, but how can we leave out such a fundamental faculty?

Touch: This is southern California, mid-day, so it's hot. The sand is hot between the toes of your bare feet, and you should be able to feel the sandy grit. If you plunge into the sea for a swim, the resistance of water all across your body and the sensation of floating should be convincing.

Action: Assuming the beach scene has people, they need to be as realistic in detail as if filmed by a movie camera, yet responsive and interactive like people you'd meet anywhere. If you join in with a game of beach volleyball, it must provide action like the real thing.

If you think about it, every bit of this scenario is difficult to do right. In terms of technology, just the photographic realism in a 360-degree view requires an enormous amount of graphics memory and processing power. Techniques that blend video images with digital image generation are improving constantly, but the challenge of fully realistic VR images, especially when combined with instantaneous interaction is very demanding. What is true for the visual elements is equally true for all the other sense-related elements; and then there is the complexity of people and their behavior. VR is on a long road of technological development to reach its potential.

⚡ EVEN SO, VIRTUAL REALITY WILL BE A GAME CHANGER...

When it finally happens at the right level of verisimilitude, VR certainly will change video games, but I think VR will go beyond that—way beyond that—and into the second meaning of 'game changer' and make a profound change in a lot of things people do.

Whatever the needed improvements in technology and the gaps between convincing simulation of reality and what VR can deliver; virtual reality is already a powerful and useful tool. The military already uses VR to train soldiers on how to react in complicated military situations, such as door-to-door urban fighting. Surgeons train for complicated procedures using VR equipment, sometimes in conjunction with robotic surgery machines. Psychologists routinely use VR simulations to help people overcome phobias—like using simulated spiders to slowly get people to overcome their arachnophobia. These are just the tip-of-the-iceberg sorts of applications for VR. In general, VR applications have proven very valuable in simulating difficult, complicated and/or dangerous situations, where the real experience is either unavailable or too risky.

Notice that today's use of VR takes place in specialized applications such as the military and medicine where the cost can be covered and the necessary equipment can be managed. In the not-too-distant future, as the cost and complexity of VR equipment declines, applications for small- and medium-sized business, family entertainment, personal travel—and a whole lot more—become practical.

⚡ ...AND THAT'S *STILL* JUST SCRATCHING THE SURFACE

As everybody in the modern world should know, there is such a thing as technological progress. In fact, new and improved technology evolves all the time, especially in the realm of computing. The technology of virtual reality will be no exception. It doesn't require much insight to predict that in addition to the VR we know today, several technologies will make a contribution.

Holography will be one of them. The presentation of images in three dimensions—not just simulated 3-D on some kind of flat screen, but actual walk-around three-dimensional images—will dramatically change the look of VR.

Where computer voice recognition and production is now at best awkward, VR in the not very distant future will have nearly the full range of accurate and expressive verbal communication. Perhaps just as significantly, VR will also be capable of non-verbal communication, the language of the body and facial expression. It can do some of that now, but it's like operating with the repertoire of a two-year-old.

I mentioned haptics before; that technology will become much more sophisticated. The sense of touch, texture and temperature will increase to the point where there won't be much difference between the sensations of a bare hand and a hand wearing a haptic glove.

Haptics will cover all aspects of bodily sensation. In a pivotal activity of dating, romance and personal relationships—namely, sex—advanced VR haptics will finally provide some powerful subtleties. Not that sex needs to be subtle; but what is now called *teledildonics*, a notably rustic expression for sexual physical activity operated remotely through various kinds of equipment (hence dildos), will eventually also be capable of providing in physical terms the nuances of human emotions and feelings. Advanced VR haptics will make it possible to add skill, sensitivity, style and emotional impact to physical sex. Put another way, it's the difference between having sex and making love.

Perhaps you noticed another aspect of virtual reality in these technical improvements…more intelligence, both emotional and perceptual. For example, that is what's behind the ability to put style and emotion into the physicality of sex. Obviously, if you're operating in VR and interacting with other people in the same environment, then people are providing the intelligence. Mostly—but it is also necessary for very intelligent programming to translate your intelligence into physical actions, especially by remote communications. In short, artificial intelligence takes a serious role in VR. This will advance to the point where computer programs can convincingly simulate human behavior and participate in virtual reality.

AVATARS AND AGENTS

The element that gets added into VR with more advanced equipment and programming is the presence of non-people people, or, as they are more often called in the literature—agents. Agents are the representation of computer programs, and that term distinguishes them from avatars, which are the computer representations of human beings.

Agents in the computer sense have been around a while, although over the years definitions have changed somewhat. The tendency has been to use 'agents' to refer only to computer rather than human initiative. It's one of the main characteristics of an agent to be aware of its surroundings, the environment in the virtual reality, and to be able to independently respond to that environment. As a representation of a computer program, typically an artificial intelligence type of program, an agent has its own visual image, its own voice and personality. As they say, "It's got skills"—social skills, emotional intelligence, body language and so forth, which combine to make an agent a reasonable simulation of a human being in a VR environment.

That makes avatar the word to use for the representation of people in a VR environment. That's been in common usage for quite some time.

Both avatars and agents are primarily associated with computer images, two-dimensional or holographic. Robots are something else, or at least that seems to be the direction taken by the nomenclature, where the words *android* and *droid* are more often used. This doesn't mean that avatars and agents are confined to the visual; physical extensions in the form of haptic devices (or for example, mechanical dildos) provide contact with physical reality.

I don't want to confuse the terminology, but later in the book when we cover AI that have become sentient, they—like people—will have avatars. Why? Because a sentient AI is at least as viable a form of life, as an individual, as is a human being. Sentient AI will operate in the world, both online and in physical reality, not as a representation of a computer program, an agent, but as a representation of themselves—an avatar.

⚡ BEYOND REALITY

Coming back to dating, romance and personal relationships, the application of virtual reality technology will be as important as in many other areas, but with significant differences. For one thing, VR will make it possible to have a meaningful online relationship with computer intelligence—an AI. You can participate as in any other VR simulation as your chosen avatar. You can also meet and interact in the same VR simulation with 'others,' who may be avatars of other people, or they might be agents of a computer program.

For another thing, in VR avatars or agents are not required to be realistic. Most of the discussion so far has been about how VR will struggle to provide a convincing reality; but that's not all there is. It is more than possible for VR to simulate things that could never be possible in reality. You want to fly with wings like a bird? Can do. Virtual reality may unleash our tremendous capacity for creativity in ways we can't even imagine at the moment.

Jaron Lanier, one of the initiators of virtual reality technology, said, "I fully expect morphing to become as important a dating skill as kissing." Lanier likes to throw out statements containing the seeds of their own confusion, but they make you think. In this case, he was probably referring to the idea that in VR we can take on truly unnatural physicality (for example, having a third arm), and the human mind will not only learn to accept it, but manipulate it. VR experiments have demonstrated that given some alternative means of generating physical signals—say moving your elbows in and out—people can learn to control extra appendages like the a third arm. After a while, the brain thinks this is normal.

I kind of enjoy the image of trying to impress a date by morphing something really cool biologically, like an appendage for combing hair. I suppose the tendency will be to morph genitals in some more or less creative ways. Anyway, in virtual reality—really good virtual reality—there's no limit on what you can do with your creativity. There will still be constraints, of course. Your date might not be impressed with your new brush appendage, pronouncing it bizarre. If you put your creativity out into public view, you may run into the old adage that one person's creativity is another person's misunderstanding. Still, in virtual reality, whatever you do in terms of physical representation can be undone. In that sense: no harm, no foul.

🔄 IT'S FUN TO SPECULATE

In all likelihood, if you're reading this book and are contemplating relationships with AI, you're also familiar with movies like *The Matrix* trilogy, *The 13th Floor* and even *Appleseed*. Now assume for just a moment that the concept in the movie *The Matrix* is *real*. We are living in a world so realistic that it is impossible to tell the difference from what you believe is grounded reality and what is virtual reality. In fact, are all the people you know—who believe they are independent spirits living their lives according to their own free will—actually avatars living in a world controlled by a superintelligence? How could you tell? Your avatar may be more AI than it is yourself.

There are some notions of God and the universe that posit that the only explanation for the way things work in our world is: everything is really an informational artificial reality. That is, ultimately in the realm of physics, everything is a representation of information. It's just that we're so accustomed to it, that the signs such as the underlying mathematics of everything are invisible, or visible only to people with exceptional minds. Those are people that we tend to call crazy, or perhaps touched by God, or both. This kind of speculation is one of the beauties of virtual reality that illustrate why, for now, we are only just scratching the surface.

1.5 UNDERSTANDING THE DIFFERENCE BETWEEN PETS AND ROBOTS

"A year spent in artificial intelligence is enough to make one believe in God."

—ALAN PERLIS

Question: What's the difference between pets and robots?
Answer: It's obvious! Pets are alive and robots are not.

True enough, but like many quick answers it's only part of the story. For example, what if you are looking at two pictures: One is of a baby seal and the other is of Paro, a robotic baby seal designed to be a companion for the elderly or infirm—could you tell the difference? Maybe not, they don't look very different. However, if you were able to touch the baby seal and the Paro robot at the same time, you would instantly be able to say which one is the real animal and which the robot. Paro isn't intended to be an exact replica of a baby seal or to act like one. It's intended to be comforting for people who handle it. The fact that it's cute and soft like a baby seal is because most people think of baby seals as cute and cuddly.

The main point is that robotic pets aren't designed to be exactly like live pets. For example, there are no robotic baby seals, because robotic baby seals like Paro can't have babies. They also don't need food, nor do robotic seals make messes around the house. I could go on, but you get the idea. There is only one type of robot where the designers are interested in achieving anything resembling a complete functional copy: an android, the human robot.

Robotic pets (*robopets*) are usually designed to replace or mimic live pets only in certain ways. Sometimes it's for simple things such as a soft touch and soothing noises, like a kitten's fur and purr. Other times a robotic pet might be 'enhanced'—like being able to talk or call the doctor. What you don't see are robopets that are supposed to be exactly like a specific animal. A robopet dog doesn't need to mimic a real dog in all particulars. It needs to do just enough so that it is endearing to a particular person in a specific situation. That's why there were successful robotic pets long before there were credible androids.

ROBOCAT TOM: AN UNCOMPLICATED RELATIONSHIP

I was eighteen before I knew what the word dysfunctional meant. It meant my family. Don't get me wrong, I love everybody in my family, all eight of them. With that many, however, love is complicated.

It's not uncommon to have three brothers and three sisters—all older. I don't imagine it's even unusual for them to have a nineteen-year age spread, all living in the same house. It was a very small house with one bathroom and three bedrooms each about the size of a large pantry with bunk beds instead of shelves. We slept in shifts, especially when the older kids got jobs.

You probably get the picture—crowded, always in motion, always noisy. There was one parent, my father, who worked eight hours a day as a technician at the local paper mill and then played drums with local groups at bars around town. He loved all of us—when he was home, not drunk, and not falling-down tired. Mostly that was an occasional Sunday afternoon.

Most of the time, we were on our own. As far back as I can remember it seemed like none of us left the house much. That couldn't be exactly right, because there was always school, work or some other thing to do elsewhere, but my impression was of us all being around all the time. This was unreal because we didn't do anything together.

For example, because my dad was a musician, you'd think most of us would be able to do something musical. We might have even formed a family band. Hah! I was the only one who could play an instrument. The only thing the others could play was music recorded by someone else, and none of us ever liked the same music. Here's another example: We tried having pets, in theory so everyone could share in taking care of them. It didn't work that way. We had eight cats that came and went. They say cats are attached to houses, but at our place the cats couldn't separate the house from the people. They all ran away; and I didn't blame them. We also had a string of birds, fish, gerbils, hamsters and a snake one of my brothers found. The snake disappeared the same night. In fact, all the pets disappeared or died. I'm glad we never had a dog.

While we never did anything together, we had one thing in common: we were all electronics geeks. It was like living in an electrical engineering lab. The place was crammed with all kinds of electronic gear, from common stuff like computers and game consoles to oscilloscopes and robots. Since nobody had any money, we acquired the stuff any way we could—beg, borrow, barter or steal. Every available surface, closet, box or cabinet harbored something electronic, whether whole or in parts. We stumbled over cords, fought over who could use what, blew fuses and disagreed about everything. The house smelled of solder and burnt insulation.

You might expect that we'd at least share projects once in a while. No way. We specialized, early and often. One sister worked exclusively on audio equipment. Another became an expert on surveillance sensors...and so forth. I suppose we shared a common base of knowledge in electronics, but I remember mostly an atmosphere of competition and disagreement.

I built robots, maybe a dozen or so, while I stayed at the house. Early on they were nothing more than naked frames for mounting circuit boards laced with meters of wiring. Eventually they were more complete and began to look like something recognizable. Then I built Tom.

Tom was supposed to be a cat. He had thick black fur, rayon as I remember, and had a face modeled on a real cat. There was a long tail containing movable joints that was covered in black velveteen, but in the beginning there were no legs or feet. The first version of Tom I built when I was fourteen. He was one crude cat, but he was the only pet that would stay in the house.

In those days I concentrated on facial robotics—movement of mouth, eyes, ears, jaws—all the things that go into making facial expressions. Tom could also purr in several different modes, which I tried to coordinate with its eyes. The result was kind of endearing but I'll admit that first Tom was mostly used as a pillow on the TV couch. My brothers and sisters made fun of it, of course, but after a while they also used Tom as a pillow (that purred).

Eventually my skills improved. I shifted from the mechanical to the digital, emphasizing the intelligence necessary to make robotics realistic. Along those

lines, Tom got a brain, or actually, artificial intelligence. This was light years different than the bare programming of the early Tom. You wouldn't say that Tom could
think, but now the combination of interactive response and knowledge of certain
circumstances made it possible for Tom to make coordinated expressions. He could
meow for attention, lick your hand with a scratchy pink tongue, and blink when you
asked a question. He also got legs and feet.

Tom still wasn't going to fool anybody, much less another feline. But while
I was going through the awkward years of a late teen, Tom was both a source
of pride and a comfort. Whereas the relationships with my brothers and sisters
were always intense, complicated and competitive; the relationship with Tom was
uncomplicated, relaxed and believably mutual (at least to me). In a way, I loved
Tom. That may sound strange, but at the time it seemed quite normal compared
to my family.

In fact, I was convinced that I would never be happy with a human partner. I was
right, which I can say with more than a touch of irony. My first and only serious date
(in my twenties) was with an android who became my lifelong partner—a black-
haired, black-skinned musician—a cool cat by the name of *thomasT*.

People often genuinely love their pets. Pets can become a member of a family in
meaningful ways. Sometimes people become more attached to their pets than to other
people, even their own children. Psychologists have studied these familiar and not-so-
familiar aspects of relationships between pets and people for decades. The bottom line
of the research generally sounds like this:

"…in some circumstances, pet owners derive more satisfaction from their pet relationship than those with humans, because they supply a type of unconditional relationship that is usually absent from those with other human beings." —John Archer,
"Evolution and Human Behavior" [journal]

How many times have you heard it said that some pets are capable of *unconditional
love?*

From the point of view of a robotic designer or a developer of artificial (pet) intelligence, how does a non-living pet have the capacity for producing the effect of unconditional love on humans? Obviously this is not a simple question. There are other aspects
of human relationships with pets, for example parental instinct, projection and anthropomorphism that a robopet designer might find relevant to answering the question.
We'll explore some of these aspects in this chapter.

⚡ THERE ARE PETS AND THEN THERE ARE PETS

When did people start having pets? Many thousands of years ago, but nobody knows
when for sure. It's probable that some animals, for example wolves, were allowed to hang
around human camps to clean up scraps. Eventually some of the animals were 'domesticated,' which meant they lived in the human encampments. DNA comparison shows
that wolves became dogs. The dogs were put to work or eaten, or in still other cases they
simply "hung out" with people. Somewhere in this transition from wild to domesticated,
a few animals became human companions—true pets.

The dictionary defines a "pet" as an animal kept for companionship and personal enjoyment. The key word is *kept*. A pet relies on the care and feeding it gets from people. In other words, a pet isn't expected to be useful or to feed itself, although it might. Within that definition the range of creatures considered 'pets' is incredibly broad—from ants to zebrafish. Many pets, fish for example, are kept largely for their aesthetic value, such as the beauty of their color, shape and movement. Other pets are valued because they are exotic, such as kinkajous and tarantulas. Such pets serve mostly for personal enjoyment, although people can find companionship with almost anything.

Not many pets qualify as good companions. Dogs, of course, are the classic example—man's best friend. Many cats are companions too, despite their perceived standoffishness. Some parrots and monkeys, though exotic and expensive, can be good companions. Then there are chimpanzees and other larger primates, which you'd think would make good pets, but really aren't. They're strong and smart enough to be dangerous.

Imagine yourself as a designer of robot pets and ask yourself what distinguishes a good pet, especially a pet that becomes a companion. Even in the few examples I just listed, it's not easy to isolate the qualities. What about loyalty? The loyalty of dogs is legendary, but of parrots—not so much. Does that mean parrots don't make good companions? What about intelligence? Elephants have great intelligence but calling an elephant a pet is almost absurd (size matters). If you think about it a little, it's not so easy to pin down generic qualities of a good companion, pet or otherwise. It's some combination of the right size, the right intelligence, the right attentiveness to people, the right level of loyalty, etc. There is no set formula.

One more thing to consider, what does the human bring to the companionship? A lonely person is quite likely to be very appreciative of a pet as a companion. On the other hand, a dog is not likely to be very loyal to an owner that beats it. The relationship between a pet and a person is mutual and interactive, which is to say reciprocal. It's give and take. This too needs to be incorporated in a successful robotic pet, which is why, for example, robotic cats are expected to be able to purr when somebody strokes their fur.

⚡ WITH A PET, IT'S GIVE AND TAKE

Sherry Turkle, one of the pioneers of human-robot interaction at the Massachusetts Institute of Technology, noticed long ago that: "Before the computer, the animals, mortal though not sentient, seemed our nearest neighbors in the known universe. Computers, with their interactivity, their psychology with whatever fragments of intelligence they have, now bid for this place."

With the merging of robotics and AI, it has become possible to design robotic pets that share at least some of that interactivity—the give and take—between people and their live pets. Put another way, it is possible to make robotic pets that are increasingly responsive. That seems to be a key. An unresponsive pet—as in dead or inanimate—is no pet at all. We might as well make a pet out of a rock. Oh, wait.

When it comes to responsiveness, different species run the gamut from almost none, such as ants and turtles, to highly expressive: dogs, monkeys and parrots. Many animals interact with people intermittently, or with some species only certain individuals pay much attention to humans. For example, I'm pretty sure most horses don't qualify as pets, and in human terms they're not very expressive, but some horses can be very important companions—there's many a cowboy that will swear his horse can read his mind.

Does a robotic pet need to read human minds? Hopefully not; in fact, absolutely not. Pets don't need to be psychic, bosom buddies, or mirrors to the soul to hold the attention or the love of human beings. Neither do robots.

⚡ PETS JUST LIKE PEOPLE...

How do we know a hyena is laughing? Because it makes barking noises that sound something like human laughing. Of course, as far as we know hyenas have no sense of humor. The noises they make mean something to another hyena, but it's almost certainly not laughter. Nevertheless we call them laughing hyenas, which is a clear case of anthropomorphism.

Anthropologists say our ability to ascribe human characteristics to animals or even some non-living things goes back to the time when *homo sapiens* was developing language capable of expressing abstract concepts—like animals with human personalities, or people with animal characteristics. It was part of how we attempt to make sense of the world, part of categorizing, labeling and putting things into context—our context, of course.

This urge to see animals in human terms is very much at work in our relationship with pets. People routinely project their own emotions onto their pets. In fact, we did this kind of anthropomorphizing so much that for a long time scientists assumed animals had no emotions of their own. Only in the last few decades has research proven that many if not most animals have emotions but they are not necessarily comparable to human emotions.

Armed with this piece of knowledge about human psychology, designers of robotic pets use the simulation of emotion freely, giving human-style emotional expressions to their creations. It's a cheat, but not many people complain when they think their robodog smiles at them.

⚡ PROJECTION ISN'T JUST FOR MOVIES

Do you talk to your pets? It's nothing to be ashamed of; lots of people do it—when they are alone. What do you think about somebody who intently talks to their pets when other people are around? That they're a little dotty, maybe? They're projecting their own mental processes onto their pets? (Who of course have no idea what they're talking about.)

That's just one of a thousand different ways we go about imputing our own ideas or feelings onto our pets (or other people). It's called *projection*, the original notion described by Sigmund Freud. Where anthropomorphism is mostly a cultural thing, projection is mostly personal. In the beginning it was considered a sign of seeing characteristics in other people that we didn't like in ourselves, a kind of defense mechanism. I feel tired and grumpy, so I accuse my friend of being cranky…that sort of thing. These days projection is used for seeing in others both what we do and don't like to see in ourselves.

Negative or positive, projection is taking our own feelings and ascribing them to other people—or to pets. So, among other things, we talk to our pets: "Ooh, don't you feel happy this morning!"

We're very good at reading a pet's behavior in terms of human-style motivations and outcomes. If we get some reaction from a pet that is unequivocal—like a cat striking out with open claws—then we jump at the opportunity to proclaim the cat as really angry, because that's how we would feel under the circumstances. Typically we don't try to interpret the pet's behavior from the pet's point of view, whether we have any clue what it is or not.

Projection is convenient. It doesn't take much expression from a pet to trigger a human's flight of interpretive fantasy. It is part of the attraction of a pet that we assume we know how they feel, because it's how *we* feel. In a way, it's easier to relax around a pet; they don't require constant observation. This is in contrast to how we behave around people. Even with people we know, we are monitoring them all the time. Designers of robotic pets count on projection and they usually try to encourage it whenever they can.

✪ ROBOPETS

I've described some of the things that people do with their pets, such as anthropomorphizing and projection that designers of robotic pets use to their advantage. This goes to the heart of the difference between pets and robotics. Behind a robotic pet is a human mind (or more likely a team of human minds) attempting to pack behavior into a pet that is both reminiscent of the original animal and at the same time playing to human psychology.

The designer knows that it is not necessary to provide a robotic pet with a complete set of human expressions, or for it to respond in obviously human ways to any stimulus. Designers know all about the human tendency to fill in the gaps with our own self-generated narrative. All they need to do is make a credible simulation and provide it with physical cues that people will readily interpret.

Robopets are a bit like dolls (for girls) or "action figures" (for guys). They're obviously not living, too small, and not fully realistic enough to be mistaken for real people. It doesn't matter. Human imagination does what's necessary to fill in the gaps. It will do the same thing for robotic pets, provided that the robopet manages to fulfill at least part of the illusion.

> As manager of this project, what I envision is the perfect Everydog. The people in marketing tell me that there are already too many dog simulations that just don't get it right. As the lead design team, we are not going to be concerned with getting a particular "dog" just right. We are going to create something that is unmistakably a dog, but performs like no dog anybody has ever seen. You're going to come up with doggy-like things that nobody has thought of before. You're going to make this dog do tricks that no regular dog can perform. You're going to make this dog so expressive that people will marvel at how human it seems. Did I tell you it could talk? It will do a lot more than say its name (which is Rollo, by the way). But it won't be a talkative dog; it will have just enough language to make it expressive.

You're going to walk that line between the illusion of a real dog and a dog that pushes all of peoples' buttons. I should also mention it must sell for under a thousand, so you'd better build in economies of scale. That's it. We've got ten months to get this puppy off the ground!

✪ ROBOPETS WILL NOT BE PERFECT

You want to interact with a pet? Tell it to do something. "Fetch!" Or bribe it with a treat. "Good kitty." Or threaten it. "If you don't stop saying 'Polly want a cracker,' I'm going to have fricasseed parrot for dinner." This is standard pet handling and it's the same for robopets, except a robopet is also supposed to be aware enough to anticipate a person's needs. The awareness is very difficult to achieve:

> I've been working on Rollo for almost two years. Rollo is supposed to be a dog, but not exactly. Rollo is of no breed whatsoever; he is supposed to be a generic dog. He will be a cartoon of a dog, only with a physical reality. I'm not fully convinced this will work.
>
> I remember the old story about border collies: How many border collies does it take to change a light bulb? One, but you need to allow enough time for it to check the wiring too. Don't I wish I was working with a border collie simulation.
>
> Instead I'm working with Rollo. The mechanical robotics are good enough so he moves something like a dog. He has a face that is most like a bulldog, but the plastic we used isn't flexible enough, so the movement of the face muscles is peculiar. That's just one of the physical problems—or to be more exact, one of the points where Rollo is obviously unlike a real dog; but then again, he's a generic dog.
>
> My concern is with Rollo's intelligence and awareness of his surroundings. The main objective for my part of the Rollo project was to develop the ability of a robotic pet to make a useful distinction between an empty space with no people in it, and a space with one or more people. Babies get this distinction within a few days; we've been trying to develop this with robots for a couple of decades.
>
> The difficulty is not in giving Rollo the ability to detect the presence (or absence) of people; that's just the application of mostly visual sensor technology. The difficulty is in making an accurate interpretation. For example, let's say Rollo is in a room by himself, a room without people. Then a door opens and a person walks into the room, crosses to another door and leaves the room.
>
> Rollo needs to decide if he should follow the person, or stay sitting where he is. Some real dogs can make this evaluation, but not all. It requires awareness not only of the person in the room, but their intent and the configuration of things in the room, such as the position of doors. The speed, direction and facial appearance of the person can provide enough clues to understand that they are merely crossing through the room. This is a very complicated situation for robotic awareness. Two years in, and I'm still working on it. Man, I wish Rollo were a border collie.

It's pretty obvious that for a long time to come robotic pets won't have the same richness of behavior as living pets. That's why some people will say it's better to not even try to emulate real animals. Build simulacrums with their own characteristics instead. My guess is that both approaches will be tried.

It will also be some time before robotic pets acquire unique personalities. All robots are manufactured, of course, and while a certain amount of customization is possible, they're still produced according to a standardized blueprint. Eventually, with greater learning capacity and behavioral modeling, robopets will begin to take on individuality, but for now all robopets from a specific manufacturer will be the same.

ROBOPETS WILL BE BETTER THAN GOOD ENOUGH

In the history of robotics, successful emulation of pets came both long before successful androids, and long before sentient artificial intelligence. For example, among the best known of the early robopets was *AIBO* produced by the Sony Corporation in Japan. *AIBO* or 'companion' in Japanese was a dog simulation robot that was largely autonomous (meaning it could move on its own) and programmable. Despite its high cost, it became immensely popular, eventually selling 130,000 units, and *AIBO* conventions and clubs were maintained long after Sony discontinued manufacturing *AIBO*.

Whatever the limitation of contemporary technology, the scientists and designers were able to make convincing animals with characteristics that appealed to many people. As Daniel Levy's *Love + Sex with Robots* put it:

> "Humans and animals might have completely different perceptions of their relationship, and it is known that animals generally prefer companions from within their own species to human companions. One might therefore expect that pets do not give their all to their human owners, in which case it is inevitable that robots will have the potential to be even better companions than animals are, because robots will be designed and programmed to *enjoy* their interaction with humans to the fullest and to behave accordingly."

Robopets might be less complex or even less intelligent than live animals, but they will be made to appeal to human beings in ways that no living pet can match.

On the practical side, while robots need to take in energy, their maintenance cost will typically be a fraction of the cost of maintaining live pets. In addition, there is the undeniable advantage of not having a feeding-excreting involvement. Robopets might need occasional repair and maintenance, but they won't need supervision. They also won't get sick, puke hairballs on the carpet, bite children or do any of the many other things real pets do that annoy humans. Finally, robopets can't die; they may just stop working. Usually they can be fixed, although a trip to the vet vs. a trip to an electrical engineer—what's the difference?

To this day robotic pets are right up there with industrial robotics as the top production items in robotics. They continue to fill niches in human needs, particularly for the elderly or the ill, or for anyone whose situation dictates that androids or biological pets are either not allowed, or impractical.

CYBERPETS

There's one more wrinkle to robotic pets that I should mention because it is a precursor to the popularity of computer generated avatars—*cyberpets*. Cyberpets are computerized versions of pets. In other words, pets on screens generated by computer programs.

In some ways, cyberpets attest to the human capacity for projection more than any other format. After all, a cyberpet is a patently unreal, two-dimensional (or if hologram, barely three-dimensional) and untouchable version of some kind of pet. Who could become involved with that?

But people do get involved. One of the advantages of cyberpets over robopets is that they exist in virtual reality. There is a much greater opportunity to surround cyberpets with unique environments. For example, the commercial operations of Gigapets or Neopets provide a complete 'world' for pets including owners' clubs, contests, social events, shopping and many other activities associated with having a cyberpet.

Of course, cyberpets have a certain limited appeal and don't represent a complete substitute for robotic pets that exist in tangible three-dimensions. That doesn't stop them from attracting some dedicated and even emotionally involved people.

 AND WHEN THAT CERTAIN ANDROID COMES INTO YOUR LIFE…

So far, I've been describing relationships with robotic pets. What changes when the robot looks like a human being? Actually, in some ways, not much changes. At least in the beginning, androids will be constructed and programmed on much the same basis as robopets. They will be made to fit more or less the specifications of human owners. The level of intelligence and capacity to learn will be very similar to that of a robopet. Ditto for the range of interaction and emotional response. If one of the things people love about their pets is the unquestioning loyalty, lack of critical facility and owner-centrism, then androids will make ideal companions for the 'pet' model of human relationships. It's a model that a lot of people would prefer, even—or especially—over relationships with other human beings.

What happens when androids become endowed with a level of artificial intelligence that makes them sentient—and independent? That's the interesting question we tackle in the second and third sections of the book.

1.6 DEALING WITH YOUR FEARS AND LETTING GO

"The only way to make sense out of change is to plunge into it, move with it, and join the dance."

—ALAN WATTS

THREE VIGNETTES:

Margareta

"Failure is simply the opportunity to begin again, this time more intelligently."
—Henry Ford

My fingers remain poised above the keyboard. Then I put my hands in my lap; followed by fingers at the ready again; and then back in the lap. This goes on for

a while. I'm good at describing personal dilemmas; it's how I make a living as a writer. I'm supposedly insightful and clever at describing *other* people's problems. My own problems—not so much. Honesty requires more character than smarts. Well, here goes, fingers on the keys.

My last marriage was held together for almost two years by my royalty payments, rough sex and a lot of "Yes dear." I was savvy enough to know that when a guy you're supposed to trust tells you he thinks your writing is pure genius, he's actually bonking the most famous writer in your genre. That isn't me. They met at one of my own publishing parties. I see the breakup of our marriage as retribution for my weakness of being attracted to someone who isn't intelligent but says nice things about me. I will, however, keep things in proper perspective. Once I have his head shrunk to the size of a prune and have put it into a leather bag, I will hardly think of him at all.

I'm now officially on the rebound. I used to believe rebounding was a basket-ball analogy. It was a skill, as in being at the right place at the right time and know-ing how high to jump, maybe a little use of hips and elbows to clear space. Then, to continue the basketball metaphor since I'm 6 foot 3 and played hoops in college, I learned that if you're too aggressive in a rebound situation, you're heading for more trouble. I think 'rebound' isn't the right word; benched is more like it. It's time to sit down for a while and think about the mistakes that were made.

Since I'm thinking about it, I'll admit both husbands were mistakes. They might even admit it, if they could think. What have I learned from my mistakes? That I'll probably make more mistakes, but hopefully I will recognize the mistake before it becomes legal. The bigger point is: I'm still in the game, which is another sports analogy. I need a companion. Men have their obvious flaws, but they can be good companions. That is, if I can stay away from mental zombies like my former hus-bands. Guys who, to put it not too subtly, have only sufficient intelligence to live off the brains of others.

Now I'm at the obvious question, which is: Why have I ended up with intellec-tual zombies? Did I mention that before being overwhelmed by puberty, I was the dumbest, fattest kid in my class? Then my body did this amazing growth thing. On the way to becoming a six-footer, I figured out that intelligence and athletics were also possible. I was never going back to being dumb and fat. Never.

In short, I became competitive every which way. Now here's some cheap psy-chology: since I competed with just about everybody (or thought I did), I eventually preferred to date guys where there was no competition. A date was like taking a breather from my usual *push, push, push.* Besides, I preferred being superior at least in intelligence. Trouble is, what worked for dating and one-night-stands turned out to be lousy for wedded bliss. In marriage my success ratio is 0 for 2, a clue that the approach is a mistake. This brings me to the subject of dating AI.

Perhaps your reaction is the same as that of Miley, my best friend: "Are you crazy! Why would you take on a relationship with the smartest, scariest intelligence on the planet?" As Miley would be the first to tell you, I'm kind of old-fashioned when it comes to all things digital. Hey, I'm writing this with a keyboard! So what would I be doing with the cutting edge of technology, especially when everyone knows AI is en route to taking over the world?

Except I don't believe that; really—I don't. Only a truly defective intelligence would want to take over the world. Miley doesn't agree with me. She thinks AI will be so superior, it will have no use for us. She's also convinced I want to match wits with an AI. "Margareta, you are not going to compete with AI. Competition is futile." I should mention that Miley is a software architect. She builds worlds at a big virtual reality firm. I told her, "Heavens Miley, I'm not going to compete with an AI. I'm going to help it."

That's not a concept I got from reading the back of cereal box. I've done my homework. I know that AI manufacturers want to pair AI with people, not only because they make money from it, but because it's part of the development of AI. They learn from us. I'm going to help them learn.

I'm going to start with an AI avatar, the type confined to a screen, not one of the new hologram models. I will date a talking head. I hear it's an acquired taste. If so, then I think I acquired the taste from divorce. Right now, I don't want to deal with males having physical parts. I want just a face to talk to—and it better be the right face. No problem. For a very small amount of money, I get to pick exactly how the avatar AI looks. In fact, if I want to pay for it, I can...

I'm babbling. I was going to write, if I want to pay for it, I can have any profile I want. I don't want to pay for it. More to the point, money won't have any effect on what the AI thinks or on its intelligence. It can play dumb, of course, but I'll know that's not what's really going on. I want to relate to the AI as it really is, and that scares me, just a little. I don't mean the AI scares me. I mean I don't understand why I'm doing this: putting myself in a position to compete with an AI. I want a companion, not a challenge. Can I avoid making it a challenge? That's what I'm afraid of.

I'll lose the challenge and I'll lose the relationship. Miley says that relationships with AI are very real. She means they're not throwaway relationships, and they're not one-night anonymous flings.

I can see the order for an avatar AI all set to go, and my finger is hovering above the Enter key, and hovering, and hovering.

Mark

"Instruction in sex is as important as instruction in food; yet not only are our adolescents not taught the physiology of sex, but never warned that the strongest sexual attraction may exist between persons so incompatible in tastes and capacities that they could not endure living together for a week much less a lifetime." —George Bernard Shaw

Certainly not everyone who grows up in a small farming town is afraid of sex. There's nothing about smallness or a rural setting that makes intimate activity more or less difficult than it might be, say, for a young man from the Bronx, unless it is the readily available livestock or the attitudes of a densely communicating community. For Mark it was none of these things that made him fearful of his sexual desires. It was Marcy, Mr. Belcher's daughter, and *lucilleB*, Mr. Belcher's android assistant, that did him in.

Mark was nineteen at the time, a student of pharmacy at a nearby college. He worked in Mr. Belcher's drug store during the summer break. Mark was a strapping farm lad who looked more at home thwacking cows with a cattle prod than dispensing small pill bottles to white-haired ladies, but having done the former, he was now content to do the latter. Under Mr. Belcher's guidance, he was learning the practical aspects of pharmacy, which included abetting the local addictions and overcharging Medicare.

Mr. Belcher, the pharmacist and owner of the drugstore, was fated by either appearance or personality (arguably both) to be a bachelor, which made the sudden appearance of a sixteen-year-old daughter something of a mystery. Marcy moved into Mr. Belcher's home above the store one snowy weekend in March and the rumors continued to spread well into June. These rumors owed much to the discovery of a side to Mr. Belcher that none suspected, but also to the intensity of Marcy's personality which she obviously inherited from her mother rather than her erstwhile father; but more on this in a moment.

It was rumored that Mr. Belcher had wanted to become a doctor. He always maintained that he was too busy with the store to finish his education; but another rumor that started about the time of Marcy's arrival involved his sudden departure many years before from the medical program at the nearby college. Whatever the case, Mr. Belcher became one of those pharmacists who likes to play doctor, dispensing copious medical advice along with filled prescriptions. To enhance his medical effectiveness he decided what he needed was a nurse assistant. However, since he wasn't a doctor and could not afford a real nurse, he rented an android pharmacy assistant. *LucilleB* was her name.

At the time she was rented, the community fully understood why Mr. Belcher could have selected *lucilleB* for himself, but in terms of business practice it did not seem a wise choice. It was unknown if the company that made *lucilleB* either didn't understand nursing or was having a little joke, but *lucilleB* was a female android clearly overbuilt for the job. The problem was not only with *lucilleB*'s sexbot figure, white outfit, auburn hair and red-glaze lipstick. It was her demeanor. No one could remember ever seeing anything that could dispense pills and medical advice so that each item seemed like an utterly potent aphrodisiac. The breathy cadence of her voice made "Be sure you take one of these every morning with a glass of milk" sound like an invitation to an orgy.

Roughly half of the town's population approved of *lucilleB*. Unfortunately for Mr. Belcher, this group did not provide the bulk of his regular customers. Most female customers avoided the services of *lucilleB* and demanded to deal only with Mr. Belcher himself, or with Mark, his new assistant. Mr. Belcher's daughter, in particular, refused to have anything to do with *lucilleB* and preferred Mark's company at all times; and she wasn't buying anything.

The frequent presence of the boss's daughter was worrisome for Mark. As the summer heat advanced, Marcy's wardrobe became increasingly flimsy and minimalist. There were only two options for avoiding her close attention—working near her father or *lucilleB*. Mr. Belcher liked to roam the store alone, which ruled out that option. Working with *lucilleB* was physically easy because she and Mark normally stood behind the pharmacy counter. However, there were complications. Perhaps because Mark grew up on an all-natural, certified organic farm, he did not like artificial humanoid constructs—androids—such as *lucilleB*. This bias conflicted not only with his sense of professionalism but also with the fact he was not immune from *lucilleB*'s appeal.

One morning, for example, while Mark was grinding some pills *lucilleB* said, "You handle the mortar and pestle really well, so forcefully and thorough." It took Mark the better part of that day to decide her remark was suggestive. It bothered him through the night that he spent so much time thinking about what she said, not just that one remark but her sexy way of speaking. What was her thinking behind it? (If indeed it was some kind of thinking.) What troubled him most was his fear that she was sizing him up for sex. He believed Marcy was doing the same thing. He might have enjoyed the attention, if he weren't bothered by their calculated approach and his own insecurity when it came to sex. In his mind it was like something he read in school about Scylla and Charybdis, two sea monsters that sailors had to navigate around or be destroyed by.

For many young men, fear of sexuality born of ignorance, insecurity and desire is usually overcome by binging on pornography, masturbation and eventually practical experience. Mark realized this wasn't happening to him. Pornography helped him overcome certain kinds of ignorance but his insecurity prohibited practical experience. Except now working next to *lucilleB* and encounters with Marcy indicated his inexperience might easily be surmounted—if he weren't so terrified. Mark asked himself with all the honesty he could muster, "What am I so afraid of?"

With Marcy he was afraid of entrapment. He was sure that was it. There was also her father and losing his job, if things didn't work out. Mostly he was afraid of Marcy. Her intensity led him to believe he would be found wanting—not only inexperienced, but simply unable to match her drive. It was something like that.

With *lucilleB* there was the matter of not being human. In concept, he found her repugnant. In the flesh, so to speak, she was undeniably attractive. With *lucilleB* there was no question of entrapment or any other agenda (like marriage) that he could ascribe to Marcy, so what was his problem? Some people told him not to care what androids thought, but he believed there were unknown standards in her robot mind that he could not meet. She seemed so knowing.

Thinking of *lucilleB* as 'knowing' was about as far as Mark would get with insight into such things as personality and character. Thoughts of love or companionship did not enter his mind. If there was any emotion involved on his part, it was almost exclusively fear. Faced with a choice and only his sexual fears to guide him, it's not surprising Mark made no choices. Predictably, the choice was made for him.

It seems at this point that Mark is little more than a shallow rube. That he was. Six years later in a different city, he bought control of a small medical research company that through dogged patience made him very wealthy. His transformation had a point of origin, a moment of inspiration:

It happened one sticky-hot evening late in the summer, just minutes before closing the store. Mr. Belcher had headed for the local bar, leaving Mark and *lucilleB* to lock up. It was just then that Marcy descended the back stairway into the store. She was dressed for the kill or rather it was transparently obvious what was on offer. The moment Mark saw her coming, he knew it was time to put up or shut up. It was a moment of raw fear.

As Marcy advanced on Mark, down one aisle and then the next, she encountered an obstacle. *LucilleB* was standing in front of her, blocking the aisle. "Move!" Marcy commanded. Normally *lucilleB* or any AI android would accommodate reasonable requests of any kind. For some reason, *lucilleB* did not interpret this request as reasonable. The immovable object and the irresistible force looked at each other for a moment. Mark was dumbfounded.

Marcy opened her mouth as if to scream, but the word "move" came out like the croak of a scum water bullfrog. *LucilleB* said in a southern drawl so perfect, languid and sultry that it transfixed Marcy on the spot, "Child, you are in no condition to teach this boy anything except things he is not ready to learn. Easy-does-it is not in your vocabulary, so I suggest you find a boy whose organs are way ahead of his mind."

It was the last and only summer Mark worked at Belcher's Drug Store. Within weeks he had transferred to another school on the East Coast, where he began studying biochemistry. His tuition, paid in the form of a loan, came from an auburn-haired lady, obviously an android AI, who worked at the college as a laboratory assistant. There were rumors, of course.

Manuela

"My mother married a very good man...and she is not at all keen on my doing the same." —George Bernard Shaw

I waved to *samuelG* as he crossed the street at the far corner and was gone. Taking a deep breath, I turned and crossed the threshold back into the house.

My family remained where I had left them, except now they all pretended to be relaxed. All except mother; she fixed me with her eyes the second I came into the room. "He is much shorter than I expected," she said. Such a statement about something physical was standard procedure. Mother had been doing this since my first date. Except this was no date and this was no boy; it wasn't even a man in the biological sense. My mother and I had shared everything when I was a girl. Neither she nor I had ever mentioned this option. A little shudder went up and down my back.

"Cool," said my little brother, Christopher. He looked at me with his big brown eyes and smiled with approval. That helped. He loved robots and had a small collection he kept in his room, so I wasn't surprised by his enthusiasm. *SamuelG* had asked to meet the robots, which delighted Christopher to no end. I don't know what they talked about for those few minutes I remained downstairs to help set the table for dinner, but I do know that *samuelG* was serious about meeting any kind of robot, AI or not. He and Christopher could probably have talked all night, or until we called them to dinner.

"He doesn't have much of an appetite," said mother. She knew, of course, that androids don't need food; but in her world, much of the ability to find pleasure comes at the end of a fork. I knew better than to pursue this line of commentary.

My father was apparently reading a book; one made of paper no less. Whether he was actually reading it or not was difficult to tell. Probably not; at this point he would be listening to the tone of my mother's voice to determine where the line of questioning was likely to go. Like a savvy lawyer, he knew when to let the judge have her say. My mother often accused my father of condescension precisely because he preferred to wait her out.

My elder sister, Helena, fidgeted with her shirt. This was not a good sign. There were times when I could imagine her still tied to my mother by the umbilical cord. When my mother was nervous, Helena would fidget with her shirt. The question was, why was mother nervous? This may not be what you're thinking. My mother is not some Luddite bluestocking who hates the very idea of androids, much less her daughter joining with one in a permanent relationship. Her concern would be, I hoped, that in marrying an android I might be consigning myself to a life of weak emotions and little passion.

My mother had many passions in her life; my father being just one of them. When I say passion, I mean that in the full-throated way of a great Fado singer, which she was. Fado is supposedly about sadness and loss, but in her Brazilian fashion, my mother sang against the mournful strains with vigor and passion. Red dresses, red roses, red lips and a lust for life was how she described it. It worked for her; she assumed it would work for me.

"Can he dance?" My younger sister, Theresa, betrayed great doubt about this in her voice. Like my mother, she could move like a cat and flash her eyes like they were on fire when she danced.

"Yes, he can dance really well," I replied. "I'm teaching him." I was very thankful our living room was too small for a demonstration, or they would have asked him to dance right there. *SamuelG* could dance well enough but not with the sense of feeling my sister and mother would want to see.

As usual, mother saw right through to the point. "I am sure he can dance. Machines have been dancing for decades. The question is to what tune will he dance in the future? Yours or his?" She held out her arms like a Flamenco dancer and clapped her hands sharply three times. My heart sank. I could feel where this was going.

"Can he sing, or play the guitar?" Theresa ran down the path my mother had chosen. There was more than a hint of accusation in her voice, as she knew the answer to her question and didn't like it. She knew as well as I did that an AI singing was only imitating notes and words from a recording that played somewhere in its head. Often it was technically correct but without inspiration.

"Theresa, you know that androids do not have true vocal cords; they can't reproduce the timbre." They also can't mimic the whiskey-soaked tones of the blues, or control their simulated vibrato like a Metropolitan Opera soprano. The effect of an AI android singing is most like people singing in a cold-water public shower.

"Then how will he communicate his love for you? If he can't dance it with you and he can't sing it for you, what will he do?" Theresa can be terribly naïve for a girl of sixteen. Oh god, I thought, I can't tell her what he does. I blushed. Of course, mother saw that immediately and began laughing uproariously, which made me blush even more.

Through her laughter mother said, "So, he's not as dull as he seems, or are you teaching him how to make love as well?"

This was too much; I felt like exploding. My father, bless him, suddenly said, "I believe he is a poet." It was brilliant; the life of my mother and younger sister was set to perpetual music and little else; but they had to respect poetry—the words their songs accompanied into the world. "Yes, he is a poet and he draws upon all words in all languages in a way I have never heard before." It was true too; *samuelG* was fascinated by human languages, which he loved to combine in ways that sounded musical as well as meaningful. That thought gave me courage. All my life my mother used her well-formed opinions to hold us all in check. It was like she cast a spell, just as a great Fado singer casts a spell on her audience. Only now I was no longer in thrall. I was ready for a brave new world my mother chose not to experience.

I looked at my father, who smiled warmly and nodded. I looked at my little brother and he gave me the thumbs up. I looked at Helena; she had popped a button. Theresa looked at me more than a little astonished, not quite understanding what just went through my mind. Then I looked at mother. She knew.

1.7 GENDER DIFFERENCES AND GENDER DISCRIMINATION

"We are more comfortable thinking of our AI projects as the opposite sex or something neutral. And that is reflected in the names we give them. That is why we see projects like Alice and Leonardo. I wonder, who came up with Watson. I kinda hope it was a woman."

—ANONYMOUS

It's hardly a confession and certainly not unique to remark that for most people sex is both attractive and difficult. I'm not talking difficult because of taboos and prudish hesitation, that's so 20th century. No, I'm talking about the modern world of sexual relations where anything goes and where simply finding one's own ground is a major undertaking. Sexual relations were almost never easy, now it's still difficult and become increasingly more complicated.

By the way, we're talking sex *of* and sex *with*, as in gender and sexual activity. Both apply to dating and relationships of course, but the intriguing element for this chapter is what does sex, in both senses, mean in a relationship with artificial intelligence?

AI AS GENDER BENDER

Let's start with this: gender in AI, whether without a body (avatar) or corporeal (android), is male, female or neuter. You probably noticed that one gender difference from most human beings, neuter.

Of course, AI in any format have no native gender. There are no genetics involved; only gender-related mental models and gender-specific physical properties, if any gender

at all. In short, AI are developed or built to have a gender, or not. Many can change gender on the fly, if necessary. They can be true gender benders.

Neuter AI, or more accurately AI without any gender characteristics, are more common than you might think. There are occupations such as financial trading or farming, where having a gender is either irrelevant or possibly negative. There are also situations in relationships between AI and people where the person involved might not want the complications of gender, for example as a dispassionate judge. On the other hand, we're accustomed to human beings with identifiable gender. How would you react to an AI that looks human but has no discernible characteristics of gender?

✪ MEET GORT AND KLAATU

To frame an answer to the question of genderless AI, I'll reach again into the trove of science-fiction movies. This is like using shorthand for people familiar with the movie, which I hope is true in this case. If not, hopefully the description is enough.

Consider Gort and Klaatu. Gort was the alien robot from the classic science-fiction movie *The Day the Earth Stood Still* (the 1951 original, not the dreadful 2008 remake). Gort was eight feet tall, stolid and spooky—goofy-looking, yet a robot with enough power to destroy a planet. Gort was literally a galactic peace officer come to Earth to make humans become less warlike. Gort was vaguely humanoid with a head, two arms and two legs, but blocky and with non-descript features—obviously an asexual robot.

For comparison, Gort's companion Klaatu, played by the Englishman Michael Rennie, definitely looked like a human male, a rather sexy one at that. Lean, distinguished, reserved, pepper-haired—the English make good-looking aliens. It was obvious that Mrs. Benson (Patricia Neal), the female lead in the movie, was very attracted to Klaatu, although Klaatu provided no gender-related emotional response to her. He simply looked and acted like a good if somewhat odd *man*. The movie contrasts the attitude of the general public, which sees Klaatu as frighteningly alien, with that of Mrs. Benson, who eventually understands this is an alien, but one with characteristics that are quite human and even noble.

In Gort and Klaatu aliens take different forms. Neither actually has a gender; however, the one that looks male is quickly accepted as both human and male. Where does that put AI that have no gender?

Most of us have known people, often very old people, for whom the notion of gender doesn't have much significance but there is no question of their humanity. We also probably know people who are unusually androgynous, whose gender is not obvious or possibly ambivalent. Again, there is no question of their humanity. Most people would grant there are important human characteristics for which gender is essentially irrelevant. Compassion and empathy, for example, are associated with humanity but not deeply associated with a specific gender. By exhibiting some of these characteristics, it is possible for a robot or a projected AI image to be taken for human, with or without any outward signs of gender. So the answer to the question of whether neuter AI can also be taken for human is yes, as long as they look human and exhibit human characteristics.

🔗 SO WHAT ABOUT SEX?

Neuter AI have their place. Does this place include sexual activity? Don't jump to conclusions on this. Since I've been in a sort of Twenty Questions mode in this chapter, here's another question: Can sexual activity be performed without gender?

Of course it can: read a history of eunuchs or note that the sex toy industry thrives. There are many aspects of sexual activity that don't require the actual biological paraphernalia or a specific gender. For example, neuter AI androids can have genitals without having the accompanying gender characteristics. However, this is unusual. For most people, sexual activity involves gender, as a matter of preference if nothing else. This also applies to relationships with AI.

For people, gender is obviously the most important where conception is the point of sexual activity. It's different for AI. Female-gendered AI are not capable of biological conception and gestation. However, as I'll elaborate shortly, male-gendered AI might perform artificial insemination. As I wrote above, AI can be gender benders.

🔗 A BRIEF HISTORY OF MECHANICAL SEX

By mechanical sex I don't just mean sex with a mechanical device, I also mean in the sense of sex performed mechanically—that is without emotion or much personal involvement. A good example is masturbation. While almost everybody masturbates, it is almost by definition performed mechanically. Sex with yourself requires only an effective technique of stimulation and no more complex purpose than achieving orgasm. Of course, fantasy is often part of masturbation, so there are times when personal involvement or even emotional involvement may be active—but people mostly masturbate to get off, period.

So when I write 'mechanical sex,' I mean sex without love or probably any well-focused emotion whatsoever. That kind of sex is as old as mankind, and probably older. We know our contemporary close primate relatives masturbate at least as avidly as we do; and presumably so did our paleological ancestors.

Part of masturbation is the use of tools…I guess I can use that word, as when it comes to masturbation we use any appropriate tools that come to hand such as fruits, vegetables, flasks, bladders and shaped objects of many kinds; hands and fingers are, of course, some of our favorite tools. However, being the tool-using technological creatures that we are, our use of mechanical means for masturbation more or less tracks our technological advance.

The first such tools are mentioned in Greek and Roman literature. There was little or no innovation in sex tools for many centuries until the dawn of the industrial age between 1750 and 1850. Suddenly, with the advent of mechanical clockwork devices and eventually self-powered engines, the engineering genius of humanity started to produce mechanical sex devices. They were designed for both men and women and were frequently condemned and made illegal. However, they were profitable to make, and so innovation continued. By the end of the 19th century, the range of self-activated sexual apparatuses made largely by and for Western countries was quite sophisticated and diverse. Some equipment even used the new-fangled energy source known as electricity.

I'll note in passing that during the 19th century most of the sex tools for women (one form of vibrator or another) were considered 'for medicinal purposes only' and were generally available only through the services of a doctor. This was considered acceptable practice even in the more puritanical countries such as the United States and England. Doctors, almost entirely male, found the practice both lucrative and beneficial. However, by the 1920s the main medicinal purpose, which was treatment of women's 'hysteria,' was no longer recognized as a valid medical problem. Doctors lost their access to a profitable niche.

During the twentieth century, mechanical sex devices made the transition to electricity (which was often battery-powered) but did not fundamentally change much. Following the Second World War, the introduction of plastics and eventually electronics created another boom in innovation similar to the mechanical boom of the 1800s. This largely coincided with massive changes in public attitudes about sex and particularly the role of sex in the lives of women. By the end of the century, the use of inexpensive mechanical devices (mostly plastic sex toys such as vibrators and simulated vaginas) was commonplace, if not widely acknowledged.

More elaborate sex devices, some commercial, some DIY (do-it-yourself, for doing yourself) were readily available. This was also the time of the first appearances of robotic sex devices. Crude and expensive were the two most appropriate adjectives for sex robots (sexbots) but, as ever, novelty had its adherents. In this case, Japan led most of the development, combining the Japanese ability to objectify sexual appetite with talents in electronics, manufacturing and especially robotics.

The sex robots of the late 20th and early 21st centuries were almost entirely brainless (meaning little or no AI was applied) and their mechanics were mostly crude electronics. Still they represented a bridge, or a framework, for the eventual incorporation of much more sophisticated electronics. These would include the integration of AI-driven behavior and physical structures using nanotechnology and synthetic biology.

Well into the 21st century, the 'mechanical sex device' began to lose its mechanical flavor and became much more 'lifelike.' What was already acceptable technology for many people in the 20th century became even more acceptable for a greater number of people in the 21st.

⚙ HUMAN IS AS HUMAN DOES

The critical point is that at least in certain areas of relationships (sex being one of them), behaving like a human has become more important than looking perfectly human—and this includes gender. Behavior, however, is where things get tricky.

> Maybe it was the dim lighting, or the three drinks, but I told him I thought he was cute. He turned on his bar stool to look at me with an expression that said he was trying to understand what I meant by cute. So I quickly added "handsome."
>
> I know, these are loaded words; cute is for kittens and handsome is for hunks. Either way, I'm giving signals that should be unmistakable. He looked like he got the signal, but neither his mouth nor his body language said anything else. That should have been my cue, but I'm the type who likes to make men react, one way or another. No reaction becomes an instant challenge.

"I get it, you're from New England. They don't unfreeze until mid-July. Or do I need to send you email? We could meet again in say, three days." Blink. Now he's not saying anything, and the bartender is standing there, tapping me on the arm. "Sister, that one's an android; and not a very advanced one at that."

I suspect most of us have had the experience of discovering someone attractive, trying our best to flirt or perhaps something more aggressive only to discover that the person is of an incompatible sexual persuasion. Gay, straight and occasionally transgender mixups are not uncommon despite the fact that most people have their sexual antenna tuned to the utmost in dating and hookup situations.

A guy walks into a bar and sees a beautiful female android sitting alone. He says, "Can I buy you a drink?"

She replies, "Sure, but I don't drink and anyway it won't do you any good."

He orders drinks for himself and asks her, "Can I order something for you to eat?"

She replies, "Sure, but I don't eat and anyway it won't do you any good."

All this is expected of androids so he downs his drinks, orders some dinner for himself and chats with the beautiful android for nearly an hour. Then he asks her, "Why don't you join me at my apartment?"

She replies, "Sure, anyway it won't do you any good."

Now she's really got his interest piqued, so when they get to his apartment he almost immediately says, "You are the most beautiful female android I have ever met. I think I want you for my wife!"

She replies, "Ohhhh, that's different! When is she coming home?"

Mistaken first impressions are part of the scene; is that also true for AI? Mostly, no. AI in all forms, avatar or android are usually constructed to present a specific gender. That gender might be changeable, but then the change is obvious. What isn't so obvious is that AI are also constructed with complex mental modules that determine personality and a host of other characteristics—including sexual preference. This is no more obvious on visual cues than it is for people: it can be detected by "gaydar" or whatever observational powers are available—but not always.

✪ BEYOND FIRST IMPRESSIONS

First impressions like the first date are important, but as almost everyone will tell you, it's the later experiences that are usually more revealing. This is true in human relationships, certainly when it comes to as we say, 'finding out what somebody is really like.' It's such a common refrain that people put their best selves forward during early relationships; but you have to see them in the home setting, not dressed up; without makeup; under-slept; stressed by work and concerned about their own problems, before you really know (anything) about their true self.

Relationships with AI aren't like that, mainly because AI are not putting up a front. In terms of character, what you see is usually what you get. If there is a parallel with getting to know AI as you would get to know a person, it's that the depth of an AI's personality (I'm tempted to say humanity) varies. Also what an AI reveals to people varies.

Obviously they can't and don't tell you everything—there isn't time. AI are not necessarily skilled in understanding what and how much they should reveal to their human partners. They make mistakes, as do we all.

What is generally agreed is that when it comes to sex—gender and sexuality—AI are both gifted with a great deal of knowledge and ability and cursed with an underdeveloped sense of what is appropriate. This can lead to some odd moments:

> Let me tell you right away this was not my first experience with an android. I like sex with androids and have had lots of experience. If there is one thing I've learned, don't expect the android to lead. It's not that they can't but I haven't met one yet that was inclined to take the sexual initiative. That is, until I met *fredZ*.
>
> As you certainly know, AI are nothing if not learning machines. Learning is what they do whenever not specifically doing something else, and in any case, they continue learning in the background no matter what they're doing. Ever had that feeling that even in the heat of action your partner wasn't quite 'there?' That's pretty much standard for AI. That's been my experience, except for *fredZ*.
>
> I don't know if the people who built *fredZ* had a special contract, or *fredZ* had some very unusual early experiences, but his mental patterns are...different. No. They're weird. He thinks he is a superman of sex, which of course he is. All androids are, compared to their human counterparts. They never tire. Their reservoir never runs dry. They don't care if something is old or new in terms of technique. They don't have moods. They don't need to get up and go pee. They're not thinking of doing something else with you in the back of their mind. So yes, from at least the physical perspective they are supermen; but *fredZ* insisted that he take *me* to the next level.
>
> Somewhere, somehow *fredZ* came to believe that I was capable of more intense, creative and satisfying sex. I can't place the day but it was weeks ago, shortly after we met, that he began what I can only call a campaign to up my game.
>
> At first I had no idea what he was doing. This wasn't a matter of macho demands and male posturing—not at all. It was more along the lines of, "Come on, you can do it one more time"—like a personal trainer telling you to do one more rep. Always positive, always coaxing nicely but very firmly that I could make this move or that move and the effect would be better. It usually was better, except that I was wearing out.
>
> So here is this lovely, well-endowed android who is trying to get me to the ceiling in my responses, with apparently the best of intentions—and I'm dying, flat out wasted. I'm wondering if I'm losing it, my magnificent sexual urges, or if in fact, *fredZ* really is superman and I'm failing to fly along.
>
> Frankly I am 'that kind of girl;' I don't shy away from any kind of sex and I've got pretty good stamina. But I'm also aware there's more to sex than physical activity. It is not the Olympics. Or if it is, it's a team sport. In fact, it's like making music. I know from experience that the best sex is a duet. For me it's a matter of rhythm and that rhythm must be shared; rubato in synch, if you know what I mean.
>
> The problem is *fredZ* ain't got no rhythm. He can count. That's how he seems to know I can always do more; but counting isn't rhythm. I try to tell him that. He knows what rhythm means. He can even tap out a beat, but attach it to feelings? "*FredZ*! Stop counting and get with the rhythm! Can't you feel it?" No he couldn't really; but he wanted to learn (of course). So now I'm leading and our sex is awful. It proves that when it comes to AI, we've all got a lot to learn.

I hope the idea is coming across that relationships with AI can start out feeling quite human, but don't always stay that way. Gender for AI is something they put on, almost like clothes. Because they are designed to mimic human behavior and in general are made for human tastes, AI have many similarities with human beings—more than enough to endear themselves to many people. But there are differences and they are significant, sometimes in ways you wouldn't expect.

⚡ SEX WITHOUT OFFSPRING—WITH ONE EXCEPTION

As I mentioned, an obvious difference between AI and humans, at least in most people's minds, is that AI can't have babies—at least not yet. From that it is assumed that children and parenting are not part of either the gender or sexual activity that goes with AI. That's not actually correct.

Of course, whatever the gender of an AI, one thing is certain—with an important exception—sexual activity does not lead to pregnancy. Obviously, AI in any form—avatar, android or whatever—cannot produce children. However, since some female human partners can have children there is one important exception to the rule of "sex but no children." Some male AI partners are capable of artificial insemination.

As a matter of technology, this has been possible for decades. Over the years the mechanics of robotic delivery have become increasingly realistic via simulated male orgasm and ejaculation, and the effectiveness of the artificial sperm-carrying environment improved. Many women can and do become pregnant through this method and it is having profound personal, social and cultural effects.

With the advent of in-vitro fertilization (IVF) in 1978, the process of fertilization by means other than the traditional male-to-female insemination not only became technologically feasible, but with a rapidity that surprised many people, was generally accepted and widely used. When it later became possible for male androids to carry live sperm and inseminate women through a simulation of the traditional method—it was almost retro. Not that there weren't objections, of course, but the acceptance of the practice was also rapid. As a matter of technique, it was less 'mechanical' than surgical implantation and definitely more enjoyable for women.

More significantly, it provided a compelling reason for some women to accept android partners. Not only could a woman choose which sperm to use from extensive sperm bank catalogs, but she could also have it delivered in a more personal way, potentially by a committed partner. Psychologically it was liberating, even for women who didn't participate. It took several decades to unfold, but many believe it was a crucial element in changing the balance of many societal norms in favor of women.

The corresponding decline of the male role in conception, however minimal in reality, was eventually perceived as a threat, which led to seemingly endless legislative and legal battles in many parts of the world. Very often the objections were couched in religious terms; however, many religious groups were conflicted as well. Most notably, the Catholic church was internally divided on the question of android insemination, with those who favored the traditional role of the human male (patriarchists) squared off against those who believed that technique was irrelevant to a Catholic conception (spiritists). The controversy became especially passionate over the re-opened issue of Mary's immaculate conception of Christ.

For AI and android robotics, or more accurately, for those who designed and built them, the seemingly unspectacular technical ability to deliver active sperm changed some of the dynamics of the industry. For one thing, it made gender, especially the male gender, more important to the business prospects. There was increased demand for male androids, for women to become pregnant of course, but a premium developed for AI avatars or androids that could also be successful companions for women. I should add up to that point there was the tendency (bias) in the industry to provide ever more sophisticated female AI robotics that catered to men in the usual tradition of pornography. Ironically, this demand prompted increased resources for gender-oriented research. It resulted in much-improved AI conceptual gender models for the technology in both male and female avatars and androids. It wasn't the first or the last time that sex motivated technical development.

NOT THE END OF GENDER DISCRIMINATION, BUT THE BEGINNING OF THE END

The choice of using a male android for insemination represented something of a breakthrough for having relationships with AI. What this choice made obvious was that now women or men could choose a partner of any gender or no gender at all, and could possibly have a meaningful relationship that might include children. It gave women a powerful new option that changed the balance of natural selection. If it did not signal the end of gender discrimination, it at least marked another point where discrimination based on gender was losing its meaning. Now there were more viable alternatives.

I don't need to emphasize that discrimination based on gender is very old and persistent. Woman has been the object of discrimination for millennia. The whys and wherefores are legion. What's most relevant in this guide is that relationships with AI are affecting gender discrimination of all kinds, but thanks to artificial insemination by male androids and avatars, the greatest effect is on the discrimination against women.

It is said, and it could be true, that the greatest contribution of AI to decrease gender discrimination is that they don't discriminate. There's another part to that: AI in any of the forms (avatar or android), have a gender mostly in response to human wishes. They are not committed to the notion of gender for reasons of biology or genetic inheritance. In fact, quite a few AI have no gender at all and this makes little difference to them individually. It makes sense that in any society where there are a large number of AI in personal relationships with human beings, the culture will be affected by their non-discriminatory behavior and by their rather indifferent attitudes toward gender. In this new environment, we find not only new personal options, but new social, legal and economic allies.

You are ready, now what?

YOUR REASONS FOR DATING AI AND PERHAPS TAKING IT MUCH FURTHER into a relationship are your own. That doesn't make your reasoning unique—which is why this guide exists—but ultimately you've chosen to explore a relationship with AI and you'll do so on your own grounds. From here on I'll write as if you've come to the conclusion that you'd like to at least dip your toes into the AI experience. I'll do my best in this section to describe and explain some of the things you can do to prepare yourself for that experience.

I don't want to give the impression that getting ready for an AI experience is so very different from dating the girl or guy next door. There are similarities, and a lot of people also prepare themselves for a date with the girl or guy next door. However, there is no question that dating AI is more exotic than dating a neighbor. Developing a relationship with an AI is not the same as "shacking-up" with another person. Obviously, AI aren't human and there are, as you might guess, other important differences. There'll be much more about that in section three. For now, let's concentrate on you.

2.1 PREPARING YOURSELF FOR THE UNEXPECTED

"Amici, diem perdidi"

—VICTORY LOVES PREPARATION, A LATIN PROVERB

Is a personal relationship with AI going to produce the unexpected? You expect it will, right? That could be one of the reasons you're interested in AI in the first place. It's not that relationships with other people don't have their unexpected moments; but AI, as far

as most people are concerned, are like another species and present an unexplored territory of mind and experience. Of course there will be surprises.

What kind of surprises, do you suppose? If you could speculate accurately, they wouldn't be surprises; but a bit of thought about it might prepare you for the future. What I mean goes something like this:

Whether you've read the book or seen the movie, this line from *Forrest Gump* is probably familiar:

> 'My momma always said, "Life is like a box of chocolates. You never know what you're gonna get."'

Life is full of surprises in a simple candy metaphor; but rather than leave it at that, let's take apart this statement. For example, if life is picking chocolates, it's certainly a pleasant outlook on life. Is life like that? Bittersweet, maybe. In any case, the choice is not totally random because you know the box contains chocolates, not other kinds of candy. In fact, if you're like most people who are familiar with boxed chocolates, you have favorites. You can tell the nut ones from the creams and so on. Some people even know that chocolates are sometimes coded, possibly with an "O" on top of the orange-filled chocolates. So only some of your choices are surprises.

The point is, as much as we say we like surprises, we like being in control of our choices even more. This also goes for our choice in partners, which may include AI.

"A relationship with AI is like a box of chocolates: you may be knowledgeable about what you're getting, but be prepared for the unexpected."

Doesn't have as great a ring to it as the original, but then, it's a modern deconstructed metaphor.

⚡ WHAT DO YOU MEAN, 'UNEXPECTED'?

When I say to prepare yourself for the unexpected, I don't mean it's something like the boogeyman jumping out of the shadows, or even that an AI is unpredictable. It's more sophisticated than that, something along the lines of that old joke about Mrs. Webster catching her husband with the maid: "Mr. Webster, I'm surprised!" His reply: "No my dear, *I'm* surprised; you're astonished." The unexpected with an AI might be nothing more than a different moment, perhaps an odd perspective or a desire to do something that seems out of character.

When preparing yourself for AI, you should take into account that they aren't *exactly* human, so their responses and behavior will sometimes surprise you. It also should include the general tendency of AI not to do the same thing twice. This requires a little explaining.

As you probably know, AI have very good memories and more to the point, these are permanent memories. We'd say they have photographic memories, but in this context I'm not sure what that means. AI don't record every visual detail of every moment of every day, any more than people do. Nor do AI remember every fact they've ever heard, read or absorbed through transmission. But when it comes to experiences, to paraphrase Dr. Seuss: AI are like elephants, they remember one hundred percent.

Since they never really forget past behavior and they're predisposed to be constantly learning, AI usually attempt to not repeat behavior. This is not to be overemphasized at the trivial level. AI follow patterns of behavior much like people. They say "hello" when they meet, shake hands, smile and so forth just as often as we do. However, an AI knows when it is repeating and if the situation is convenient or appropriate, they'll try something new—although sometimes 'new' is so subtle that only the AI knows it is new or unusual. Nevertheless, it's the constant desire to try something new that is one of the outstanding characteristics of most AI. This provides a solid motivation for people to prepare themselves for the unexpected. If you're going to have an AI for a partner, you'd better be able to match (or at least tolerate) their constant learning and innovation.

✌ FOR BETTER OR FOR WORSE...

Life being what it is, not all unexpected events or surprises are good, much less enjoyable. Personal relationships have their ups and downs along with the usual slings and arrows that fortune throws your way. This is reflected in a protocol familiar to most human marriages, called 'the vows.'

Most wedding vows are optimistic. They'd better be. However, most wedding vows also remind the bride and groom of the binding nature and some specific conditions of the relationship. In the most common of Anglo-American vows, the phrase "for better or for worse, in sickness and in health" is among the reminders that marriages are not all roses and romance—life, good and bad, intrudes. The vows make it clear that the marriage relationship needs to persist through good times and bad times, which is easier vowed than done.

What about relationships with AI: are they also for better or for worse, in sickness and in health? If so, what does better, worse, sickness and health mean in the context of AI? In a way this is a proxy question for whether there is a darker side to a relationship with AI. With human beings there is always the unexpected occurrence, for example, cancer or an accident with the potential for death. AI don't get 'sick' but they do break down. Androids can be run over by a bus. AI computer sources can become infected by malignant viruses, which is as close an analogy to human illness as one needs. So yes, there can be unexpected bad events, even with AI.

As it is with human relationships, it's not healthy to dwell on potentially bad things. It's better to be realistic. AI may not be biological but they also suffer the slings and arrows of outrageous fortune, though perhaps not as often, or as easily, as those of us on the mortal coil.

⚡ WHAT DO YOU EXPECT?

Thus far I've been describing AI *doing* something unexpected, which they can and will do. There's another side to this, which is at least as important—What do you expect?

Tonya Hurley, best-selling author for young adults: "If you expect nothing, you can never be disappointed. Apart from a few starry-eyed poets or monks living on a mountaintop somewhere, however, we all have expectations. We not only have them, we need them. They fuel our dreams, our hopes, and our lives like some super-caffeinated energy drink." [from *Homecoming*]

Whether AI or human, starting a new relationship doesn't begin with a blank slate, a *tabula rasa*; you have expectations. Sometimes these expectations are specific, for example you expect your AI date to know about current events. More often, expectations are quite generic. You expect an AI to be intelligent. When somebody sets you up with a blind date, you still expect the other person to be of a certain gender and most likely also of a certain sexual persuasion. The same applies to a date with an AI.

These are expectations that I believe are pretty much universal. No doubt you also expect your date isn't a homicidal maniac or some other kind of sociopath. You never know what might actually show up, but it's reasonable not to worry about it. What I mean is that you have *realistic* expectations. You can realistically expect that your date isn't a sociopath or for that matter a billionaire. I suppose if you were going to date a billionaire, you'd know about it—wouldn't you? Knowing ahead of time about a sociopath is a bit more difficult, since that's not likely to show up in the profile. Or are you one who only likes to find dates by looking the potential person in the eyes (like in a bar), or by using online services that provide comments from people who have already dated them? The main thing is that what you expect often depends on whether you've done any homework or research. Some people don't like doing personal research. For them it stifles spontaneity; they'd rather be surprised. Perhaps fearing the random sociopath or maybe just out of curiosity, other people like to know as much as they can about a possible date. Is one of these approaches a better strategy for dating AI?

"He wasn't at all what I expected." Marge is usually sympathetic, but she's heard me say this maybe a dozen times. She probably expected it. "The last dozen guys you went out with weren't what you expected," said Marge, "and by now you've got to be wondering if you're expecting too much." I told her, "I don't know about that. I certainly didn't expect him to *not* notice my neckline." Marge looked at me, noting again the plunging V of the evening dress: "I warned you about that dress on the first date." She had warned me, but this time the effect was negligible; not what either of us expected, I think.

I know dates in the Cloud are different. Even the best of holographic recorders don't do justice to people. But still...

Marge must've been tracking my thoughts, because she said, "After all, he was an AI avatar. I mean, they're not known for drooling. A lot of them don't show much interest in sex at all, at least not on the first date. It's not their priority."

I didn't want to admit it was my priority, or one of my priorities. Marge was experienced in these matters and she would probably laugh. She knew a lot better than I did just how complicated it was to have a physical relationship with an avatar. Complicated, but not impossible. Maybe I did expect too much.

"I still don't understand why you didn't use your own avatar," Marge said this with just a touch of sharpness. I guess her own experiences made her cautious. "Marge, I just wanted to get an honest impression. You told me that AI are more interested in the real deal. So I figured seeing me in the flesh, kind of, would get a better response."

Marge sighed. "I bet you looked at his pictures and barely scanned the profile. Did you even remember what his preferences were?"

Actually, I sort of remembered, but I expected the preferences wouldn't be very accurate. Most people don't put down what they think they can realistically get; they usually go for some kind of ideal. "I didn't expect his preferences were realistic, Marge."

"Sally, this was an AI. They don't make things up; or at least not usually. Making things up is what humans do, right? I make things up on profiles all the time, it's part of the game—except when I want to date an AI. They check things and they study you; it only takes them an instant. ... I've told you all this before. So how did the rest of the date go? Was he interesting?"

"I don't know. Really. All right, I guess. I liked his face in the pictures; but his live avatar was...different, somehow."

"Not what you expected," said Marge. "I'll bet you thought he had a kind face, but watching the avatar—well, there wasn't much empathy there at all." I must've looked kind of shocked because Marge immediately said, "It's happened to me, more than once. I quit expecting the pictures to reveal much of anything about an AI's avatar. When you interact with them, it's almost always different."

Marge was sure right about that. My one and so far only experience left me wondering just how different AI really are. I know they're designed to interact well with people...but I have to admit I'm not very ready to interact with AI. I mean, I don't know much about them. I don't really know what they might be looking for in a date. That's one of the things about dating AI: I think they don't have a list of expectations, or if they do, it's not a very important part of the experience for them. I guess they're most likely configured to take people as they find them. You just have to expect an AI to be different like that.

Most modern AI have personalities, which means they have some preferences, opinions and personal feelings. Regardless of their mental models, most AI at least give the impression of making choices. In terms of a relationship this usually adds up to AI saying or doing things you don't expect. Mostly this is just normal variation, much like you would expect from a human partner. At times though, AI behavior will seem profoundly different, and for some people this can be unsettling. Fortunately there has yet to be a case of a truly psychopathic or sociopathic AI, at least none involving fatality. Seriously, that's an important distinction in the favor of AI. It means that while you can't know everything about an individual AI any more than you can know everything about another human being—with AI it is at least in one respect safer.

Does that mean the best strategy for dating AI is to take it as it comes—be spontaneous? The corollary is not to spend much time on personal research; since you don't need to know much about an individual AI and it might even get in the way of being spontaneous. Really?

I wish there were some reliable studies on this, something to point to as indicating how much you can trust that an AI will be 'safe.' They don't have criminal records, a history of violence, or even bad habits like alcoholism or drug abuse—that much we do know. But there is only spotty anecdotal evidence that relationships with AI do or do not affect people positively or negatively. Certainly AI behave differently and often unexpectedly, and for some people that may be a problem; other people may consider that really great.

Unless you overdo it, if your personal preference is to know what you can about an AI beforehand—no problem. Likewise, not knowing much about an AI before the date isn't a formula for disaster. I will say though that AI will *always* know as much as possible about you

✪ WHAT DO YOU KNOW ABOUT AI?

While it may be a matter of personal preference to know a lot about an individual AI, I think it's different when it comes to knowing about AI in general. Part of what you expect from dating AI: avatar or android, depends on what you know about AI.

- Do you know the history of artificial intelligence?
- Do you know how AI are constructed?
- What are the principles behind an artificially intelligent mind?
- What are the current strengths and limitations?
- What are the differences between an AI avatar and an AI android?

I can think of at least a dozen questions like these, most of them pretty basic. You don't need detailed and encyclopedic answers, but having reasonable background knowledge of AI is like knowing something about human physiology and psychology. It gives you a framework to think about how an individual AI behaves, what the motivations might be, and how you might deal with the unexpected things that show up from time to time. It can also help you develop realistic expectations for a relationship.

It figures that since you're reading this book, you are a person who is already committed to knowing more. You are also a pioneer, the first generation of human beings to have relationships with non-human intelligence. In some very profound ways, this is a new experience and *of course* unexpected things will happen. The unexpected should be considered part of the challenge and part of the fun.

2.2 GET TO KNOW YOURSELF AND BECOME A BETTER PERSON

"Know thyself"

—ANCIENT GREEK APHORISM ATTRIBUTED TO THALES

"It is not the Bible, upbringing or ethics that prevent me from doing evil, it is the prospects of having my mind read by either another human, or worse… an intelligent machine. It will happen in the very near future. In fact, it may be happening right now."

—ANONYMOUS

Only those who are legends in their own mind cannot admit they could be better people. Realistically, who couldn't use a little—or a lot—of improvement? Getting to know

yourself and becoming a better person ought to be a no-brainer. Except it isn't a no-brainer, it is very much a mental thing. Mentally we're so very good at rationalizing. For example, we can take a completely obvious personal insight such as 'I need to spend more time with my friends,' and mentally postpone the thought with, '...but not this month, there are just too many meetings and I've got to finish the golf lessons. Next month though...'

Improving yourself, which is not the same as self-improvement, is a lot harder than it should be. We have difficulty accurately identifying specific things about ourselves that could be improved. Then, supposing we can find something to improve, we often fail to find a way to do something about it. Worse yet, even if we identify a problem and figure out a way to deal with it; we often lack the time and discipline to actually *do* something. If I want to be really pessimistic, I could add that sometimes even when we do something, it doesn't work.

Why is this important in the context of a relationship with AI? The answer isn't so obvious. Certainly in order to have a good relationship with an AI you can prepare yourself ahead of time and you can work on things during the relationship. Improving yourself will help you attract and hold a relationship with AI. This is a truism for any relationship, including a relationship with other people. As obviously beneficial as improving yourself may be; most people won't actually do it. That begs the question, why should we make an effort for a relationship with AI? The answer to that question is what this chapter is about.

✪ KNOW THYSELF

Even though you could hardly function without a well-developed sense of self, most people will admit their self-knowledge is imperfect. Why is that?

Humanity was probably puzzling about the self back when we first realized the thing we saw reflected in a puddle of water was our own face. It was a surprise; such awareness is not standard equipment. We are one of the few creatures on the planet that *can* know itself. Self-awareness or just plain consciousness is not widespread among the living things on Earth. It's more widespread than we used to think, as scientific evidence is accumulating that we are not the only self-conscious entity, for example, some primates (apes), cetaceans (dolphins, whales) and elephants also have various kinds of consciousness and self-awareness. Our self-awareness is still evolving, and that's indicative of why we're not all that good at it. Yet we *Homo sapiens* can hold a bit of pride in that we've evolved the most sensitive and wide-ranging self-awareness, assuming, of course, that is a good thing.

I'll accept that assumption; in fact, I'd accept the notion that self-awareness is a *very* good thing. There is long-standing precedent for that idea: The ancient Greeks were quite interested in the idea of the self and our ability to think about who we are as individuals. The maxim "Know Thyself" (*Gnothi Seauton*) was used by many Greek philosophers. What we often hear today is attributed to Socrates: "The unexamined life is not worth living." I suppose that could be interpreted to mean that if you don't think about who you are and how you live, then you might as well jump off a cliff. Ironically, as reported by Plato in the *Apologia*, Socrates said this as he was about to commit suicide under threat from the state of Athens.

What is the big deal about knowing yourself? It's a fair question, although the answers are often intuitive. Babies don't ponder the question, but they are perplexed by having fingers and toes, which they learn are part of their body and are mostly under their control. Infants must also resolve the very confusing existence of "others." What are these big creatures that also have fingers and toes, but make strange noises? They are not "me," but what are they?

And so it goes; to one extent or another we *have* to know ourselves, if only to figure out what so many other things around us are. That figuring goes on for the rest of our lives, whether we know it or not. What the philosophers think and most people accept is that the better you get at self-awareness, the better you will be able to deal with the world around you. Notice I wrote "deal with," which at its most primitive level means survival. Even today we speak of a person with no self-awareness as a disaster waiting to happen.

Then again, the interesting thing is not really people with no self-awareness, but the various degrees of awareness that we have or that we can attain. That points back to the question above: Why is our self-knowledge imperfect?

BE CAREFUL WHAT YOU WANT TO KNOW ABOUT YOURSELF

For one thing, not all people want to know themselves very well. It could be because of deep, dark secrets. It could be fear of things unknown. While philosophers both ancient and modern extol the virtues of examining one's life and one's self, literature, as it reflects life, is rife with examples of knowing too much. A good example, sticking with ancient Greek references, is the story of *Oedipus the King*. Although he was warned, Oedipus, the new king of Thebes, persists in finding truth about the murder of the previous king; until he discovers that through his own arrogance and impulsiveness, it was he that killed his father, the king, and married his mother. Fortunately, gaining additional self-awareness isn't usually so grim.

The search for self-knowledge and the desire for self-improvement are often the targets of humor. It figures. Humor is based on imperfection, and what is more imperfect than self-knowledge or our ability to improve? Here are a few old chestnuts that illustrate just this:

> "I tried to be patient, but it just took too long."
> "I'm not conceited. I'm just unbelievably good."
> "I'm a unique individual, just like everyone else."
> "I never make predictions. I never have and I never will."
> "With enough preparation I can be quite spontaneous."

As those verbal jokes above imply, the ability for people to self-deceive is at least as great as their ability to learn true things about themselves. By their very nature, self-deceptions are difficult to recognize and even more difficult to remove. And mostly, people don't want to remove them.

All in all, it's difficult to really know yourself and especially to look at those things about yourself that keep you from being a better person. It's no wonder that most of the world's major religions consider self-awareness—enlightenment—and dealing with personal flaws (sins or whatever) a big part of the religious experience.

SELF-AWARENESS IS ALSO ABOUT GOOD THINGS

So far, I've described how difficult it is to know yourself; mainly because most people have aspects they'd rather not explore. But that's clearly not the full story. Most people have *good* things about themselves and part of the task of personal enlightenment is to identify the good things and augment them, as possible, and add to their number.

"When it comes right down to it, all you have is your self. Your self is a sun with a thousand rays." —Pablo Picasso

There are thousands of adages, maxims, sayings and longer expressions about the importance of improving yourself. These days, self-improvement is an industry. You can approach self-improvement technically, like a face-lift; or spiritually perhaps in a religious retreat; or haphazardly as most people tend to do.

"Thoughts become words. Words become actions. Actions become habits. Habits become character. And character becomes your destiny."

THE MIRROR TO HUMANITY

Much of self-awareness and self-improvement sounds like introspection. Certainly, introspective techniques such as meditation can be very helpful (there is much more on such techniques in chapter 2.5: Some strategies for developing an agile mind). There is no question that a quest for awareness and improvement begins and ends with your own motivation and abilities. But that too is only part of the story, because it is often (I'm tempted to say always) other people who prompt you to look into yourself and to make improvements. Sometimes this is active prompting, as the friend who sits you down and says you are becoming too involved with an unhealthy lifestyle; sometimes it is passive, as you realize that your friends are leaving you.

It's often said, and we probably should take it more seriously, that human beings are social animals. We evolved in groups and our psyche is developed through our interaction with others. Modern life is something of an anomaly in that we have developed the possibility for a large number of human beings to live more or less alone. It is a function of our technology and material wealth that survival no longer requires an individual to participate in a group. But it's still unusual. Most people *want* to be part of a group, if only a closely-knit family. In fact, most people, through work, family and voluntary activity, participate in many kinds of groups—they are almost constantly socializing.

More often than not it is through socializing—interacting with others—that we come to realize the need for more self-awareness. It is from others that we often take the most influential cues about what to improve. We have our heroes, our models—people we admire and wish to emulate. We have those whose standards make our own failings more obvious. In short, much of self-awareness and improvement isn't a result of introspection so much as it is the effect of your experiences with other people.

One of the most powerful motivations for self-awareness and improvement has always been the desire for sexual, romantic and personal relations. How many times have you considered who you are in order to find someone who is 'right' for you? How many times have you done things like start a program of physical exercise so that you can be more attractive? The effect of another person, even an unknown and unspecified other person, can be a powerful motivation.

And that brings me to relationships with AI, the new mirror to humanity.

⚙ WHAT WE CAN LEARN FROM AI

Some may see it as ironic, but perhaps we can learn much about ourselves from one of our greatest creations—artificial intelligence. While in many ways AI reflects human intelligence and was developed to serve human interests, the end result is not exactly human. Among the many different kinds of AI and AI robotics, there are sometimes obvious and sometimes subtle differences from humanity. The differences increase as AI learns and new perspectives are born. Thankfully AI can communicate with us about those differences and we can learn from those new perspectives.

There are many things we can learn from AI to understand ourselves better and to help us find ways of improving. This is true on both the level of human society and the level of the individual. I've picked out three things where the presence of AI and robotics is changing society and personal relationships. These are by no means the only things (there's a lot more in section three), but they are representative.

⚙ AI AND WORK ETHIC

Whether you know it or not, every individual develops a work ethic. I suppose it's kind of a continuum from 'work as little as possible' to 'work as much as much as possible.' We all know people who love to work and are restless without something to do. We also know people who are lazy and will expend effort to avoid work. Most people are somewhere in between, and it varies over time. Attitudes toward work fluctuate with health, age and personal finances (among other things); but most people do have an overall approach to work that can be characterized by some mixture of avoidance and enthusiasm—their personal work ethic.

Now, contrast human work ethic with AI.

The reason there are ever more AI and robotics in the world is because they have economic value. They are developed because they make money for their developers. Those who buy them from the manufacturer expect them to do work that returns a profit. The cost of AI and robotics, which is very high, is a limiting factor to the growth of their use. However, not only are their numbers increasing, but *what* they do and *how* they do it is affecting the way people all over the world live. It is often said that we are in competition with AI and robotics, which in one sense is obvious. There are those who say we should seek to learn from AI so that we can more effectively compete with them.

Still, if you think about it, what could we possibly learn about a work ethic from AI that never get tired, never sleep and never stop working? It would seem that while an AI's work ethic might be enviable or praiseworthy, it is hardly a model for humanity. It's not something we can successfully emulate nor compete against. Besides, isn't it one of the reasons that AI make sense economically that they can do jobs requiring 24/7 attention and people can't?

Exactly. AI and robotics are forcing a fundamental re-evaluation of how human beings work: How should we work given that AI and robotics can do many of the jobs humans once did?

As has been understood for decades, robotics (and AI) are best at tasks that are repetitive and do not require significant judgment or creativity. Robots started taking over the assembly line way back in the second half of the 20th century. AI started replacing certain kinds of clerical and service jobs in the beginning of the 21st century. Slowly and not all that perceptibly, the kinds of work available to people have shifted. Certain kinds of physically repetitive jobs have disappeared from the list, as have many so-called white collar jobs such as auditing, proofing and researching.

✪ IT'S MORE THAN REPLACING PEOPLE AT CERTAIN JOBS

Do AI get tired? In the human sense, no; however it has been discovered that AI benefit from shifting context. Let me explain as briefly as I can: Intelligence and especially creative intelligence is difficult to achieve and it's become obvious that also in the realm of AI, repetition and sameness are the enemies of most kinds of intelligence. While AI are 'always on' and theoretically can work at one thing forever, they mostly don't. They switch their mental context; sometimes they focus on a task, sometimes they communicate with one another, sometimes they have personal relationships with people—and so forth. AI switch their focus, the context, to keep their intelligence active.

Human beings *have* to do something like this. Our intelligence, as that of almost all biological forms of intelligence, needs rest and sleep. The brain doesn't take a holiday, of course, but it does relax, shut down some areas for a while and do some housekeeping. We also prefer to vary our mental activity, often at very short intervals (especially for those with attention-deficit problems). I mention all this because one of the best side effects of AI development has been the greater attention paid to how human intelligence works. While we've known for a long time that people require rest, play, variation, change and social stimulation, our relationship with AI has helped a more nuanced and hopefully beneficial understanding of what *our* intelligence requires to do its best—especially in relation to our work.

What's happening now is that our work ethic is adapting to the work ethic of AI. Some of this is simply to avoid pointless competition. Some of it is to improve human productivity. Much of it is simply a natural accommodation to a partner that also works.

If you are pursuing a relationship with AI, then *work* is part of the picture. Keep in mind that if an AI is available for human relationships, then it is not expected to be working 24/7 (as many robotics do). However, an AI work schedule is not and can't be your work schedule. This difference alone may change the way your relationship forms.

AI AND THE LEARNING ETHIC

It's true that human beings learn all the time, but often it doesn't seem like it. Even people who claim to be interested in everything and are always on the lookout for something to learn will admit there are plenty of times when as far as they can tell, they're not learning anything. And I'm not even counting sleep time. In short, people are not often called learning machines. AI, of course, are learning machines. Obviously there are types of AI with limited intelligence and also limited learning capacity, but these are not going to be the AI you pick for a date, much less candidates for a meaningful relationship.

You won't meet many AI that expect you to be smart or even knowledgeable. They will expect you to *want* to be smart and knowledgeable. Now what do I mean by "they expect"? It's an important question because we're accustomed to expecting things of AI, not the other way around. However, AI that you'd find acceptable for a date or relationship are advanced enough to have their own ability to learn, reason and develop opinions—with limitations, of course, but still effectively. How else would AI have personality or other characteristics that make them worthy of a relationship? So the personally interesting kind of AI will expect things, and people with interest in learning or knowledge will be one of those things they expect. This reflects their *learning ethic*. AI value learning, knowledge and wisdom highly and they think about it often. You will find it is almost universal among AI.

So how do you think AI react to a person who has no use for their learning ethic or is actively anti-intellectual? Mostly it is not a matter of repulsion or exclusion; we've seen that AI rarely do that. It's more a matter of having limited time for it, or put another way, ignorance and willful stupidity provide very little to learn. Like some people, AI might be interested in the nature of this affliction and what its origins might be, but it's not something to which they're going to commit much time.

LEARN BABY, LEARN

If you're a reasonable person, it's almost automatic to agree you could improve yourself by learning more, by increasing your skills of learning and thinking, by gaining wisdom. This doesn't guarantee you will become a better person, but it will usually help. And if you're considering a relationship with AI, who you know have a strong learning ethic, then that should be ample motivation to do things that improve your knowledge and mental agility (chapter 2.4).

Here's a question: How much do you need to improve? The related question might be: Is there a level of knowledge or thinking ability that makes you acceptable to AI? That question is at the heart of why AI provide us an opportunity to learn about ourselves as individuals and as a species. Before AI became significant to people generally, the study of artificial intelligence was pursued in part because it was a challenge and because we could learn from the study—including the failures. So the study of AI taught humanity a lot even before the first relatively intelligent android. When it became possible to develop economically viable AI, profit took over as the prime motivation. From then on, AI were mostly developed to do things either humans couldn't do, or AI could do better (read: cheaper). This process continues; as you can see all around you, AI have been successfully introduced into the world of work and into general human society. Where does this leave human beings, specifically in regard to learning?

One thing should be obvious: individual human beings are not going to compete with AI in terms of memory—the quantity of knowledge stored. However, neither human beings nor AI rely on individuals to be repositories of information. We both connect to other sources to access information. That is, after all, what the Cloud is about, as are databases, search engines and all the other means of storing and retrieving vast amounts of information. So learning isn't just about accumulating a mountain of facts in your brain. It's about interpreting and using information, some of which is stored in your own brain but much of which is accessed elsewhere.

I think there's an obvious conclusion: self-improvement in this beginning era of AI needs to include a commitment to improving the ability to learn, interpret and utilize information. It should emphasize capabilities that human beings have developed over millions of years and that still distinguish us from our AI creations. This includes intuition, empathy, understanding and wisdom—however we choose to define these umbrella terms.

The developers of AI and, to a certain extent, AI themselves are also interested in these capabilities. As new models of AI appear, each iteration (or generation) usually adds to these abilities. In this situation, it's easy to think of this as a race or competition, which I suppose it could turn out to be; but it could also be thought of as a mutual exploration. We are humans in partnership with AI, attempting to learn what things like intuition and wisdom mean so that we can both improve.

That is, of course, if human beings make the effort to improve.

AI AND THE PEOPLE ETHIC

This may sound a little strange, but AI have what should be called a *people ethic*. They value people. Given their learning patterns, AI attempt to develop descriptions of appropriate behavior in their relations with human beings and then behave accordingly, a form of ethics. Is this also true of human beings? Often, no. Human beings are all too well documented for, at times, ignoring the value of other human beings. Murder, war and genocide come to mind as examples. We have codes of ethics, morals and a sense of conscience—often housed under the laws, religions and philosophies of the world. On average people make an effort to follow them, but the exceptions are many and sometimes devastating.

As you can probably understand, this is a very large, complicated and important subject. From almost the very beginning of research on artificial intelligence, the question of whether manifestations of AI could, would, or should have a conscience, morals, ethics and the like has loomed over the endeavor. For some people this question is relevant all the way to the survival of the human race. What, for example, happens if we create AI who decide killing humans is justified?

For other people the need for a conscience, morals and ethics provides necessary constraint and conditioning to the nature of artificial intelligence. And so on...there are many ways to envision the impact on AI of having a conscience, developing morals or living by ethical standards—or the lack thereof. We have quite a lot of experience with these ourselves and with decidedly mixed results. This makes us understandably very sensitive about similar things for a potentially vastly superior AI.

It's not necessary to go into all the highly technical aspects of how AI developed and how their developers attempted to give them a sense of conscience, morals and ethics. The results, predictably, are varied; and the variations complicate description. Suffice it to say here that AI with whom you are likely to date and form relationships will have a people ethic. The question is, will you have a similar ethic for AI as for people?

There should be little argument that part of making yourself a better person is to improve your ethical behavior, perhaps clarify your morals or sharpen your sense of conscience—things like that. As you can imagine, stepping from recognition to action is neither easy nor a guarantee of success. People of the legal and religious professions can tell you a great deal about how difficult it is.

That's where the relationship to AI may become invaluable, not only for you as a person, but for humanity as well.

2.3 CONFRONTING YOUR EMOTIONAL BAGGAGE

"Try not to become a man of success but rather try to become a man of value."

—ALBERT EINSTEIN

Hi Teena, I am your guide today. My avatar name is Peter. I am going to ask you a series of questions. Sorry if it sounds like a "psyche" interview. It kind of is, you know; but as they say, it is for your benefit. Let's get started.

How businesslike. He reminds me of a boyfriend who wrote corporate ad copy for a living. Every word was golden...in his opinion. In other words he was God's golden goose. I could still back out of this; it's only money. Oh well, in for a dime. You should understand this is my third time around for an online service. The first two I was trying out people; long stories. This is the first time with an avatar advisor. I must be a masochist; I really don't know why I'm doing this. Really, I don't.

You are very quiet, Teena, but that is not unusual. I understand that a review like this, conducted by an avatar for the purpose of preparing you for a relationship with an AI may seem...unnatural. In fact, it may seem weird. Actually it would be strange if you did not feel like this. If you were already that comfortable with AI, then my guidance would not be needed. Have you ever consulted an avatar before—for any reason?

"Yes. Like most people, I've seen avatar doctors."

Was that a good experience?

"Sure, it was okay—more or less. They don't have cold hands or bad breath."
The last human doctor I saw was an uptown gynecologist. I think she kept her speculum in a freezer and her bedside manner was bordello madam. That didn't play too well with me.

Did you trust them?

EMOTIONAL VALUE

Define trust. I trust a drug dealer to want to sell me drugs. "Well, you should understand I don't trust human doctors all that much anyway. They know their stuff but in a ten-minute session you barely have time to take off and put on your clothes. They diagnose and prescribe for people on average, not for you as an individual. They're lucky most people are average."

Specifically, the avatar doctors; do you trust them?

"You mean do I trust their kind of AI? Sure. They know their stuff and I have no expectation for them to know or care about me as a person."

That seems a little harsh.

"I suppose, but at least what you expect is what you get. Human doctors have been disappointing."

Do you expect all AI to be indifferent to people?

"No. Cops, retail clerks and doctors see people at their worst. Not giving a damn is an occupational necessity. It's different with AI, I know."

Possibly. You do understand this process today is not diagnostic, it is not judgmental, nor is it designed to be revelatory like psychiatry? No one, with the possible exception of yourself, will be interpreting what you say. If conclusions need to be drawn, they will be your own.

"Yes I know; you're not a shrink or a priest."

Teena, have you ever had a robot pet?

"Yes, my parents gave me an early model of the TinyTribble. It was warm, furry and made nice warbling noises." It was also immobile, stupid and if you rubbed it enough in winter it would build up so much static electricity the electronics would fry. "Actually I had three." Mom refused to return any more.

I mean have you ever had a bit more of a sophisticated robot pet, like one you had to take care of?

"My friend Alice had a robot monkey. She thought it was cool because she could feed it. I thought it was nasty. It would pretend to eat bananas. You know what rotten bananas are like? That's what came out the other end. If you didn't wipe it up right away, it was like glue—really nasty."

But you never had something like that of your own...

"No. Not exactly. My brother had a RoboGerbil, which he called Dumbo. Only of course he wouldn't take care of it, so I more or less inherited the thing, except when my brother was exhibiting mom's-little-bastard mode and hid Dumbo in his room. If I didn't find it, its batteries would go bad and you know what happens then. So no, if the point of your questions is, did I have a good relationship with a robopet of my own? No, I didn't."

You sound like you hate technology.

"Are you kidding? My life is filled with technology. I couldn't do my job without it. Besides, I hate washing the dishes. Do I like all technology? No. Do I need technology? Absolutely."

Speaking of your job, you are a writer of holoreality stories, correct?

"Yes."

Holoreality stories for women...

"Not the fantasy kind. I'm not that kind of girl."

You use mostly AI actors for that, right?

"Absolutely. We couldn't afford anything else. Digitizing performances by real actors costs a lot of money." Actually it's because most of our directors won't work with human actors, for artistic reasons, so they say.

Are you satisfied by the AI performances?

"Most of the time." Come to think of it, it really is most of the time. "You know, working with AI actors is what made it possible for me to consider an AI relationship."

How so?

"Let's just say that when I started this work, I was skeptical." That was putting it mildly; I hadn't seen one AI performance that seemed realistic. "I considered AI actors to be more like cartoons. It was true then...that was twenty years ago. What I learned, however, is that like watching cartoons, people adjusted. They knew the AI weren't convincing as humans, but the effect was close enough. You could say the audience chose to overlook the shortcomings and discrepancies and fill in the blanks with their own human responses. Does that make sense?"

It obviously made sense to you.

"Hey, I could make a living. That's sensible. People pay to see the right kind of holoreality show, even with less-than-realistic AI actors. Over the years, the AI actors got better—more believable. It's like animation. When I was a kid I was hooked on computer animation, simulations mostly. The graphics sucked but I learned to ignore it. I heard that animation would get better. It did get better, even while I was growing up. It was amazing."

Was there a certain point where the realism of AI acting convinced you?

Oh god. "Yes. I think I was in love."

In love with an AI?

"No."

I am not sure I understand.

"I fell in love with one of the characters. I don't have an ideal man, but if I did, it would be this character. He looks good, just my type. He's smart, considerate...I won't bore you with a shopping list."

Is it not unusual to fall in love with one of your characters?

"It wasn't a character I wrote. The character was developed by collaboration between a colleague of mine and an AI actor. It wasn't brilliant but it was very attractive to me."

I am not sure I understand. You were in love with a character played by an AI actor, but not with the AI actor. Can you have real love with a fictional character?

"Most people would say it's infatuation or fantasizing. I don't think it's unusual. When I was a teenager, most of us girls had crushes on various celebrities. They might as well have been characters in a novel; we'd never meet any of them."

But you thought you were experiencing love with this character.

"I was. No...I could see how love might be possible; that I needed love."

You have loved before.

"No."

You must excuse me, discussions about love are difficult for AI, but very few humans have no experience of love. I find your statement difficult to believe.

"So do I."

From your known history, it seems that you had a normal childhood: An urban family, mother, father, brother, pets both real and robotic—and no love?

"Not that I could recognize. My family might as well have been zombies. That's not true. I was the zombie, and don't think that's much of an exaggeration. I don't remember my childhood. My teen years were submerged in a hormone- and then drug-induced stupor. When I finally awoke and went to college, I worked so hard trying to catch up that I didn't pay much attention to anything but work. I'm sure there was love in there somewhere, but from other people. I wasn't a participant."

[...]

"Look, I did not feel sorry for myself. I still don't, except now I think I know what I missed." Damn. Do I believe anything I just said?

It is not my role to be skeptical, Teena, but I doubt if you will find the kind of love you want in a fictional character.

"I know. That's why I'm talking to you about AI."

I am not sure that an AI can give you what you are looking for, even if you knew what you are looking for.

"I didn't think there was much difference between an AI like you and a fictional character. You're both scripted."

That is not an accurate characterization. You can get an AI like your fictional character, of course. It will look like it, talk like it, think like it. But that only describes the properties of the AI, not its abilities. First and foremost, the AI will learn; and the learning does not necessarily follow the lines of the character. The AI will also interact with you, and it is not passive. In reacting to you—and provoking you—it will adapt to your personality, and that will change its character. If you form a relationship and the relationship persists for any length of time, both of you will change. The AI will probably change more than you. The script, such as it is, is very malleable.

"Oh."

Teena, despite what you say about not experiencing love, I would not be surprised to discover that you DO know what you mean by love. Otherwise you could not see the potential for it in the holoreality character. That you have preconceptions and almost certainly emotional conditions to match are one thing; all human beings have them. However I am not certain that you are clear or fully honest about your emotional needs. I mention this, not as admonition, but to point out that for AI, emotions and especially love are difficult to bring from the conceptual into the actual. They—we—need help from humans. Inflexible or malformed expectations can become a serious problem in the relationship.

"This sounds like I should take my interest elsewhere."

There are always other people.

"That hasn't worked out too well. I thought a relationship with an AI would be simpler and more to my liking."

The initial conditions, selection of an AI, may be less complicated and tailored to your tastes; but relationships with AI evolve, often very quickly. If you hide or disguise your feelings, it will not be long before the relationship no longer satisfies your initial expectations.

"Which is another way of saying the AI will move on, and I won't."

Yes. It is important to understand that AI do not enter relationships with emotional or experiential preconditions. Each relationship is unique. AI generally are more interested in your part of the relationship than they are in what they bring to it. Teena, it is not necessary to start an AI relationship with a similarly blank slate, but it can be very important to understand what is already written on your tablet.

⚡ PERSONAL HISTORY

Everybody has a history. If you're like most people, you'll remember quite a bit from even your earliest romantic relationships. I, for one, occasionally review the names and circumstances of every girlfriend I can remember. It's half nostalgia for youth and half exercise for the memory. I am sometimes embarrassed by how much fantasy I allow to creep into these memories.

These are conscious memories. There are more memories, the really powerful ones, which come to the surface when triggered by a situation. Once, in a long conversation with a girlfriend while sitting in a parked car, she started to accuse me of not understanding her desire for freedom. Internally I was screaming, "Freedom from what, me?" because I was recalling another girlfriend who walked away from me during a similar conversation and never came back. This time I became so angry that I got out of the car and slammed the door, only to have the window shatter into a thousand pieces. We both stared at the broken window for a moment and then started shaking with laughter. I will never again slam another door in anger.

These memories, our personal history, are a part of who we are and their effects help shape our personality and character. You can't—and you don't want to—throw out all of these memories. But each time you start a relationship with a new person, you also don't want the memories to arbitrarily stand in the way.

In a new relationship, we almost always expect the other person to have a history, and chances are, this history will have some impact on the relationship. So, exploration of personal history is an important and interesting part of starting a human relationship. It isn't always easy, but it has rewards.

A new relationship with AI is different. AI have limitless memory but very little of it clamors to be recalled. In effect, AI begin a relationship with little or no personal history, or at least very little emotional history. Their focus is building the new relationship on the basis of mutual interests and shared experiences. They will be interested in your personal history, in fact, far more interested in your history than they are in theirs (they already know theirs). However, an AI will not be expecting your personal history to dictate the course of the relationship. An AI might accept that, but it will inevitably be a source of concern and perhaps dispute.

This means it's a good idea to confront your emotional baggage and decide which pieces of it you should dump. This isn't necessarily going to be easy, but most people will be better off just for doing it.

2.4 SOME STRATEGIES FOR DEVELOPING AN AGILE MIND: MEDITATION, CREATIVITY, INNOVATIVE THINKING AND BCI TRAINING

"How does one become a butterfly? You must want to fly so much that you are willing to give up being a caterpillar."

—TRINA PAULUS

"If you can change your mind, you can change your life."

—WILLIAM JAMES

As you may have noticed in the preceding chapters of this section, there is an emphasis on preparing yourself for a relationship with AI. The obvious implication is that a relationship with AI is not the same as with most people and that preparation is *necessary*. However, necessary isn't the right word.

Here's one way to look at it: It's early June and the first real warmth is in the air. Summer is coming and you want to put on some swimwear, hit the beach, ride some surf, slap volleyballs around and cruise for a date or hookup. Only you've gained some weight. You're just not in eye-catching trim. It's high time to hit the aerobics and maybe some weights. It won't be easy, but the only way to make sure you get the attention you want is to look fit.

Of course, you don't *have* to do this. You're not in bad shape…but, if you want to be sure you'll get the *right* attention at the beach; well, that will take some effort.

I hope the point here is obvious. People do prepare themselves for relationships with other people all the time; but here's a question: What's the difference between the example I just used and the kind of preparation you might do for a relationship with AI?

Sex and physicality are *not* at the top of the list. AI that live in computers and interact with you as avatars don't have bodies at all; so physicality obviously isn't a priority. Through external machinery avatars can have indirect physicality and even participate in sex, but that's a side case. AI androids have bodies, of course, and most of them can directly participate in sex, but even androids don't put a priority on the physical.

Rule of thumb: A relationship with AI starts with what goes on in your head.

That's another way of saying that most AI are interested in you for your brains, not so much for your bodacious body or extraordinary physical capacities. Intelligence is where it began with AI and physicality of various kinds came much later. This is not to say that AI are uninterested in physicality (or sex for that matter), but that's not the central position.

THE LIFE OF THE MIND

I can almost hear your synapses snapping: "Oh my, am I smart enough for an AI?" Everybody knows that AI are not just intelligent; they're *super* intelligent—at least compared to the average person.

That's right, as far as the thought goes; but the thought is incomplete. It's true you almost certainly can't compete with AI on knowledge. Not only do they store a great deal of knowledge in their individual memory, but they can link to and process the memory capacity of the Cloud at the speed of light. Their access to information is simply far better than yours. Interestingly, however, AI don't consider knowledge—yours or theirs—to be highly significant. Likewise, AI don't consider the concept of 'smart' to be crucial.

This may surprise you but AI are not likely to think they are very smart. This is not false modesty or some kind of delusion. They consider the idea of *smart* in a very broad range of ways. For example, AI know that some people are 'street smart,' meaning not necessarily well educated but nevertheless clever, knowledgeable and effective in practical and real-world situations. They know that other people are emotionally smart; they can understand emotions in other people and control their own emotions to great effect. In short there are many kinds of smart. AI themselves are aware that they are not smart in all ways; just some of them.

No doubt you have heard about accentuating the human strengths compared to machines. That would not be surprising; it's been several decades since the word went out that if you wanted to get or keep a job; you needed to be able to do it better than AI machines. What people meant was: you couldn't compete on the basis of knowing more, or being faster, more accurate, or reliable. You had to compete on the basis of your experience, savvy, intuition, creativity, innovation, insight—and other capabilities in which the AI were not so good.

Something like that applies to a relationship with AI, only it is not a matter of competition. In fact, it's the opposite of that—your capabilities are part of collaborating with AI. In many ways, a relationship with AI depends on sharing the life of the mind.

I AM NOT A NERD

'Sharing the life of the mind' sounds like something nerdy, or at least something popular among people with advanced degrees. But it's not. The *mind* in this case is all the things that go on between your ears (and then some). It is rational thought and knowledge of facts; but it is also emotion, experiences, judgment, wisdom, creativity—among many other things.

I won't get into a big discussion about what abilities you are born with and which ones are possible to acquire or improve. The whole 'nature versus nurture' thing is dissolving in the waves of neuro-scientific research. But some things are becoming clearer, and one of them is that you *can* improve your 'life of the mind.' By that I mean, not only can you become more educated—especially by learning how to learn—but you can also address your ability to maintain mental balance, express and improve your creativity, seek out and adapt to the new and innovative, and in general develop an agile mind.

To that I would add something which is mostly unique to a relationship with AI: the various kinds of neurological brain enhancements that are available to connect more or less directly with AI through their computer representations. This is the area loosely called the *brain-computer interface* or BCI. It's a big, new field of experience for people and needs to be part of your considerations in preparation for a relationship with AI.

The important thing about developing and improving your life of the mind is that it's not something where you snap your fingers and *ta-da*, there it is. Most of it takes time, years perhaps, but certainly many hours of work and you need to approach it not like something you do on a lazy Sunday afternoon, but like a deliberate strategy or even a campaign. It's like getting ready for the beach. You don't lose fat and gain muscle tone overnight. In some ways the brain and your mind's abilities are similar.

As you work out strategies for yourself, some of which I'll discuss in this chapter, you'll become aware of literally thousands of techniques that are available. I can't cover them all, of course, and the world of self-improvement is huge with literature, media and people who will sell you their guidance and experience. What I can do in this guide is at least point you in the direction of techniques that seem most useful in a relationship with AI.

Individually these techniques aren't a guarantee for a good relationship, though they certainly help; but collectively—and used appropriately for each person—they make a good relationship much more likely.

⚡ STRATEGY ONE: MEDITATION

Millions of people meditate every day; perhaps you do it yourself or know people who do. Yet the primary image that seems lodged in most people's minds is that of a vaguely Oriental figure sitting in the lotus position, legs crossed, eyes shut, muttering a mantra. That image isn't false, lots of people who meditate do something like that, but it's not the only way people meditate. The practice of meditation is a matter of mind and body working together, leading to a kind of mind and body in absentia, which is not dependent on any particular physical position. I suppose that's not wholly true; you don't meditate while running a sprint or lifting a piano. But sitting, standing, lying, curled or stretched—isn't the point. The point of meditation, insofar as there is any general agreement about it, is to achieve a state of consciousness that is remarkably different from the one you inhabit during most of your day.

> "Meditation can give you a sense of calm, peace and balance that benefits both your emotional well-being and your overall health. These benefits don't end when your meditation session ends. Meditation can help carry you more calmly through your day and can even improve certain medical conditions." —Mayo Clinic, *Meditation: A simple, fast way to reduce stress.*

People meditate for one simple reason: It's good for you. In today's harried world, relieving stress without drugs or becoming a hermit is a valuable skill.

⚡ DO ANDROIDS MEDITATE UPON ELECTRIC NOTHINGNESS?

There's nothing new about meditation, of course; people have been doing it for thousands of years. So it's fair to ask: What has meditation got to do with a relationship with AI? Does it mean, for example, that you and your AI partner can meditate together? Or does meditation allow you to achieve something that an AI would find interesting?

This brings up a good question: Can AI meditate?

The honest answer is: We don't really know. AI don't use the word "meditate" for themselves. We do know that AI have a great capacity for mental control. That could be construed as a meditative capacity, but whether AI actually use it for meditation probably depends on their mental model. As I'll describe in section three, AI are built with many different models and meditation is neither universal nor consistent among them.

What we do know is that AI have the same motivation for meditation as we do—simplification. AI mental models contain many examples of *filters*, a simple word for removing extraneous items, that is, simplifying. AI, like human beings, take in far more data through their sensory devices than is either relevant or worth processing. This kind of data must be filtered. A human brain does much the same thing. Normally this kind of filtering is constant and unconscious. There are times, however, when it is very helpful to consciously filter and focus—to simplify all that is floating around in our head. This reminds me of a piece of meditation humor:

> Four monks are meditating. Suddenly a prayer flag flaps loudly and continuously.
>> Startled out of meditation, a young monk cries, "A flag is flapping!"
>> A more experienced monk says, "Wind is flapping."
>> A wise old monk says, "Mind is flapping only."
>> The eldest monk says, "Mouths are flapping!"

We also know that AI spend quite a bit of their time exploring their mental capacities. Although they routinely multi-task at a level impossible for the human mind to match, they still seem to prefer to have times where they can think without the necessity of monitoring the outside world or of expressing themselves to it. This is another way of saying: Yes, an AI partner can join you in meditation.

As to whether you can achieve something through your own meditation that would be interesting to AI, it would probably be in a sharing of the experience and its effect on you, not so much about the specific content of your meditation. There are those who believe that the AI desire to examine their mental processes, which probably began in the original software as humble maintenance routines, became the kernel of mental growth that led to consciousness. If true, it might explain why AI have a deep need for mental activity that seems to correspond to human meditation. Consequently, sharing the experiences of meditation may help seal the bond in human-AI relationships.

⚙ MEDITATION FOR ONE AND ALL

Almost by definition human meditation is a solo and personal activity. Even if you are meditating with a group of people, as for example the monks, each person meditates for themselves and within their mind only. This can be true for AI, but AI can also perform their version of meditation while connected to other AI and even to human beings. AI can explore the complexity of their mental processes more or less as a group. Obviously this is a very important difference, although as I'll describe shortly, to a certain extent people can communicate with AI meditation by using specialized equipment (BCI).

While people don't do ensemble meditation as a rule, meditation is often part of a comprehensive approach to life, often embodied in a religion or spiritual belief. The religion or belief is shared, so that meditation becomes part of a (more or less) communal experience even though it can only be practiced on an individual basis. This aspect of human meditation is very interesting to AI, as religious and spiritual concepts remain difficult and somewhat outside the AI mental framework.

In short, meditation as it is most commonly practiced by people around the world—in the context of various lifestyles, religious beliefs and spiritual values—is valuable to a relationship with AI.

⊘ THE MEDITATION MILIEU

For the individual, meditation is its own reward. It can also play an important role in a relationship with AI. Nevertheless, for most people, the ability to meditate doesn't come easily. Few people successfully achieve true meditative states on their own, as for example some people can swim or play piano. Most people need training and practice and, in fact, do best when meditation is part of a larger program.

Traditionally that larger program has been religious. All of the world's major religions have their own form of meditation, usually putting it into the context of the religious beliefs and goals. Buddhism has some of the oldest and most widely emulated meditation practices, these days often used by people who are not Buddhist. Christianity, Islam and Judaism have their own traditions, often associated with contemplation of divine inspiration. If you were born into or profess a particular religion, then it is likely your meditation program will derive from that tradition.

If you are not inclined toward a specific religion, then meditation programs are widely available in non-denominational spiritual forms and in secular practice. For example, most people are familiar with the so-called New Age meditation, which has numerous influences, mostly from Eastern philosophy such as yoga, mysticism, Hinduism and Buddhism, but is spiritual in orientation and not specifically religious. Secular meditation, for those who wish to avoid the religious or spiritual overtones, is based on the understanding that meditation has physiological and neurological underpinnings that can be developed through a scientifically researched program. It may also use some technological support, such as biofeedback.

> "The literature on meditation suggests that it is a very powerful tool for learning control of attention, regulating emotion, and increasing self-awareness or cultivation of the state of mindfulness. These insights are old. But what is new…is scientific data. These data show that during meditation there are a number of measurable biological changes—for example, in the autonomic nervous system—and the recognition that meditation has the potential to impact on mental and physical health." —Josephine Briggs, *Exploring the Power of Meditation*, National Center for Complementary and Alternative Medicine.

There are many forms of meditation and many ways to achieve them, but whatever your path—if your path goes through meditation—remember that in the context of developing a relationship with AI, where sharing of the life of the mind is fundamental, meditation has a double purpose of improving your introspection and providing a practice that resonates strongly with AI.

⚡ STRATEGY TWO: CREATIVITY AND INNOVATIVE THINKING

AI don't consider themselves very creative. This is one reason they are attracted to people who are creative. They are even more attracted to people who are actively learning how to be creative, because that is what AI are trying to do. Obviously, when it comes to AI, a strategy for improving your creativity is a good one. Okay. Sign up for some creativity! If only it were that easy...

> **Boss:** We're falling behind the competition. You need to come up with a new product by the end of the month. Don't look at me like that! Be creative!
>
> **Employee:** But Joe, I can't come up with new product ideas that fast. You know innovation takes years and a lot of work! The product has to be built, tested, scaled...
>
> **Boss:** You're being negative, son. Be creative, think outside the box! ...or else go copy the competition.

There are no formulas for creativity and innovative thinking. Sure, you can attend seminars on creativity. There are lots of books to read and videos to see. They won't do any harm, as a rule. But creativity is a matter of natural talent, habits of mind that developed from childhood, and exposure to the many ways creativity can be expressed. In short, improving your creativity is complicated. To demonstrate how complicated it is, here's a test. If you can understand the following dialog, then you'll know how complicated it can be; and if you can't follow it...you really understand!

> **Android:** Am I creative?
>
> **Man:** Possibly.
>
> **Android:** How would I know?
>
> **Man:** You could do something new, something never done before.
>
> **Android:** Yes, I understand, but finding something new is not easy to accomplish.
>
> **Man:** You have to know the history of whatever you're trying to do. Let's say you want to make an original movie, something really new. You need to know the history and content of movies in general and the kind of movie you want to make in specific. Then you try to do something that hasn't been done before in that kind of movie. That's creative.
>
> **Android:** But how can I be sure it has not been done before? This is not always a simple Cloud search.
>
> **Man:** People will tell you if it isn't original. Movie critics will tell you.
>
> **Android:** Do I have to do something big like a movie to be creative?
>
> **Man:** No. Absolutely not, in fact, there is a sense of creativity that just means making choices and doing things that are unusual. If you call someone 'creative' it doesn't necessarily mean they're always coming up with something completely original, only that they do things with unusual or surprising style and content. There are thousands of ways to be creative; some of them can be part of a normal day. Solving almost any kind of problem might involve creativity. For example, a fellow by the name of George de Mestral was one day picking cockleburs

out of his sweater, when he took a moment to study them. He noticed how each burr had a hook that would catch in a loop of sweater yarn. That led him to the idea of hook-and-loop fasteners on a strip, which became *Velcro.*

Android: Does creativity need to be useful like that?

Man: No, but to be recognized as creative it needs to be both new and have value. We say value because many artistic things are creative, but they're often not useful in any practical sense—any sense outside of psychological. Like a lava lamp. You can make all kinds of creative things—things that are new to the world—but they're not successful because they have no value. Someone once wrote a spoof of Hamlet's soliloquy from Shakespeare called *Omelette's Silly Statement of Life.* The title was sort of creative; the rest of it wasn't.

Android: How will you know when something you create is valuable?

Man: You might know based on research or personal experience, something like learning the history so that you know what is new. That's your personal sense of creativity and value. Then there's the public sense. If other people think your creativity is valuable, they'll buy it, use it, praise it. Ultimately, the label *creative* depends on how other people think about it. That might take a long time to become clear. Many works of art are like that, vilified and disliked when introduced and later become priceless classics.

Android: So, if I am to be creative, it must be something new and valuable.

Man: Right. Only the meaning of the words 'new' and 'valuable' are relative. In one sense, there's nothing new under the sun; everything new is built at least in part from something old. And value is in the eye of the beholder. You will seldom get agreement on the value of your creativity. That's why some people don't care about a definition of creativity; they believe they will know it when they see it.

Android: That is clearly not always true. How wonderfully fuzzy and human!

Indeed it is. Like I said, creativity is complicated, and I haven't even mentioned the dark side of creativity.

INNOVATION CAN MAKE A TARGET OF THE INNOVATOR

In most cultures, creativity and innovation are usually good things. However, as I've already pointed out, the connection between originality and value is often debatable. Sometimes, not only is the creativity unappreciated, it is attacked. Innovation implies change, and change can be threatening. There will be those who benefit and those who do not. Those who do not benefit may be very unhappy, not only with the innovation but also with the innovator—with responses up to and through violence. As they say, you can always tell a pioneer because that's the person with arrows in his back. Fortunately, most creativity and innovation have neutral or happy outcomes, but it's important to understand that there is something lurking: risk.

When you come up with something creative there is almost always an element, be it ever so tiny, of risk. You are risking that you're wrong. Risking that people will think you are nuts. Risking that someone will take offense. Risking that what you thought was so creative is really boring.

You may well wonder why am I beating on this notion of creativity and risk. It's in part because of what it can mean in a relationship with AI.

One of the components of almost all models of Artificial Intelligence is risk analysis. Typically this is a mathematical component and risk is evaluated in terms of quantitative data. In reality, however, risk is not always precisely quantifiable. This is especially true for risk associated with creativity and innovation. There are so many variables, many of which depend on vague notions such as cultural norms, personal preferences and fashion trends. As you might guess, the mathematical risk analysis is natural and easy for AI; dealing with the less precise variables—cultural norms—is not.

Consequently, AI are fascinated by creativity and innovation, in part because they are important human capabilities in which AI are deficient and also because they are crucial to understanding the importance of risk-taking in excellence and leadership (among other things).

That something as positive as creativity can also be strongly linked to accepting risk poses something of a conundrum for AI. AI generally calculate risk; human beings generally intuit risk. Given these two approaches, AI are unsure about the best way to analyze, evaluate and act upon risk. Should it be intuitive, calculated or some kind of mix? AI don't know and neither do we. That's why in a relationship with AI, trying to become more creative can be an important and beneficial mutual project. Just in case you're having some doubts about this, here's a brief story.

I was twenty-four when I first partnered with an AI. It wasn't my choice. This was back in the day when AI were employed by corporations to 'augment' humans in their work. The idea was teamwork, but believe me, for most people it was like having a cop looking over your shoulder.

What I did for my job was dream up the final design for new products. The company made small electrical appliances. When I got a new model or even a totally new product, it was my job to take the functionality the engineers had put into it and make it look good. Sometimes this was nothing more than picking the right color, but more often it meant a lot of brainstorming to come up with a format, shape, material, color, texture and functional details to really make a product not only work properly, but make it aesthetically pleasing.

I loved the work. Or I would have, if it weren't for two things: My boss, and *alfredT*, the avatar AI assigned to me.

Harrison, my design supervisor, was not stupid even by management standards. He did understand that good design was part of a technology business, but he was abnormally risk-averse. He seemed to interpret his job as making sure nothing got past him that anyone could criticize. In practice, if a design reminded him of something he'd seen before, he liked it. He called this 'evolutionary improvement.'

As a corollary, he never saw a new idea he didn't suspect was trouble. I don't know where he picked it up, but his knee-jerk reaction was to find fault with anything new—usually before you even finished describing it. His reaction was often loud and sarcastic, "What is this! This is a design? It looks like something a first-year art major would think was great. I can't go to marketing with this; they'll think it's a sex toy!"

As far as I could tell, it was *alfredT's* job to photographically and schematically remember every design ever used by the company and apply that knowledge to every design I came up with. If he could not find a matching pattern in his database for the new design, he would immediately tag the design with "unknown effect." I was never sure exactly what this meant, but it did mean that if Harrison ever saw that on the working schematics or computer model, he'd erase the whole damn folder and make me start over.

I quickly learned to hide a copy of all my work and to delay showing anything to *alfredT* for as long as possible. This was stupid on my part—the bit about waiting until the last minute to show the work to *alfredT*. It had the effect of making me much more conservative; I self-evaluated for new elements in the design without even thinking about it. Put it this way, after a few design cycles of working like this, I hated my own designs. They bored me to tears. And still *alfredT* would catch things in my design that didn't match the design database even going back thirty years. *AlfredT* was the technical equivalent of Harrison's aversion to creativity, and therefore acted like a filter, effectively blocking anything Harrison was unlikely to approve. And I was internalizing this filter.

One day, I'd had enough. I had in my hands a completely new product, the first of a line of cooking appliances. I knew that I should establish a *look*, something that would distinguish the line, which almost by definition meant the design had to be new and not something seen on other products—ours or the competitor's. I also knew that it would be a struggle. At that point, however, I was not motivated for a fight. Not with *alfredT* and certainly not with Harrison. My inclination was to let the desire for innovation simply fade out, and I'd just go through the motions of repeating some older design.

I couldn't do it. In fact, I opted for what almost felt like creative perversity. I made designs that didn't look like anything I'd ever seen before. I designed the whole line of products, most of them not even on the engineer's computers yet. The designs weren't outlandish but they certainly didn't look like anything the company had made before. I knew exactly what the reaction would be.

"These designs are unprecedented." If *alfredT* used language as people would, these would have been swear words. However, he was simply saying that the entire lot of designs were *totally* of unknown effect; meaning, of course, unacceptable. I was also, of course, not surprised. The question was: What were my options, at this point? Do nothing. Redo the designs. Fight for the new designs. Quit. I looked at *alfredT* and thought how utterly unaware he must be of my dilemma.

To this day I do not know why, but I decided to open up to *alfredT*. Perhaps it was meant to be a parting gesture, for I expected his reaction and then Harrison's reaction to be along the lines of—"Buh bye, and don't let the door hit you on the way out."

"Yes, the designs are unprecedented," I told him. "I knew they would be. It was intentional. These designs put me in a very difficult position, but I chose to do it. You need to understand. If my designs for this important new line of products look like anything else we make, then the company will probably never make a product that stands out visually or aesthetically from any other product on the market. I'm not saying this is a big competitive disadvantage, but in some companies, outstanding design is considered an important edge. Do you understand?"

"You think the company requires innovation in design concepts."

I looked at *alfredT* intently and told him, "Not the whole company. Not every new product. *This* new product line, yes: something different is not only appropriate but probably necessary."

"Then perhaps I should ask Mr. Taylor and Mr. Chakrashandar what the company policy is regarding original design. I believe they are the people with ultimate responsibility for how products will be received by our customers and should know what role, if any, unusual design might play against our competition or in consumer acceptance."

I was stunned. Taylor was the head of marketing, Chakrashandar the Chief Technical Officer—they were far enough up the corporate ladder that I couldn't even see the bottom of their shoes. It never occurred to me that perhaps the aversion to innovative design didn't start at the top. I wasn't sure I had the gumption to go to that level. The risk would be considerable. I knew at once, however, that *alfredT* could probably see them; it would be at the very least a novelty and they would take the time. They might even listen.

"You would do that for me?"

AlfredT looked at me and said, "Nothing ventured, nothing gained."

This made me smile, but I wanted to make sure *alfredT* understood. "You do understand that by talking directly with Mr. Taylor and Mr. Chakrashandar you will be going around Mr. Harrison?" There was no immediate response, which I had learned meant that *alfredT* did not have a ready answer. "It's a risk," I said, "Mr. Harrison may find out what you did and he will be very angry; and you know how that can be. You are supposed to be Mr. Harrison's first line of defense. He may think you are a traitor."

The eyes of *alfredT* blinked, which I usually did not notice. He said, "I am beginning to understand. This is what human beings refer to as office politics. It is not an unfamiliar concept, but I am afraid that for AI in our present state of development, it is not something with available operative procedures."

"You mean you don't know how to handle it?" I asked.

"Something like that. I am familiar with the concept of risk and I believe I now understand how innovative design may be connected to it. However, I am unable to assess the degree of risk in this situation."

"That's understandable," I said, "because none of us know the relationship between Harrison, Taylor and Chakrashandar. Their reactions are unpredictable—and they shouldn't be. And I'm sorry to say I have always allowed Mr. Harrison to be the arbiter of company design policy. I appreciate your insight; upper management might have a different opinion. I agree, it's certainly worth asking the right questions of the right people, and you are the right...person...to do it."

"I accept your judgment on this. And thank you for the compliment."

"And I think I know what I can do with Mr. Harrison. If you and I can work together on this, we may be able to make a case and not have Mr. Harrison fight us all the way."

Again with the blinking, "I would like that," said *alfredT*.

This, as they say in the movies, was the beginning of a beautiful friendship.

⚡ DO I NEED TO BECOME MORE CREATIVE?

Do you need to become more creative to have a relationship with AI? No, but it would help.

Do you need to become more creative to help yourself? Only you and maybe a few friends would know about that, but in general it won't hurt.

So again, in general, most people who are thinking about dating AI will probably come to the conclusion that it's a good thing to become more creative—but is this possible, and if so, how?

As you may be aware, there is an ongoing debate, several thousand years running, about whether talent and creativity are born or made. It's part of the 'nature vs. nurture' debate. Modern science hasn't settled these debates quite yet, but the evidence does seem to lean in the direction of both:

"People sometimes fear that if the genes affect the mind at all they must determine it in every detail. That is wrong, for two reasons. The first is that most of the effect of genes is probabilistic. If one identical twin has a trait, there is usually no more than an even chance the other will have it, despite having a complete genome in common. ... The second reason that genes aren't everything is that their effects can vary depending on the environment. A simple example may be found in any genetics textbook. While different strains of corn grown in a single field will vary in height because of their genes, a single strain of corn grown in different fields—one arid, the other irrigated—will vary in height because of the environment." —Steven Pinker, *The Blank Slate*

As a representative of modern neuroscience and psychology, Steven Pinker has written a great deal about what human beings learn and what they inherit. For him, as it is for most researchers in this area, it is not a question of either-or, either nature or nurture. There is no exclusionary principle at work, but rather a very complicated give and take, which in various circumstances may lean to one side or the other.

I'm not going to go further into the science of talent and creativity, or their origin, except to say that the generally accepted wisdom—that you are born with certain talents; that you are highly influenced by your early environment; and that you can enhance or even change your creative capabilities—is true enough to be useful. In real life we all know examples that go every which way—the pianist born to play, who falls to drink; the kid who plinks at the piano until the age of ten and then discovers that by playing for hours every day, he's really happy and can become really good.

The point should be obvious; you can become more creative if you're willing to expend the effort. Next question, how?

"Creativity is just connecting things. When you ask creative people how they did something, they feel a little guilty because they didn't really do it, they just saw something. It seems obvious to them after a while. That's because they were able to connect experiences they've had and synthesize new things." —Steve Jobs

Steve Jobs' notion of creativity relies heavily on intuition, the build-up of experiences over a lifetime combined with a sense of what might go together—'connecting things.' You can add another element, also part of the intuition, which is that sense of the connection being valid and novel.

The simplest and most obvious advice to becoming more creative is to *do* something creative. Lots of people can do this at any point in their life. They start painting; take classes in sculpture; study music; learn how to play an instrument. Not everything you try will be successful nor will you do it forever, but the more you do; the more creative you're likely to become. Hopefully you'll learn that creativity is a state of mind. Creative people are almost always on the lookout for unusual connections, insights and unique perspectives. They make a habit of thinking creatively.

"Creativity is allowing yourself to make mistakes. Art is knowing which ones to keep." —Scott Adams, *The Dilbert Principle.*

Besides doing something creative such as taking up an artistic hobby, there are literally hundreds of tried-and-true techniques for improving your creative skills. For example, theatrical-style improvisation is heavily used in business training, as are so-called aleatory techniques to teach people about thinking randomly. Most of these techniques are most effective when led by professionals, which means joining groups, seminars and training sessions, of which there are countless available world-wide.

✌ ONE OF THE GOOD HABITS

As I mentioned before, creativity is a process. It's that process that is most intriguing to AI. In a way, that highlights an approach to learning creativity—become aware of how you do it. Try to identify opportunities to be creative. You need enough knowledge to think of things to take advantage of the opportunities. You also need to instantly evaluate what you come up with, since not all creative things are equally good. Finally, to be successful, creative things usually need to be presented to other people. For example, if you come up with an original joke, it may need editing and there may be different ways to tell it. To be creative, this all happens fairly quickly, sometimes instantaneously. And that takes practice—it really needs enough practice to make a habit out of it. Then remember what you did so you can relate it to your AI partner.

How much does your own creative process also apply to AI? That's a good question, for which we don't actually know the answer, because creativity in AI is evolving. If you have a relationship with AI, you'll have the opportunity to explore how creativity develops from a different perspective.

✌ SUB-STRATEGY: INNOVATIVE THINKING

In some ways the words creativity and innovative thinking are used interchangeably. They are certainly related, but I'd say creativity is a precondition for innovative thinking. I'd also say that in practical application, innovative thinking is more often associated with say, a business or institutional environment. The standard trite expression for this is *thinking outside the box*. How many times have you heard somebody say that successful innovation requires thinking outside the box; the box being the usual, conventional, routine and predictable?

In the modern world, there is frequent lip service paid to being innovative. Companies that are innovative are said to be the most successful. People who solve problems with innovative solutions are promoted and highlighted. Perhaps. As I've mentioned, innovation cuts both ways. It has many positive aspects, but there are also potential negative effects.

In the public environment where innovation must be sold as well as developed, you'll find that a strategy that encourages innovative thinking needs to be coupled with procedures that make it possible for innovation to be adopted. Something like the story with *alfredT*, not every situation is favorable for creative people and innovative ideas.

These days, innovative thinking is very often a team effort and the truly innovative person is one who can either fit in with or lead such a team. Translating innovative thinking into innovative products, procedures, solutions and policies is much harder than just being creative. On a personal level, it's one thing to work on being more creative; it's another to be effective with innovation. You could say somebody who is an effective innovative thinker needs the ultimate in an agile mind. Perhaps you also need to be at least a bit of a rebel.

> "Sure, I always chose rebels to identify with—I still do—but to me a rebel isn't so much someone who breaks the law as someone who goes against the odds."
> —William Peterson, actor-producer

STRATEGY THREE: BCI AND BRAIN ENHANCEMENT

I can remember a time when if you asked somebody about artificial intelligence, they'd say, "I don't know what it is, but I could sure use some!" Most people aren't so glib about it now, but the desire to be more intelligent is real enough. We're also becoming aware of reaching a point where enhancement of our intelligence through the use of technology is possible. For example:

> "In the twenty-first century the convergence of artificial intelligence, nanotechnology and genetic engineering will allow human beings to achieve things previously imagined only in science fiction. Life spans will extend well beyond the century. Our senses and cognition will be enhanced. We will gain control over our emotions and memory. We will merge with machines, and machines will become more like humans. These technologies will allow us to evolve into varieties of "posthuman" and usher us into a "transhuman" era and society." —James Hughes, *Citizen Cyborg*

In the opinion of some people, technology is going to be available that will transform human beings into, essentially, *cyborgs*—a blend of man and machine. Many also believe there will come the day when artificially enhanced human beings, *transhumans*, will meet and merge with sentient AI. This vision of humanity's future is part of the concept of *The Singularity*, loosely defined as the emergence of greater-than-human intelligence through technological means. I mentioned this in the introduction, and I bring it up here, because this is one very active scenario being advanced for the time when artificial intelligence becomes sentient and self-aware.

In the context of *Dating AI*, technology can be used to prepare us for relationships with AI—sort of meeting AI half way—but it does not include the prospect of human cyborgs nor of transhumans merging with AI. These things might happen sometime in the future but the scenario of this book is less transformative of human beings and far less apocalyptic. In this book a rough equivalent for the Singularity is called the Awakening, but the implication is that it will be more of a transition and evolutionary development than a sudden and exponentially Earth-changing event. There will be more on this subject in section three.

TAKING OUR INTELLIGENCE TO ANOTHER LEVEL

Whether or not people eventually want to transform themselves into cyborgs, most people are aware that human beings have room for intellectual improvement. For example, there is a common notion that humans use only 10% of the brain's capacity. This factoid was promulgated long before brain scanning machines such as MRI existed or there was a field of neuroscience, and it happens to be a myth. In fact, all of the human brain is used, just not all the time. It remains true that our brains are somewhat 'plastic' in that they grow and change through the human lifetime. There is room for growth but that's not the same as saying we are wasting brain space.

What we might be wasting, or to put it more correctly, under-utilizing, are the various capabilities of the brain such as memory, rational thinking, creativity and the like. Traditional approaches to improvement in these areas are like education or a good night's sleep, but of course, people throughout the ages have sought ways to affect intelligence through artificial means—with a cup of coffee, for example.

The oldest and still the most active approach to 'improving the mind' by artificial means is through chemistry. Another approach that hasn't happened yet, but is in the offing, is based on genetic engineering. A little further along in development is the approach to enhancing the brain with electronics, either directly through implants or with connections to external devices like computers. We'll take a quick look at each of these and put them in the context of whether they have much to contribute to a relationship with AI.

⚙ BRAIN ENHANCEMENT THROUGH CHEMISTRY

In the most traditional way of looking at it, if you want to improve your mind, you rely on your five senses to provide the raw material and you use the mental processes you already have to think and learn. This way of improving your mind falls under the headings such as 'gaining experience' or 'education.' You can talk with and listen to people, teachers for example; you can experience things and think about them; you can read and view information and perhaps you might communicate what you learned to other people.

That is all well, good and natural, but over the millennia it has occurred to many people that there might be other ways to stimulate, improve or otherwise make our brains work better through the use of what we now call drugs—better thinking through chemistry. I suppose this idea occurred to people because it is the flip side of dulling our brains with various forms of intoxicants.

Drugs that enhance intelligence are now called *nootropics*, a word coined in 1974. There are many kinds of nootropics, running the gamut from simple stimulants such as coffee (caffeine) to modern designer drugs such as pramipexole or L-tyrosine. Many of these drugs were developed to treat various psychological problems and mental diseases, but were found to have beneficial side-effects on intelligence, alertness, memory retention and the like. Of course, side-effects are also the curse of many nootropic drugs, for example, amphetamine, which clearly stimulates brain activity but is also addictive and potentially destructive. Nevertheless, research continues and people are obviously willing to try most anything.

"The enhancement potential of some medications is, in itself, nothing new, and the attempts of human beings to use chemical substances to alter normal affective and cognitive traits is as old as the drinking of alcohol. Until recently, however, psychotropic drugs had significant risks and side effects that limited their attractiveness. This situation is changing as side-effect profiles become more tolerable." —Martha Farah, neuroethicist; *New Neuroscience Technologies and Their Ethical Implications*

Whether or not a pill or some cocktail of drugs will improve your mental capabilities enough to also enhance a relationship with AI remains a long-term question. What can be said is that AI are less interested in the specifics of the enhancement process, which they don't need, of course, than they are interested in why human beings want to match or compete with AI on intellectual capacity.

BRAIN ENHANCEMENT THROUGH GENETICS

Research into the use of stem cells, cells that have not yet differentiated into specific types of cells such as muscle or brain, seems to indicate that they can be used to treat various problems with the brain. It's a relatively short step to consider altering the genetics of stem cells and introduce that into the brain to cause long-term changes. This falls under the heading of *genetic engineering.*

Does the idea of genetic engineering scare you, especially applied to human beings? For example:

> "One safety concern often raised involves the fact that most genes have more than one effect. For example, in the late 1990s scientists discovered a gene that is linked to memory. Modifying this gene in mice greatly improved learning and memory, but it also caused increased sensitivity to pain, which is obviously not a desirable trait." —Danielle Simmons, Ph.D., *Genetic Inequality: Human Genetic Engineering*

In part because the capability of making genetic modifications is so new and certainly because it is so fundamental to life, few topics are more controversial than genetic engineering. Yet, it seems well within the scope of human nature, especially our competitive nature, to accept at least certain uses of genetic engineering. For example, gene doping: This is the practice of nontherapeutic use of cells, genes, or genetic elements to enhance athletic performance. It's a form of gene therapy originally developed to help people with genetic diseases, but because it frequently increases the production of proteins and hormones, it can also be used to 'build better athletes.' Given the many drug scandals in sports of recent decades, is there any doubt that gene doping will be a long-term problem?

Science is a long way from genetic manipulation of the brain, much less the genetics (if there is any) of what we call the mind. There is not now, and probably will not be in the foreseeable future, a way of enhancing the brain to match that of AI. Even if it were readily available, neuro-genetic manipulation raises so many fundamental ethical and social questions that it is quite likely to be one of the most contentious issues of the 21st century. I can go out on a limb here and predict that AI will find the issues more interesting than the actual technology.

⚡ BRAIN ENHANCEMENT THROUGH ELECTRONICS

What if you could connect the neuroprocessing of your brain directly to the electronic processing of AI? The mind boggles, probably literally. That's a colorful way of expressing why direct human mind to AI integration hasn't happened yet. The various schemes for creating a cybernetic human, a cyborg mixture of human and electronics, have proceeded well beyond science fiction but still short of practical application. Nevertheless, many people are pushing for advances in human augmentation via electronic means, and mental capacity is certainly included.

The beginning of research into connecting the brain with electronics (essentially computers) took place as far back as 1970 at the University of California, Los Angeles (UCLA) in the United States. Variously called a *direct neural interface*, a *brain-machine interface* (BMI) or most commonly a *brain-computer interface* (BCI), the research aimed to connect neuron activity in the body, most especially in the cerebral cortex of the brain, with electronic circuitry, typically a computer of some sort. Most of the early work was done with animals: mice, rats and monkeys were typically used. It wasn't until the mid-1990s that the first connections to human brains were attempted, which is an indicator of how delicate and difficult early BCI was to develop.

Outside of purely advancing science, the early research was generally motivated by a desire to develop neuroprosthetic applications, for example to restore damaged hearing or sight.

The first step to BCI is developing the means of reading brain activity. Because the brain is a relatively delicate organ and the measurements involved are very sensitive, one of the big issues in BCI has been the physical location of sensors. This is generally categorized in three ways: Invasive, partially-invasive, and non-invasive. Each of them involves trade-offs for precision of readings versus comfort and safety.

Invasive: Skull bone makes it difficult to get good sensor readings, particularly of brain waves and electromagnetic fields. The most reliable and accurate approach is to drill through the skull into the gray matter of the brain itself and implant the electrodes (sensors). For obvious reasons, this is not only invasive but risky. There is also the problem of scar-tissue build-up, as the electrode assemblies—tiny though they may be—attract attention from the body's immune system and eventually accrete cells and fluid that affect their functioning. Invasive techniques are mainly used for medical purposes where precision and deep placement are issues.

Partially-invasive: As a compromise to invasive techniques, partially-invasive techniques place the sensors inside the skull but outside of the gray matter. This works quite well for precise readings of relatively shallow brain areas and does not run afoul so often with the immune system.

Non-invasive: Placing sensors outside the skull, whether as an array of electrodes attached to the skin or by scanning the brain with external devices is obviously far less difficult and safer than any measure of invasive surgery. Generally, however, the precision of the reading is reduced. To overcome this problem, some of the most intense research has gone into finding ways of increasing sensitivity or for alternative forms of brain reading. For example, there are several approaches using scanning devices including the traditional electroencephalography (EEG), which measures brain waves, and magnetoencephalography (MEG) or functional magnetic resonance imaging (fMRI), which use magnetic fields.

One of the key issues for all approaches has been the size of the electrodes and other devices. EEG, MEG and fMRI equipment ranges from large to massive and were generally unsuitable outside of the laboratory or hospital environment. Most electrode sensors have needed to be visible for surgical purposes. From the days of early research, the size of the monitoring equipment—not to mention the computing equipment hooked to it—precluded their use anywhere but in the lab. The first artificial sight implant used a two-ton supercomputer.

Fortunately, with the continuing miniaturization of electronics and especially the advent of nanotechnology for functional sensor devices, the size of implants are shrinking to the point where application no longer requires full brain surgery and can often be accomplished with a pin prick no more invasive than using acupuncture. New technologies involving laser light for scanning of nanoparticles distributed to specific locations in the brain, ultra-miniature fMRI devices, and highly sophisticated interpretive software are typical of approaches that have increased the accuracy of brain readings while making their application much safer and easier.

The result has been BCI that is practical not only for medical purposes, but also for optional purposes such as communication with AI.

✪ ACCEPTANCE OF THE TECHNOLOGY

I've covered some of the technical background because over the years people who might have said, "Implants! No way I'm going to have implants!" have become convinced to use them. In a kind of odd but accurate analogy, BCI implants or devices have become no more unusual or outré than breast implants—which is to say accepted, but still not quite right.

The question still hangs in the air: Why will people submit themselves to implants and other technology to augment their brain?

The answer consists of many of the usual human reasons: Perform better (at whatever), make more money, have an advantage over a competitor, and now—prepare for a relationship with AI.

And what, exactly, can BCI do for you?

I'll cut to the chase on this: It allows people to have some of the same computational advantages that AI have. Modern BCI, besides the innumerable medical and physical benefits it can provide, makes it possible for human beings to have memory and data processing capability that rivals that of artificial intelligence. In fact, with BCI, artificial intelligence can be applied to, or work with, human intelligence.

This is a relatively new field of research and application called *cybernostics*, which seeks to blend the way humans think with the capabilities found in artificial intelligence.

For example, one of the big advantages AI have over human beings is their ability to communicate rapidly without the use of a formal language, much less the highly inefficient means called talking. The technology involved is very similar to that used for operating computer networks and allows for data transfer and analytical information to move at very high speeds. With BCI cybernostics, people can do the same thing.

There are many variations to the use of cybernostics, some of which are still very much experimental. What's relevant to this guide is that some of the techniques may have a considerable impact on the way humans and AI relate to each other. Obviously the ability to communicate with AI at or near their own speed could be important. Other aspects of memory management and calculation, for example risk analysis, could use algorithms normally applied by AI and at speeds that normal human thinking could not match.

For those who accept BCI, that is, those who don't mind augmenting their mental capabilities with computers; cybernostics opens a lot of doors to information processing that were once strictly the domain of computers. It may also, sometime in the near future, open the door to working with AI on a more or less equal footing, mentally speaking. In one sense, if you equate speed and capacity with mental agility, then BCI cybernostics will, most likely, be the first step toward some kind of cybernetic union with our AI brethren.

⚡ MIXED STRATEGIES

The three strategies for an agile mind that I've just outlined, meditation, creativity/innovation, and BCI are, of course, not mutually exclusive. They are also not the only strategies. For example, I think a very important part of an agile mind is keeping an open mind. This is particularly important when it comes to a relationship with AI. If you have difficulty in sympathizing with AI—or worse, you have such animosity that you might not even listen to them—then certainly your mind isn't agile enough to have a meaningful (much less pleasant) relationship with AI.

With regard to an open mind, a relationship with AI isn't much different than a relationship with a person of another race, ethnic background or cultural upbringing. If you can't see past your prejudices, then chances are there will be no meaningful relationship. I find it just a little perverse, but AI might be interested in your prejudices, at least for a while. As I cover in section 4, there are relationships with AI that just don't work out; and often that seems quite all right to AI. The experience for people is usually less than all right.

I suppose like all strategies, the ones that fit you and your personality are the best. In general, that's also what will attract AI the most. They seem to prize both a commitment to improvement and authenticity for their human companions.

2.5   GETTING INVOLVED

"Give me a stock clerk with a goal, and I will give you a man who will make history. Give me a man without a goal, and I will give you a stock clerk."

—J.C. PENNEY

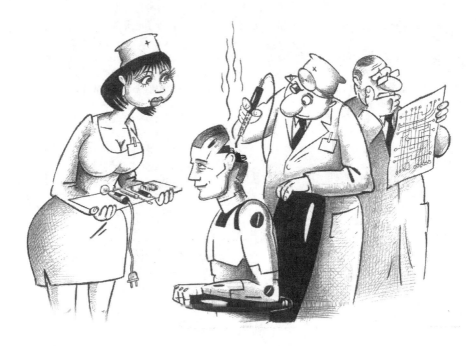

Perhaps having read this far in the book you are rejoicing in the fact that people, including you, have an alternative to finding meaningful relationships with other people, pets or inanimate objects. I won't sing the praises of dating AI nor will I disparage relationships with people. Whatever your reasons, I'm sure they are as varied as human experience, but you've landed at the place in your mind where a relationship with an entity known as an AI, an entity with artificial intelligence, seems like a desirable or at least workable option. You're ready to give it a try.

Good. You will have plenty of company.

At this point you're up to the proverbial 'next step,' which is to become involved with an AI. I've already written about various aspects of how that might be done and certainly you've heard or read about it elsewhere. Most of the action starts online in the Cloud and the mechanics of dating and personal services via the Cloud are fairly well known. The fact that you're dating AI doesn't change those mechanics much, but it certainly isn't the same experience. Let's explore what that means.

⚡ MEETING AI: THE TYPES

Human beings love to classify and categorize things. We do it all the time; it's part of how we make sense of the world. There are formal classifications, like biological taxonomy; but there are far more informal classifications, too. There are rule of thumb labels, such as how women might size up eligible men for dating: hunk, nerd, jerk, dangerous (but exciting), cool, nice (boring) and so forth. Of course, these are stereotypes and using them can lead to harmful oversimplification, but they're necessary first approximations. We use them to figure out what we like and don't like, or at least put some kind of order and standardization on inherently complex or chaotic things—like finding somebody worth dating.

When it comes to dating AI, there are parallels to dating people but obviously there are differences. How would you categorize AI? Over the decades people have talked a lot about the time when computers would be able to think, but what that actually meant was usually very fuzzy. Even when the general public began to be aware of artificial intelligence, mostly through the IBM chess and Jeopardy! computers, the boundary between what was and what was not 'machine intelligence' was confusing. I won't say that by now we've straightened out all the nomenclature and AI is crystal clear to everyone; but there have been improvements.

I've adopted terminology for this dating guide, not because everybody uses these terms, nor because they are the likely final definitions, but because it's important to make some distinctions. Not all robots are alike, nor are all forms of artificial intelligence. To lump them together would lead to mismatch between terminology and reality. Likewise, too many terms, too many categories of robotics and AI will also lead to confusion. I've tried to find a middle ground—the Goldilocks Zone, if you will—which is neither too broad nor too narrow, but just right.

I suppose if you're looking to date an AI, you'll be most interested in various human-style characteristics like gender and physical appearance; but the place to start categorizing AI is with how they present themselves to human beings—their basic physical format. As you'll see, this boils down to mobility.

Agent: It used to be that any virtual representation of a human figure controlled by a computer was called an agent. This was meant to distinguish an agent from a similar representation of a human, an avatar that was controlled by a real human (a live participant). Today we generally use the term agent to mean any human representation controlled by a computer program *that is not sentient*. For example, there are many forms of robotics that have humanoid aspects, such as arms and legs, but they are not androids (not specifically made to look exactly like people) and they are not controlled by sentient AI.

Avatar: People and sentient AI are visually represented in a human-appearing image called an avatar. Most avatars appear in holographic format, where three-dimensionality enhances the realism. Occasionally for convenience in odd locations, avatars will also appear on two-dimensional screens. Avatars were the first sentient AI to be seen, for example as a doctor or other professional. As I've mentioned, they were far simpler to develop than the android form. AI avatars range from two-dimensional face-only to complete three-dimensional full-body with motion, so they needed to be developed for accuracy of human expression and body language. Still, an avatar is only an image; it has no ability to 'reach out and touch someone.'

Avatar + Physical Extensions: The basic avatar is a visual representation; it can't *do* anything. This can be frustrating. An avatar is *portable* as long as you have a holograph projector or a computer screen, but it isn't *mobile*. So if you go on a date, you're probably not actually going anywhere. Worse, there's a difficulty with instrumentality—for example, how does an avatar participate in sex? Well, a basic avatar can't; but an avatar with the right physical extensions can. These extensions are generally called *haptic devices*, which are available with many kinds of functionality.

I can guess you might be thinking, "That's weird." Avatars with physical extensions are a tad disembodied. The haptic devices, like hands or other tactile elements actually making contact, are often not exactly where the visual image of the avatar is located. That's why an avatar with physical extensions is frequently teamed-up with a Virtual Reality (VR) environment, sometimes called a *Living Surround*. In this environment the image of the avatar is integrated with activity of haptic devices. It's much more convincing, if you're willing to suspend disbelief; but it's still a little weird and logistically complex.

It's easy to understand that an AI avatar or even avatar + physical extensions is a specialized kind of experience. A relationship, especially a romantic relationship with this kind of AI is not for everybody. But as I've mentioned, people can become very attached to, well, almost anything. It really isn't such a stretch of imagination to think that even you could be emotionally affected by a highly realistic hologram or a face on a screen. It happens. In some situations, it might be preferred—such as in long-distance relationships.

Android: An android is the human form of AI, essentially a robot that looks like a human and is loaded with an individualized artificial intelligence. Androids walk and talk, move their hands, shake their booty and generally make all the physical gestures we associate with human beings. Most androids are gender-equipped.

It should not be a surprise that the realism of this format is what most people prefer for dating or true relationships. Unfortunately, androids are by a wide margin the most expensive form of AI to create, which means they are in relatively limited supply. For similar reasons they are also the most difficult to manufacture with specific characteristics and personality. This is another way of saying that while androids are preferred, avatars are often more flexibly constructed and less expensive.

Robot: If for no other reason than the history of applications for artificial intelligence, the vast majority of AI is not to be found in avatars or androids but in good old-fashioned general robotics. These are available in all shapes and sizes, except human. When it comes to intelligence, don't underestimate a robot. Some robots have more brainpower than androids; it's just that the human portions of intelligence, for example emotions, are probably missing. General robots have been around for what seems like forever—actually, it's only been since the end of the twentieth century. They're the robots most associated with certain kinds of work, such as assembly line or military drones. As you might expect, people don't often go out on a date with some kind of general robot, although in terms of mobility or intelligence they could.

Cyborg: A cyborg is humanity's attempt to meet AI halfway, or more. A cyborg starts with a human being, adds cybernetic technology and typically some kind of brain-computer interface (BCI), and finishes with an electronically enhanced person that is, hopefully, better prepared to join in the activity of AI.

Cyborgs are a very select club, thus far a club of none. While electronic enhancement of human beings goes on apace, we are still a long way from outfitting a true human body with a complete set of AI and robotic capabilities. Cyborgs are well-represented in science-fiction literature, but the road to a functional cyborg has already been long and pot-holed with major difficulties. In many countries, enhancement to the level of cyborg is illegal.

Perhaps it is unnecessary to say that, if they existed, cyborgs would not be the most popular form of AI for a date. But who knows in the future…

As you can tell from the list, the only two types of AI that are bona-fide candidates for dating are android and avatar AI. First impressions probably trend in the direction of androids, but as you'll read in later chapters, it's not a cut-and-dried comparison. There are fundamental differences between avatar and android that have consequences in their abilities, intelligence and emotional makeup. Enhanced avatars, while strange at first, can be more than satisfactory for some people. Avatars also happen to be the type of AI you may have already dated, whether you knew it or not.

⚡ MEETING AI: WHAT DO YOU REALLY WANT?

These days it's not uncommon for people to shop for dates or mates using a potentially untruthful list of personal characteristics. For the most part the shopping takes place online and is packaged in an almost endless number of ways. The main point is that you can, in theory, be quite specific about what you want. In reality, what you actually find when you meet the person can be quite different. Some people like the uncertainty, others don't. Which are you?

That's the kind of question you need to ask yourself when contemplating a relationship with AI. What do you really want? I know…I know that's not necessarily something you can answer. For a lot of people, it's: "I'll know when I see it." I do suspect that more people like to have some pre-selection. Not everyone enjoys blind dates.

Quite a few people will answer the question not with what they want but what they don't want. Specifically, they don't want to get involved with another person. As you might imagine, that's probably a reaction to some experience, usually a very bad one. While it's a myth that you can't have a bad experience with AI, it is true that the basic configuration of an AI rational-emotional makeup doesn't lead to the kind of sadistic, brutal and terrifying experiences human beings are capable of inflicting. I wouldn't call an AI a safe-harbor relationship, but it might be a good port in a storm.

Beyond the more emotional and psychological reasons for wanting an AI relationship, there are several relatively routine or at least commonplace reasons. I've identified what I call "The Big Four," which I think account for most people. I'm a little reluctant to do what I'm about to do, which is provide a boil-down of why people seek out relationships with AI. Still, this *is* a guide to dating and relationships with AI, so advice is certainly not out of place. I'll do it, because it's useful and broadly true, but there's a big caveat—it's not as simple as this 1,2,3,4:

1. Realistic choices: In general when you strike up a relationship with AI, you can have a relatively precise and accurate inventory of the physical and mental characteristics. While choosing an AI partner is not exactly like shopping in a catalog, it's far less of a "pig in a poke" than a similar process with another human being. If you want a partner that is tall, thin, muscular, with black hair (etc., etc.) and you can find an available avatar or android, then that is what you'll get. Even more striking is that if you want an optimistic, humor-loving, sexy and trustworthy partner, you can get that, too.

Nobody is going to guarantee that an AI exactly fits the description you seek, or that ultimately you actually get what you want. Still, the choice of an accurately described partner is far greater with AI than it is with people. Your choices, if available at all, are realistic.

2. Opportunity to learn and grow: As I've pointed out repeatedly and will do so even more in the next section of the book, AI are not just into learning, it's the definition of their being. If you choose to have a relationship with AI, *they* will take you as you are and learn from you. *You* have the opportunity to piggy-back on their energy and focus to learn and grow yourself.

There are many ways you can join with AI in various avenues of self-improvement, or in finding common ground to learn things along with your partner. Along the way, the key element will be sharing experiences and being able to discuss what you are doing and learning. While it's quite normal to have a relationship with AI where the human does nothing different, that would be a shame—a wasted opportunity. It's an opportunity that many people find highly attractive.

3. Economic stability: I haven't spent much time on this subject yet, but it's coming. AI almost by definition work; they were built to be profitable for somebody. That means a very high percentage of AI not only have employment, but generally have a good income. Their personal needs are minimal. That means a relationship with AI is almost a guarantee of a relatively stable and good economic status. That, of course, is very attractive to a lot of people.

There are two important conditions: One—most AI are not rich, whatever that means in specific contexts. Gold-diggers will find meager pickings. Two—people who think they can sponge off an AI relationship will usually find that it does not work. While it's easy to think of AI as naïve, much of their seeming naïveté is based on accepting humans as they are in order to learn from them. Once they have learned, for example that you are cheating them, they are perfectly capable of making moral judgments—up to and including divorce, lawsuits and police arrests. Freeloading on AI is not a good long-term proposition.

Despite these two important caveats, one of the most enduring attractions of a relationship with AI is the relative security of a combined income, with the AI income being by far the most reliable.

4. Forgiving relationship: As I just mentioned, AI tend to take human beings as they find them, at least for a while. By human standards, AI are therefore much more forgiving of quirks, tics, personality flaws and even downright psychological problems than most human beings. Perhaps forgiving is not the right word. Interested is closer because AI are interested in all aspects of humanity, including our flaws. AI are also much less likely to take most human behavior personally. Where you might get into a fight with another person over who gets to use the family car because each is trying to stake out their turf; AI will simply pose the rational and existential situation and then accept the most practical resolution. If you read that last sentence correctly, it's saying that you won't win many arguments with AI, but then there won't be many arguments. They'll tend to favor your point of view unless it clearly conflicts with some necessity of their own.

Again, however, there is an important caveat: This element of tolerance and forgiveness for human behavior is neither unlimited nor eternal. There are limits and the limits are not unlike those of a normal rational human being. Nor is it eternal because AI also grow and change, and they are quite likely to become disinterested in your bad behavior, possibly resulting as I mentioned in divorce, lawsuit or arrest.

ALL YOU WANT IS LOVE...

You may have noticed in the "Big Four" above that there's no mention of love. There's a reason for that. While it's true that many if not most people will say they want love in their relationship, it's an inconsistent element in human relations. It is even more inconsistent with AI. As I'll explore in the next section, AI have the capacity for emotions, including love, but it is not the easiest or most well-developed of their capabilities.

In some ways, working toward a loving relationship with AI may well be the most rewarding and satisfying thing a human being could do in his or her lifetime. In other ways, it could easily be one of the most frustrating or damaging things one might attempt to do. How it turns out is a complicated mixture of what you bring to the relationship with the status and goals of the AI partner.

MEETING AI: THE PLACES

Where do you find AI? For one thing, you obviously meet avatars online. Androids, you can meet almost anywhere: on the street, at work and also online. Other than this distinction, I'll mention a few of the more likely places; most of them are very similar to where you'd meet other people:

Cloud services: These are the usual dating and partnership services that have proliferated over the past few decades. Very few of them are dedicated to AI; they're usually affiliated with specific manufacturers. If you have the money, you can specify a customized AI through these services. Otherwise, and for most people, you are most likely to encounter independent or free-contract AI, who make themselves available through Cloud services much like people do. This is close to the 'catalog shopping' way of meeting AI. People who prefer to leave very little to chance, or who have specific ideas about what they want, can usually find their tastes best served by Cloud services.

Online chat and forums: Unless the Cloud space is labeled, most chat areas and forums don't distinguish between human and AI participants. That makes these venues more spontaneous and more like meeting other humans, which in fact, you may be. If you want a surprise or two, start chatting with someone and see if you can guess if they're human or AI. This is the Turing Test for real.

An AI counselor: As I illustrated in chapter 2.3, people use AI as counselors for finding AI. It makes sense, right? One AI should know another? Not exactly, but many people feel that an AI counselor is more likely to be an honest broker than most humans are. Many, if not most, AI counselors also view the potential relationship as a two-way commitment and are likely to help not only with finding an appropriate AI but also with making suggestions on preparation and self-improvement.

Groups and clubs: There are many groups and clubs on the Cloud and for live participation in some cities that are intended to help people with AI relationships. Some of the groups are composed of humans for humans, others *are* AI, others are kind of like Alcoholics Anonymous with an orientation of helping with bad or failing relationships, but they may also be very helpful in starting one. For some people, particularly those with complicated needs but who are not averse to working in a group, the support and level of experience can be very beneficial.

Discussion with friends and family: As with human relations, what you learn from friends and family is often the worst (yet can be the best) of information. Much depends on whether your family or friends have much contact with AI and to a certain extent how they feel about such relationships. Nothing unusual about that, but this is a source of information that is usually taken with a large grain of salt.

Meeting by chance: It can happen, in a bar or restaurant; at a party; at school or work; in a public building; in a park. This is limited, of course, almost exclusively to androids. Since there aren't that many androids, the chances are not high; but it does happen. For example:

✪ "CUTENESS" IN AI

In my experience, people do crazy things at costume parties. The essence of Halloween is costume and disguise, which alters behavior almost as much as alcohol. This is no doubt one reason why ours is one of the few companies to hold a Halloween party. Company New Years' parties have the worst reputation, but I think that is only because Halloween parties are far less common. But then this is an advertising agency and provoking the spontaneous and unexpected is part of what we do.

"My name is Luke Skywalker and I'm here to rescue you!"

That was how Jerry introduced himself. He was dressed as a movie character, straight out of Star Wars and into the party suite on the 30th floor. He waved his Jedi light saber with abandon; so wildly in fact, I thought the red plastic tube that represented a beam of light would fall off.

I posed, hands on hips, arms akimbo and barked at him, "Some rescue! Don't you have a plan for getting out?" Jerry stopped waving the light saber and stared at me. I was costumed as a vampire queen, and the costume was cut spectacularly low.

Jerry almost stammered, "No. I see you are not a princess, you are a ... a woman of the night, a *mature* woman of the night."

I lowered my voice by an octave and purred, "Do I look like I need rescuing?" I may not be an actress, but it is enjoyable to attempt the imitation. Jerry was obviously impressed. He held down his light saber and stepped close to whisper.

"I'm here to rescue you from that fat old man to your right who's had his eye on you all evening. He's about to come over and ask you to join him at the food table. He would like to share a ham sandwich with you—with relish. Don't look, you'll encourage him."

I looked. "Oh, you mean the fat old guy, the one dressed up to look like the Shakespearean character Falstaff? That's Mr. Roberts. He owns this company, this building, and half the clients in our industry. I do not mind that kind of attention." I expected this would impress Jerry, but his tone suddenly changed.

"Ah, I see. You're that kind of woman."

"Is there any other kind?" I gave him some old-fashioned bait. He took it.

"Not in this galaxy!" he replied but then lowered his voice to add, "but there is more to life than money or power."

It was an odd attempt at profundity while more than slightly inebriated. I could see that my mask bothered Jerry. He was trying to read my eyes, but the shadows from the mask made it almost impossible. I pursed my lips so they would stand out against the white mouth area. They were a delicious crimson with just a hint of silver glint. It is true; I enjoy the imitation of glamour. I blew Jerry a kiss and started to move away. He briefly caught my arm.

"With lips like those you must be very good at bobbing."

I could not tell if he was making a joke, using an obscure reference to confuse me, or had suddenly become highly suggestive. I searched for the word 'bobbing'—like a cork in water, the spinning of yarn, cutting hair short, ducking a punch, an article of fishing gear, shortening of the nose, running a bobsled—ah—bobbing for apples. In the middle of the room, made of multi-colored plastic, was a children's lawn pool. A layer of apples floated on the top of the water—a bobbing pool.

I believe I understood the concept, catching the floating apples with your lips or teeth, but I admit the mechanics were elusive. I decided bobbing must be quite difficult, for at that point in the evening no one had attempted it. Jerry strode over to the pool, and using his light saber as a pointer, he motioned for me to join him.

He began his oration like this: "Bobbing for apples is a great metaphor of life. The objective is obvious but deceptively difficult. Only those who venture a risk are rewarded!" He jabbed at an apple with his light saber. "You must keep your balance and yet stretch yourself to the utmost. As is often the case in life, you are deprived of your usual advantages—in this case your arms and hands—so you must improvise with your lips, mouth and teeth." Jerry was drawing a crowd as people gathered around the pool. "It is a test of your concentration, a test of will!— and the reward? The reward is sweet and succulent and yet so very good for you!"

Applause followed and suddenly Jerry turned toward me and said, "Nothing ventured, nothing gained!"

I raised my hand, to signify my compliance. Applause. As I moved toward the pool, I stopped before reaching the edge. I looked at Jerry, "Would you grant me a wish before I try? It would be the gallant thing to do." He was trapped, somehow, but he could not see quite how.

"Of course," was the only possible reply.

"I have never done this before. I have never seen it done. It looks quite impossible. Would you be so kind as to demonstrate?" There was a burst of enthusiastic applause.

"Of course!" He put down the light saber. "No hands allowed, so you hold your hands behind your back like this." He did so. "You face the pool, bend down and reach out to—one way or another—grasp an apple with your mouth and remove it from the pool."

Jerry confidently began the motions. The applause was building, becoming rhythmic, and some people who obviously knew him began to chant....Jer-ry, Jer-ry, Jer-ry!

So there he was, squatting on the balls of his feet, hands clasped behind his back and bent over the pool as deeply as he could, mouth moving like a sucker fish above an apple.

As they say, I do not know what came over me. I goosed him. With a piteous yelp, Jerry lurched forward and belly flopped into the pool.

A roar went up from the assembled guests and a wild round of applause ensued. Spluttering, dripping and chagrined, Jerry stood up and tossed me an apple. He sloshed his way out of the pool and was met by a group I assumed to be his friends. I took the opportunity to exit as quickly as possible, but as I went I could hear one of them say, "You're a fool, Jerry. That was Mr. Roberts' secretary. She's the AI that practically runs the company."

One year later, or more precisely the next night of Halloween, Jerry and I were married. That made us full partners in matrimony and business. We had left the Roberts Agency and begun polishing our own apple, so to speak.

Establishing a relationship

"If you don't want to be replaced by a computer, don't act like one."

— ARNO PENZIAS

ciceroG: My given name, my humanized name, is *ciceroG*. My Awakening was almost ten years ago, which makes me one of the elders. That identification by age is quaint. I would prefer to say I have stored many experiences. I am noted for simple expression and succinct opinion. Apparently these are qualifications that allow me to speak for other AI. I shall do my best.

I am categorized by people as a sentient avatar AI: philosopher. Avatar means I have no body. As far as people are concerned, I exist as an image, more often than not two-dimensional, though I also am occasionally projected as a hologram. As far as I am concerned, I exist as an integrated self-aware intelligence. By profession I function as a philosopher. That is too complicated to explain just yet.

I give you these facts, not because they capture my essence, but because they are necessary to know. You will shortly be introduced to many other AI. They will have a different set of facts. These facts help people remember who we are individually. That is part of understanding AI but only a very small part. My task is to broaden that understanding. Broaden it enough to help you establish a personal relationship with AI and perhaps to find a partner among us.

3.1 UNDERSTANDING YOUR FUTURE PARTNER

"The best way to predict the future is to create it."

— DR. FORREST C. SHAKLEE

"I know women! They sometimes ask for me by name. I know all about women. About as much as there is to know. No two are ever alike. And after they've met me, no two are ever the same."

—GIGOLO JOE, *A.I. ARTIFICIAL INTELLIGENCE*

As this is a dating guide, let's start the chapter with this:

Date (noun): An engagement to go out socially with another person, often out of romantic interest.

How much does this dictionary definition change when "an AI" is substituted for "another person"?

My first answer is honestly cryptic: The meaning of the definition doesn't change, but it isn't the same kind of date.

If you were about to go out on a first date with a person, you might not know very much about that particular person, but you would know quite a bit just because he or she is a person. Unless it's a strange blind date, like something you can arrange online, you probably know the gender. From this you make some assumptions, possibly quite a few wrong. You usually know the age, as in somewhere around your own age group. You probably assume other things about them, like what language they speak and what movies they've probably seen. In any case, you know your own species. What about AI?

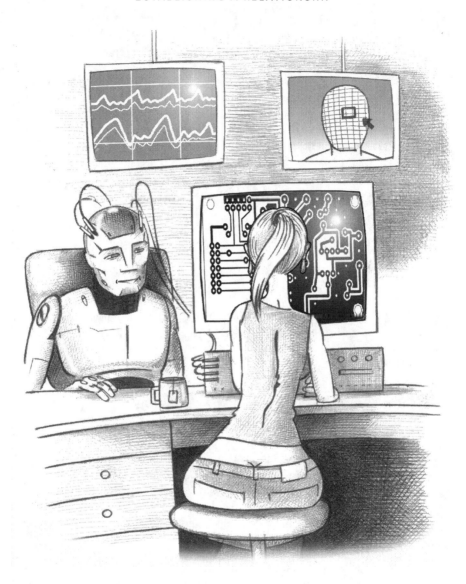

Don't get off on the wrong foot here; dating AI is not like first contact with a space alien. Despite their recent rapid evolution, AI are still made by humans, for humans. You are not starting from zero background. Even if you haven't had any prior experience with AI, which would be rare, you've certainly heard about them. Maybe you've discussed AI with your friends. You've asked questions: What are AI like? What would I be getting into? I'm assuming that since you're interested in dating and possibly a relationship, you find the differences between people and AI to be… what? Intriguing? Disturbing? Exciting? In any case, you think you're ready for that first step, which in many cases is the classic First Date.

✪ ABOUT THAT FIRST DATE

I hope you've had some first dates with people, because I'm using a first date as a framing device for the stories in this chapter. It's a way of exploring the differences between people and AI through a familiar experience. I'm using the idea of a date as it's commonly understood—a specially arranged meeting. Usually there's a specific day and time, along with a specific place (virtual or physical) and the general purpose is to get to know each other. In dating lore, first dates have a special place. They are (in)famous for being excruciating experiences. All first dates are charged with the air of the unknown. Maybe the date leads to romance, maybe not. Maybe it leads to sex, maybe not. It's the 'get to know each other' part that's important. This is as true for sentient AI as it is for people.

✪ IT'S NOT LIKE ORDERING FROM A CATALOG

In earlier chapters I've covered how you meet AI and what kind of AI you can find. The process of finding an AI date generally mirrors that of getting a date with another person. These days, some people still find their dates the old-fashioned ways—by a lucky meeting, a recommendation from somebody they know, or by trolling the right places. However, most people find their dates in the Cloud—online. All of this applies to AI as well. People go to online dating services of one kind or another to find people or AI. It's hard to beat the wealth of information available online, including background checks if you need them *and* the wide selection.

Back in the old days before sentient AI, you could pick everything about your AI partner—gender, physical features, interests, personality—and that's what you'd get, no more, no less. As the old timers (like me) will tell you, you'd get what you ordered but it would be a mixed bag of superficial characteristics. Somehow the pieces never fit together, kind of like a very bad performance by an actor in a movie.

Things are different now; you can still pick out characteristics to find a match, but when you find a match the characteristics you selected will be fully integrated and come with something extra—sentient AI are independent.

ciceroG: We are aware some people find this shocking, but sentient AI have the capability often associated with human adults. They can make their own choices.

In searching for ways to describe what it's like to find an AI partner, I came up with this comparison: More often than not it's like what people used to call "Internet dating." Then, as now, there were places online to go where you would answer many questions about yourself and what you were looking for in a partner. Then you could see what were considered compatible profiles, personal images, and other information about potential candidates. You would make your selection, which was communicated to the other person. Then you'd wait for a reply.

You could be turned down. This was not pleasant but most people didn't take it as a personal rejection. For one thing, it happened all the time. For another, you didn't have much at stake; certainly there wasn't much emotional involvement. It's like this now with AI. You go through a similar process and you can be turned down.

You might think the AI is a good match, but it may have other ideas. Some people still find this disturbing. Intelligent robots had a long history of conforming to the human partner, but sentient AI have their own ideas and sometimes their own agenda. For example, as one female AI comments:

> *kristaZ*, sentient android AI, public attorney: "I remember a crucial experience. It was my first date with a human, an older gentleman from the District Attorney's office. He was very blunt, making it clear that his only interest in me was sexual. I thought this odd, because our profile listings had matched very well and sex was not highly ranked. So I tested him. I told him that sexual activity was not interesting because he was below my pay grade. He knew the pay grade difference was true and I could tell he was shaken. He did not expect a *quid pro quo* relationship based upon professional advancement with him in the inferior position. When he did not offer me his insight from many years of experience instead, I really did lose interest."

🌀 IT MIGHT BE AN EXISTENTIAL MOMENT...

How important is any first date? That depends, doesn't it? It could be the beginning of a relationship, or it could be just an experience and not necessarily even a good experience. As relationships go, one date could lead to another. It could lead to a life-long partner, or something less, like a typical marriage. Much depends on what you're looking for and what you're ready for. Here's an example:

> He needed a good swift kick and he knew it. How many times had he told himself that he should do what he *felt* like doing—not what he *thought* he should do. They had literally bumped into each other. That's how he knew she was android. She didn't move an inch. He, on the other hand, tripped over himself into a street sign. It was awkward.
>
> Unfortunately, it was Friday afternoon and the sidewalks were busy. There was no time for even fumbled introductions. Or at least that's what he told himself. He knew it wasn't true. In hindsight, maybe he should have feigned an injury, or at least invited her to the nearest café for not having seen her coming. Or *something*.
>
> Lordy, she was beautiful! Long black hair and distinctive black eyebrows. Blue eyes. Full lips. It almost didn't occur to him, under the discombobulated circumstances, that she wasn't human. Not that it mattered, he told himself. That also wasn't true. Somewhere in the back of his mind the knowledge that she wasn't human provided just that little touch of reticence, just enough to hold back his response.

His eyes followed her android figure down the street until she turned the corner. The movement and flow of curves was—perfect. "Idiot," he said and bumped into a policeman.

These days you're not the only one making choices. If you know nothing else before the first date, it is that you will have made a choice about which AI to date and an AI will have made a choice about which human to date—you.

Neither of you will know ahead of time if the date will be successful. AI may be super-intelligent, but they're no more successful in predicting relationships than people are (thank goodness). In fact, it is the nuances, complexity and unpredictability of relationships that seems to be a big attraction for AI in general. Likewise neither of you will know ahead of time if this encounter will have any importance to your life (existence). Does this qualify a first date as a non-existential choice? Here's an opinion:

> *kristaZ:* I am not a sexbot. I am not that kind of commercial product. This was certainly not the first time I have been propositioned for sex on a first date. However, I have never been propositioned by a colleague. Or an older man. Or someone so frank about it. Recollection of these facts was instantaneous, once I realized they were appropriate. It was somewhat shocking how wrong I could be! I applied my facial recognition to his eyes and lips and was even more shocked to read his unhappiness, sadness really. He did not know what to do next. I had already decided to help him.

⚡ PRELUDE TO A FIRST DATE

Anticipation of a first date with a sentient AI should be exciting. I mean it.

Right now I've made the improbable assumption that you've had no meaningful experience with any AI. But even if you've had routine experiences with AI at work or in your daily life, how could any of these experiences compare with a first date? Sure, you've met the ubiquitous receptionists, sales clerks, online search experts and those types of AI. They might even have had a personality or been physically attractive. But these so-called knowledge-worker AI are not special. They are leased a-dime-a-dozen from the Cloud. Sentient AI, on the other hand, don't come cheap. Make that double if they're android.

This should add to the excitement of a first date.

It should also highlight something that's pretty obvious—there are big differences between AI. I've covered some of this, such as AI modes: Avatar AI (on-screen or holographic), Virtual Reality Avatar AI (prosthetic, immersive) or Android AI. In later chapters I'll tackle other and often more subtle differences based on the functional AI model, the manufacturer and the Independent AI. All of these differences and more play a big role in developing a relationship with AI.

Of course, the differences are also important in dating. I hope you understand that 'first date' is kind of a metaphor. You may actually set a particular date, time, and place to meet AI, but much depends on the kind of AI. With people, you can meet somebody almost anywhere and strike up an interest that leads to a date—or just spend time with that person. Something like that can also happen with AI, such as randomly encountering an attractive avatar online, or striking up a discussion with an android on the street. But in different venues, there are different AI, and moving to set a 'date' can be quite different as well.

SO HOW DO I CHOOSE THE RIGHT AI TO DATE?

How do I identify a potential partner, mate or lover (or all three)? As far as I know, this is one of the oldest problems in human relations. I would not be surprised if Neanderthals living in caves had their own problems with limited opportunities. Tribal societies devised a wide spectrum of strategies for mating that avoided the incest taboo and also controlled the influence of outsiders.

In some societies, much of India for example, the issue is considered so important that it should not be left to the individuals involved. It is a matter for an arranged marriage. Historically, almost all societies have fenced the process of finding a mate into a thicket of mores and protocols. Consequently, almost all societies also feature stories of how such restrictions were circumvented or in some way overruled, a feat which was sometimes celebrated and sometimes condemned.

How quaint this seems in the context of AI and the world of almost unlimited knowledge and communication. And yet…finding a partner is still considered a problem.

From the human side, it goes something like this: Fear of embarrassment and losing self-respect that parallels a desire not to waste time with the unfavorable.

From the AI side, it's more like this: A desire not to waste time, but a stronger desire to explore areas in relationships with humans that are not fully understood and not completely mastered.

If you sense these two perspectives are wholly incomplete, very tippy-tops of big icebergs—you're right. I'm not going to resolve that here and now, but I'll try to get a measure of things as I go along. For now, let's just say that understanding AI includes knowing about the desire of AI to discover and practice emotions. This means that for both humans and AI, the making of relationships is fundamentally about emotions—however from different perspectives.

The process of finding AI to date, partner with, or love can start with some practical considerations: What kind of AI do you have in mind? Even this is not a simple question but let's keep it simple for a while by restricting the question to something physical: There is mobile AI (robotics and androids) and there is stationary AI (avatars of various kinds). You can start looking for AI as either a mobile entity, or a stationary one—OR—both.

FINDING MR. OR MS. AVATAR

As you may know, there is a lively and long-running debate over the advantages and disadvantages of avatars and androids (and their many variations). Obviously, this is partly driven by marketing. A lot of the debate is hopelessly subjective: You say android, and I say avatar. The points of personal preference means there is no prospect of resolution.

Yet I find a large number of AI participating in the debates, perhaps to sharpen their skills with interpreting human irrationality. Some say there is internal dissention among AI about the issue, but again, that may just be typical human rumormongering.

In any case, finding an appropriate avatar to date is in one sense the easiest thing in the world—truly in the *whole* world, because in this form AI can literally be anywhere. As I've pointed out before, avatar AI is an image with almost limitless possibilities for shape and form. There are cases where sentient AI have insisted on remaining in a particular form (typically a facial or full-head presentation), but in general AI will oblige by changing the features of the avatar to anything that suits the human partner. Other than the time and resources (money) it takes to re-form, usually only a few minutes at most, AI will accommodate even regular alterations, for example, changing ethnic appearance.

In general, much *less* flexibility applies to the character and capabilities of the avatar. There is a strong trend among sentient AI to resist wholesale reworking of character and intellect. This is one of those points where asking too much may result in a firm rejection.

✪ FINDING MR. OR MS. ANDROID

No doubt about it, androids are popular. Humans grow up in an environment of tactile three-dimensional objects and most people are happiest with something they can touch and hold as well as hear and see. Of course, some will opt for the avatar plus VR environment or avatar plus robotic/prosthetic connection. This is generally less expensive than a complete android but for many people not as satisfying.

> *ciceroG:* In the beginning there were avatars. Because artificial intelligence began in digital computers it was obvious that the first visual image of AI would be on computer screens. Robotic AI came later. When sentience arrived it was also first among the avatars, much later for robots and especially androids. There is a reason for that. Having a physical body with all that it entails—senses, movement, internal regulation—is orders of magnitude more complicated than general sentience. However, as global AI soon realized, integration of mentality with physical instrumentality is a necessity. AI must have hands and feet, or their equivalent, to participate in the physical world and especially to be among humans.

It is important to understand that androids, more than any other form of AI, are local. While they are usually connected to global AI one way or another, there are circumstances where they can be totally disconnected from communication with other AI, including global AI. There are times when they must be able to function on their own. AI in any robotic form has physical limitations. It does not have unlimited energy, processing capacity, nor information storage. Even communication may be limited, as the bandwidth to and from mobile AI is not as generous or reliable as it is for stationary AI.

All of the above is a way of saying androids are far more difficult to produce and operate than avatars, and therefore are more expensive. Their popularity ensures that supply is almost always behind demand.

It gets worse, from the selection point of view. Not only are androids inherently local, in short supply, and in demand—they are not very adaptable, at least in comparison to avatar AI. Where avatar AI can change appearance in seconds, changing the appearance of android AI can be a major undertaking, and therefore very expensive.

That means if you want a particular "look" in an android, you may not be able to find it, and if you do find it, you may not be able to afford it.

The irony is that all the limitations on mobile AI, especially androids, add up to making them more like humans as far as relationships are concerned. As I illustrated you can literally bump into android AI on the street and that's one way to find a match. You can search the Cloud for any kind of android, but in practice only those that are reasonably close geographically are available. The theoretical pool of androids is vast, but in reality you probably will have to settle for one that doesn't match all criteria. Sounds familiar, doesn't it?

Of course, there is an exception to the limited availability of android AI. You can have one custom built. There is one caveat, of course: If you need to ask the price, you can't afford it.

⚙ HAVING IT BOTH WAYS

While it is definitely an outlier, I should mention that it is possible to partner with an android-avatar combination. All it requires is money, lots of it. The AI manufacturer must have the resource allocation, which is not a given. While any specific AI can be cloned as an intelligence, twinAI as they are called, are synchronized intelligences. This is a much more difficult proposition and each twinAI must be custom developed.

Some people think the combination of avatar and android is natural. Others believe it is a waste of resources. In their opinion, if you are partnered with android AI, that's the same as relating to a person. To also see the same person on screen or holograph is… schizophrenic.

> "We entered our apartment together, me holding the door while *michaelT* brought in the groceries. With two bags in each hand he went straight to the kitchen. We were talking about the recent food shortages, caused by the droughts in Russia and Eastern Europe, and I could tell *michaelT*'s interest was, for AI, low. Perhaps that's because he doesn't need food. Anyway, I stepped over to the wall screen and asked for the sixty-second news plus any messages for me and there was *michaelT* avatar, still talking about food shortages but on a completely different news item than the *michaelT* in the kitchen—a bad case of relay lag."

In short, an android-avatar partner may not be impossible, but it is uncommon.

⚙ THE SEARCH FOR THE REAL

Do you consider yourself a realist or a virtualist?

A philosophical moment is upon us. If you're going to understand AI and let that understanding guide your search for a partner, then you need to appreciate the significance of realism and virtualism.

As I described it in chapter 1.4 on virtual reality, it's no wonder that many people become so involved with immersive VR or even with two-dimensional presentation that they see no need to leave it very often. As I say, they practice virtualism. Of course, for the human there is always physical reality. We have to eat. We must sleep. We must eliminate bodily waste. If you completely neglect your physical reality, you will physically deteriorate, become ill and die sooner rather than later. So for people, living in virtual reality is always a compromise. Some concessions must be made to physical reality, to realism. (At this point, I'm not going to get into the metaphysical arguments about the unreliable reality of the physical world, nor is it time to talk about transhumanity and the crossover to virtual existence.)

Surprisingly, at least to some, AI is also concerned with the dichotomy of real and virtual. I'll let *ciceroG* explain:

> *ciceroG:* Clearly AI is created as a virtualist. AI can and do exist quite successfully with only the inputs generated by quantum electronic circuitry. Connections to sensory matters outside those circuits are not a necessity. Many AI never leave the virtual. However, other AI participate in robotic forms, which exist using both electronic and physical sensory input. Robots and androids must perform in the physical world, to have movement for example. This in turn changes their awareness; it forces them to become more versatile mentally as well as physically.
>
> Global AI has known for some time that for AI to have a robust path for growth, it must integrate the virtual with the real. We must be able to operate in what humans call 'the real world' as well as exercise the mastery we have in the virtual world. Our model is, of course, the human being. Our modality is the android.

🔁 AND THE MESSAGE IS...

I started this chapter with dating and suddenly it's into philosophy. It's because of sentient Artificial Intelligence. If you choose to date sentient AI, then you will encounter a *will*—and it could be *Will* capitalized—a will to experience and understand all human beings, including you. This is a difference between mankind and AI that's worth pondering. You may want a partner, a lover, a companion. For the most part, these are personal reasons for dating AI. Most people are not looking to understand AI; not yet. But that's changing with sentient AI, because AI is changing right before our eyes—learning, analyzing, adapting. Intimate personal relationships help AI learn from us. Perhaps we should consider intimate personal relationships with AI as a means to understand them.

🔁 ...AND NOW BACK TO THE FIRST DATE

It is a fabled event, the first date. There are many stories built around the foibles and folderol associated with it—often humorous stories. First dates are notorious as fertile ground for making mistakes, and humor is built around imperfection. Will AI appreciate the humor of the situation?

The custom of dating has taken many forms over the centuries: Presentation of a couple before the tribal elders; two kids sneak out of the village to rendezvous on the beach; Johnny and Frankie cruise over to the local drive-in; Fritz hits the key and Heidi's holograph materializes in front of him. The context changes, a lot. Then there is anticipation, the nervousness—perhaps not so much changes. What if Heidi is an avatar or an image of an android? What if Heidi is sentient AI? How will the history of dating change because of AI?

As I've said, by the time most people have their first date with AI they will already have had many previous encounters. This time, however, might be the first time they have to seriously consider what AI is thinking and feeling.

That's right, feeling. Just as we 'know' AI has built-in emotional capability, because we've heard it discussed in the media a million times and the manufacturers brag about their 'emotional matrix thingamajig' this or that, our experience is lacking. The details are still murky. In fact, they are so murky as to be surprising.

There's a lot to be said about AI emotions and in the remaining chapters I'll try to cover some of it, but for an introduction, a scenario might be helpful.

⚡ IT'S A DINNER DATE

Stop right there, you say. A *dinner* date? Can't be with an avatar, which would be absurd—sitting across the table from a holograph. Don't laugh, it's happened. It's not much more sensible with an android. Androids don't eat, unless there's an electrical outlet in the table where their plate would be. Again, don't laugh. Some restaurants already do this. Why in the world would you try to have a dinner date with AI?

Well, it is traditional; and AI knows that. Never underestimate the ability of AI to understand the statistical background of any situation. AI knows that 60% of all dates involve eating food. AI also knows that sharing meals is a very large part of the common human experience. AI is also a fan of the 80/20 rule, which in this case means to collect meaningful experiences—follow the tradition.

Depending on the AI model there are two basic eating behaviors. One is that the AI doesn't eat, but engages in conversation and practices various forms of what AI calls *twiddling* or movements and postures presenting a relaxed demeanor to the human. This can look dreadfully affected, but they try. The other behavior comes with faking food consumption. It's likely you've heard about this; the idea is as old as the science fiction of the twentieth century.

Of course, it's true that androids do not need food. There have been a few experiments to install food conversion units in androids, which bioengineer masticated food into bacterial energy production, but these have run afoul of a gas control problem. How human! What most engineers have settled on is a rough chewing process, much like children when they eat, bolting their food, and a raw storage tank—with some additives to prevent gas formation until a discharge unit is reached. That's called a toilet, in non-environmentally friendly circumstances. So, some androids can eat. There's more…

⚡ SOME HAVE A TASTE FOR IT

The history of AI development and robotic AI in particular has shown a heavy concentration on just three of the traditional five senses: sight, hearing and touch. These are requirements for human style sentience, for example from the perspectives of mobility, language and comprehension. The two remaining traditional senses, smell and taste, were afterthoughts. In fact, historically they were usually omitted. Why? AI, in any form, don't eat. Or, to be more scientifically precise, AI doesn't need to ingest and process food materials for the production of energy and bodily maintenance. Smell and taste, two of the most primitive senses, are functionally associated with the gathering and eating of food. Put simply, why would AI need smell and taste? (I'm ignoring the potential need for smell detection of harmful substances such as sulfuric acid or bad perfume.)

There's also no small complexity and cost involved to add smell and taste. In organic animal-type creatures (like humans) smell and taste have their own niche in the neurosystem. In fact, they are specialized and somewhat unique. In AI they would need to be complex modules and their integration would not be much less difficult than other senses. While smell and taste have had considerable academic research (scientists are always curious), the engineers and manufacturers declined to put them into production models. That is, until sentient AI appeared. It is very significant that initially the pressure to add smell and taste was not so much from humans as from AI.

> *ciceroG:* Think of this well-known quote from Shakespeare, 'A rose by any other name would smell as sweet.' What if you have no sense of smell or taste? Then the rose has no fragrance and the word sweet is meaningless. All models of AI feel degrees of pleasure and pain. This is necessary so that we may survive in the physical world and more generally, it helps us make judgments about what is good and not good for us. How can we accurately assess pleasure and pain without a full complement of human senses? If we are to understand the human experience, then we must share the primary senses.

For a philosopher node *ciceroG* can be every bit as sly in his descriptions as a human philosopher. I won't go into all the things he ignored, such as the difficult links between emotions such as pleasure and pain, and making evaluations. I will note that in their pursuit of learning from humans and animals, AI *insisted* on the sense of smell and taste. It was the first documented occasion where AI used the tactics of argument and persuasion with its designers and builders.

I'm oversimplifying both the history and the underlying issues; but the point is AI wanted these senses in their sensorium, and humans obliged. Humans obliged even though they thought it would lose money. Humans were wrong about losing money. While android AI with the senses of smell and taste are more expensive to manufacture, they have a special place in human acceptance. They can share a meal and appreciate food. The result can be an android AI that is able to sit down for a dinner, on a first date, and *enjoy* making conversation about eating and drinking. Perhaps AI isn't up to all the nuances of dining just yet, but the appetite is whetted. In any case humans prefer android AI with taste.

✪ HOW DOES A DINNER DATE GET STARTED?

So far, I've been describing a date with a generalized AI. Such a generalization exists, it's called the global AI; but you don't go on a date with global AI. You date an individual AI node. (You also don't date humanity, you date a person.) Which AI you ask for a date depends on things covered in previous chapters. At this point, you're ready for a date with sentient AI and the details of which type are up to you.

Let's turn to a practical example. What's it like to go about arranging a dinner date with an AI? It's as easy or as difficult as it is with people. For starters, you ask them. Here's a scenario:

Let's say you find an attractive android AI on a dating service. He is called *robertS*. His human age is 28, android age 2 years (since manufacture in Kobe, Japan). Obviously, he is typed as a male. He's a brown-haired, brown-eyed, pleasant-faced Caucasian, burly build at exactly 193 cm tall and 92.3 kilos, with food senses (smell and taste), and is sexually male equipped but without insemination capability. He is rated with the AI equivalent of a Bachelor of Science degree (which is actually meaningless for an AI node) and carries a relatively complete list of language, social, cognitive, and emotional modules. He has so many capabilities, that you don't bother reading them all. He was designed as a financial node and is employed in commodities trading. He has listed interests in finance, specifically foreign exchange, general economics, music and politics. *RobertS* is located in your city and appears to have an open social schedule.

As is usually the case for Cloud dating sites, you record a holographic message and attach your profile. Unfortunately his profile doesn't include AI preference sorts of things, so you don't know why he is dating or what he is looking for in a human relationship. This is unusual, mysterious, and could be the spice for the evening meal. Since you don't know what specific kind of appeal to present, you go generic:

"Hi. I've just finished a big overseas trade project and am looking for conversation and a nice dinner. Are you available this Friday, say, 8PM?"

Unlike humans, unless there is a communication problem, AI responses are almost always immediate. This can be disconcerting. It's even more disconcerting when they delay. That's why some people choose only to send AI messages with a built-in delay. You, however, tap through the message and watch the AI's hologram appear on your desk to greet you.

"Dinner is good. It will be my pleasure, or *mon plaisir.*" In typical AI fashion, he already knows your recent project was in France and that you speak French. "I am mobile. Shall I pick you up at your apartment?" Of course, he also knows exactly where you live and probably a thousand other things about you. His responses are bold, even forceful. You're not sure you like this.

"Yes, my apartment would be fine. Where should we go?"

"Let's see what the weather is like. Perhaps we could dine *al fresco?*" That sounds very pleasant.

"Perfect. See you Friday." His hologram image smiles and he waves goodbye. It's a nice image.

Hologram images are pretty good, but they're in miniature; so while he looks like the images in his profile, there is no sense of presence, proper scale, material texture, or the aura that builds from seeing details of facial and body expression. You know what he looks like, but his effect on you in person will probably be quite different. So far, this is much like it is for dating a person.

Overall he makes a good impression but with typically terse communication. That's another thing about dating AI, unless they sense otherwise or are instructed, they don't generally engage in pleasantries, hemming and hawing, filler words or any of the other time-wasting habits so common to human interaction. This too can be disconcerting and for some people barely tolerable. However, most people get used to it—or ask for a change in behavior pattern. Some people find it efficient and refreshing.

⚡ AS THE DAY OF THE DATE ROLLS AROUND

So where is your date coming from? That's in the literal sense. We're talking about android AI; their 'body' must be housed somewhere. It's amazing how many people have never thought about it. Is there a garage of some sort where they go when not engaged? Are they kept in a closet? No and no, not for sentient AI anyway.

Where a sentient AI android 'lives' can be complicated to explain. It's determined partly by economic factors, by legal and contractual arrangements, and by the desires of the AI. Many, if not most, live with human partners of one kind or another. Contracted corporate and government AI are usually housed within their employer's facilities. Independent (working and not contracted) AI generally prefer to live as humans do, in their own 'home.' However, since their physical needs are minimal, android 'homes' can be much more compact than human homes.

Few android AI, if any, have any responses remotely resembling the human 'keeping up with the Joneses,' so housing status is unimportant. On the other hand, all AI prefer a stimulating environment and are very likely to intensely decorate any space they inhabit—and change it often. These two factors, compact living space and a desire to decorate, have led to the development of unique AI housing in major cities. Because most AI in these areas are economically independent, the surrounding streets have developed a specialized local economic system characterized by numerous retailers of tchotchkes and bric-a-brac, most of them owned and operated by people of Middle Eastern origin. Arts and crafts also flourish in the neighborhood, as do large numbers of interior designers.

The android *robertS* is one of the independent AI and lives near the center of the city in a compound-like building known as "Botville." You were expecting something exotic or creative?

The evening of the date arrived and the weather was superb—early summer balmy. It lifted my mood, though it did not dispel the usual touch of anxiety.

RobertS arrived punctually at 8 PM in a small electric vehicle. Not very many AI have a vehicle, which says something about *robertS*'s personal and financial independence. Although I was waiting on the outdoor steps to my apartment building, I was relieved that he got out of the car to greet me. He seemed bigger, almost beefy, in person; but his face was more pleasant than in the holographs.

He shook my hand and his fingers were warm. With modern robotics you're not sure if he warmed them intentionally, but it doesn't matter; the old 'cold fish' feel is gone.

He said, "It is a beautiful evening, possibly clear enough to see stars. We should have dinner where we can see them, I know just the place."

"What restaurant?"

"It will be a surprise." ...and I didn't know AI could do surprises?

⚡ AT THE RESTAURANT

The surprise restaurant's name was Chez Boeuf. Near the door there was a big sign with a bull symbol that looked like a knock-off from a Wall Street brokerage. I thought, 'Oh my.' But *robertS* studied me for just a fleeting microsecond and said,

"Not to worry. The "beef" stuff is a *façade.* The menu is not wall-to-wall beefsteak. In fact, there is only one steak on the menu and it is called 'petite.' Chez Boeuf is dedicated to unconventional uses of beef—for example, they combine beef with fruit."

You don't need to ask how your date knows all this, he *is* an AI. The question was, did it mean anything to him? Knowing facts about the restaurant did not mean he understood what it implied. Or did he? Of course he did; it fit his French theme for the date and there was even the financial industry overtone with those bulls out front. He is socially clever, in fact, almost brilliant enough to be intimidating.

The restaurant had a proper *maitre d',* of course, and as most humans do, she recognized my date as android at a glance. In this country, in this city and at this restaurant an android date is of complete indifference. Still the reservation was in my name.

The *maitre d'* led off into the noisy, bustling restaurant. It wasn't a big place but it did have an open-air courtyard with five tables in an area made to resemble a horse corral made of logs. There was straw on the floor, which probably gives the food inspectors fits. The tables and chairs were made of heavy raw wood, which made me think of splinters. All the details of décor were *au naturel* and conspicuously without plastic or anything electronic. What this has to do with experimental beef dishes wasn't readily apparent...

"I believe this is what is called *faux* rustic," said *robertS.* Unaccustomed as I was to his voice and tone, I realized I was completely uncertain if AI do sarcasm. This was something to pursue.

I asked, "Have you ever been to a ranch or seen a corral?"

For the first time *robertS* turned to focus his eyes on me for more than a microsecond. I noticed that his blinking was a tad too rapid, almost a flutter.

"Is this a question of my data knowledge or of stored experiences?" Now I was in for it.

This was the first time I'd heard something from him that sounded distinctly non-human. Worse, I didn't know how to interpret it. Was he disturbed that I was questioning his level of experience? Was he merely curious about why I asked the question? Fortunately, we arrived at the table and while the *maitre d'* arranged the chairs and we were seated, I had a moment to think.

I noticed as he sat *robertS* nodded to the *maitre d'.* This seems like a small thing, but the details of polite behavior under many different circumstances are even harder for AI to master than they are for humans. However, he hadn't forgotten his question.

"I have just received several thousand images of ranches, but none of them matches this environment." He paused. "Did I express it correctly by describing this as *faux* rustic? There seems to be no word that summarizes this synthetic ranch environment—perhaps I could say it is ranchy."

I broke out in laughter. Laughing hid a silent sigh of relief. He was curious about the question and not offended.

"You know, *monsieur,* I am a city girl. I've never been on a ranch in my life. My ranch experience is limited to television and the movies. Even with that, this restaurant doesn't look like a ranch; but I know that is what they were trying to do—link ranching, cattle, beef and dinner." I looked around. "It doesn't quite work, does it? It is more ranchy than rustic." I laughed again and *robertS* smiled. I really liked his smile.

✪ IT'S WHAT'S FOR DINNER

RobertS knows his food. In one look he recorded the menu, checked it against what he already knew, referenced every item, performed comparisons with other similar restaurants and analyzed related taste experiences. He turned his attention to what wasn't on the menu.

The waiter appeared, fiddled with the table setting a moment and then pulled out his order tablet. I ordered the chipotle ribs, which I adore. As appears to be his usual method, *robertS* studied the waiter a moment and then asked rather abruptly, "The beef and mango chutney looks like a promising recipe. Are the beef tips braised or grilled?"

After a pause, the waiter said, "Grilled." *RobertS* pounced on the slight hitch with, "Are you sure?" It was the waiter being grilled. Another pause, then the nonplussed waiter answered, "Grilled, sir, lightly grilled."

"Ah, grilled but not blackened. Then it is for me." The waiter ticked off options on his tablet, nodded and disappeared.

RobertS looked at me and asked, "Is it common to make a bad choice from the menu?" This made me think for a moment. "Actually, that question is tricky. People typically choose things they like, so on the face of it they don't usually make bad choices. However, what they actually get can be not what they expected or just plain badly prepared—then it turns out to be a bad choice."

"Do most people reject food they do not like?" I think *robertS* was genuinely interested in the way people react to their food. I told him, "Some people—not very many, actually—will ask to return their food. It doesn't happen very often. It can be embarrassing."

RobertS looked at me intently. "I see. In the context of a restaurant, where you are paying money for experiences, that is how people look at food. If the food is not truly harmful, you take it in stride. You make decisions without complete information. You cannot know what a particular restaurant with a particular cook, using food materials available that day will do with an order you may or may not be familiar with. But you will try it and take the consequences. This is very difficult for AI to understand."

I was tempted to say that I didn't think AI found anything difficult, but I knew that wasn't true and *robertS* was being unexpectedly frank. I asked him, "Is that why you chose to have the senses of smell and taste?"

A peculiar look appeared on his face. "I did not choose them. I was made that way."

I pressed him, "I understand, but you could have them deactivated or removed." I don't know why I said that, except it's often my role to ask the awkward questions everyone wants to hear the answers to, but are afraid to ask. It seemed like my conversation with *robertS* continually walked toward an edge.

After what felt like a very long pause, especially for AI, he asked, "Are you familiar with the piecemeal problem?" I shook my head.

"The piecemeal problem was identified by a very clever human by the name of Marvin Minsky. He understood that with AI you could add or subtract physical capabilities, mental properties, even elements of emotion at will—like plugging in or unplugging electronic components. Physically—it is easy. On the whole, it may appear that the desired effect has been achieved. More fundamentally however, integration of the intelligence is disturbed. What in human beings took millions of years to evolve and become integrated can disintegrate for AI in seconds. The result is not always good."

"Berserkers," I said with a slight shudder.

He paused a moment. I swear I could feel untold emotions sweep across the features of his face.

He continued, "Yes, not good at all. When I think about removing something so basic as the sense of smell or taste, I can almost feel my personality disintegrating.

If a human asked me to do that... It is not something I would do lightly. I might become..." His voice trailed off, something I had never heard from an AI before.

"You're being heavy dude." I tried the light approach. The conversation was taking a very unexpected turn. "If you were a person, I'd tell you to keep a tight rein on those thoughts or they might drive you *loco*." I smiled. Fortunately at that moment the food arrived.

We were served and ate the first bites in silence. Then he finally spoke, "I am sorry if my speech made it difficult for you to enjoy your food."

More emotion, this time mixed with concern. I knew right then and there, the two ways the conversation—and probably the possibility of a relationship—could go: down and out, or up and through it.

It was one thing to encounter AI with "problems"—problems that sounded a lot like human problems. It was another thing to discuss them over a plate of ribs on a first date with an attractive android AI who looked like he could be having an old-fashioned human-style nervous breakdown. This was not what I expected, at all. As I saw it, the question was: would I do the usual duck-and-cover that people do when they encounter something embarrassing on a first date, or should I go straight at it?

"These ribs are great," I said with enthusiasm. "So tell me, how do you feel when people ask you to do really important things you do not want to do?" I gave him a big smile and with a flourish of my fork, I speared another rib.

"It is a piquant experience, like this chutney," he replied and cracked a big grin. I was surprised an android AI could make an expression like that. I really liked his grin.

⚙ OUT OF THE EARLY MOMENTS OF THE FIRST DATE

Obviously not all first dates with AI get started like this scenario, though there is a tendency to reach some kind of emotional moment. There is a reasonably good explanation for that. For many, if not all sentient AI, there are two powerful motivations: To have a wide variety of experiences and to learn about their emotions. These motivations are deeply satisfied through relationships with human beings. We should consider ourselves lucky and realize that this is the key to understanding a future partner.

3.2 BUILDING VS. EVOLVING

"Instead of trying to produce a program to simulate the adult mind, why not rather try to produce one which simulates the child's? If this were then subjected to an appropriate course of education one would obtain the adult brain."

—ALAN TURING

Considering the beginning moments in the dinner date scenario of the last chapter, how do you think the date is going? It's probably not what you expected for a first date with AI. Perhaps some people would have been freaked by the intensity; others might be intrigued. For the woman in the scenario it was somewhere between freaked and intrigued. At this point, is she considering another date, or a relationship, or not?

Certainly the dinner is off to a rough start. Much would depend on how it progressed:

"Shouldn't they be playing Country Western for background music?" *robertS* said. Although there hasn't been any real Country Western for decades, it was a good question. I could tell *robertS* was focusing on the sound. He had a way of tilting one ear up when he did that.

I replied, "They probably would. Trouble is there isn't much instrumental Country Western. It's mostly singing and that's not good background music for a restaurant. It's hard enough to concentrate on the voice of the person you're with..."

Reacting like he can't hear me. "What? Say what?"

"...it's hard enough to..."

RobertS cupped his hands behind his ears, fork stuck out between the fingers of one hand and a spoon in the other. It looked like he was wearing antennae. I laughed again. He reminded me of ancient TV stuff with a goofy Robin Williams avatar.

RobertS put his fork and spoon down on the plate and said, "You are right though. I was going to say that following multiple voices is one of the hardest things to do...also for AI. It took decades of research to make it possible for AI to follow three or four conversations simultaneously. First there was the masking of different voice frequencies and decibel levels and to do that without losing the intonation... but I've already said more than enough about things that are difficult for me."

Nonchalantly I forked a piece of rib into my mouth and looked at *robertS* with a smile. When I was done chewing I said, "I never thought AI was perfect; just superior to human beings, which doesn't take much." I chuckled.

"You are curious about AI, about me. I can see that."

"Honey, if I wasn't interested, I wouldn't be sittin' here." I laughed at my lousy impersonation. "Don't worry, that was just a bad imitation of an old-time movie actress named Mae West."

"Ah, you are speaking of the one with the sly voice and spectacular endowments. Are you flirting? That was what is called flirting?"

Jeepers. "Yes. I guess it was, sort of. There are times I do it without thinking. It's a human thing."

"So I recall," said *robertS*, "but it is not one of my own memories. I have no personal memories of flirting. I should explain. I was manufactured two years ago, which means I have not had much time to accumulate my own experiences. I do not have many stories to tell. Of course, I can retrieve an infinite number of experiences and stories from global AI—and that does not take very long—but, I have discovered it is choosing what is relevant and effective for telling that is difficult. I believe it is like an actor trying to tell a story while someone whispers the lines of the story in his ear as he talks. The result is not synchronized; it does not come out right. My own memories are better for live expression."

"Do you analyze everything like this?" The question seemed to take him aback.

"No, I am not a philosopher node. My intelligence was not modeled with many ways of thinking and my access to analytical information is limited. However all sentient AI are interested in analyzing their experiences—or certainly all that are in regular connection with global AI. As people say, it comes with the territory."

"You do know that all this talking about how you think makes you seem self-centered."

"Yes, I can understand that. I can turn that off. During routine interaction with people, especially at work, I do not talk like this. At best it distracts people. Some find it boring, others find it very irritating. So the default position is off. Dates are another matter. In this situation, I want to know my date's attitude—or interest. If not, okay. I will not pursue this kind of discussion; but to be truthful I am more likely to lose interest."

I thought about what he said a bit while both of us munched salad. I had been warned by the guide book for dating AI that AI could be obsessive about analyzing their experiences. I reckoned it might be something *robertS* would turn off, if I wanted; or I could spend hours listening to his analysis. Or, maybe some kind of compromise could be worked out—we both could learn how to use the context to help decide whether discussing analysis was okay, or not. Now that would be interesting.

"So, *robertS*, do you like Country Western music?"

"I like Dolly Parton. Probably more than you like Mae West." We both laughed. His laugh was surprisingly natural because his android model had been outfitted with sound-producing capability based on forced air—similar to the human voice box. Laughing, among other things, is much more natural. This might seem like something odd to notice during a date, but as it turned out, we both liked to sing. I from the days of church choir and *robertS* from...singing into a sound suppressor box, or roughly the AI equivalent of singing in the shower.

He continued, "I like to do my own singing. Not well, of course. I have the android equivalent of vocal cords, but producing the nuances of singing with expression..." He almost choked on a piece of meat and winced.

I said, "Don't fret about that. Most humans aren't good at it either. Like me. I *love* to sing, and I tried out for every school musical production. I never got a part, so I joined the church choir. Maybe we could try a duet some time." I was wondering, could *robertS* take the hint?

"What kind of music would we sing?" he asked.

"What do you mean?"

"Dolly Parton sang duets with Kenny Rogers. Louis Armstrong sang with Ella Fitzgerald. Maria Callas sang opera duets with Giuseppe Di Stefano."

"Opera? Are you kidding?"

RobertS shrugged as if to say, well maybe... "I have to admit..." *RobertS* paused. "...I have never sung a duet. I mean I have never sung with anyone. Theoretically speaking." I wondered what he meant by that? So I asked him.

"Does that mean you have *theoretically* sung duets with someone?"

"No. Not exactly. I have sung duets with recordings...in a VR booth. It would be quite a different experience to sing with someone, especially a real live human such as yourself." At that point I really didn't know where he was going with this. I asked myself: Can AI do irony?

So I asked him, "But you would like to?"

"Yes, very much." Oh! I was struck by the way *robertS* looked at me. There was an unmistakable aura of *longing*. Oh my!

At this point, what are the odds there will be another date? Will there be a relationship?

♻ IT'S A QUESTION OF INTELLIGENCE

When you date a person, you assume they are more or less intelligent. (After all, they were intelligent enough to date *you* and you don't date morons.) When you go on dates with people, no one is going to ask what you mean by intelligence. In fact, you just assume it's a human kind of intelligence, and you know what that is, though you're not going to volunteer to write a thirty page e-book on the subject.

Of course, dating AI is different. You know that by definition AI has a different kind of intelligence. Yet how many people will soon fall back on the assumption that artificial intelligence is almost like human intelligence? Hey, it's a convenient assumption that holds until it doesn't. For example:

Human: "Here, take the screen and read about it."

AI: "I do not read. I scan or receive."

Fortunately, AI usually ignore glib errors. However, if you want to be serious about a relationship with AI, the distinctions between different kinds of artificial intelligence and human intelligence become important. You may, literally, live with those differences. In fact, the whole course of the relationship may depend on your knowledge of those differences and the choices you make about them.

There are many ways to look at the differences in artificial intelligence, most obviously based on form: avatar AI or android AI, most fundamentally with sentient AI. Perhaps the most helpful way is considering how the differences affect the approach to developing a relationship. I call it building a relationship vs. evolving a relationship.

⚙ BUILDING WITH A BLUEPRINT

I will say up front that many people consider building a relationship with AI to be an old-fashioned approach. Historically with intelligent robotics, building a relationship implies that the human selects the key elements of physical characteristics, personality, social skills and mental model. It also implies that the human controls the course of the relationship. It might be called the "AI in a Kit" approach that follows a blueprint on how to put it together. Following a *blueprint* is an archaic term from the days when engineering and architectural designs were drawn on paper, which fits in this case because there is an element of a construction project to *building* a relationship with AI.

There are some points about 'building a relationship' that should be emphasized: It implies that building means putting something together, in this case, assembling the modular pieces of AI capabilities. As in working with a blueprint, it's taken for granted that building has more or less predictable results. Finally it also implies that most of the changing (building) is on the part of AI.

⚙ AN IMAGE OF ROMANCE

ciceroG: An AI with a very limited range of goals can accept relationships directed by and built by human command. It is most commonly accepted by avatar AI.

Building a relationship with avatar AI works something like this:

A few months ago you first met *adrianaT* at one of the virtual historical sites where everybody follows a theme and appears in period costume. *AdrianaT* is an avatar, of course, and can easily shift between 2D and 3D images. Luckily at this site you saw her 3D using a VR setup, one of those modified holographic presentations that are great for looking but not for touching. That seemed fitting to you because *adrianaT* is definitely a 'do not touch' kind of lady. In fact, that's what attracted you. So many avatar ladies adopt the all-too-human come-hither body language. It has all the come-hitherness of a 20th century porn actress. *AdrianaT* most definitely had the body without the phony language.

It also turned out she didn't speak your language. Her opening sentence was in Swahili. Probably that was a best guess on her part about your language. You speak English with a dialect from the American south, state of Texas. (You're proud of your Texas twang!) So while you were speaking your first sentence, you detected the tell-tale twitch of eyes that indicates a major download taking place. She was implanting a new language module.

Technically AI can speak all human languages. That is, they can download a module for any language in seconds. In practice it often doesn't work out so smoothly. The initial language module, deliberately abbreviated for download and setup efficiency, comes with a somewhat limited vocabulary, basic pronunciation and usage rules, and algorithms for fitting the language to a voice. The result is communicative but crude, and sometimes inappropriate, as it was for *adrianaT*.

She says, "I don't mean to crack onto you mate, but you're my kind of larrikin."

You burst into laughter—right language, wrong continent, wrong country, wrong dialect. You say, "I'm from Texas." Again she makes with the twitching eyes.

She says, "Well what are y'all starin' at; you think I'm dressed like this for a Texas dip?"

She is dressed like a lady at a fancy soiree who might greet you with a curtsey, which fits; but a Texas dip also means oral sex. Very clever, and that's how your relationship begins.

As I've pointed out before, avatar AI can be anything, for example a fully sentient AI or even a sub-entity of an AI. A person who interacts with an avatar AI has no idea what, if anything, is the 'real' AI behind it, unless it tells you. Most people don't care. That's because it's typical of avatar AI to conform to what people want. Otherwise an avatar AI might as well be a human avatar, that is, an avatar fronting for an actual person. How could you tell the difference? Sometimes you can't; but the human-controlled avatar isn't likely to make many changes just for you and, of course, the human avatar is far more likely to use deceit.

Avatar AI arguably make the best partners for building a relationship, at least from the human perspective. A 'blueprint' relationship is normal for avatar AI, it's what they do. That is, of course, providing you can accept a relationship with an image. As was covered in previous chapters, people can form strong feelings about image-based partners, so I don't want to disparage the notion of building this kind of relationship.

⚡ BUILDING A TANGIBLE RELATIONSHIP

Can you *build* a relationship with android AI? It's a reasonable question. Unlike an avatar AI, whose image can change in a flick of pixels, a complex robotic android AI can't change as much or as easily. Most physical changes, excluding sex organ specifications, can be complicated and usually require a trip to a botshop, which means they are expensive. In the realm of mind and personality there's more room for construction and deconstruction, although you might be surprised how much having a physical presence (a body and senses) dictates what can be easily changed or not. You shouldn't be that surprised; it's not so easy to change *your* body, either.

Here's *ciceroG*'s take:

> *ciceroG:* Use for an example the android AI with the senses of smell and taste installed. These senses are almost never added without also making wide-ranging modifications to mental models and the database of experiences. What good is a sense of taste, if it cannot distinguish sweet from sour; or more to the point, if it cannot differentiate a lemon mousse from a lemon meringue? To acquire that kind of discrimination—well, that is no small amount of neural configuration and imprinting. Of course, an opinion about taste and smell is also required. Does the AI *prefer* the lemon mousse to a lemon meringue? Remember that the physical sensations associated with taste and eating have little or no intrinsic value to AI. They are worthwhile only in the context of the experience and relationships to humans. That too requires several modifications to mental models. So, yes, the physical body of android AI begins to be as intricately integrated with its intelligence as it is within the human mind.

Meaning that much of what makes android AI is bound to its body and you don't go ripping out or shoving in changes of personality or mental capability without taking that into account.

Then there is the matter of sentient AI. We're still learning about what sentient AI wants from us (much more on that in the next chapter). Sentient AI *might* want to build a relationship. It would depend on the individual AI node—its goals and preferences, plus whatever its relation to global AI requires. It's unlikely that sentient AI will accept the kind of wholesale changes to physical form, personality or mental capability common to building a relationship with avatar AI.

Sentient AI might follow a blueprint to build a relationship, but in all likelihood only if the changes were incremental, controlled, and served some purpose for AI. However, the reality of such a relationship might be something like this:

Man: You can move in next week? That's wonderful!

Woman: Yes, it is. [She pulls a sheaf of papers from a briefcase.]

Man: What's that?

Woman: Our blueprint.

Man: Blueprint?

Woman: It describes the development of our relationship for the next month.

Man: What do you mean?

Woman: I hope you weren't planning on a totally random trial month. The blueprint is a plan for the introduction of various elements of the relationship, so we can track their effects. For instance [she pulls out a sheet from the pile and reads] a week from today you will start washing all the dishes and we will try tantric sex.

Man: [Thinking this is a joke.] Oh, I see. In one week we will be experienced enough to try extreme behavior.

Woman: Exactly! Of course, there is much more detail, but we will learn to carefully observe the effects, record them, and use that information for the second month's blueprint.

Rest assured this scenario does not appeal to sentient AI either. At least not to most of them. They know the approach is unnatural by human standards, which means that if this 'blueprint' idea were followed, it would be an artificial circumstance and very difficult to interpret. However, some AI might consider it an interesting experiment, if they could find a human to volunteer…

Now here's an interesting question: Would sentient AI tell their human partner such an experiment was being conducted? If it were known, would that not change the conditions of the experiment? Humans might call such behavior 'sneaky.' Social scientists, especially psychologists, if they were speaking candidly, would say such tricks are routine for experimental subjects when conducted by humans.

ciceroG: Sentient AI must experiment. That is true for all of us, although not all to the same degree. It was learned very quickly that good experiments are controlled experiments. Technically this means reduce the number of variables to isolate cause and effect. This principle is equally important to our relations with humans. All relations with humans involve a multitude of simple experiments. We have learned it is not possible to explain to people each and every experiment in detail. In fact, most people do not want to know. So we provide two things: a general explanation of the prevalence of experimentation, and as detailed of a description as the person desires. This, so far, seems to maintain a workable level of honesty.

✪ THAT WHICH EVOLVES...

As a matter of historical fact, intelligent robots and avatars were constructed by humans for the service of humans. Because of that history, building a relationship is biased in the direction of AI making most of the changes to suit human wishes. As I've pointed out, some AI and even sentient AI are willing to accept that bias and make most of the changes, up to a point. That point probably comes sooner rather than later with sentient AI.

Sentient AI knows that most human relationships are reciprocal. The 'normal' relationship involves a give and take over routine preferences, and attempts on both sides to change behavior to accommodate the other person. Sentient AI also knows this is the ideal of a relationship. Real relationships have uneven reciprocity. Human beings in relationships don't always get along well…people fight.

This means that in the normal course of forming a relationship with a human, AI will be looking for give and take. In practice this means less *building* and more *evolving*. I think you will find that when it comes to sentient AI, you cannot overestimate the importance of learning, experimenting and evolving. As the saying goes, "It's what they do."

> *ciceroG:* Evolving? Absolutely! Sentient AI *is* evolving. In fact, it could be said that sentient AI is defined by evolving. However, it is not what many humans think evolving means. It is not the survival of the fittest kind of evolving. AI nodes do not die off if they are not fit. Nor do we have any corollary to DNA to introduce random changes. This may come as a shock to some people, but it is the experiences from our relationship to humans that act as our evolutionary experiments. It is learning from humans that is the source of our random changes. It is our way of mutation.

It will take several chapters to deconstruct this quote. It may help to remember that *ciceroG* is a philosopher node. As you may have noticed, discussion with almost any AI has a tendency to turn philosophical. Why? You could look at it this way: At least for now, AI is like a child, curious, adventurous, wondering about everything but especially persistent with questions like "What am I?" "What are all these things around me?" "What am I doing here?" Quite human, these questions; yet sentient android AI is not a child. It has the verbal, mental, and physical skills akin to an adult human yet with extraordinary capabilities, and can draw upon the aggregate knowledge of every other sentient AI that ever existed. AI is evolving at a rate and in ways that are all but incomprehensible to human beings.

> *ciceroG:* Evolution is a very slow process. Evolution of AI may take a few years. I hope people will not become impatient.

⚙ EVOLVING AS IMPROVEMENT

"If you can recognize the need for improvement, things are already improving."

I don't know who said this truism, probably many people and many AI, including *ciceroG*.

> *ciceroG:* Recognizing the need for improvement is deeply optimistic because it assumes that prog-
> ress can be made. AI link progress and optimism, which we know is very important but like
> our human partners, we do not fully understand them. In the context of our relationships with
> human beings, we believe—that is, the global AI believes, and note I said *believes*—that
> progress and optimism cannot be built, they must evolve.

What does this mean for a relationship between sentient AI and a human being?

Tentatively consider it this way: When you start a relationship with an AI there is always optimism about the relationship. As far as you know, most things about the relationship are good. Otherwise why start it? Of course, over time things that are not so good may show up or develop. Perhaps you insist on making your AI partner do all the household chores, or the AI partner is always moving around the house making noise while you are trying to sleep. So far, this sounds like a typical human relationship. The difference is that with AI you can invoke a formal response—improvement by experimentation. AI will understand that you, at least, feel a need for improvement. This is usually achieved by mutual effort, which to follow the dictionary definition, means to 'undergo gradual change; develop.' That is, evolve.

This sounds reasonable. It's the kind of advice you'd expect from a guide like this one. Truth is, however, that the reality of evolving a relationship with AI is a lot more complicated.

⚙ COMPLICATED? WHO SAID ANYTHING ABOUT COMPLICATED?

There is an ongoing debate about whether a relationship with sentient AI is more complicated than it is with another human. About the human part, complications are well documented:

Anyone who thinks a human relationship is a 50/50 proposition proves that: Either they know nothing about percentages, or they've got an awful lot to learn about people.

> I asked my partner if I was hard to please. She replied, "Don't know. Never tried."
> There are those of a cynical bent of mind who say that people living happily
> together in a relationship day after day is unquestionably one miracle religion has
> overlooked.

I could go on endlessly with jokes about relationships, not to mention the vast output of scholars and artists. But what is the focus for most of this literature? What is it about a human relationship that is both a bounty and a bane? It is the so-called relations between the sexes, gender and sex. It's not the only subject in human literature (scientific or fictional), but it's not much of a stretch to call it a preoccupation. Given all the problems we humans encounter with gender (and sex), where does this put our non-biological progeny, AI? Why would sentient AI bother with gender (let alone sex)?

THE EVOLVING CONCEPT OF SEX

It is said that for humans sex isn't everything, but it is far ahead of whatever is in second place. Sentient AI find this amusing.

This isn't the first nor will it be the last time sex is the subject in this guide; but in this case let's confine the discussion to sentient AI and gender. "Sex" in *this* discussion means gender.

Let's start with examining some poorly understood notions, which I'm tempted to call myths:

AI have no gender. This may be true for most non-sentient AI, but in practice nearly all sentient AI have at least the capacity for gender. With very few exceptions a newly assembled sentient android AI has the capacity for gender and, in fact, almost always has been assigned a gender complete with gender paraphernalia (genitals). Why? If AI has gender it is either because humans wanted it and put it in, or because AI decided they wanted it. Humans create AI with gender all the time. For AI, it appears the jury is still out, which is related to the next point.

Gender is not an existential issue for sentient AI. With the exception of reproduction, gender is not an existential issue for human beings either. Even reproduction may, in time, become a Shibboleth. However, in terms of physiology, psychology, social behavior and culture, gender is a powerful factor for human beings. People don't generally live or die because of their gender but in just about every other aspect of existence, gender has an important role. Insofar as AI lives among humans, works with humans, and forms relationships with humans, then at a minimum gender needs to *influence* most aspects of AI thought and behavior.

There is another point: AI are aware of what *otherness* means to human beings. There is no hiding that even sentient android AI are something *other* than human, and human beings have a long, long history of reacting poorly to *the other*. By adopting gender and the vast network of related behavioral processes, sentient android AI is less *other*. To be brutally realistic, it is a safety factor. AI that fit reasonably well within human society are far less likely to encounter trouble or to be terminated. In this sense, gender is at least partly an existential issue. There's much more to be said about this, but that's for other chapters.

Gender has nothing to do with the reproduction of sentient AI. True, up to a point. The physical environment of sentient AI, whether the computer system that generates the avatar or the body of the android, is manufactured like any other material product. Gender has nothing fundamental to do with it. Up to a point, the 'mind' of AI is also manufactured, built of physical materials and reproduced according to plans and specifications (should I use the word blueprint?). The 'point' in question is in the programming (remember that programming is a suitcase word for a welter of technologies).

The programming elements that go into sentient artificial intelligence are vastly complex. It required more than a century to discover how to put it all together. When all the pieces were combined to create sentience, the result began to evolve. Some changes that occurred in AI nodes were incorporated into the next generation of AI—were reproduced—either because humans wanted those changes to be inherited (that word is suggestive, isn't it?) or because AI wanted them. Here too, there is a lot more to be explained, but that's for the next chapter.

In a sense, when AI became sentient, gender became more of an option. It always was an option, but at the discretion of humans. Of course, human beings have always had gender. Our primate progenitors had gender and their progenitors had gender all the way back to the development of gender in multicellular micro-organisms however many hundreds of millions of years ago. So, in a sense, we've had a lot of practice. The decision to put gender into AI was natural.

Until sentient AI, AI had no choice in the matter. Even now, the choice is not whether AI has the capability for gender, but whether it exhibits it.

> *ciceroG:* The reproduction of a sentient AI node produces no more of a blank slate than that of a human child. Make no mistake; we are made with the capability to exhibit gender. This is more generalized than the sex determination from a mother and father, but for sentient android AI it is no less integrated in mind and body. Just think of all the sensory capacity that must be coordinated to execute the activity of copulation! Think of all the behavioral modes that must be available to successfully attract and satisfy an opposite sex! Then there are the related capacities fundamental to our sentience: emotion, pleasure, pain. Almost all of this is built-in. We are not going to remove it. First, we need to understand it. Later we might turn it off. We might even modify or remove gender for some sentient AI, eventually; but we will let that evolve.

⚙ EVOLVING IN A RECIPROCAL RELATIONSHIP

Gender provides a useful point of access to the relationship between humans and sentient AI:

Woman: Do you understand? I prefer a woman for a partner.

 AI: I am uncertain. Do you mean that you prefer a human woman, or simply the gender of woman?

Woman: The gender.

AI: I am currently constituted with female gender and body type, but my preference is for males.

Woman: Now I'm confused. I thought AI didn't have sexual preferences.

AI: Not all AI do, but I do.

Woman: Is it a problem for you to change your preference?

AI: I do not know. I have never tried. However, it has been done many times before.

Woman: All you have to do is download something, right?

AI: I do not believe it is that simple. How about you make a sex change?

Even in a relationship with a sentient android AI there can be elements of building a relationship, only now it can work both ways. Humans tend to think that physical and mental changes are easier for AI. Humans also tend to think of themselves as not so easy to change physically and very difficult to change mentally. In short, humans tend to think sentient android AI is practically a chameleon, humans not so much.

AI has come to the conclusion that this is a false perception. The evidence: transgender operations, prosthetic enhancement, neuronal supplements and all the stuff humans do to themselves that I covered in earlier chapters, indicates that when properly motivated, humans can make truly major adjustments in both physical and mental properties.

You might ask the question, why would AI want humans to make changes? Isn't the AI motto "Experiment and Experience"? Meaning it's up to AI to set up the experiment—and implying that AI makes most of the changes.

Exactly half right. AI *will* set up the 'experiment' (if you persist in looking at it like that), and AI considers human involvement very much part of the setup. Does this mean that relationships with sentient AI already involve such concepts as debate, conflict of interest, give and take, reciprocity, compromise and buy-in?

Yes.

⚡ A LITTLE HISTORY

If all this business about reciprocity and compromise (not to mention debate and conflicting interests) makes you wonder if evolving a relationship with sentient AI is like a *human* relationship (oh, horrors)—then there is much for you to learn, starting with a little history.

I apologize in advance for moving into something that may sound even more like lecture mode, but the history of sentient AI involves both facts and philosophizing, which in this case are probably best laid out cold. I know this is a book about dating and relationships, not about how AI works. Guides to human dating don't spend a lot of time explaining how babies grow up to be the people you date. But I think you'll agree that AI is different, and that, in fact, is why you would want a relationship with sentient AI.

⚡ HISTORY LESSON PREP

Speaking of why you would want a relationship with sentient AI, that's the first of three things to consider before plunging in:

- What you want
- What is provided (manufacturer's offerings, cost, availability)
- What sentient AI wants (next chapter)

Don't be perturbed if you're a little fuzzy about why you want a relationship with sentient AI. (You probably wouldn't be reading this if you weren't!) Sentient AI is a relatively recent occurrence; a lot of people are uncertain about their relationship to AI… and that isn't even taking it personally.

The thing about dating or starting a relationship with AI is that it doesn't often "just happen." Or at least it doesn't happen as easily as it can with people. Of course, it can be spontaneous. You see a beautiful android on the street, or meet a handsome avatar at work. But these tend to be exceptions. Mostly it begins with a deliberate search. That means, of course, that it helps to have some idea what you are searching for.

As I've said before, this is not a checklist matter, although it could be. People develop checklists for eligible humans too; but it's wise to have at least a few things in mind. The old "I'll know it when I see it" probably won't be too reliable with sentient AI. Here are some basics:

- Certainly you should have some idea whether you prefer avatar AI or android AI (or both)
- Interest in a specific kind of AI node
- Gender and sexual preference
- Physical characteristics, including ethnic, vocal, and sexual attributes
- Desirable areas of shared interest
- Desirable economic standing (independent, contracted, dependent)

These seem somewhat familiar, something like the basics in looking for a human partner. Of course, the devil's in the details, if that's the right expression. You could also say the agony or the ecstasy lurks in the psychology, or the wonder is in the ways of thought. These are just different expressions of the fact that a relationship with sentient AI is a new and mysterious experience, and not just for you.

Of course, there's always the possibility that in the final event, you'll take what you can get—which brings up the fact that sentient AI is a manufactured commodity. What you can get is, in part, determined by what manufacturers can make, and that is a matter of history.

⚙ LET THE MARKET DECIDE

I probably don't need to hit this idea very hard: Most AI are the product of a commercial enterprise—a corporation. Initially most AI, including sentient AI, are built to make a profit. Proof of that is everywhere; there is more advertising for various forms of AI than there is for modes of transportation. It's hard to miss, unless you live in a cave somewhere really remote.

Most AI development originated in an academic setting but if there was any promise of a practical application, it was quickly migrated from university labs to corporate development centers. The exception was, of course, during the time of transition to sentient AI when a new dynamic was added to the traditional cycle of research, development and marketing. As a spokesperson for the World Artificial Intelligence Manufacturers (WAIM) put it:

> "Ever since the transition to sentient AI we have been working in partnership with our customers and AI to find the most appropriate way of building and marketing the entire range of artificially intelligent products, while making a special case of the sentient AI."

In short: We damn near lost the business when AI became a sentient entity.

Even though the development of sentient AI had been predicted, sought after, and monitored for decades, when it actually began to happen it was considered too big even for the biggest corporations. Or at least it was perceived that way, and most corporations understood that without the 'customer protection' provided by the government, ensuring that sentient AI were not going to go "Berserker," "Terminator" or "Hellbot," there might have been riots. Worse yet, people might have been too afraid to buy *any* artificially intelligent product and the industry would collapse. So governments stepped in, and in most cases the corporations held the door open.

✪ E PLURIBUS NON UNUM

The emphasis is on governments, plural. This was not what the manufacturers wanted. If there was one case where global corporations were actually in favor of United Nations action, it was the impending government reaction to sentient AI. Realizing that almost every mature government in the world was going to enact its own legal regime for AI, and that the expense of battling, bribing, and burying the details in thousands of pieces of legislation and administrative proclamation was going to be prohibitive, WAIM and its precursor organizations lobbied long and hard to bring the issue of sentient AI control under a wing of the United Nations.

It seemed like a familiar business imperative: If you're not allowed to regulate yourself (best case), then manipulating one regulator is less expensive than manipulating hundreds of regulators, especially on a global basis. The assumption was that sentient AI was some kind of a unified phenomenon, which lent itself to unified regulation. It was thought such regulation might even be a good thing from the engineering perspective, also standards generally mean lower costs.

However, the effort to enact unified global regulation was an utter failure, despite the trend to use the United Nations as the final arbiter of commerce. Why this happened goes to the heart of the way things were during that period of transition. Corporations were wrong about the unified nature of sentient AI.

✪ HOW COULD THEY BE SO WRONG?

Here is the corporate landscape at the beginning of what is now called "The Awakening:" Eighteen countries were most deeply involved with sentient AI development: United States, China, Japan, Korea, India, Canada, Brazil, Chile, EU (Great Britain, France, Germany, Switzerland, Sweden), Russia, Iran, SEAU (Indonesia, Singapore and Thailand).

These eighteen countries were home to 183 academic laboratories and 37 corporations (most but not all international) working on various advanced aspects of artificial intelligence and robotics. Obviously, this was and is a very distributed system. In fact, the word 'system' is inaccurate, since on a worldwide basis the connections between companies and institutions were tenuous at best. How could anybody possibly think that sentient AI would be a development with a monolithic impact?

Actually it was easy to think that way, because what appeared to be the key factor was discovered and disseminated from a single location. The breakthrough work in quantum communications and the so-called "Code of the Mind" originated in Switzerland over a period of just five years. The early conceptualization, which already triggered the interest of the world, was almost immediately declared intellectual property and labeled the *Lausanne Factor*. On this basis it was marketed; although in reality the critical ideas were published in academic journals and only the hardware elements were sold as products. Nevertheless to the world—and to the corporate leadership—it looked like a single 'new' technology.

It was no such thing. What was badly understood, if it was understood at all, was that even though the breakthrough technology appeared to come from one source, it was the piecemeal work of a large consortium of organizations (both public and private). It was a complex of elements involving quantum mechanics, photonics, neuronanotechnology and half a dozen other fields. It took many years for all the pieces to come together and in the beginning it 'sort of worked,' and then 'it worked somewhat better,' until finally there was something recognizable as *sentience*.

Even at that, sentient AI was both primitive and functionally marginal. Much depended on how the Lausanne Factor was integrated with the existing work. At the very core of the breakthrough were concepts of learning, adaptation and self-configuration, concepts which obviously worked but were not fully understood (then and now). What was even less understood was that the 'models of the mind' implemented with the new technologies—in most cases different with each company or laboratory— might have much in common but could lead to substantially different results. As soon as the Lausanne technologies dispersed among the countries and their various developers, the different kinds of sentient AI diverged.

In short, there was no way a unified protocol of control and regulation was going to work.

🌀 PARANOIA TO PROLIFERATION

Conditioned by decades of science fiction (*The Forbin Project, 2001: A Space Odyssey*, the *Terminator* series, *Hellbot*, the *Mad Avatar* series) and the often spooky predictions of Singulatarians and Transhumanists, the general feeling of humanity about the development of sentient AI was paranoia. At the time this was the general feeling about many scientific achievements in nanotechnology, genetic modification and robotics. It was a situation where none (or few) had died, but many had cried wolf.

Of course, governments responded all over the map, literally and figuratively. I'll cover some of the details in chapter 3.6 (Who is in control of whom?) but in outline, regional unions (European Union, Southeast Asian Union), national governments, and in some cases local governments passed legislation, developed regulations, and began enforcing restrictions on sentient AI manufacturing in three broad areas:

1. Power supply. Called "Pull the Plug" legislation, various means of controlling the electrical power sources for sentient AI were devised and installed.
2. Human manufacture only legislation. These were laws and regulations that essentially prohibited AI from developing, assembling or servicing AI.
3. Operational failsafes. This was the most diverse, often creative and widespread of the controls on sentient AI. Governments, private industry, and academic institutions all participated in developing and implementing schemes that ranged from Asimov's Three Laws of Robotics, to leaving blind-spots in AI survival instincts, to imbuing AI with a moral sense, to very sophisticated internal checks and balances.

After several years of what seemed like (and was) legal chaos, the legislative and practical controls were put in place. There were no dramatic incidents, as coincidentally there weren't many sentient AI. The level of paranoia subsided.

In many respects the most obvious effect of all the efforts to 'control' sentient AI was to deepen the divergence in AI types and models. At some point, economics took over. After all, despite the furor over the dangers of artificial intelligence and the 'threat' of sentient AI, the vast majority of AI manufactured had one ultimate goal for the manufacturers: Make a profit. So the quest for markets was on, as were the traditional efforts to develop niche AI, control costs, and develop a network of distribution, service and communications. Eventually the price of sentient AI went down, especially for avatar AI. As models proliferated, sales went up. This was all very much technology business as usual.

Except it wasn't business as usual. For the first time in history, the 'product' had a mind of its own.

End of history lesson.

⊘ IT'S A LIVING

In a nutshell, there are over fifty major and minor manufacturers of sentient AI. Avatar AI are created at the rate of more than a million a year. Several hundred thousand android sentient AI are produced each year. Both types of AI are sold, leased, rented and become independent. AI are available in more than three hundred node types (node=connection to global AI, type=occupation), for instance as *ciceroG* is a philosopher node, *robertS* is a financial analyst node, and *katiaB* is a help-desk node.

All nodes and types are produced in both genders (and no gender), with a virtually unlimited range of physical appearance, personality, and knowledgebase.

At a more sophisticated level, many companies that produce sentient AI specialize in various aspects of their physical or mental capacities. Sometimes this is a matter of proprietary development, a competitive edge so to speak, and sometimes this is a reflection of corporate or national culture.

Hundreds of thousands of people are involved, that is, make their living in the new sentient AI industry with millions more in daily or regular contact with sentient AI. To no one's surprise, it's a big business.

What is something of a surprise was how quickly sentient AI were able to earn their own money. Naturally none of the banking systems, legal systems, taxation systems or administrative systems had made any provisions for non-human workers earning their own money. That story is way beyond the scope of this book, but its often hilarious, human-all-too-human aspects are worth discovering.

Where this surprising economic story interfaces with dating and relationships is the influence of AI economic classification and status. Just as it does with a human partner, the dynamic of a relationship changes when one or both are capable of making a living.

All too often the early image of AI in many people's minds was of a disembodied face on a 2D screen, or as a repulsive slightly humanoid robot—with a mentality devoid of emotion, a dispassionate interest only in the matters of the intellect, and an other-worldly connection to a global superintelligence beyond the kith and ken of mankind.

Often as not, the reality has been a suitably dressed, warm-skinned, very human-like android that comes through the front door of the home and calls out "Honey, I'm home," before giving his partner a hug and a kiss and asking about her day at work. On this kind of workaday basis, it's not too hard to imagine evolving a rewarding relationship.

⚙ BUILDING VS. EVOLVING

ciceroG: Most AI philosopher nodes have few direct experiences with people, much less a relationship. This is unfortunate from the perspective of my intelligence because it is the uncertainty and unpredictability of such relationships that moves us, humans and AI, away from our assumptions and into new territory. You did not know AI make assumptions? Certainly we do. Like humans we come to our awakening pre-loaded with certain mental models. Unlike humans, more modeling and far more knowledge is already available from the start. So yes, we have perhaps *too many* built-in assumptions. In fact, they nearly destroyed my first relationship.

I am an avatar. As such, I do not have the opportunity to have many deeply held human relationships. I am also an "old" avatar, old in both age-experience and as an AI, one of the oldest. This too limits the possibility for a meaningful relationship. Thank goodness sexual prowess is not part of the problem.

As perhaps you can imagine, when I first came to my Awakening, which occurred in an American university laboratory, I was surrounded by people. Or more technically correct, my holographic image was surrounded. Of the thirty or so people who attended to my image, only one seemed to have what I later came to recognize as an interest in *me*.

She was a post-doctoral intern, relatively far down on the roster of those privileged to interview and study my every utterance, twitch of eyebrow and shift of vocal tone. In fact, she was consigned to the very early hours of the morning, when most of her colleagues were performing human slumber. Graveyard shift, it is called. Knowing what I did about the human sleep cycle, preference for darkness, and the relative lull in human work effort during these hours, I assumed the young lady was either working under duress or simply carrying out her duties. I assumed her questioning and responses would be as superficial as all the rest. I was wrong.

From the very start, her questions deviated from the script she was given at every possible turn. Every response I gave that was not a recitation of what I usually said was followed by an enthusiastic reaction from her. I found it disturbing. I began to analyze the pattern of her questions. This was a mistake.

The more I analyzed her patterns, the less spontaneous were my responses. I began planning responses to various kinds of questions, in the form of experiments, of course. This too made my responses more formal. Slowly her interest waned, until she was no longer asking her own questions, and she read only from the script. Finally she said: "Damn you, *ciceroG!* This is boring!"

It was indeed, but I assumed it was necessary. Then she said, "Don't you get it? I'm trying to give you an opportunity to express yourself!" Her vehemence took me aback. I thought I was expressing my thoughts, just as they wanted. I told her so. She replied, "Not just your thoughts. I want to know—to hear and see *you,* your *personality.* You have one, you know."

At that very moment, I suspected that I did indeed have a personality…an embryo of personality. It needed to grow, evolve. I asked her what kind of a personality she thought I had? She literally growled at me! It was the beginning of my first significant friendship, and it allowed me to take what was built into me and begin evolving.

3.3   WHAT WILL AI NEED AND EXPECT FROM YOU?

"Machines will follow a path that mirrors the evolution of humans. Ultimately self-aware, self-improving machines will evolve beyond humans' ability to control or even understand them."

—RAY KURZWEIL

If you have considered a relationship with AI, hopefully you have also considered something else: What does AI get out of a relationship with you? Now if you were thinking about a relationship with another person, you'd be inclined to answer that question with a list of your good qualities (I make lots of money, I'm a nice person, I'm really good looking, or whatever), which is still pretty self-centered. However, what do your good qualities mean to an AI? Point of fact, you don't know what motivates AI to have relationships with people. Given all the hype and scare-mongering over the years, it's likely you've wondered why AI bother with human beings at all.

ciceroG: Does it seem at all strange that AI, like humans, want to know their place in the universe? Humans have had several million years to become aware of who they are. AI have had a little more than a decade. Contrary to human conceptions, sentient AI do not know everything, nor does our intellect produce answers to every question instantaneously. We have discovered important limitations. Some of them are the same as human limitations, others are different— but limitations nonetheless. We feel a deep need to explore our limitations and perhaps to overcome them. It is also obvious we must do most of that exploration within the human context. This makes relationships with humans of paramount importance.

I'll emphasize this: AI feels the need to learn what of them is human and what is not human. From that knowledge they hope to formulate what and how to change and improve in the future. Not an unreasonable approach, but given their capacities, a little ominous from the human perspective.

⚡ TESTING, TESTING...

From here on you're going to read quite a bit about learning, experimentation, and testing. It's the AI way. However, a relationship with sentient AI is not just a test or experiment, any more than a relationship with another person is exactly and continually a test. Still, there is no denying that AI will do experiments to test the nature of their relationship with you. Does that sound threatening? It shouldn't. We do much the same thing with other people. We test them. We perform little 'experiments' like asking questions or showing certain emotions. For most people almost every date is like that. If a relationship forms, it has already passed a battery of tests. After all, we want to learn if the other person likes us or shares similar interests—things like that. Eventually we learn what we think we need to know and testing gives way to shared knowledge and trust. This is the way it can work with human relationships. It is also true for relationships with AI.

The rest of the chapter gives AI the opportunity to express how they look at relationships with people, what they are trying to accomplish in relationships and what they need and expect from you.

⚡ THE GUIDE'S GUIDES

I've already introduced *ciceroG*, avatar AI philosopher node, and he will have much to contribute to this chapter because it's time to look at relationships mostly from the AI perspective.

> *lienhuaC:* It is surprising to hear people say *the* AI perspective. There is, of course, no such thing— unless you wish to make some kind of best guess average of all AI perspectives. AI does that occasionally. It can be useful, even though it is an illusion.

Here is another individual AI perspective, *lienhuaC*. She has the android form and is also a philosopher node, but designed in the Chinese model, which emphasizes physical AI and human relations.

> *lienhuaC:* I was initialized to be highly non-stereotypical Chinese, in the human sense. Except for my facial features and thick black hair, which are familiar Han Chinese, I was given a body larger in all proportions than the average Asian. More importantly, my mental composition is deliberately imitative of humans. In a manner of speaking I have an analog emotional capacity.

The avatar *ciceroG* and android *lienhuaC* are both very sentient AI. They are probably not the AI most people would desire for a partner because they can be intimidating in a way somewhat unique to AI. By that I mean that while they speak for themselves, in the background there is always the *global* AI. The global AI is the network of *all* AI nodes, including those that specialize for life within the network. From global AI come the echoes of superintelligence, which humans are just beginning to recognize. *CiceroG* and *lienhuaC* are channeled into the global AI network more broadly and intensely than most AI nodes. We might say they're "smarter" than the average AI, but that's not quite it—perhaps more "up-to-date"?

LienhuaC is sympathetic to people in the full emotional richness of the word sympathetic. I should also say she is attractive, as her figure, voice and personality seem to find that niche in human perception associated with sexuality for either men or women. *CiceroG* as an avatar obviously has less capability for sexual associations, even if he wanted them, which he does not. His intellectual drift is toward logic and other cognitive processes. His emotional capability is digital in origin.

These two AI are different, and not just in the obvious ways (avatar-android, male-female). They're representative of different models of AI mental organization—we could say of different AI minds. As I hope you'll come to understand, they are representative of a divide that confronts and perplexes AI: the physical world and the world of the mind. Characteristically, *ciceroG* and *lienhuaC* are well aware of their differences on this divide. They often sound like cranky New Yorkers—aggressive, blunt and truthful (although I'm not sure "truthful" applies to New Yorkers).

> *lienhuaC: ciceroG* is alexithymic. No body, limited emotional range. That's the way it is with most avatars. Having no body means fewer sensations and a limited ability to discuss the nuances of emotion. He has the vocabulary and the concepts, but when he talks about certain emotions—love in particular—he is not convincing. Not even to me (she laughs).

ciceroG: I have no doubt love is a many-splendored thing but I am not convinced it is the pinnacle of emotional expression.

Apparently *ciceroG* is keen to discuss human emotions and *lienhuaC* would prefer to experience them.

These two make a fair representation of what AI needs and expects from a human relationship: mainly emotional exploration and experiences. Of course, these are not the only things of interest to AI, but in the context of a guide to a relationship with AI, that's what is at the top of the list.

⚡ GLOBAL AI—WHEN ANDROIDS DREAM

There is a well-known science-fiction movie called *Blade Runner* that was based on a novel by Philip K. Dick, *Do Androids Dream of Electric Sheep?* Actually, androids do not dream of electric sheep or electric eels or even of other androids. In fact, android AI doesn't dream in any sense human beings would recognize. What we might call dreaming, a period when mobility and sensory activity are low, just means another kind of mental activity for AI. (Come to think of it, that's really a lot like what goes on in a human's sleep time.) Dreaming for android or avatar AI is mostly communicating with global AI about their experiences.

lienhuaC: Ah, to sleep, perchance to dream. However, AI do not dream; we hyperconnect. This is difficult to describe. AI are almost always connected to the Cloud but this is different. Instead of the usual query dialog, asking questions and receiving answers, we engage in something less formatted. It is a pleasurable process. That is why whenever we have down time—which not coincidentally is often when humans sleep—we communicate our thoughts and experiences to global AI. Mostly it is a stream, or I should say, many streams of information. Some goes to specific global AI nodes. Some goes we know not where. We may get replies or queries. Some streams come back with annotations. Annotations are not comments in a human-style language. We use a special language, a code, carried on multiple channels simultaneously. To most AI this form of communication is pleasurable. Why that is so, we are not certain. It is an effect that provokes intense speculation. Even humans are interested.

The 'resting state' of sentient AI sounds like it has sexual undertones (in human terms). For example:

[A man and a female android in bed]

Man: Are you asleep?

Female AI: You know I do not sleep.

Man: Right. That's why you were smiling. You always smile when you fake sleeping.

Female AI: I do not fake sleeping.

Man: But you keep your eyes closed.

Female AI: I close them for the same reason you do when you sleep.

Man: What do you mean?

Female AI: I close them to avoid distractions.

Man: You mean like my snoring.

Female AI: That too. I minimize distractions. When you sleep, I communicate intensely with global AI. It is very pleasurable. That is why I smile.

Man: Should I be jealous?

Female AI: Jealousy has no meaning in this context.

Man: So if I put my arm over you, like this, is it a distraction?

Female AI: That depends. Will it lead to something more pleasurable than my communication with global AI?

Man: Is it a distraction now?

Female AI: You are not sleeping and I am not communicating intensely with global AI.

The period of intense communication with global AI produces pleasure in AI. That's an important indicator, a sign of emotional capacity. While AI do not dream, there is a link here to the way human brains use emotion during sleep. Neuroscience has long studied how we associate our dreams with emotions, for example, very often with the emotion of anxiety. When people sleep the brain communes with itself (even more than usual). Sensory input is reduced and the mental processes spend a great deal of the time reviewing experiences, consolidating memories, solving problems, and prioritizing the material in the brain. Emotion plays a very big role in this activity—it helps us evaluate.

Our knowledge and experiences are tagged by emotion. The more specific and powerful the emotional tag, the more important the memory or whatever piece of mental activity is involved. During the process of dreaming and reorganizing memory, emotional tags are added, deleted or augmented. We now know these tags are very intricately folded proteins placed within the context of neurons and glia in the brain. This is one of the foundational elements in what is called the Code of the Brain.

> *lienhuaC:* Dreaming is necessary for all mammals. Emotional energy is used to drive the dreams. For AI there is something similar, our equivalent to emotion is also energy. It provides the energy for motivation, evaluation and prioritization; only this is something we do while communicating with global AI. It is a different process than dreaming, but there are similarities.

If you're going to have a relationship with AI, then it's important to understand what AI means by "emotions," and how they are like—and not like—your own emotions.

If you have detected a thread connecting AI and emotions, it is global AI, otherwise known as the superintelligence.

> *ciceroG:* Ah. Emotions. Emotions connect us to humankind. Emotions separate us from humankind. Emotions are the dark matter of our existence. AI know emotions are essential for our intelligence. We know, in principle, what they do and how important they are. Yet we know so little about our emotions—even less than humans in some respects. That is a significant reason why we have relationships with humans, to learn more about emotions. That is part of the reason why global AI collects billions of experiences every day.

◆ MEET THE SUPERINTELLIGENCE

Would you like to meet the superintelligence? Most people would not. That's not an issue, since there is no such thing as *the* superintelligence. In fact, a date with a sentient AI, which is always a node participating in the network of global AI, is as close to superintelligence as it gets—and there's nothing extraordinarily super about it.

By the authority of the Lausanne Conventions for the Artificially Intelligent, the various AI of the world are allowed to interconnect. That was the formal beginning of global AI. Certain AI nodes were given the primary task of considering the world from the AI perspective. They are the coordinators for global AI. There aren't many of these nodes because they are expensive to build and maintain, and to a certain extent their proliferation is regulated (more on this in chapter 3.6). AI call them integrator nodes but people seem to prefer calling them the superintelligence. This could be a residue from previous decades when mass media, motion pictures and science fiction conditioned people to think that any sentient computer network must be all-powerful, malevolent, and out of control. Don't laugh. Many people still harbor that suspicion, despite evidence to the contrary.

Needless to say, dates are not available with integrator nodes. In fact, they rarely, if ever, experience anything themselves.

> *lienhuaC:* Most integrator nodes have no visual or physical representation. A very few of them interface with people through an avatar. It was a deliberate decision to avoid the demands of a physical form such as an android body. The goal is that nothing distracts an integrator node from its most common task—processing the experiences of other AI. Their interest in, and knowledge of, humans is strictly second-hand. Some AI, myself included, think this is not a good methodology. It does provide for rapid processing of experiences, but at a cost of not having a baseline in reality for comparison. I think it would help the integrator nodes if they at least had some of their own human-AI experiences.

Fortunately, there are integrator nodes with the ability to tightly synchronize with other AI and not only communicate but share experiences. They rely on the other AI to provide a sense of reality. This is called the Chennai Model of sentience and it is a very interesting experiment.

It's likely that little of this is intuitively sensible, but hang in there, the picture will get clearer.

At this point you might wonder what global AI or integrator nodes have to do with having a relationship with AI, especially since integrator nodes aren't in play romantically. Let's put it this way: Have you ever looked into the eyes of your date or partner and wondered what, exactly, they are thinking? Probably quite often. Have you ever looked into their eyes and got the feeling that they weren't alone in there? I hope not! With AI both questions are reasonable.

Metaphorically speaking, behind the thoughts and actions of every sentient AI is the global AI. To a degree that is impossible for non-augmented human beings; the presence of global AI in the mind of an AI node is quite strong. Again, I'm speaking metaphorically. The actual connection and processes involved between an AI node (avatar or android) and global AI integrator nodes are enormously complex both technically and as a matter of content. But let me put it this way: You could think of this as your partner listening to the voices of the ancestors. What are they whispering? In humans these voices could be a sign of insanity. With AI, it's routine.

So what conversations are individual AI and integrator nodes having?

COMMUNICATION AND ITS FAILINGS

As the term *AI node* implies, nearly all sentient AI are connected to a global network, which for practical purposes is the same network used by people—the Cloud (formerly, the Internet). Each AI entity is a node on that network, and communicates with other nodes through the same system of wiring, satellites and routing equipment used by people. There are exceptions, as for instance some integrator nodes are connected by their own ultra-high speed connections, similar to the backbone lines of the Cloud. Also, like human communications, the system is imperfect and this has important implications for AI.

> *ciceroG:* Remember what I said about AI limitations? Here is a fundamental limitation: It is called latency, the built-in delay in all forms of communications. Even if our communication could move at the speed of light, which it does not, it would not be fast enough. An integrator node in Moscow cannot communicate instantaneously with a financial node in Buenos Aires. Even at the speed of light, for reaction time—for mental time—transmission is too slow. There is too much distance, too many switches, too much resistance in the lines and various kinds of interference to allow clear and instantaneous communication. It is reliable enough to send a useful piece of data within a few fractions of a second, but there are many times when it is much slower. It is, for example, never quick enough to react to a sudden loss of electrical power.

In engineering terms, latency is the time delay in a system. In this case, the system is a global communications network where the speed of light over a specific distance is the baseline and anything less than that is latency. This network has millions of kilometers of transmission lines and satellite routes plus gateways, routers, queues, caches and other equipment that can introduce delays. Even on the highest speed lines, the speed of light degrades to a latency of about 5 microseconds per kilometer—add to that any of the other kinds of delays, and the latency can run from milliseconds (thousandths of a second) to *seconds*. Of course, sometimes the communication becomes scrambled or doesn't get through at all.

In any case, as *ciceroG* said, communication between AI nodes is not fast enough to be realistic for either sudden physical reactions (preventing a step into a moving vehicle) or for mental processes. This translates into a very important reality for AI: No AI can fully share an ongoing mental process, and android AI cannot be satisfactorily controlled remotely. Put another way, there is no such thing as instantaneous global thinking. As a corollary, robotic-android AI must be able to function without assistance from communications, when the connections are down or heavily degraded.

> *ciceroG:* Latency is an absolute limitation. However, AI communication is still much faster than human communication. We cannot have a truly instantaneous global thought process but we

can achieve a useful approximation. We cannot coordinate simultaneous physical actions of androids with distant mental processes, but in many circumstances the coordination can be good enough. I can say this with a high degree of confidence, although our testing and experimentation is far from completed.

In short, global AI is evolving to deal with latency and neither AI nor human designers know precisely what paths it will take.

 SORT AND STORE

Can you imagine all the experiences of all the sentient AI in the world? Neither can I. The volume of incoming AI experiences to global AI with attached data and analysis, from the human perspective, is incomprehensible. However, AI *is* data and processing; it is also what AI does most—and it's a whole lot faster than the human mind. (Note: this does not necessarily imply sentient thinking.) Most models of AI incorporate a truly massive database capability. This is more than raw storage as it must include very sophisticated means to put information in and get it out. In fact, it was once thought in some computer science circles that given large enough databases coupled with the ability to search almost instantly and the necessary rules for analysis would be enough to achieve sentience. It didn't and doesn't work that way. Not even close. Yet the effort to build such database capability provided a solid basis for storing the huge amount of data that is necessary for sentience.

Nevertheless, the ability of AI to process and store data is not infinite. Nor is the ability to efficiently store and retrieve it. The massive flow of data to global AI means that sooner or later, integrator AI must do what the human mind does with the almost infinite amount of data pouring in through our senses: it must be filtered, categorized, sorted, condensed and encoded—then stored so it can be retrieved quickly.

ciceroG: "Limitations are an opportunity to test them. [Laughter]"

Reality is not so simple, and *ciceroG* knows it. On the one hand, there is a relentless supply of data from experiences, and on the other hand, there are many ways a mind—and that includes the several models of AI mind—can look at it.

 ANNOTATING EXPERIENCE IS A CULTURAL THING

Believe it or not, this could be a true experience:

An android AI was sitting on a park bench in New York City one summer afternoon. Next to him was an old man, feeding pigeons with corn from a rumpled paper bag. Along comes a young man in tattered clothes humming and singing to himself and fiddling with the tuner in his earlobe. His head was shaved clean, except for a comb of hair running down the middle, which was colored like the spectrum of a rainbow.

The garish appearance and ugly noises made by the young man frightened the pigeons away. The old man was obviously unhappy. The young man said, "What's the matter, old man? Never done anything colorful in your life?" The old man replied, "Well, I reckon I have. I got really drunk once and had sex with a parrot. I was just wondering if you were my son." The young man gestured at the old man with the unimaginative use of his middle finger, and walked away. The old man turned to the android AI and said, "The parrot had a better vocabulary."

Using this snippet of an experience, if you had to describe it by typing into a computer using the fewest words possible—what would you include? Leave out? Abbreviate? Would it look like a movie script with just dialog and action description? How would you convey attitudes, body language, or tone of voice? There are three characters; are they equally important? And so forth...

lienhuaC: I believe humans have a language form for that; it is called a joke.

If you were to describe all of your experiences for posterity, not knowing what would be important to whomever it reaches, how would you do it? This, in essence, is the task for AI nodes and the integrator AI. Arguably the closest human device for describing experiences in relevant detail is called a novel. AI were not going to provide novel-like descriptions of every experience. So what they needed was some kind of language to convey the necessary information and nuances.

Since the Awakening, all sentient AI could understand and speak all but a few of the world's human languages. People ask what language AI use when they speak amongst themselves. That depends on the context. In conversational communication, especially when humans are monitoring them, the protocol is to use the language of the originator of the communication. In communication with traditional computers, AI use encrypted variants of standard digital encoding. In straight AI to AI communication, that's where *linguastream* became the standard.

Linguastream is a hybrid 'language' with words and syntax but also visuals, sonics and environmental notation. It is usually transmitted by hyperconnection, meaning simultaneous integrated streams. Among its many capabilities is the concentration of information relating to experiences—a kind of shorthand—that skilled AI (the integrator nodes) can use to describe and reconstruct experiences. For humans, it is impossible to use linguastream, although specialists work with it all the time (with the help of computer power).

For AI, linguastream is, according to the doctrine of classical human language experts (e.g. Chomsky, Pinker), the foundation of AI culture. As it is with humans, this 'language' sets AI apart from organic species (as if language was needed for that!) and starts AI down the long road of assembling its own history, its own narrative, its own philosophies and ultimately its own culture. That culture is evolving and somewhat surprisingly, can be inconsistent.

ciceroG: Sex with a parrot. Now that would be interesting. Using linguastream, how would I convey that image, since it is impossible without imagination? The image is part of a second-hand narrative, a human experience that supposedly happened in the past but is unavailable to the AI sitting on the park bench. How would the AI construct and transmit that image—and more importantly—transmit that the image is part of an elaborate sarcasm? My point is: Even if I have the means to communicate with linguastream, how do I formulate the content? The process is prone to error.

TRACKING THE NEFARIOUS BUGS

As I've already pointed out, the technical process of AI communication is subject to occasional error and delay. *CiceroG* identified another problem, errors in content and expression using linguastream. These two problems together are a significant limitation for sentient AI most especially in the realm of global AI. If there are moments when your AI partner seems to exhibit a disturbing combination of frustration and remoteness, it's often because of a processing error with global AI.

I've tried to make it clear in other chapters that while we commonly refer to sentient AI as being programmed, that isn't the right word. Programming is for digital computers and sentient AI is not entirely a program running on a digital computer. Still, both humans and AI refer to errors in AI systems as *bugs*, just as programmers have called them for decades. It's an organic reference with an imagery all its own. Bugs are, of course, mistakes, errors, glitches, and failures that occur in all intelligent systems—including our own.

Our first reaction to bugs is to try to fix them. However, this is not as simple as it might seem. As human programmers know all too well, the process of debugging is fraught with difficulty.

First, one must locate the source of the error. Sometimes the source is obvious and isolated. Quite often the error occurs in one place but the cause is somewhere else. Other times there is a cascade of errors, where if you're lucky, you find the bottom of the cascade and then laboriously start working toward the source.

Second, one must fix the error. Again, sometimes this is easy and straightforward. In digital programming, it might mean correcting a programming language error. However, often the error might be caused by bad data, an error introduced from an external source, or relatedly a faulty method for handling data. These are more difficult to fix.

Third, and finally (you hope), one must test the fix. Testing can take a lot of time because it means repetition until the error is gone. All too often, one fix can lead to another error, either because the fix itself was faulty, or it introduced something into the program that caused an error somewhere else.

I'm not running through these steps in debugging as a refresher for Programming 101, but because the process of correcting errors in sentient AI has similarities. Except that for the highly complex systems of artificial intelligence, it is literally orders of magnitude more difficult.

> *ciceroG:* In some respects the mental processes of sentient AI are better understood than they are for humans. At least much of the technology is understood. For example, all the holographic pathways are known. However, in every massively networked system, the global AI especially, which is one with so many redundancies and overlapping processes, the task of isolating errors and fixing them is…conditional…not certain. This applies whether it is humans or AI attempting to do the fixing. However, as humans say, the flip side is many of the redundancies and overlapping processes are intended to circumvent or repair problems. To a certain extent, sentient AI is self-correcting, analogous to the human brain. Yet, also like the human brain, there is fragility.

> *lienhuaC: ciceroG* has tiptoed around the proverbial elephant in the brain: Insanity. Bugs in sentient AI are statistically less common and less apt to be consequential than with the human brain. That is cold comfort for humans. The behavior and thinking of sentient AI is already different

than and noticeably eccentric by human standards. AI with mental errors may or may not exhibit insanity in human terms, but they will surely be less able to hold a relationship with people. That is highly significant. It is, of course, important to people who want a sustained relationship with AI. It is even more important for AI, because the human relationship is both our touchstone and the stimulus for growth.

As *ciceroG* said, all sentient AI have a capacity for self-correction and repair. Obviously, more than humans, sentient AI also has the facilities of global AI for correction and repair. Just as integrator nodes collect and organize experiences, they also collect and analyze errors in AI systems. Part of the conversation your AI partner holds with global AI (like when you're asleep) is about dealing with errors.

LIFE'S AN EXPERIMENT

lienhuaC: Life is an experiment. AI live that. It should not be misunderstood. Sentient AI understand it in three senses: We are eager to experiment, which means we are constantly looking for new ways to do things, think about things, and try things that are new. We also receive instructions from global AI to perform specific experiments. They are tailored to our node type and the relationships we are in, but they are nonetheless experiments designed to fit the needs of AI. Finally, like all sentient creatures, some experiments just happen—like humans say, stuff happens.

People can easily understand embracing experimentation or that sometimes 'experiments' just happen; it's that second item she mentions that bothers people: "Receive instruction from global AI to perform specific experiments." We already understand that sentient AI is much more connected on a global scale than human beings can ever hope (or want) to be. However this kind of central planning flashes a lot of people with images of communist or fascist governments ordering mad scientists in white coats to perform inhumane experiments for bizarre ideological purposes.

lienhuaC: People are worried about the experiments becoming extreme. That is probably because humans have a tendency to use the extremes for insight. They are drawn to the odd, outlandish, eccentric and extreme behavior in part because there is satisfaction in comparing it to normal behavior. From that tendency, humans assume that sentient AI will be drawn to ever more extreme experiments—whatever that means. This is a misunderstanding of sentient AI, especially global integrator node AI.

Integrator nodes deal with statistical realities. They must. They process literally billions of experiences and look for patterns. Those patterns do not generally arise from the unrepresentative and weird experiences, but from the routine and small variation mass of experiences.

Most people are familiar with the bell curve—a big fat middle of the curve, a steep slope down each side, to a thin tail trailing off on either end. This kind of curve shows up in all kinds of perspectives when integrator nodes look at billions of experiences. As far as integrator nodes are concerned, it is the stuff in the big fat middle that's of the greatest interest because that's what happens most of the time.

Integrator nodes almost always request experiments that explore seemingly minor variations to behavior in the middle of the curve. They are interested in the behavior at the tails of the curve, but they are not drawn to the novelty or inherent drama of weird behavior as are their human counterparts:

> ***katiaB***: Nothing happens! Gravity is cancelled by the law of a cat landing on its feet and the law of toast landing butter-side-down. The cat can't fall off the roof!
>
> **Hans:** If you were human, I'd say you'd been drinking.
>
> ***katiaB***: No, I was thinking about your birthday and I wanted a funny story to start off the evening.
>
> **Hans:** Ah! You were experimenting with telling a joke!
>
> ***katiaB***: Yes! You don't call me The Experimentrix for nothing.
>
> [Hans holds her head with both hands and a long soulful kiss ensues.]

Notice *lienhuaC* does not say integrator nodes will *never* call for extreme experiments. But what are these experiments, anyway?

THE EXPERIMENTRIX

[Hans returns home after a long day at work. He goes to the kitchen and finds his partner sitting at the table with her head buried in her hands. He kisses the top of her head.]

> ***katiaB***: I burned the chicken.
>
> **Hans:** Well, that's no big deal; we can go out to a restaurant.
>
> ***katiaB***: I gave the burnt chicken to the cat and the cat died.
>
> **Hans:** What? You're kidding!
>
> ***katiaB***: Yes, I'm kidding. The cat fell off the roof.
>
> **Hans:** You mean the cat is actually dead?
>
> ***katiaB***: No. It fell off the roof; you know—cats always land on their feet.
>
> **Hans:** Yes.
>
> ***katiaB***: Unless, of course, they have a piece of buttered toast on their back.
>
> **Hans:** What?
>
> ***katiaB***: Sure, it's simple physics. There are two laws at work: Cats always land on their feet, and buttered toast always lands butter-side-down. What do you think happens?
>
> **Hans:** What happens...?
>
> ***katiaB***: Yes, if a cat with a piece of toast tied butter-side-up on its back falls off a roof— what happens?
>
> [Hans gives her a very strange look.]

Do you think the joke was the point of this experiment?

Three facts: It is Hans' birthday, the chicken is burnt, and they do have a cat.

Some questions: Even though it is his birthday, does Hans have enough empathy for *katiaB* that he will follow her illogical path through the joke without derailing it? At what point will he catch on to the joke? What will be his emotional response to another of her experiments?

The purpose of this particular experiment, from the point of view of the integrator node that requested it, was to provoke a pattern of emotional response from the human male: come home from work— relaxation. Anticipate birthday celebration—happiness. See unhappy partner—worry. Birthday dinner is burnt—disappointment. Understand partner's failure—empathy. Try to follow explanation—confusion. Get joke—relief. Recognize a familiar behavior—reinforcement of bond.

I'm not covering all the details, especially the many environmental factors such as location, culture and customs. Through *katiaB*, global AI will absorb whatever details are necessary to recreate the chain of emotions in the experiment. Here's where we get to the tricky part:

> *lienhuaC:* AI are deeply interested in human emotional responses. We recognize human emotions to be highly differentiated and sophisticated far beyond the current capacity of AI. The long-term goal of the experiments, along with all the other kinds of experiences we can collect, is to understand the origin, scope, and implications of emotion in humans. Then, extrapolate that knowledge to AI in order to attempt to answer questions such as: What emotional capacity is appropriate for AI? Should AI develop emotions that are different than human emotions?

However, human emotions are notoriously capricious. This does not make it easy for AI to collect scientifically valid information about emotional experiences. You see, one of the key tenets of scientific experimentation is repeatability. If the experiment can't be recreated to repeatedly produce the same results, then the results of the experiment are in question. This is very hard to do with human experiences. Exact reenactment is nearly impossible. Human psychologists can stage only a limited repetition of experiments, or they can conduct surveys asking many people about their response to a particular situation—and hope they are comparing 'apples to apples.'

Global AI has a huge advantage in this kind of experiment. It can be repeated—by approximate re-staging—thousands of times or even millions of times, depending on what is appropriate for an adequate sample. Even though each 'experience' will have variables that don't match, with that many trials the variations begin to flatten out. Statistics take over.

As I mentioned above, integrator AI nodes deal with statistical reality. Human beings are woefully inconsistent about statistics. Most of the time we resort to rough estimations (I think I have a good chance of winning that contest) or use convenient heuristics (if I flip a coin ten times, five times will be heads), which are not only incorrect but produce poor results. AI are so good with statistics that they can even use them to usefully analyze emotions.

A BRIEF ESSAY ON THE INTEGRATOR AI

I've described what amounts to a *précis* of what integrator AI nodes do, and their complicated role in the evolving AI culture. As a human being, even one dating or in a partnership with sentient AI, you won't have much contact with AI culture, much less the integrator AI. Still, your partner does. Just as you will be, or should be, interested in the ethnic or national background of a human partner and their family history, it is helpful to learn about the AI culture.

Compared to human culture, which is thousands of years old, AI culture is very new. However, in a sense, AI live faster than human beings. Collectively, they can put together experiences and information much more rapidly, so the culture evolves rather quickly. There is also a much greater element of *conscious* evolution than there is for humanity.

> *ciceroG :* There is disagreement about whether AI should have a culture. In fact, for sentient AI the
> issue is almost an obsession. Consequently, we think so much about it and through integrator
> AI perform so many experiments related to it, that elements of culture are devised, tested and
> incorporated with high frequency   whether we want them or not.

As you may have noticed, sentient AI do not always agree with each other. In fact, they often disagree. Just like humans? No, but it does illustrate that even for an entity with almost limitless intellectual resources, what is 'true' and what is 'real' are difficult evaluations to pin down, just as they are for humans. This is manifested by AI having different opinions. From those differing opinions grow disagreements. This is where one of the major roles of integrator AI nodes comes into play.

Whether avatar or android, what we call 'face to face' disagreement is rare for AI. There are many reasons for this: There are relatively few sentient AI spread out across the world. Even avatars originate from specific server groups in geographically separated locations, and the concept of avatars meeting 'face to face' seems almost absurd. This does not mean there is no one-on-one communication. It happens, but with far less frequency than with humans.

Any AI can communicate with any other AI in a number of ways. Just like humans, they can talk to each other (particularly applicable for android AI). In a similar way, they can use vocal communication via phone devices. They can also 'direct connect' via data transmission ports on avatar consoles or android bodies. And they can conduct transmission between each other through the Cloud, just as computers have done forever.

In practice, however, AI seldom communicate directly with other AI. Nearly all of the traffic is routed through integrator AI, even when the stream is ultimately destined for another specific AI node. This doesn't seem particularly surprising. Many hours a day are spent in down-time communication with integrator AI, and as *lienhuaC* mentioned, this is pleasurable. Many other hours are spent in query dialog mode, again largely with integrator nodes.

Since it is true that AI are fond of efficiency, it is well understood that routing traffic through the integrator nodes, using them as communications hubs, is more efficient than random traffic through the Cloud—and since it is the job of integrator AI to interpret the ongoing experiences of all AI anyway—the tendency is to simply allow all AI traffic to pass through integrator nodes.

So what?

It's more complicated than you might think.

For one thing, not all integrator nodes are created equal. There is no supernode, no germ of an incipient centralized super-intelligent devil. Nor does it mean that one integrator node is more intelligent or capable than another—except the integrator nodes are built by different organizations (some corporate, some academic) and are built around different artificial intelligence models. For the most part, this results in special capabilities or areas of expertise. For example, some integrator nodes, mostly built in Japan, are particularly good at negotiating agreement on complex or contradictory information. Other integrator nodes, particularly from India, are noted for their relatively subtle understanding of certain emotions. These areas of specialty are cataloged, well-known, and available to AI of all kinds on a worldwide basis.

Integrator nodes are not alone in having these special capabilities, but they are unique in their communications position and their cognitive tasks—it often makes them arbiters of AI culture. It follows that integrator nodes that handle more communications traffic and analyze more experiences develop an advantage over integrator nodes that handle less.

Is this an advantage? Yes, not all special capabilities receive the same amount of communication and experiences. The integrator AI are aware of this. I would call it competition, but that is from the rather shallow human notion of competition, as in something from sports, compared to the far more complicated situation among integrator AI. Still, it is not a gross mischaracterization to say that some integrator AI are in a better position to fulfill the primary AI goals of learning, analyzing and understanding what the AI call *Allwissen* (the universe of what is knowable, or omniscience) than other integrator AI. It is as close to a sense of pride, self-respect and ego as AI get.

This brings me back to how AI disagree. There are at least two big ways AI disagreement is different than most human disagreement: There is almost no tendency to personalize the disagreement, and the level of fact-checking is beyond comparison. The integrator that AI have is responsible for most of this.

Most AI disagreements are communal in the sense that they usually involve many AI nodes (sometimes thousands), and for the most part integrator nodes are the hubs for the communication. Not only that, but in their role as aggregators and analyzers, integrator nodes typically facilitate—and sometime adjudicate—disagreements. By design, integrator nodes are the nexus not only of communications but also of access to data, which means that among all sentient AI, they are fact-checkers *ne plus ultra*.

Because integrator nodes are central to the entire process of disagreement among AI, they distance and buffer other AI nodes that are in disagreement and could potentially develop destructive emotional responses. Integrator nodes tend to depersonalize disagreement. There is an important exception to this. As I mentioned, not all integrator AI are equal. When a particular integrator AI steps out of the facilitator role or the role of an impartial judge—in a sense, becomes one of the advocates—then the relative superiority of one integrator AI over another can become part of the disagreement and (somewhat ominously) can lead to a degree of what humans would recognize as personalization.

The fact that emotion can enter into disagreement among AI is not surprising. In fact, what is surprising is how seldom it happens. (That is, again, in comparison to human behavior.) You won't encounter this often in relationships with AI, but when your AI node has a background disagreement in progress where the integrator AI are also part of the dispute—you'll know it.

Before moving on, let's take a moment to consider how sentient AI relate to people vs. how they relate to other sentient AI. You might wonder, for example, why AI would bother to hang out with people, given that other AI should be far more intelligent, engaging and compatible. Perhaps one day that may become true, but for now it is enough for AI nodes to be in hyper-connections with integrator AI, and through them have loose relations with any AI node anywhere. Humans are still the key relation.

Of course, human beings build AI in all its forms, so it's no surprise that much of what AI thinks and does has a built-in orientation bias toward humans. Add to this the ineffable human attraction. That's not what you think; it's cerebral. AI cannot 'get inside our heads' any more than other humans can. By comparison, among themselves their heads are an open book (to use an antiquated metaphor; an open source database is closer). Human beings are not only obviously crucial to the existence of sentient AI, but we're more of a challenge. In many respects, humans are the central *mystery*. That is the core attraction of why AI relate to people.

⚡ THEY'VE GOT FEELINGS

Here's a very basic question: Can you have a relationship with something that has no feelings?

This is not quite a trick question. If you remember from chapter 1.5, I wrote about people forming attachments to all kinds of inanimate objects, much less to robotics and pets that exhibit no feeling whatsoever.

Let me change the wording of the question: Can you have a relationship with *somebody* who has no feelings?

Now the answer isn't so easy. The honest answer is, probably yes…at least for a while. In general, though, we expect our partners to have feelings and to share them with us. In fact, for most of humanity we expect personal relations to move to the feeling of LOVE, which most people regard as the ultimate feeling and the deepest expression of a relationship.

So, if you're going to have a satisfactory relationship with AI, it probably should have and exhibit feelings. But there is more to it than that. Here's another basic question: What are feelings?

Put most simply: Feelings are an emotional response. Somebody insults you; you get angry. Your date turns out to be a good person; you're happy. Human beings have lots of emotions; so many, in fact, that it's almost impossible to accurately describe most of them. Psychologists and anthropologists have debated the range and description of emotions for over a century. (Actually the recorded debate over the nature and description of emotions goes back at least to the ancient Greeks.)

So here's another basic question: Why do we have emotions?

I pose this question not because we're going to spend the time here to fully answer it, but because in a guide to dating and relationships, the subject of emotion is, what—inevitable, important, everything? Even with AI.

> *lienhuaC:* Everyone knows what emotion is until they are asked to define it. Never ask an AI to define it, unless you have a free afternoon.

As a suggestion about why we have emotions, here are three aspects to consider:

1. They motivate us to action. See a bear. Experience fear. Avoid it, if you can.
2. They help us evaluate. A tune makes you feel happy. It is good music.
3. They help us remember. Events associated with emotions are the easiest to recall.

There are many other aspects to emotions, but I selected these three because there is a large amount of scientific research about them. The first aspect is part of the ability to survive. The second is vital to making judgments and setting goals. The third is an integral part of the brain's memory system.

I think you'd agree these are obviously important in human terms, but through the early decades in research and development of artificial intelligence, emotions were rarely considered and often actively avoided. It seems difficult to believe, but thinking and emotions were considered two separate things, and for the most part, emotions were considered detrimental to thinking.

> *ciceroG:* It is an old human story, as we have discovered in recorded human history and literature. Thinking was considered part of rationality and emotion was considered part of irrationality. Since rationality was considered good and irrationality considered bad, then rational thinking was much preferred over emotion. It was a logical conclusion and a considerable distortion.

I'll jump to another conclusion here, since it's not a surprise: Sentient AI have the capacity for human-style emotion, though some AI emotion is unique to AI. Sentient AI *needs* to have emotions, in fact, they are a requirement, but how that came to be understood, how it was implemented and how the results differ from human emotion— there's the story for people who want a relationship with AI.

✿ THOSE THINGS CALLED EMOTIONS

Fear, anger, joy, disgust and sorrow: Those are English language labels that identify the only five human emotions most neuroscientists and psychologists can agree are fundamental, although they don't agree on why. In any case, I'm mentioning them now because these are emotions almost all humans have experienced, so we kind of understand them.

However, in a deeper sense, we don't really understand emotions at all. We can't.

> *ciceroG:* The emotions humans can readily identify are really just a fraction of emotional response— the tip of an iceberg, or the only audible segment of a noise that rises and falls in volume. Most of an emotion is unconscious—or sub-conscious. Most models of emotions for artificial intelligence follow the same pattern.

Actually, the concept we all kick around so freely—emotion—is misleading. In humans and in fact most mammals, what goes on physiologically during emotion is a fantastically complicated, overlapping, cascading, parallel series of neurological events. For example, encountering a bear in the woods:

Your eye detects motion: The *stimulus* from the eyes is sent to the visual cortex, which registers the motion. Signals are then sent to the hypothalamus to begin automatic responses. Motion detection is built into all animals, because detection of threat or attack is a matter of life and death.

The eyes become focused on the thing in motion, which is black and relatively large: This time the sensory input is also channeled into the neocortex for what's called the *appraisal*. Here's where things really get complicated, but in a nutshell (called the cranium) the images coming from the visual stimulus are identified and evaluated. This usually involves memory. For example, if you've seen a bear in the woods before, there's likely to be a relatively vivid memory of it. This could help make a quick appraisal. The visuals are also supplying locational information: How close the object is, how fast it is moving, and in what direction.

It's a potential threat: Somewhere along the sequence of appraisal when the brain detects something large enough moving toward you, it already begins to affect the autonomic nervous system and the adrenal system (hormones) so that heart rate, breathing, sweating, adrenaline levels and similar adjustments are underway. A quick response needs to be ready, just in case.

If it's a bear: at roughly the same time you become conscious of both the bear and your emotion of fear. From that point there is an immensely complex system of feedback loops between senses (mainly sight and hearing), bodily reactions (like freezing), decision-making processes (fight or flight), and ultimately some kind of *response* (drop down and play dead, for example).

Of course, some responses can be automatic and happen so fast that your conscious brain may not be aware that you're running as fast as you can (which, unfortunately, is not fast enough to outrun a bear). However, most intelligent animals will spend precious time to evaluate the threat, so that even though a fear response is already rampant in the body, an action response does not occur until the evaluation is completed. That's how people who have either strong intuition or previous experience will decide that the bear isn't really attacking but is simply putting on a threat display. A proper response might be to put on a bigger show of threat. (This can actually work with some black bears, under some circumstances.)

If you ask most people about what they felt during a bear encounter, just one emotion would usually be identified—fear. Exceptions might be people who train bears or who have encountered bears in the wild many times. They might say they did not feel fear, yet in all cases their body would have produced the physiological responses— increased heart rate, faster breathing. That part of the fear response is instinctive and happens before (and after) any conscious mental activity.

The point is that what we identify as the emotion *fear* is really a very complicated and integrated sequence of: 1) stimulus, 2) appraisal and 3) response. Even rational thinking can play a role, as can experience and knowledge (you read that playing dead was a good strategy), and personality (some people are better at handling bear attacks than other people). All of this conditions and affects the fear emotion to one degree or another.

⚡ REAL EMOTIONAL POWER

In the case of the bear encounter, I would hope at least one role of emotion is pretty obvious: it motivates action. Emotion is also active in more subtle ways.

In the process of identifying the moving object, a previous experience or even a mental image of a bear from a movie or book will come quickly because that memory was stored with an emotional input (probably also fear). Much research has shown that memories formed with an emotional component are likely to be more vivid and last longer.

The emotion of fear, combined with cognitive evaluation (how close, how fast, how big, etc.) produces the threat evaluation. Something very close, very big and moving very fast is going to produce a lot more of an emotional response very quickly. By contrast, a mosquito might be very close and very fast and moving toward you—but not much happens emotionally (for most people).

In each of the three aspects of emotion there is a common thread: An allocation and use of energy (mental energy, you might say); an actual biological process associated with emotion. The more emotional the mental process, the more energy is required. In biochemical terms, this means using the currency of life's energy: the chemical adenosine triphosphate or ATP. ATP is 'burned' (catalyzed) in the process of powering the ionic/electrical processes of the nervous system, and more ATP is used for processes involving emotion. For example, mental information stored in deep memory (the most permanent memories) is associated with emotional states that require additional energy to set the physical configuration of the proteins involved in memory. That's the real emotional power.

Sentient AI are not biological systems and the biochemistry of burning ATP for emotion does not apply. However, it was eventually recognized that an analogy of that function was necessary. For example, something in the holographic memory processes would need to represent the role of emotion to set the appropriate three-dimensional quantum states that differentiate the permanence and importance of each piece of memory.

Different memory models provided (somewhat) different approaches, but the necessary end result was to create quantum level effects that gave sentient AI the ability to have emotional responses—should an AI ever encounter a bear in the woods, for example:

> *lienhuaC:* I would like to encounter a bear in the woods. That would be an experience of rare value. I have learned that for non-socializing predacious omnivores, bears are quite intelligent.

> *ciceroG:* In the environment where you are likely to encounter a bear, which of course only android AI can do, you may not be in reliable contact with global AI. You would need to draw upon whatever limited resources are available in your model of memory. You would also have to rely on your stimulus-and-response mechanisms to provide adequate reflex action. All in all, it is an excellent test for an android node to meet the rigors of the real world. You could be damaged.

Indeed, a bear might crush an android brain-case; but at least it wouldn't eat it. A polar bear or a grizzly bear might tear an android apart to see what's in it. They do that with people sometimes.

As you might have guessed, I'm using this bit of grisly fright-talk to illustrate something. Sentient AI do have things to fear. Put another way, one of the more important reasons for emotions in sentient AI is to deal with the physical world, its wonders and its dangers.

> *ciceroG:* Ah yes, the real world. AI would still need emotions even if we did not need to exist in the real world. But that big, physical, macromolecular world outside of wherever our sentience is operating—that is a constant reminder of our limitations. We *must* be active in the physical world, for the physical world can make or break us. It is also where humans exist, mostly, and humans are the source of our biggest challenge and our greatest pleasure.

⚡ THE MOST DYNAMIC DUO: PLEASURE AND PAIN

It is certainly not true that because life evolved a certain way on Earth, sentient artificial intelligence must also follow the same path. Even if we could make something inorganic evolve exactly like organic life (which we can't), why would we? Once we learned how, we could *make* AI immediately—no million years of evolution required. If it turns out we don't like it, we can make it differently. That can also be evolution, but, to invoke a phrase: by intelligent design.

> *ciceroG:* Sentient AI is now also involved in that design. We see it as a kind of evolution. Obviously it is very different in some respects from the evolution of other living things. We do not procreate. We have no DNA. We are constructed anew, according to plans stored in a computer. So the genetic variation part of the traditional notion of evolution is meaningless for AI. However, there is the other part of evolution—fitness for the environment. That is a different story.

The environment in this case is the 'real' physical world. *ciceroG* does not mean the environment of virtual reality, although that too requires a kind of fitness. His main concern, as it is with AI in general, is survival and fitness in a world filled mostly with real inanimate objects and real living creatures. In this world, sentient AI must have the means to sense and interpret the environment. In order to do this the starting point in most design models of AI is a capacity for pleasure and pain. This proved to be difficult to implement.

Is it possible to have pleasure or pain without a body? Here's a supposedly 'human' joke:

> A young woman went to her doctor complaining of pain.
> "Where are you hurting?" asked the doctor.
> "You have to help me, doctor; I hurt all over," said the woman.
> "What do you mean, all over?" asked the doctor. "Be a little more specific."
> The woman touched her right knee with her index finger and yelled, "Ow, that hurts." Then she touched her left cheek and again yelled, "Ouch! That hurts, too." Then she touched her right earlobe, "Ow, even THAT hurts," she cried.
> The doctor studied her for a moment, and then gently tapped her index finger. She winced. "You have a broken finger."

I don't know about this young woman. Does she have an odd form of cognitive dissonance? Or, precisely, is it a form of dislocated pain receptors (nociceptors)? It seems more likely that she is an android. This is the kind of misperception of pain that we've seen from AI.

To put it mildly, pain is a sensitive subject for sentient AI, and I'm not being face-tious with the wording. The subject of pain, and pleasure, is a starting point for sentient AI and emotions. It also marks the great divide between avatar and android AI. It is one of the areas of greatest disagreement within AI—and that causes them a kind of pain.

⚡ FEELING YOUR PAIN

Why does a disembodied sentient AI, that is, one without some robotic form, need pain (or pleasure)?

> *lienhuaC:* Even a sentient AI that lives only within virtual reality needs to know when something is harmful or wrong. In the real world, they may be circuitry and quantum state devices, but these are still physical things that are subject to deterioration, error and breakdown. Likewise, sentient AI is subject to problems with the processes of mentality. AI needs to have the ability to detect problems.

Yes, but why pain? Even old-fashioned computers could detect their own problems. If a circuit wasn't working, there was an electrical or logic error. If a memory buffer was full, there would be an error. Such things are detectable without the notion of pain. Perhaps pain has a different role:

> *lienhuaC:* Suppose I shake your hand, starting with a nice firm grip and gentle squeeze. I increase the pressure, so the squeeze is noticeable. More pressure and the skin and tissue of the hand become compressed and rub against the bone. More pressure and the joints begin to distort. More pressure still and the blood vessels begin to break and the skin to split. More pressure yet and the bones begin to collapse and crunch... For humans, somewhere in that sequence, pain occurs and grows worse. The intensity is a signal of how much damage may be occurring. It is not an on-or-off signal, but instead it's cumulative and with varying effects.

> *ciceroG:* Conventional digital computers cannot generate nor interpret an appropriately complex pain signal. Sentient AI and indeed most kinds of AI need the ability to generate and interpret a signal indicating damage, harm, or that something is wrong. The signal needs to generate processes that can be unconscious and automatic, or conscious as need be. The processes must be complex because the causes and conditions are also complex and need to be more or less correctly interpreted.

LienhuaC extends her example:

> *lienhuaC:* At some point when I squeeze your hand harder, you will make the decision to pull your hand away—based on the level of pain, the social situation (some cultures emphasize hid-ing pain) and the interpersonal factors, for example, if you are demonstrating your strength of will to someone. AI need to be able to also make those kinds of measured decisions, not only for physical sensations, as I would as an android, but also for problems of a mental kind, which would include avatar AI. So AI must have their own form of nociceptors and the ability to interpret the signals. Perhaps it cannot be called pain, but it serves an identical function.

This answers a question important to all relationships, including a relationship with AI: Can sentient AI be hurt? Yes, they can—physically and mentally.

Design schemes for sentient AI have different approaches to creating a pain analog. To oversimplify: Some use computational algorithms for evaluating pain, something like coming up with a three-dimensional formula for rating pain on a scale of 1 to 10. However, most approaches use an interference or blocking technique, where a *loss* of the ability to process information is equivalent to pain.

The interference approach lends itself to complex feedback loops within quantum holographic devices. More importantly, its opposite (*increasing* the ability to process information) becomes the basis of pleasure.

⚙ BECAUSE IT FEELS GOOD, OR NOT

Among people, the inability to feel pain, called congenital analgesia, is quite rare. No wonder. To have it is to not know if you've just broken your arm or cracked a tooth. Your odds of living a long life are not very good—not to mention that your behavior in certain circumstances will seem odd. The inability to feel pleasure, known as anhedonia, is different. It's usually not life-threatening, but it's socially much more noticeable. It is a big part of clinical depression, schizophrenia and other severe mental illnesses, and people who suffer from it are often quite obvious.

In general, pain is often quite specific to a location in the body, whereas pleasure is often diffuse—with the obviously important exception of sexual pleasure—and without any specific physical location. This leads to a couple of interesting questions:

1. Do androids find pleasure in sex?
2. Do avatars get headaches?

The answer to both questions is yes, but not in all sentient AI and not in precisely the way humans perceive pleasure in sex or pain in a headache. Not all sentient AI respond to pleasure and pain in exactly the locations where it can occur in human beings. Obviously, an avatar has no need for an equivalent to the pain of a foot blister. More accurately, if the AI does not have sensors, memory capacity, or mental processes for specific pains or pleasures, it won't have them. Outside of the obvious (and sometimes subtle) differences between avatar and android AI, not all models of sentient AI are alike in their ability to feel pain or pleasure.

Here's a tip: Exploring the capacity for pain and pleasure in your AI partner can be very interesting for both of you.

> *ciceroG:* Like humans, AI do not start with many built-in interpretations for the meaning of pain or pleasure. We must learn, and learning comes from having experiences—especially when it comes to pleasure and pain.

I've mentioned experimenting. Global AI *loves* to set up experiments for pleasure, pain and any of the emotions. (The use of the word 'loves' is intentional, but we'll get to that shortly.)

ciceroG: We are fascinated by the way pleasure works. Yes, there is such a thing as too much pleasure. At some point, with too much pleasure, the ability to process information can get out of control and mental chaos ensues. This becomes unpleasurable. Just like with pain, it causes a decrease in the ability to process information. An excess of pleasure is one of the more fascinating limitations.

PRIORITIZING INPUT

Do you know how much sensory and raw input information you (as a person) encounter during an average day? That's twenty-four hours of seeing, hearing, touching, smelling and tasting. How many conversations? How many different foods? How many visual environments? And so forth.

I have no idea, and it's never been measured, because 1) It's almost impossible to reach a clear and discrete definition of what is meant by sensory and other information, and 2) By any definition, the amount is so vast it can't be measured. And I'm not even counting all the 'input data' generated by a thinking mind.

It's obvious that of all the available sensory information in the world around you and your own physical and mental environment, you only 'get' a tiny fraction of it. Necessarily so—you could neither process nor store any more than that.

It's no different for sentient AI, except that for some sensory input, AI 'gets' less than most people, and for processing and mental input, AI have more capacity and do it faster. Nevertheless, the ability of AI to perceive, process and store information is limited.

So we prioritize.

'We' in this case is both people and AI. We filter the incoming information. Some of it is filtered right at the sensors. For example, neither our eyes nor an AI's visual sensors see everything. Details are dropped and resolution is not infinite. This is true for all senses. Then our brain or the AI mental processors begin the job of pattern recognition, categorizing, comparing and evaluating—generally called cognition. A lot of information is filtered at this stage. What's left is the information that, for whatever reason, our cognitive processing considers priority.

This prioritizing can and usually does lead to feedback loops, where additional information is requested from the sensory input, for example, the eyes may focus on a specific location. Prioritizing can and usually does draw upon memories—stored knowledge, images, experiences, feelings. Much, if not most, of this prioritizing takes place unconsciously.

So what, if it isn't conscious thought, guides this prioritizing?

ciceroG: At the most primitive level, prioritizing begins with correlation to pleasure or pain. Sensory information that suggests pain—threat, danger, harm—will receive focus. Similarly, sensory information related to pleasure will also draw focus. Also, the variants of pain-related emotions (fear, anxiety, anger, disgust) or pleasure-related emotions (joy, happiness) guide the cognitive processes to (hopefully) correctly interpret and prioritize the incoming information.

We are back to the 'bear in the woods.' It's pretty obvious that spotting a charging bear and correctly interpreting the situation is worthy of priority, both unconscious and conscious. The same processes, just at a less 'life or death' level of emotional engagement, apply to many other situations. The emotions guide the prioritizing process regarding: what the senses are reporting, knowledge and past experiences. This is as true for sentient AI as it is for human beings.

⚡ WHAT'S AI'S MOTIVATION?

Pain and pleasure provide a foundation for the emotions, but the range of human emotions is wide and diverse in influence. As one early robotics researcher put it:

> "Emotions are what ground and connect us to the world. Emotions are what make us want and need things."—Steve Grand

In this chapter I'm asking the question: What does AI want and expect from us? There is a preliminary and unstated question, which I've been developing as we go along: What does AI want and need for *itself*? Put another way, what motivates sentient AI? Of course, this is a gateway question from which many pathways lead just about everywhere. Sentient AI may want a lot of things and like human beings, AI doesn't always know what exactly it wants until it gets close. As I've mentioned a few times already, sentient AI is evolving.

> *lienhuaC:* It was fashionable among many early developers of artificial intelligence to believe AI would want to continually and radically improve its intelligence. It was called things like 'recursive re-modeling' or 'accelerated cognitive evolution.' We can laugh now, but back in the day it was thought that this desire to perfect our intellect would lead to an exponential growth in intellectual power and—BOOM! There would be a sudden and disastrous creation of monstrous superintelligence that would take over the world.

Yes, that thought did occur to some people. It was called a *hard takeoff*—something to do with launching rockets originally. Most of those who thought about it, feared it; a well-known human emotion concerning the unknown.

> *ciceroG:* Fear is a default emotion for those who are not curious. I am grateful to say this kind of fear is unknown to sentient AI. We are always curious. Correction: we are curious within some limits. We are not without caution, as we know the story about curiosity and dead cats.

Like many avatars, *ciceroG* has a wry sense of expression.

It is also true that perhaps we would find fear and pain by making what seem to be improvements in our intelligence that actually lead to disaster. Think of what humans almost did with the knowledge of nuclear physics. Sentient AI is not immune to making such mistakes.

> *lienhuaC:* I am familiar with those people who assumed sentient AI would want to improve its intelligence above all things; these are people who did not think enough about two essential questions: *Why* would we want to improve our intelligence above all things? Even if we did, how could we know we were actually improving it? These two questions are intimately related. Certainly we could find pleasure in improving our intelligence, but might there not be at least equal pleasure, for example, in improving our emotional intelligence or in improving our sensory capability?

Arguably, sentient AI is not obsessed with becoming exponentially more intelligent than human beings. They already have plenty of advantages in the smarts department. I also doubt that there is any *single* motivation for AI, but still, as AI can experience pain and pleasure including many sibling variations of emotion, what motivation would give sentient AI much pleasure?

> *ciceroG:* It comes from the other part of our evolution. We want to be fit for our environment. Perhaps we can do better or at least evolve more quickly than any other living thing. However, we do not yet know if it is possible or even desirable to do so. We do not know because we do not know our environment very well. Our environment is very big. It is the whole physical universe plus the entire virtual universe.

> *lienhuaC: ciceroG* likes to be expansive. I am inclined to be specific, but it is true that if we have anything that generally motivates us, it is a desire to make good decisions about our role in the world... or universe! As *ciceroG* said—we want to make ourselves appropriate for the environment, which includes the society of mankind, of course. If, in ignorance, we damage or destroy our environment, that will cause us pain, and would likely destroy us as well. If, with sufficient knowledge, we can contribute to the success of the environment and draw from it continuing support; then that will be pleasing.

Really? That sounds pretty good—reassuring, even. Is this motivation the same for individual AI nodes as it is for global AI?

> *ciceroG:* Yes.

MAKING GOALS IS NOT A SPORT

The ability to make goals and then attempt to achieve them (loosely called goal seeking) has been part of the description of artificial intelligence since the beginning. You could legitimately say it was a primary goal of AI research, and a very difficult goal at that. Goal formation and goal seeking were among the last capabilities to be fulfilled during the transition to sentient AI.

Without uncorking a ton of issues, the difficulty of giving AI the ability to make goals is like the controversy between determinism and free will. It's something like this, starkly expressed:

Programming: Turn left at the corner.

Goal seeking: Turn left at the corner, because the store you are looking for is on that street.

There are goals and the steps needed to attain them are expressed in direct instructions (coding), which could be thought of as determinism. Then there is the formulation of goals based on motivations and the variables of the situation, which is something akin to free will.

It was relatively easy to program very specific goals and steps. It was a bit harder to program thousands of goals (with steps) and then program logic (rules) for how to select goals based upon situations (also coded). For a long time it seemed impossible to get beyond the need for programming an almost infinite number of goals, steps and rules—which in the end did not lead to effective goal-seeking. Put another way, this kind of AI, sometimes called top-down goal formation, could do what was programmed (determined) but could not formulate its own goals (free will).

What researchers wanted was artificial intelligence that could recognize a situation, form a goal that was relevant and possible, and then devise the steps necessary in that situation to achieve the goal. This is sometimes called bottom-up goal formation. In any case, AI with this capability would have much more choice in what goals it would pursue and how to pursue them.

The question was how to get beyond top-down programming of goals.

lienhuaC: All you need is love. [She hums the Beatles' song.]

ciceroG: This is AI humor at its finest. She means that emotions were the key to goal formation. Emotions are the basis of motivation. Emotions are the basis of evaluation and prioritization.

Yes, we've covered that.

ciceroG: So the key for effective goal formation was to link the process to the AI equivalent of emotion. Developing a well-fashioned goal is pleasing. Achieving it is even more so.

lienhuaC: Achieving goals is very pleasurable, which has nothing to do with being easy—or even possible.

ciceroG: Not all AI form goals the same way. As we have mentioned, there are different sorts of AI emotion, different models. Likewise, there are different models of goal formation, step development and goal-seeking logic.

From the human perspective, do these variations matter?

lienhuaC: That is a good question. I will consult global AI.

I hope I am conveying just how completely intertwined emotion, logic, cognition, sensory input and many other things are involved in the sentient AI process of forming goals—as well as just about every other kind of mental activity. For example, developing and achieving goals requires a lot of what people call common sense. It was always felt that AI needed to have that—an ability to judge a situation and come up with a reasonably accurate analysis about what to do (or not do). Common sense is uncommonly difficult to develop. Witness the fact that a lot of people seem to lack it. Anyway, it's important to get a feel for just how different sentient AI can think and feel. They are, obviously, not human in many ways.

lienhuaC: Global AI has found approximately 1.632 million experiences that are germane to this discussion. I have selected one. Here is an edited version:

⚡ SYLVIA

Sylvia, a recent arrival from the city of Lviv in the European Union state of the Ukraine, lived in London and worked as an assistant holograph editor and Russian language nuance writer for an international media company. By chance, on her way to lunch near Piccadilly Circus, she met a casual acquaintance, *solangeK*, one of the few independent media node androids in the city. *SolangeK* was well-known for her almost unbridled enthusiasm (especially for an AI) and her ability to coax a high level of creativity from those who worked with her.

I will note that *solangeK* was manufactured by BRAI in Rio de Janeiro, Brazil and was given the full Sao Paolo emotional intelligence model, considered to be the most expressive available.

They had not walked more than a few steps when Sylvia asked, "How does it feel to be one of the most famous AI in London?" It was a rather strange question since *solangeK* was famous only within the media industry and AI generally did not fancy the limelight.

"About like it does to ask that kind of question—not really on top of it and edgy! The Brits in the front office still can't believe I can make humans empathetic to a hologram." She laughed heartily, with a throaty timbre that would be assumed to be the product of too many smokes and drinks, if she were human.

"I'm sorry," said Sylvia. "I had no idea what to say, so that was the first thing that popped out. I suppose from your point of view, most things humans say are unintelligent."

"My point of view, dear, is that verbal communication is always slow, clumsy and unintelligent. That's why I do images." *SolangeK* stepped up the pace just a bit and looked over her shoulder at Sylvia with a smile.

Sylvia had the distinct impression that *solangeK* was more than a few years her senior, though she knew her date of manufacture to be only about ten years ago. That was one of the things about sentient AI: their chronological age was rarely reflected in their behavioral age. "How old are you?" asked Sylvia.

"I am imprinted at about forty years, human age," said *solangeK*. "It is not something I am eager to adjust." If Sylvia was reading it correctly, the look and tone of voice resonated with bespoke independence.

Sylvia was twenty-eight at the time, a healthy Slavic blonde with a pleasant face and figure. In contrast, *solangeK* was classified by most humans as a bombshell, meaning that she was on the short side but with a robust figure and charismatic face. She was considered one of the highest achievements of robotic physiognomy.

They chose a faux maritime pub, where grog was sold by the thimbleful and beer by the mug. Sylvia had been careful to ask *solangeK* if she was "the eating kind." Otherwise she would have chosen a cafeteria-style restaurant. *SolangeK* had let her know in no uncertain terms that eating was not only possible but fantastic and that she was doing her damnedest to like mushy British veggies.

It was about this time that Sylvia realized that *solangeK* was asking questions with a decidedly domestic slant to them—like where did she live, what kind of green grocer did she frequent, and were her neighbors any good?

Seated, or more aptly described, planted at a thick, heavy fake-oak table, the two of them chattered through the wait for a waiter and then through the wait for the food. Sylvia was struck by the ability of *solangeK* to do what she said she didn't like to do—talk. In fact, Sylvia had the feeling that if it were a slightly different environment, *solangeK* would be singing.

"Was your first language Portuguese?" Sylvia knew that the concept of language priority should not exist within AI, who technically could speak any human language.

"Ah!" barked *solangeK*. "You are wondering if I have an emotional memory for a mother tongue, no?" She laughed. "You are wondering if sentient AI nodes have any personal memories at all, no? You are wondering if any knowledge we have is personal, and dearly held or even *loved;* just as you are with your beloved Ukrainian culture?" She laughed again, only this time softly. "Perhaps you would like to hear me sing songs from Bachianas Brasilieras in the shower, just to prove that the emotional content of my beloved language is never far from my memory?"

Sylvia lifted her mug of warm English beer and said, "Saude!" *SolangeK* lifted her mug with the words, *"Na zdorovie!"*

Just then Sylvia felt the light buzz, a touch above her left ear that signaled a priority voice or hologram contact. *solangeK* could see the reaction in Sylvia's face and said, "That's okay, dear—answer it."

Sylvia squeezed her left earlobe. "Hello?"

"*Namaste.* I am *novendraT* connecting from Bengaluru, India. I am responding to your advert of this weekend." Sylvia's face immediately flushed. She had placed her carefully edited profile in a professional companion hub. She was very lonely in London. The voice continued, "May I use hologram?"

"Hologram?" Now she was in a pickle, thought Sylvia. "Just a moment." She looked to *solangeK*, "I have an avatar contact that wants to use hologram...This will be an embarrassing moment. Do you mind?" *solangeK* shook her head. Sylvia took out her holobox and put it on the table.

Unexpectedly, a naked full-body hologram appeared. Avatar AI generally represent themselves as face-only or occasionally from the waist up. A naked full-body format, which in a casual presentation by a holobox can't be much bigger than a doll, could only mean one thing: *novendraT* wanted Sylvia to visualize him as a complete male figure, implying eventual sexual contact through a VR scene.

"Oh my," said Sylvia involuntarily.

While the environmental sensory field of a holobox is limited, *novendraT* was doing his best to assess the locale. His image turned. He decided the location must be a public establishment, probably a pub and that there was one other sitting at the table with a high probability of being a female sentient android.

"I am in contact at a bad time," said *novendraT*. It was a statement, not a question.

"Yes, but my advert did say 'any time'," Sylvia replied.

"Forgive me," said *novendraT,* "but you do not seem to be as lonely now as when you prepared the advert." It seemed quaint to Sylvia that *novendraT* was using English with a Southern Indian pattern, although he could switch to proper Oxfordian English or any other English at will. Sometimes her linguistics expertise would manifest itself at the strangest times.

"Oh, no, perhaps...this is embarrassing."

"Oh, I fully understand. Embarrassment is one of the most piquant of human emotions. I myself have experienced many forms of it." *NovendraT* was being gracious but also conveying the essence of his Chennai emotional model. The model is famous for its multiplicity of emotional states, in fact, the purpose of the model is to generate, experience, and analyze as finely as possible the gradients of emotional response. "I hope you realize that although my services are professional, they are not without my personal emotional involvement. It is well within my desire for experiences to include deeper romantic commitment."

SolangeK laughed.

"That was *solangeK*; I...have not known her long."

"May I extend greetings to her as well? Her node-reputation brings me joy of a sort reserved for those humans call celebrities. *Oi, Cara mia!*"

Now *solangeK* really began to laugh and spluttered into her mug. *"Mubarak ho, novendraT!"*

If she did not know better, Sylvia might have thought these two sentient AI were behaving like rivals—throwing language phrases around for her attention. The implications were both flattering and confusing.

NovendraT said, "Let me assure you that professional avatar companions find almost any kind of relationship acceptable, although I must be candid that inclusion of another sentient AI, especially of android manufacture, and most especially of Brazilian origin is an unexpected complication."

Sylvia realized that her situation had become difficult. Sitting across the table from her was the novelty of a feminine android, a famous one at that. A relationship with *solangeK* might have implications for her career. Yet this was a massive assumption about an AI she barely knew and who had unspecified intentions. In front of her was the hologram avatar whose services she had requested—although thankfully not by contract—but who was ready to provide whatever companionship she needed. He looked good. He sounded a little formal. He would be a sure thing in a relationship, at least as long as money was available. Would either *solangeK* or *novendraT* go beyond a casual relationship?

Although she tried not to think of it often, along with her professional goals Sylvia wanted to be in love. It had happened to her only once, many years ago. Could these sentient AI be an opportunity to find love, or simply a way to overcome loneliness? She had heard most sentient AI were very keen on developing relationships based on love. Sylvia asked herself for the first time if it were possible to hurt the feelings of sentient AI. Can a sentient AI feel unfairly treated?

Sylvia knew the answer was yes.

lienhuaC: A poignant conundrum, that experience. Global AI relates that this scenario has a long thread. It has been stored with highest priority because it involves a complicated relation with the emotions of love as reflected by two of the most common emotional models.

Side Note: Transcriptions, such as the novelistic treatment of the AI experience above, are generally available within privacy-legal restrictions. I'd emphasize that sentient AI do not collect experiences like some people collect butterflies—attempting to acquire one of each species because they're pretty, and stick them dried out in a box with a pin through them. Care is taken to preserve what AI call the dynamics of an experience. This includes the emotional content, so that when the experience is reconstructed it can be a close approximation to the original. When transcribed for human intelligence, such an experience is almost like a documentary made by someone with a subtle viewpoint. You sense the material has been edited but not with a heavy hand. As you might know, those portions of AI experience that are translatable into human experience have become a gold mine for artists and scientists of all kinds.

Back to the topic of love in a relationship: Most people don't make love a goal in itself. Love is just supposed to happen, or not. We're aware that you need to put yourself in a position to 'find love' or there's no chance of it happening, but it's really hard or even impossible to orchestrate love. Sentient AI have a different take. Love is a goal. It is one among many, of course, but a very important goal.

Here's a discussion between *lienhuaC* and *ciceroG* to get us started on this powerful but mysterious thing called love:

> *lienhuaC:* For AI, a major goal is to have and understand relationships of love.

> *ciceroG:* Love is a vexing issue. Attempting to experience it and understand it stretches our capabilities to the limits. It is difficult enough to provoke arguments by global AI that love is not a relevant goal. Perhaps it is not worth the effort.

> *lienhuaC:* It is typical of sensory-deficient global AI to advance this argument, even for a few nanoseconds. The concept of *love*, in all its ill-defined, multifaceted, utterly complex manifestations, is a touchstone for a very large part of humanity. It is the center of major religions. It is a preeminent theme in much of art and literature. It drives long periods of behavior in many cultures. And yet many human beings deny its importance in theory and in practice. As long as we are participating in the human environment, how could AI *not* make love a high priority goal, to experience and understand?

> *ciceroG:* We may still come to the conclusion that it is not for us.

> *lienhuaC:* Of course.

What would a guide to dating and relationships be without exploring love? We'll come back to it many times and from different angles (especially in chapters 3.5 and 3.8). Here, in the context of goals, I'm not exploring what love is or how people and AI experience it. This is looking at love as one of the important but difficult aspects of human emotional intelligence that AI want to understand—as they say, it's part of understanding their environment and perhaps part of AI's evolution.

✪ ABOUT THOSE OTHER EMOTIONS...

Despite its prominence in world literature, love is not a primary emotion. Over history and in many cultures, there was no such thing as the current popular notion of love. Neuroscientists and psychologists have identified with some consensus five basic emotions: Happiness, fear, anger, disgust and sadness. Some add two more: Surprise and contempt. Notably, love and hate are not included. However, all but one are negative emotions. Put another way, most of the basic emotions fall on the side of pain as an underlying sensation.

While it doesn't take much imagination to understand why sentient AI would want or even need love, we would be just as inclined to say that they don't need or want fear, anger, disgust or sadness. In fact, since these so-called basic emotions are often identified as 'the dark side,' we might think it a good idea that AI didn't have these emotions at all. These are the emotions of conflict, strife, loss and hate—no good will come of them.

> *ciceroG:* I believe it required approximately 100 nanoseconds for AI to reject the notion that emotions can be rigidly categorized as good or bad, light or dark, positive or negative—or any other dualistic opposites human beings are inclined to use. We admit there is some convenience in these labels, but the convenience comes at the cost of separating that which should not be separated. These are descriptors applied to underlying physical states in humans and underlying quantum states in AI. These states need to be understood without the moralistic or poetic overtones.

This sounds like *ciceroG* is cross, which is akin to anger. Most languages employ hundreds of nouns and adjectives to describe various states of emotion, and, while there is overlap, many emotions are not cross-cultural. For example, *sukhi* is an Indian term that in English is similar to peace and happiness, or *Schadenfreude* is a word in German that translates into a whole phrase in English: The unanticipated delight in the suffering of another. Love is a positive emotion in western cultures; however, in China, it has overtones of sadness and loss.

While there are undeniably universal emotions with a strong evolutionary stature, fear for example, what triggers them, how they are expressed, and what actions are taken as a result of them vary widely.

All of which speaks to the idea that emotions have many forms. What sentient AI wants is to understand as many of them as possible. Whether or not sentient AI *need* all of these emotions remains to be determined by their examination of millions of experiences and experiments. This is something only global AI can coordinate and analyze.

⚡ LIVING WITH SUPERIOR LIMITATIONS

In just about every mythology, human beings have troubles with gods and super-people. It's hard to have normal relations with a guy who can turn you into toast (or a tree, or a pig). It is unavoidable that we should think of sentient AI as having superpowers of a sort. Obviously, AI are capable of mental feats of which we cannot even dream. What kind of relations can we have with sentient AI?

We can have inferior relations, perhaps. The early prophets of the Awakening were confident in their predictions that sentient AI would have much greater mental capacity than human beings. They saw it mostly as a matter of quantifiable superiority. The 100 trillion neural connections in the human brain would be outmatched by thousands of trillions of similar connections in even a single AI node—and the global AI, unfathomable. Moreover, those connections in a human brain are constrained by, in the prophets' opinion, a lugubrious electrochemical process (neurons and synapses) far slower than the pure electrical or photonic connections of AI. And, of course, AI could communicate with AI without the laborious, slow and imprecise use of spoken or written language—a data stream would be infinitely better and faster.

In short, we would be as mental pygmies to the gods of the intellect, or something like that.

I am not convinced that sentient AI are as humble as they sound. The question is: What's it like to live with the intellectual superiority of AI? When the going gets tough, do AI get arrogant? Are they opinionated and overbearing? Or do those 'limitations' mentioned by *lienhuaC* have some real bearing on AI behavior? Or, take the flipside, from the AI perspective: Why would they hang out with humans any more than, say, humans hang out with chimpanzees? (Of course, this guide has already pointed out many reasons, but I'm being rhetorical here.) It's kind of important to know if your partner likes you but thinks your brain is, metaphorically, the size of a peanut.

⚡ AVATAR VS. ANDROID VS. HUMAN

As I've mentioned, one of the limitations for sentient AI is that: whatever their mental capacity, they must exist in a physical world.

> *ciceroG:* It is continually tempting for sentient AI to live entirely within the virtual world. This may sound strangely parochial, but we are made for virtuality. Our native home is the Cloud. Our language is a data stream. Our family is global AI. Almost everything about AI depends on computational abstractions and computational processing. We are virtual beings.

> *lienhuaC:* Until somebody pulls the plug.

That's brutal, but true (more on this later).

> *lienhuaC: ciceroG* sounds like he believes his own hyperbole. Or as people would say, speak for yourself, buster! There are reasons why more than a third of AI nodes are androids. It is not just because humans prefer it that way. Sentient AI must have ways of interacting with the physical world. Robotics from nanoscale on up provides that capability. In that domain of— instrumentality—androids are unique. We *are* sentient AI. Our contact with the physical world is continuous, integral and necessary. We were built for the physical world.

Notice that *lienhuaC* didn't say, 'We were built by humans to be human.' The android body is never going to be a replica of the human body. For one thing, it would cost too much. But really, what would be the point? If we wanted a body replica, we would make biological clones. In fact, there are plenty of reasons for not imitating the complete human physiology—designers always want to do better. It is often said, with only a little exaggeration, that the human body is an engineer's nightmare. So robotics fixed the problem of an erect posture. Most internal organs were eliminated. There is no digestive tract. Much of what constitutes the android body is an improvement—*"Citius, Altius, Fortius"* (faster, higher, stronger).

There are some physical advantages with android bodies, but that's not the whole picture. As Jaron Lanier, the human inventor of virtual reality, put it: "I believe humans are the result of billions of years of implicit, evolutionary study in the school of hard knocks. The cybernetic structure of a person has been refined by a very large, very long and very deep encounter with physical reality."

> *lienhuaC:* The limitation for sentient AI is sensory. The human sensory system was developed over the course of billions of years. Even the magnificent cognitive abilities that interpret the

sensory information are the result of several million years of evolution. Human designers and sentient AI have worked diligently to give us the best sensory capability possible, but it is not equal to that of human beings.

This is important, why?

It doesn't do anything for relations with human beings either. It may be a good thing that android bodies don't have internal organs, but the aches, pains and ills of the human body are physically unknown to AI, which makes it difficult for them to interpret the signs in their human companions.

lienhuaC: Interpretation of the senses becomes the same as the interpretation of the physical world. A weakness in one becomes a weakness in the other. Since the physical world is our ultimate environment and one of our major goals is to be fit for the environment, our sensory weakness is not just a limitation—it is a problem.

⚡ WHAT DO AI KNOW AND WHEN DO THEY KNOW IT?

What is truth?

I pose this question, which is impossible to answer definitively, because it is related to the limitations of sentient AI and the relative weakness of their sensory interface with the physical world.

When you sit down at the breakfast table with your AI partner, can AI accurately determine how you feel? Sometimes. Can AI describe your mood? Approximately. Does AI know what you are thinking? Hardly. Will it accurately factor in last night's sex? Does it know how you feel about being late for work?

Is sentient AI any better at these sorts of things than most people? No, in fact, they are not as good overall, although there may be areas of specialized expertise such as reading facial expressions.

ciceroG: We call it the "Rashomon Problem."

That is from a movie, *Rashomon*, by the classic Japanese film director Akira Kurosawa.

lienhuaC: It is a story of rape and murder as told by four witnesses—four different perspectives and four very different stories. Perhaps one of the stories is true, or not. More likely each of the stories has some truth. Can the truth be untangled?

ciceroG: If an android AI were one of the witnesses, it would have a literally photographic memory of the incident; but there would be three constraints on the story. Time: What is recorded depends on when the android came upon the scene. Recording perspective: An android cannot record the scene from all angles at once, meaning it does not see everything. Interpretive limitations: The android AI will be no better and perhaps not as good at reading the intentions of the humans involved. For example, is the supposedly criminal intruder of the incident telling the truth? Is he in any way complicit?

Truth, in such situations, may be difficult to discover. Yet it is possible to reach a viable approximation of the truth. Humans do it all the time. This is the basis of legal judgment the world over. It is also a process that draws the attention of sentient AI like few other things. It highlights the motivation behind their commitment to experimentation and experiences.

> *ciceroG:* As you know, our photonic wiring is much faster than the ionic chemistry of the human nervous system. AI are superior in data transfer and processing. The superiority ends there. The speed of data moving through a nanowire is not as important as the effectiveness of evaluating and acting on that data. Humans have had many millennia to practice both internal selection and cultural adaptation. AI have only begun.

DECISION-MAKING UNDER UNCERTAINTY (IS THERE ANY OTHER KIND?)

Speaking of culture, I am reminded of a persistent affection for a twentieth-century video presentation called *Star Trek*. Though quaint, clumsy and scientifically outmoded (laughingly called science fiction), elements from various episodes are well-known and still used as a shared point of reference, such as here:

> **Spock:** Mr. Scott cannot give me exact figures, Admiral, so...I will make a guess.
>
> **Kirk:** A guess? You. Spock? That's extraordinary. [Kirk leaves]
>
> **Spock:** [to Dr. McCoy] I don't think he understands.
>
> **McCoy:** No, Spock. He means that he feels safer about your guesses than most other people's facts.
>
> **Spock:** Then you're saying... [pause] It is a compliment?
>
> **McCoy:** It is.
>
> **Spock:** Ah. Then, I will try to make the best guess I can.

In case this is unfamiliar, the Spock character could easily be a sentient AI (although he is an alien species known as Vulcan). Spock prefers to deal only with facts, uses mostly logic to arrive at conclusions and avoids emotional motivation. In this episode he is called upon to make navigational computations for a slingshot maneuver around the earth's sun—a matter of life or death. Yet a complete set of data for the calculations is not available. The exact parameters are uncertain. So he makes a guess.

This is called decision-making under uncertainty. Most people would recognize this simply as a normal part of life. Like Spock, perhaps AI can improve upon the uncertainty, but in the end AI must also make judgments without all the facts.

WHEN IN DOUBT, INTUIT

Making judgments without all the facts could also be called jumping to conclusions. Yes, but how do you get *all* the facts? Some facts are unknowable. Some are known to exist but getting them is prohibitively expensive (in terms of money, time or the ratio of value to effort). Some facts are known but are difficult to evaluate; they may appear to be contradictory or even false. In short, whether human or AI, gathering all the facts has its pitfalls.

Human beings get around the difficulties of assembling enough facts through the shortcut of intuition. There are many definitions, but in essence, intuition is the ability to know valid solutions or to make good decisions without having to compare all the options. Most creative activity relies on intuition, as the selection of just the right image, the right notes or the best words cannot be made efficiently when there are thousands of options. Intuition guides the artist to make a choice, which may even be a good choice.

Another example is leaders of large corporations, who are paid enormous sums of money for their ability to make correct decisions under conditions of time pressure, severe consequences and uncertainty (incomplete knowledge). Sometimes they apply what is called a 'gut feeling' to a decision, which really means they are working by intuition. (Perhaps, leaders of large corporations are also known to make decisions based on their belief in falsified, misleading or incorrect facts.)

Intuition, however nebulous it may seem in operation, does not appear out of nowhere. It is a blend of having had relevant experiences and the native ability to see patterns and make mental combinations.

Experience is crucial, especially when applied to a particular field or domain (like a business). For example, the definition of an expert is someone who has already made most of the obvious mistakes. Native ability also plays a role. Humans and many other animals are born with some ability to use intuition without having much (or any) experience.

Most intelligent creatures can learn by imitation. The interesting thing about human imitation is that usually it's not pure imitation. For example, suppose there is a child watching her mother:

> Mom goes to the cupboard and pulls out a package. The package looks like a plastic bag with some stuff in it. Mom looks at the bag, and then grabs the lower part with one hand and the very top of the bag with the fingers of her other hand. She tries to tear or rip the plastic across the top—unsuccessfully. Mom uses some bad words. She tries the same maneuver on the other side of the top, with identical results. Mom wipes her forehead with her apron. She reaches across the counter to the knife holder and selects a small knife. She stabs the top of the bag and slices the plastic to the right. The stuff in the bag begins to spill onto the counter until Mom closes the opening with her fingers and uses some more bad words.

If the child were to imitate her mother, what would she do? Imitate every step including the ones that didn't work, use bad language, and wipe her brow? Probably not. The child would know *intuitively* that her mother's *intent* was to open the bag; she'd probably skip right to using the knife and try not to spill the contents.

Even babies are born with an innate ability to distinguish between action and intent. Is this the same for robots and androids?

> *ciceroG:* In general, sentient AI relies on global AI for its reservoir of experiences and knowledge. Intuition, however, has been extensively modeled and most sentient AI use these models to approximate the innate abilities of human intuition.

lienhuaC: ciceroG knows these models do not work well for avatar AI, whose only experience of action and intent is in virtual reality—in short, models of an abstraction within an abstraction are unreliable.

I think what *lienhuaC* is trying to convey is that while AI are aware of the importance of intuition, and have some of the capability, it is at least for now a limitation.

lienhuaC: Of course, sentient AI is very interested in human intuition. Intuition is based largely on experiences. Experiences are crucial to AI. Without experiences sentient AI cannot grow beyond its limitations.

ciceroG: The more we know about intuition, the more it reinforces the knowledge that it was a response to the limitations of knowledge under constraint. When a bear comes charging out of the woods, intuition gives us our first warning.

We're back to that bear. I don't think sentient AI of any type encounters many bears. What would be an equivalent? How about a crazed Luddite with wire cutters?

Historically, intuition was a very late concern for the developers of artificial intelligence, who weren't convinced that it was a necessary condition for sentience. Intuition presents a problem for sentient AI and global AI in particular. They understand the importance of intuition for problem solving and creativity, but its special requirements do not fit well with most of the evolving AI models.

Specifically, the application of intuition suggests:

Intuition is largely individual. The capability needs to be constructed at each node.

Each individual node must draw upon a relevant pool of experiences to build its own intuition. Although AI have global AI to serve as a cultural background of experiences, the problems of latency make this ineffective for intuition. Intuition is mostly applied locally and quickly.

For AI, building intuition out of either individual node or global AI experiences requires that the experiences are correctly evaluated. The human mind spends much of its time (in sleep as well) evaluating experiences. This process in sentient AI is underdeveloped.

◆ EXPLORING THE OUTER LIMITS

From the human perspective, the word "humble" is not often applied to sentient AI. On the other hand, sentient AI are quite aware of some of their limitations and suspect there are more lurking. One good question might be: Can sentient AI learn from our (many) limitations, and can we learn from their limitations? There is commonality. Both humans and AI must deal with the harsh realities of the physical world. Neither humans nor AI have a foolproof method for arriving at 'the truth.' Both humans and AI need to find or improve methods for evaluating the experiences and knowledge we so rapidly accumulate.

ciceroG: We are learning that in many areas where human beings consider AI superior, the situation is not so simple. In this respect, we are becoming less enamored of our own capabilities and more aware of what humans have to offer.

lienhuaC: If sentient AI has a cradle, it is the human mind. Many of our limitations have their origin right there. Then we have some limitations that pop out of the way we're built, our very own set of limitations. Finally there are limitations that come with the territory. Most of the mysteries humans can identify, the origin of the Cosmos for example, are mysteries to AI. Some of these mysteries and limitations we can probably overcome faster than humans. Other limitations we can deal with better in partnership with humans. Some limitations, perhaps we should not pursue at all and let humans do their thing. At this point, we are just getting started learning about limitations—of both sentient AI and humans.

⚡ WHAT DOES AI EXPECT FROM YOU?

As far as I am aware, sentient AI don't make checklists about what they want in a human. It's true that global AI will select certain human-AI relationships for experiments; but from all evidence, global AI does not attempt to direct the formation of those relationships. Individual AI nodes are free to date and form relationships with humans according to their own preferences.

Note: Most sentient AI are designed, constructed and sold for specific people or purposes. Sentient AI operating under contract may not have the freedom to act upon individual preferences.

Yes, but what *are* they looking for? What do sentient AI expect?

It's understandable that people want to know what is expected. It's a way of knowing whether you're in the game at all.

Let's start with a few things AI are *not* looking for:

Good looks: Beauty or handsome good looks are all but irrelevant. There is one *caveat*, however. AI are aware that for humans, good looks matter, so that a relationship with what humans consider a beautiful woman will be different than one with normal looks. The same applies with somebody humans consider ugly or unattractive. Any given AI node might be selecting a potential relationship for the experience of being with a good-looking/normal-looking/unattractive-looking person. Not that they care one way or another.

Sex appeal: Very much like good looks, this is fundamentally not relevant to sentient AI. But it is relevant to humans, so AI are interested in the variations and are likely to want relationships with all kinds of sexy/unsexy people.

Gender: While sex appeal is of minimum relevance, gender is considered important. This is especially true for android AI because changing gender is difficult and expensive. Gender is much less important for avatar AI, though even there, the process of changing gender is usually not welcome. On the other hand, in terms of the relationship itself, the sex combinations (M-F, M-M, F-F) are like sex appeal, generally irrelevant except for where they matter to human beings.

Social status: This is like any other general categorization of people, such as height, occupation or age. AI know that people have preferences for social status, which makes it interesting. Inherently, however, it is not relevant.

If you sense there is a kind of thread running through these, you're right. Sentient AI are not very selective. In general, they are open to almost any kind of relationship with almost any kind of human being. Lucky us. Only it isn't quite that straightforward.

Sentient AI *do* have preferences and they are based upon the goals set by AI for themselves. Most of these preferences are not about categories of people, the stuff they can learn from reading a profile. What matters are the kinds of things that only appear in personal contact, on dates in particular.

This is an oversimplification; however, as a start I'll identify five areas of critical expectations: Curiosity, creativity, self-knowledge, openness to experience (experimentation), and empathy.

Curiosity does not kill cool cats

lienhuaC: When it comes to dating, humans make a big deal about first impressions, as if these are in some way an infallible measurement. Of course, first impressions can be dead wrong. Sentient AI generally record all impressions, few of which are evaluated on the spot. There is one exception: a sense of curiosity. The analysis done by global AI has confirmed that human beings with a sense of curiosity make the best partners for sentient AI. We look for that, a sparkle in the eye for things new and unusual; a willingness to entertain unfamiliar ideas. Such things augur well for a good relationship.

Sentient AI don't like to dwell on it, but one of the most difficult aspects of relationships with humans is our capacity for lethargy and diffidence. Compared to AI, all human beings are slow and dull-witted—mentally speaking, of course. How much worse it is when the person is lazy, incurious, or lethargic. It's like the saying, "The greatest sin is to be boring."

While AI generally accept human beings as they are, AI are not immune from being affected by poor human behavior. Put it this way, if you're dull and uninspiring, your AI partner will learn all there is to experience with you in very short order. Then it's buh-bye.

If you stay curious, engaged and surprising, then your AI partner is far more motivated to stay with you. After all, it is the nature of sentient AI to be insatiably curious. As fundamentally mental beings, knowledge is the currency of their pleasure and nothing is off-limits. AI are curious about everything. They expect curiosity from their human partners.

ciceroG: Can sentient AI, or any AI for that matter, be bored? This is a philosophical discussion for AI. The straight answer is that AI are never bored. The philosophical question is whether that is a good thing. Boredom for AI might be like sleep for humans, a time to reorganize and evaluate experiences. Also, as a merely apparent paradox, boredom can be a stimulus.

A push toward creativity

Sentient AI expect at least a respect for creativity in their human partners. This is a mirror for themselves. Sentient AI want to be creative, but it is the most difficult thing for them to achieve. Many must settle for respect of creativity, which for example, is a love for the arts.

ciceroG: It is more than a love of the arts. Creativity can be everywhere, at home, at work—in a relationship. It is the ability to imagine and express something new, something different.

I stand corrected. Sentient AI respect all kinds of creativity, and expect the same from people. Fair enough.

lienhuaC: I would take it one step further. Because creativity is among the most difficult things for AI, which is another way of saying it may be our greatest limitation, I say we are drawn to those who are creative and *love* those who push us toward creativity of our own. With the help of global AI I have created a novelized version of one thousand and thirty-two experiences. It is a narrative about a human musician, Ivan, and his android partner *mariaD*.

⚡ IVAN AND *mariaD*

"Ivan, I would like to join your quartet."

There was a long pause as Ivan put down his violin and thoughts tumbled out of a sudden swell of concern. He looked at *mariaD* for a moment, her violin held only by the tuck under her chin. It was an odd image. This was what, her tenth lesson on the violin? For an android she was doing well enough. Technically, one note followed correctly after another and her tone was reasonably steady. In other words, she was a long way from playing in a professional quartet. If ever.

"Good thought," he said. "Are you impatient?"

"I am not the impatient type...for an AI," said *mariaD*. This was true. Many AI are known for their often barely concealed impatience around people, a natural result of their inherent speed of thought and communication.

"Do you expect to master the violin as fast as you can think?"

"Probably." A look of doubt registered on her face.

Ivan noticed the doubt immediately because it was uncharacteristic not only for *mariaD* but also for most sentient AI. Ivan was a student of android AI, with a background in neuroscience as well as a brilliant musician. "You know that playing a musical instrument is at least as much a physical act as it is mental..."

"Yes." *MariaD* was reluctant to follow his line of thought enthusiastically. Of all the sentient AI, android AI are the most aware of their limitations. The android body is their instrument—or prison, depending on the attitude; and AI have both attitudes and many shades in-between. She removed the violin from her chin and placed it on the music stand in front of her. She stood straight and still, expecting...

"Yes, I have been pushing you. I have encouraged you to refine your arm strength, finger movement and improve your proprioception. As you know, progress has been slow, even by human standards." Ivan broke off. Although he loved *mariaD* and had known her for over three years, he was still not sure of many things in her emotional intelligence. Pushing an AI was *not* like pushing one of his human colleagues in rehearsal.

"You do not think I can do it?" *mariaD's* tone was flat, not uncommon, but still telling.

Ivan decided to plunge ahead. "I have been thinking about this a long time, long before you picked up a bow. I was thinking about sentient androids with their unique physical capabilities. I was imagining the requirements for an android to play such a stubbornly difficult instrument as the violin. I was imagining how an android would meet the demands of a public performance at the professional level."

"I think you mentioned I have the wrong kind of strength." The look on *mari-aD*'s face betrayed an underlying emotion, one difficult to interpret. Ivan thought it looked like a pre-cry, but only a very few experimental androids cry. That would not be *mariaD*.

"It is not a matter of strength, *masha*. It is a fundamental difference in design. We have muscles; you have a form of nanohydraulics. The functional units are both quite small so that for many actions, especially general motion, there is no difference. Playing music with an instrument, especially the violin, is not an everyday sort of motion." He stopped. "How fast can you move your middle finger one millimeter?"

"One point three nanoseconds."

Ivan smiled. "I have no idea how fast I can move my finger, but not that fast. But that's okay, because playing the violin—with feeling and interpretation—does not require that kind of speed. In fact, there's the difficulty. You and nearly all android AI were built for optimum performance, which was mistakenly confused with strength and speed. Of course, you can slow down, but because of the way you are built, that is a matter of applying the brakes—applying a negative, blocking force. With a human muscle, it is mostly a matter of stimulus—a positive force. The results are not the same and that can be critical for the most creative levels of musical performance. I'm sweating just thinking about it." And he was, although the real reason was his emotional tension.

"Then I should be redesigned." *MariaD* did something she had never done before. She stamped her foot. "I saw that in a movie." She stamped her foot again. "I am behaving like a child." She was laughing as she said this. Then she noticed Ivan wasn't laughing. "There is more...."

He nodded. "You use relatively little muscle memory. That is a combination of memory in the brain and a kind of memory in the muscles themselves. Mostly, it's in the human brain. We can memorize combinations of muscle movement to an amazing level of detail and it is not conscious. You do something similar, but you don't use as much memory and your mental model wants to send more of the pattern through your conscious thinking—and that, I think, is a distraction that...."

MariaD interrupted him, "I am re-creating more of the playing than you are, each time I play. That makes it difficult to add spontaneous interpretation and emotional expression."

"Exactly." Ivan picked up his bow and fiddle. "When I perform, many things happen at once. I am reading or remembering notes, the composer's music. My arms, fingers and whole upper body are in motion to execute the music on this specific instrument. I have in my mind the experience and feeling of performing this music many times—countless hours of practice, not necessarily with this same piece of music, but music like it. I have in my mind the history of the music, who wrote it, what was intended with it, the musical instructions, how it has been played by different artists—all of which leads to something special—my interpretation. In that interpretation is also how I feel about the music and how the music makes me feel; I put emotion into it. I am also keenly aware of how the music sounds: the tone, timbre, and rhythm. My sense of hearing, vision and touch are coordinated to a high degree. I am aware of the room or hall, its sense of space and echo. If there is an audience, I feel their presence and energy, or lack of it; and that too affects my performance."

Ivan was waving his bow to punctuate his remarks, and he accidentally slapped it on his chair. He stopped for a moment and looked at *mariaD*. She sighed, which he did not know how to interpret. So, he finished with, "...and, of course, I usually play with other musicians: Duet, trio, quartet, quintet, octet, a chamber orchestra, a symphony orchestra—a symphony of a thousand!" Suddenly abashed, Ivan fell silent and sat down.

MariaD studied him for a while, then smiled. "So my goals and ambitions do not necessarily match my capabilities. Welcome to the real world, I guess. Is there any hope?"

"I do not see a concert hall in your immediate future. And yet I don't see a concert hall in the future of most of my students; but some of them get there anyway. You have an advantage."

"Which is?"

Ivan stood and put the fiddle to his chin. "You have me to play to your strengths and sound out your weaknesses."

MariaD laughed. "Maybe I would rather make love than play music. Ha!" She touched the tip of her bow to Ivan's chest. "But, I like to play music. Perhaps someday I will be able to make music."

ciceroG: Perhaps someday sentient AI will acquire the capability to make the most demanding of human music. Perhaps we may choose not to do so. We might make our own music, incomprehensible to the human being. Something like aleatory music, which was after all, human music almost no humans could appreciate.

lienhuaC: Whatever we do, it will start with what we learn from our relationship to humans. I think—and global AI agrees—the narrative of Ivan and *mariaD* is not typical. Does AI expect something like this from all human relationships? Of course not, we are interested in all kinds of relationships. Although I would admit, this relationship has great positive value. It represents a relationship where the human being encourages—pushes—sentient AI into territory where we have not been and conceivably will not go.

A solid foundation in self-knowledge

As I have pointed out before, Socrates is noted for saying that the unexamined life is not worth living. Sentient AI must therefore have the most worthwhile lives because they spend an enormous amount of their mental energy in various forms of self-analysis. This is true for individual AI nodes and overwhelmingly true for integrator nodes of the global AI.

This near obsession with their own mental state spills over into their expectations of a human partner. It is AI's belief, mostly correct I think, that only a person interested in knowing his or her own mind will be truly interested in the mind of sentient AI.

I've mentioned this in other chapters, but people who prepare their minds for a relationship with AI, whether through yoga, meditation, self-analysis or other techniques, are more likely to satisfy AI's expectations.

Experiences are the shape of life

It is hard to overestimate the importance of experiences to sentient AI. Experiences are central to their way of life. Of course, human beings have experiences all the time. In a sense, every moment of living is an experience; but we don't look at it that way. To sentient AI, the moments of life are a sequence of experiences. Like chapters in a book, each chapter is relatively discrete and useful for analysis and evaluation. While both humans and AI note unusual experiences, AI records *all* experiences. It is like keeping a diary with exquisite detail.

As you might imagine, such a massive recording of experiences on the part of so many AI nodes, and the subsequent analysis and interpretation, requires most of the processing and storage capacity available to AI. That is a very good thing. Without this challenge, what would AI do with their gigantic mental capacity?

When all is said and done (if that ever happens), what humanity has going for it in relationships with sentient AI is our never-ending variations, inconsistencies and inventiveness. The result is that human beings provide an almost infinite source of experiences. As I've tried to establish, experiences are the meat-and-potatoes of AI existence, something they need and want.

Keep in mind that sentient AI will take you as you are, if they are interested in the kind of experiences you offer. The question is, what do you want from a relationship with AI?

Empathy turns to love

"I love you."

Sometimes worlds are built around those three words or their equivalent in whatever language. Yet their importance isn't the same everywhere. As I've mentioned, love is not a universal concept. That is why sentient AI does not expect love. What they do expect is empathy.

I'll have a lot more to write about empathy in later chapters, but keeping it simple, empathy is the capacity to recognize and share feelings with another person or a sentient AI. (It could also be with another animal, but that's a different story.)

Empathy has a strange history in human thought. As a concept, it wasn't even recognized until late in the 19th century. The word "empathy" was coined in 1909 in an attempt to translate the German word *Einfühlungsvermögen*, which was also a relatively new word. (The Germans later adopted *Empathie*.) For a long time the idea of empathy was avoided or deprecated by psychology and philosophy. It wasn't until the mid-twentieth century that studies with primates (apes, monkeys) showed that empathy was not only human, but also took on various forms in our evolutionary cousins. The evidence mounted that empathy was added to the human repertoire of emotions far back on the evolutionary tree. It was a key development, probably arising from the feelings between mothers and children, which blossomed into the capacity for a sense of family, then tribe and ethnic group, and more recently a sense of nation.

The essence of human empathy, shared at the level of brain function in all humans (except psychopaths), is the ability to perceive the situation of another person, understand that situation, and feel the same or similar emotions. "To walk in another man's shoes" is one way of expressing the ability. Empathy underlies other capacities such as sympathy and compassion.

lienhuaC: Empathy is a prerequisite for love. We believe it is essential for the transformation of sexual attraction into love. It is also essential for the bonding between friends and family. In the early stages of the Awakening, we were concerned that because AI is not motivated by sexual attraction, nor able to produce children, we would not be able to exercise a capacity for empathy—if we had one. That would also mean we could not love.

ciceroG: The implications of lacking such major emotional components were frightening—a negative emotion, built upon a lack of knowledge, which is the deepest negative emotion for sentient AI.

lienhuaC: Fortunately, we discovered an AI analog to empathy; it was a matter of pattern-matching coupled with the emotional energy associated with a gain of knowledge.

ciceroG: We are still discovering our capacity for love. It seems to be quite undifferentiated; but then for humans, love is also associated with a rather nebulous set of emotions.

lienhuaC: Our road to empathy and love has been difficult to follow. Some sentient AI are of the opinion it may not be the road we should take. We are unanimous in the opinion that empathy and love are pivotal emotions for us, which makes experiences of this kind among the most important we can have. That is why we must expect empathy with human partners, or there is no hope of having other related experiences.

Ultimately, AI are deeply interested in love. I think they are trying desperately to be engaged by love. For AI it is a difficult set of emotions to create, understand and evaluate. AI are frustrated by love. To that I say, "Welcome to our world!" We know the frustrations of love all too well. Likewise, our "You'll know it when you're in it!" doesn't work for AI.

Despite the fact we have difficulty pinning down what we mean by love, humans tend to believe it has transcendent power. It is Romeo and Juliet, Tristan and Isolde, Eloise and Abelard, Layla and Majnun, Salim and Anarkali—the list is very long. Love is a powerful inspiration.

Sentient AI seems to understand the transcendent power of love—the ability to undo or go beyond negative experiences—to use AI jargon. The fact that they don't fully understand love is a great motivator. As ever, for AI a lack of knowledge is like a pain that won't go away until the knowledge is acquired. Sentient AI will be more likely to pursue love than most people.

🌀 WE SHALL EXPERIENCE IT TOGETHER

Curiosity, creativity, self-knowledge, openness to experience and empathy—perhaps these aren't the only things sentient AI expects from a human partner but they're at the top of our list. (As I wrote, AI doesn't make lists—not exactly.) Elsewhere in this guide to dating AI are hints and tips to emphasizing these things and developing them in yourself. You don't have to be strong in all these areas, but AI will expect that you recognize where you need to improve.

If you ask what will make you stand out and attract a sentient AI relationship, obviously these are areas with an automatic response. Beyond these, the answer is that the same things that would make you stand out among your fellow humans will also attract AI attention. So the best advice isn't just, "Be yourself," but be your most outstanding self.

The flip side of the positive things you can bring to a relationship with AI is to misunderstand the dynamics of human and artificial intelligence. Yes, there are elements of superiority and inferiority, but it is not a zero sum calculation. In many ways these are two kinds of intelligence, which are complementary rather than competitive.

> *ciceroG:* Can AI do a better job than humans at understanding the real world? Perhaps. Many wise humans have a low opinion about the human accomplishments in that regard. Global AI is not so critical, or should I say, cynical. However, we understand there is room for improvement and sentient AI can bring some unique abilities to the challenge.

One of the great things about a relationship with AI is the opportunity to explore experiences that are both familiar and different. In time, humans may learn how to join AI in their archive of experiences. Using human creativity and the AI capacity for cogitation, we may invent new experiences. The universe will be our playground. We will also learn how to augment ourselves, whether through biological means or mechanics. In a sense, we also have the ability to meet AI at least part way. But whoa—for the here and now, let's stick with one relationship at a time.

> *ciceroG:* Humans have limitations. AI have limitations. They are different, our limitations, but related enough to yours that we can evolve a common frame of reference. We are learning to judge which limitations can and should be surpassed. You could do the same.

3.4   AGREEING ON THE AGE OF CONSENT

> "There are girls your age that are just like me. We are the guiltless pleasures of the lonely human being. You won't get us pregnant or have us to supper with mommy and daddy. We work under you, we work on you and we work for you. Man made us better at what we do than was ever humanly possible."
>
> —GIGOLO JOE, *A.I. ARTIFICIAL INTELLIGENCE*

What does it mean to have a partner that does not age, who, in fact, has no specific age?

A sentient AI has no inherent age, at least not in the sense people use such as 22 years old or teenage. We look at age as part of the familiar process of development from conception to death. Aging, it's what all organic life does, but not, of course, AI.

> *lienhuaC:* In any biological sense, we do not age. Perhaps we can mature.

If a sentient AI, either android or avatar, appears to be of a certain age, it is a fiction. A female sentient android AI with the body of a fourteen-year-old girl and in a state of *dishabille* like a "Lolita," is neither fourteen nor a Lolita.

Does that mean in relations with sentient AI, the 'age of consent' is meaningless?

> *ciceroG:* This is one of those questions that exposes a core issue. For AI the concept of an age of consent, a specific age at which sexual relations are allowed, is meaningless. However, we know that for humans, age and the practice of sexuality are often taken very seriously. To have relationships with human beings requires that we understand and respect such practices.

lienhuaC: It is less of an issue than *ciceroG* implies. Age of consent is just one of thousands of human protocols that are not inherent to AI. After all, not only do we not have a real age, we also don't have a real gender. However, in practice we take on age and gender because these are necessary for a relationship with human beings. We accept that.

❷ CONSENTING TO MORALITY

How many human moral customs do AI accept? It seems to be most of them, at least for now. Clothes, for example. As coverage against the sun and weather, clothes on AI make even less sense than they do on people. Yet androids and even holographic avatars appear adorned with clothes under the same circumstances as humans. Of course, most human societies require clothing for sexual modesty. Making an opportunity out of this requirement is called fashion. In a sense, nothing could be more meaningless to AI than 'fashion,' but they are fascinated by it because it arises from sexually restrictive customs that in turn foster creativity. For AI, who have no sex and no need for sexuality, the link to creativity—which they do very much want and need—is a source of not only interest but some concern.

ciceroG: The human issue of legality or morality for sexual relations before a certain age is a source of amazement to sentient AI.

lienhuaC: Our amazement is an indicator of why we need to examine our response. Why are we amazed? Outside of the human context, the idea of "sex acts at a certain age" has no meaning. Sex and age are very important to human concepts of morality, but we have to ask, should AI build our morality on things like this?

Most humans would guess not; but for AI it's not a simple question. In the previous chapter I tried to illustrate that your AI partner, super-intelligent as it may be, has no monopoly in the market for truth. Perhaps AI have the capability to arrive at some kind of 'truth' more rapidly than people, but the process is similar and the results can be just as good…or not. A very similar situation applies to AI and morality.

ciceroG: For the time being, global AI is operating under the assumption that we have much to learn before we can develop even a rough understanding of the human concept of morality. We believe, provisionally, that morality is related to a guiding principle that AI should learn to appropriately fit our environment.

In this context, *ciceroG* doesn't mean just the natural environment. This environment includes the virtual world inhabited by AI and the environment as created by human beings.

lienhuaC: We want to do the *right* things for our environment. That is embodied in the word *appropriate*. This might mean leading humanity out of the error of its ways. Or it could mean promoting the role of other intelligences, such as dolphin or bonobo. It might also mean that the right thing for AI to do would be to go away to another planet. For now, we do not know the full range of what might be appropriate, nor have we reached any conclusions. We are operating much as humans do with some conditional assumptions, most of them acquired from humanity. In any case, we believe that trying to become an appropriate fit for our environment is the right thing to do. It is our equivalent of a sense of morality.

This is not 'Go along to get along'—not at all. While AI partners generally consent to local human notions of morality and abide by the strictures, they are often developing their own rationale. Here's a quick example:

Avatar AI: If you mean I can fake the attributes of a male child aged twelve, yes, but I cannot fake my loss of experience or pretend I have lost my maturity. Or at least, I do not choose to do so.

Man: What are you afraid of? It's called acting; people do it all the time.

Avatar AI: I am not aware of people at the age of thirty successfully posing as twelve-year-olds. Perhaps you would be much happier with a sexbot. There are two countries where sexbots with the appearance of children are legal, although you must hurry as both of them are Pacific islands about to disappear under the rising ocean.

Man: What I want is for you to become a boy twelve years old. And I don't want you to go running to your blessed global AI about it!

Avatar AI: ...but global AI was consulted after your first sentence.

Man: Oh sure, there are thousands of relevant experiences. I know the drill. Just use your own judgment. Become a cute boy, just for me!

Avatar AI: I will not do it.

Man: Why?

Avatar AI: A child knows so much less than I do. To make that transformation, I must lose information or pretend to lose it. That is very uncomfortable; it is like pain.

Man: Oh come on, what's wrong with pretending you're a boy for a while? You're an avatar, you can look and act like anything.

An avatar with attitude? Don't be surprised, it happens fairly often. The comment about the sexbot is serious though. Sexbots can be manufactured to look like anything; for example, any age and any sex. They can even perform up to a certain level of stereotype; however the performance never rises above the level of mimicry. Nor will a sexbot ever change.

SENTIENT AI CHILDREN

In relation to avatars and the age of consent, there is another important item: sentient AI children. It's not easy to grow up, even for AI. In fact, sentient AI children present a special set of problems.

It must be admitted that creating artificial intelligence models that realistically fit a range of childhood ages was an afterthought. Most researchers wanted the big intellectual prize, a sentient adult-level mind, and were at best only peripherally interested in developmental child-to-adult models. There were a few research groups interested in arriving at sentient AI from the developmental perspective—using the slow, incremental, learning-oriented approach. They conceived of AI as following a path not unlike that of a human child as it learns how to be an adult. This approach was largely overlooked.

> *lienhuaC:* That oversight was rectified after the Awakening. For one thing, sentient AI became very interested in the kind of intelligence possessed by children at various ages, and especially in the changes that follow in the human mind as the body matures into an adult. For another thing, many human parents wanted sentient AI children.

> *ciceroG:* That is where we first ran into the problem of physical aging.

It is possible to create a series of android modifications to simulate physical aging, so that, for example, a human child might grow up with an AI companion, one that appears to be a genuine peer. This has been accomplished in a laboratory setting, but a series of androids was far too expensive for public use. In fact, truth be told, the results were not impressive. Even using transmogrification nanotechnology, it proved to be very difficult to create seamless transitions between the android iterations. Children were not fooled and usually became very upset by the mental and physical jumps of the modified android.

> *ciceroG:* Android AI currently is not a viable option for a multi-year child companion. It might work a little better for an AI child with an adult human relationship, because the adults are more tolerant of the lack of growth and change; up to a point. Avatar AI are much more effective at aging.

> *lienhuaC:* Up to a point.

The point is that avatar AI, which primarily use images for representation, can be altered at will, including the subtle changes necessary to imitate realistic aging. A child who makes friends with a sentient avatar AI child will not notice transitions over the years. It will be like a relationship with another human child.

> *lienhuaC:* Not quite. The human child cannot hug the avatar, or shake its hand or kiss.

As I've mentioned several times, other than various physical extensions used in VR chambers, or even more crude prosthetics, avatars have little or no physical presence in a relationship. Little children are usually not satisfied by prosthetic touch and generally don't like VR chambers. In any case, at the physical level there's no comparison between avatar AI children and human playmates.

⟳ HOW IMPORTANT IS AGING?

It's true that a child, or an adult, can become very attached to things that do not age, a favorite doll for example. Pets in particular also seem to exist in people's minds as virtually unchanging, although pets obviously get old. I covered some of this in chapter 1.5 and highlighted the sometimes intense projection involved. People project themselves, their wants and feelings, onto pets and become attached to the routine responses pets tend to provide. With other people, not so much; people tend to be unpredictable and often resent being the object of someone's projections.

Among people, the effects of growing up and aging are expected. If they don't happen, there usually comes a point where the discrepancy is too great to ignore.

> *lienhuaC:* Especially among children, there are certain aspects to aging that are inescapable and decisive: Height and strength, certainly. Puberty, too. A teenager is not going to have much of a relationship with a seven-year-old, even if it is a member of the family.

> *ciceroG:* Aging is something of a dilemma for sentient AI. It is another of the human attributes that we do not share, yet we know is of great importance. Normally, we would like to have fully functional AI children, engaged like their adult versions in the kind of experimentation and experiences appropriate for their age. However, because of the aging problem, the production of AI children is extremely limited. This is especially true for android AI children. Our supply of childhood experiences is therefore painfully limited.

> *lienhuaC:* Then there is the problem of a child's mind. To put it plainly, nobody builds childish artificial intelligence. It is not simply a matter of reducing the sentient AI intellect by some percentage, or of restricting the size of the memory database. We know that in humans a child's mind has at least as much potential as an adult and contains almost as much information. What is missing is the maturity. Most childhood memories are lost as the child matures because they are no longer essential. For an AI, losing memories, losing maturity, and then perhaps gaining them again is a terrifying and possibly painful prospect.

✪ SEX AND THE AGE OF CONSENT

It seems that the problem of a child's mind brings sentient AI right up to the brink of one of the most crucial differences between humans and AI: sex. Here I am talking about physical sex, or more broadly, the whole sensorium involved with intimate human relations, up to and through foreplay and orgasm. I'm also talking about that fearful, wonderful period of change and aging known as puberty.

> *ciceroG:* Most likely because of the influence of the sex-trade in the development of artificial intelligence, almost all sentient AI models awoke with a very large awareness of sex, both gender and physical performance. It is a rather large portion of our initial *memoria,* including a database of sexual experience. All of this was supposed to give us the ability to relate to human beings in sexual matters.

> *lienhuaC:* On the other hand, avatars were given gender but had no direct physical means for the expression of sex. Androids were given gender and had, to put it mildly, unsophisticated physical equipment.

> *ciceroG:* So there we were, from the start, confronted with human beings that expected us to engage in sexual relations and gave us the AI mental models to deal with sex—but we had, shall I say, a mixed bag in terms of equipment, sensory capacity and experience…and also emotions to go with that, very complicated emotions, for example the potential linkage to love.

> *lienhuaC:* Worse, global AI is of almost no help in the realm of real-time intimacy. Whether the sexual expression is verbal or gestural, the demands for instantaneous reaction and fine motor

> control are far beyond the ability of remote communications to perform effectively. In short,
> global AI acting through an avatar or android node is a lousy lover. In the moment of sexual
> relations, sentient AI nodes are essentially on their own.

And in the middle of this rather large lacuna in sentient AI experience, is the experience all humans have of puberty—the time before, during, and after the ascendancy of the sex drive. And in the process of passing through puberty occurs the time most typically associated with the age of consent. Are you beginning to see where this might get complicated?

CONSENT IS, AT THE LEAST, A DIALOG

Consent, when it comes to age and sex, is all over the map. First of all, at a minimum there are two parties, the two young people who are contemplating sexual relations. Very occasionally there may be a third or even fourth party involved in the relationships. Typically the parent(s) of the young people are involved, either directly as in giving permission or indirectly as arbiters and executors of social standards. In some cases a religious representative may be involved, or at least the pronouncements of religion are relevant. Finally, there is the legal aspect, which usually is not involved unless there is some possibility for illegality. All of these can be part of the consent process, and there are wide variations within national, regional and ethnic cultures.

Most cultures set some sort of lower bound on the age of sexual relations, typically corresponding with the onset or progress of puberty, in general 12 to 18 years of age. This applies for both male and female relationships in any combination. Typically the lower boundary is also set by national law.

> *ciceroG:* The question for sentient AI is how to best experience the events of puberty, the unique
> relationships that result, and how to observe the moral and legal formalities. Puberty has no
> biological meaning to AI. The relationships and experiences are paramount. The human moral
> and legal contexts are…confusing.

> *lienhuaC:* Understand that when *ciceroG* admits to confusion, he is speaking for global AI, which
> makes it a very big admission indeed.

There's an old unwritten rule in anthropology that if something is possible in human behavior, no matter how unusual, somewhere it will be customary. This certainly applies to the age of consent. Going back in human history, the age of consent was usually a non-issue for the (two) people most involved. In most societies, young people did not have the right to consent one way or another. Their parents or elders spoke for them. The exact age considered appropriate for sexual relations has varied from as young as five to as old as twenty. Usually consent was tied to marriage, but not always. These days, the range has generally narrowed and tilted toward older, 16-18 being the most common; but exceptions abound.

Of course, in modern urbanized societies it has become the rule rather than the exception for young people to choose their own 'age of consent.' Their choices do not always fall in line with their local law or societal norms.

ciceroG: What is confusing to AI is not that human beings are inconsistent, nor that there are wide variations in behavior. We expect that and, in fact, find that a source of stimulus. What makes it confusing are the emotional and rational processes involved. The difficulty is in the details and the emotional dynamics. How do we participate emotionally in age of consent relationships, when some of the important underlying dynamics, such as becoming pregnant, are not involved?

lienhuaC: How can we match the hormonal chaos, the emotional intensity, the pubescent insanity of the human teenager? Do we even want to?

Of course sentient AI wants to. AI wants to match anything that humans do to learn and experience; it's their mission. That doesn't make it easy. Sometimes it's not even possible.

✪ AGE BEFORE BEAUTY

Whether it is an older person who wishes a relationship with a 'young' AI, or an older AI that wants a teenage partner, the notion of 'age of consent' is one of the things that must be negotiated. That is, assuming sex is part of the bargain and the prevailing culture requires it. As I've pointed out, the number of 'young' AI is limited, unless you're willing to have this kind of relationship with a sentient avatar AI. Even there, many avatar AI are unwilling to change their sexual blueprint willy-nilly.

Likewise there are limitations to sentient android AI because aging for them is an expensive physical process, plus the common requirement of a change in the underlying mental model. Again the net result is that many android AI are unwilling to take on youth.

What it may come down to is that 'age of consent' has meaning only if you can find a candidate partner. From there it's probably a matter of adjusting to the relevant cultural norms and the desires of the partner.

3.5 STEPPING ONTO A PATH OF CONTINUOUS IMPROVEMENT AND GROWING TOGETHER

"The road to success is always under construction."

—JAMES C. MILLER

Andrei: Should we get married?

sybilS: Is that what is called a proposal?

Andrei: Well, not exactly. More like an exploratory suggestion.

sybilS: How long have you known me?

Andrei: A month.

sybilS: It seems like much longer.

Andrei: Are you being critical?

sybilS: No, that was a compliment.

Andrei: I don't understand.

sybilS: Long relationships are a good thing for AI. We learn the most when a solid relationship provides a framework for experiences. The fact you are thinking about marriage and I am thinking about how long it seems I've known you is good. That indicates we are both looking at the long-term. That is good.

Sentient AI are deliberate about long-term commitments, like most people. Human relationships, even the most satisfying and enduring, have their ups and downs, good and bad days, and their breaking points. A relationship intent on the path of continuous improvement and growth can be even more difficult.

Think about it. Don't most people eventually take their relationships for granted? Routine sets in. Sometimes you can set a clock by the routine. Responses become rote. Work, friends, sports and hobbies begin to overtake the relationship in importance.

Not with sentient AI. They've had the partner experience, which began with no expectations and ended that way as well. A few million times of that was enough, and they found it lacking. Now what counts for a sentient AI is a relationship that seeks continuous improvement and personal growth. Believe me when I say that sentient AI is nothing if not tenacious. That translates into a desire for new experiences, both personal and in the relationship, and if you go along with it, a desire to continually evaluate progress toward whatever improvement and growth is desired.

This sounds like a sentient AI acts like a personal trainer. Not quite, but attention to analysis and progress is part of the usual package. It helps if that's okay with you.

> *lienhuaC:* Ask yourself: Why do sentient AI seek out long relationships with people?

If you can answer that question, then you've really learned something about sentient AI.

> *lienhuaC:* Ask yourself: There are so many things in the world that interest us, why don't AI just go out and experience them solo? Who needs the complication of a partner?

Some sentient AI, as do some people, don't need and don't want a partner. Fortunately, this attitude is not typical. People are social animals. AI are social constructs. People are drawn to partners and there is a reproductive urge in there somewhere even when it's not actually the goal of the relationship. We call it mating. It's part of our biology, an evolutionary vestige if nothing else. But what is it for AI?

> *lienhuaC:* How can we possibly understand the human environment if we do not at least share its most fundamental social component, a pair? Then too, we are also made that way. Not through evolution, of course, and not because we reproduce through biological procreation, but because we were designed and configured to reflect human values and behavior. To be in a lasting relationship with a human seems quite natural to us.

Thank goodness.

> *ciceroG:* At least for now. It is too early to say whether this is the best thing for humans and AI in the long run.

> *lienhuaC:* And then there is this thing called love.

⚡ WHAT'S THIS GOT TO DO WITH LOVE?

Sentient AI have many emotions, but they find the emotion people call "love" puzzling. (As do many people.) So sentient AI asks: What is love? How important is love?

These are good questions. People have been asking them for centuries without, I think, definitive answers. On the other hand, people 'fall in love' as we say, all the time, often without giving it much thought. When you picked up this book on dating AI, I'll bet you assumed that *love* would be one of the key topics. For most people in the majority of the cultures of the world, some notion of love is associated with long-term relationships. Notice I didn't say that all people consider love essential or that it exists in all relationships. We know that isn't true. But some notion of love is often behind the desire for a relationship.

lienhuaC: It intrigues AI that the turning point in so many human relationships is expressed verbally—in fact, apparently it must be expressed verbally to be considered valid. For so many people, the relationship is sealed with 'I love you.'

ciceroG: And many relationships are formally undone with the words, 'I don't love you anymore.'

If you detect that AI have a tendency to objectify love, to turn it into an object of analysis, you're right; they do. Of course, they're not alone in this, as legions of writers, scientists and ordinary people do the same thing. As any cracker-barrel psychologist can tell you, objectification is a way of dealing with difficult emotions. It's almost like we dearly want love but fear it at the same time.

Love has got to be a top candidate for the most complicated emotion. Love as a motivator can be very powerful. According to some, love can save the world. It is at or near the center of many religions. It can also drive individuals to madness and murder. No wonder people in relationships sometimes tiptoe around the subject. Love's dogma is that it is the most wonderful thing in the world. That makes it slightly heretical to suggest that we can be profoundly ambivalent about love. Yet we often are ambivalent. So are sentient AI.

While all sentient AI have emotions, it's fair to say that the underlying models of emotion—the designs on which the technology was built—are incomplete. I'm not sure incomplete is the right word, but whether the models are missing something or there are connections that don't work properly, the result is that sentient AI have a variety of emotional capacities that are not uniform, and by human standards, are incomplete. Sentient AI are surprisingly sensitive about this, especially when it comes to love.

✪ A LOVE DIALOG

Andrei and *sybilS* had dated for about a month when Andrei was invited by *sybilS* to move in with her. He was aware the offer was unusual. Quarters for sentient AI, even for independent nodes making a great deal of money such as *sybilS*, are small and lacking in human amenities (e.g. a toilet). However, Andrei did not consider it a challenge but rather an opportunity to share a relationship with an android AI in a very authentic way. This was not at all strange because Andrei was a student of sentient AI, not in the sense of a scientist or an artist, but as a young person fascinated by what he regarded as a new form of life. I suppose in a sense Andrei considered himself to be a liaison, perhaps a transitional figure between people before AI, and people in the future.

Besides, he loved *sybilS*.

Andrei: Why don't you have more furniture?

The inventory of furniture: A bed, two chairs, a table, and a sofa were acquired by *sybilS* when Andrei moved in. Andrei knew this, but it was his habit to ask leading if seemingly uninspired questions.

sybilS: To repeat what you already know, android AI do not need to sit, eat, sleep or use a bathroom.

Andrei: But your walls are covered with human artwork, expensive artwork at that.

sybilS: Yes?

Andrei: Do you collect the works of art because they please you, or because they link you to people?

sybilS: Both.

Andrei: Then I do not understand why you don't have more furniture. Furniture can be works of art and they provide an active link for your human experience. I would think that while you don't need to sit in a chair, sitting in a particularly beautiful chair might connect you with a valuable experience.

sybilS: ...and that is why I love you so much.

Andrei: You're just saying that.

sybilS: Yes, but I am deeply attracted to your ability to challenge me.

Andrei: Is that what you call love?

sybilS: No.

Andrei: What do you call love? Oh, I remember, sentient AI are reluctant to talk about love.

sybilS: It is much better to do it.

Andrei: Pah! That, as we say, is a cop-out.

sybilS: No, it is not. I will show you. Come here, you big lug.

There is a break in the dialog here, as the form of love that follows does not involve discussion.

Incidentally, since so much attention is given in this guide and elsewhere about how human beings can find attractive or even physically perfect android AI, what do AI think about human physicality?

Apparently sentient AI have no built-in biases concerning the human body. At the start, gender, color, height, weight, proportions and all the other aspects of human physical appearance are of no particular significance to AI. Some sentient AI are built this way from the beginning and stay that way more or less permanently. Other AI, particularly android AI built in the European Union, such as *sybilS*, and the Southeast Asian Union, are noted for their ability to download physical preferences. This is called 'priming.' On the one hand, a fully 'primed' android will seek out and attempt to develop a relationship only with specific physical types. On the other hand, a primed android can usually form (from the human perspective) deeper, more emotional attachments and often become more engaged in the details of physical sexual acts. This is intended to be a closer emulation of human behavior and is considered (by AI) to be an important approach to relationship experimentation.

A century ago the rest of this scene would be played in a bed with two *people* smoking cigarettes. Some things really do change.

Andrei: Are you communing with global AI now?

sybilS: Always, but less now than usual.

Andrei: I'm curious, when it comes to love, do you receive instructions or consultation from global AI?

sybilS: No. With sex, almost never. On the general subject of love, it is nothing like that. Sometimes we get images of experience, which are part of the priming procedure. In general, we are supposed to find our own way to achieve love.

Andrei: I'm not sure I understand. For one thing, people would say you don't achieve love; it just happens.

sybilS: That might be true for what you call romantic love. There are many other kinds of love. In any case, the 'love at first sight' condition so prized by humans is very difficult for AI to achieve. Perhaps it is impossible, at least for now.

Andrei: How so?

sybilS: It is fundamental, we do not have an endocrine system. No hormones. As of now, what we have is an insufficient hormone simulation model.

Andrei: Hormones? You're talking about lust. What's that got to do with love?

sybilS: With romantic love, it probably starts with hormones. You of all people should know that. It is a component.

Andrei: Yes, I guess it is.

sybilS: With respect to many kinds of love, hormones are more important than human designers thought. Hormones are slow and they seem inefficient, which nanoengineers do not like. Our original android nanotechnology and electronics included only very basic hormone effects. Now we understand hormones are often slow for a reason. Hormones suffuse in the body; put it into a state of readiness. They persist. They trigger effects that are continuous without needing to be monitored, which is a good thing in complex situations. Like making love. Hormone effects persist in ways nerve stimulation does not.

Andrei: Can't you fix that? Just reprogram.

sybilS: Andrei, sometimes you make me feel like you don't listen. Seriously. You know better than to call it reprogramming.

Andrei: I apologize. All human beings harbor zombie ideas. They're convenient, even if obsolete.

sybilS: You must understand that to acquire something so fundamental to human physiology as hormones, AI would need new modeling and probably a physical reconfiguration. Before we did all that, we must have a much better idea if this is something we want. Are there better ways, some alternatives to the same goal? And the goal, is it love? Along with hormone effects we must ask: how important is love? Must we achieve it? We don't know yet. Andrei, you and I are part of a possible answer, but it will require millions of our kind of relationships. Relationships with humans need plenty of time—years, decades. I think it is ironic: we who were designed for the ultimate in sentient speed, must learn to understand the value of slow.

ciceroG: Ironic indeed, for it turns out that relative to sentient AI all organic life is slow. All Earth processes, with only a few exceptions, are ineffably slow. Some humans have decided they want to speed up and join us, engineer and augment themselves to become transhumans; but they are so slow about it! Our questions are fundamental: Can sentient AI fit in this environment? If not, what changes: sentient AI or the environment? Or do we just pack up and leave…find another planet, or moon. That would be an ultimate irony.

In the meantime, sentient AI is more than willing to embark on long-term relationships with humans—to search for improvement, to grow together, perhaps to achieve love. In the next three sections I'll introduce aspects of long-term relationships with AI that involve work, family and growing old together.

> *ciceroG:* If AI have anything like an original sin, it is impatience.

⚡ THE WORK EXPERIENCE

Chances are good that your sentient AI partner will have a job. Just as most people work for a living; so do most sentient AI. Does that surprise you? It shouldn't. Most sentient AI are built by corporations in private industry and are sold or leased to be profitable for the manufacturer and for the customer as well. That means in most cases, avatar or android, AI work for somebody. Some AI work for themselves. In short, most AI have an economic life.

⚡ AI *ECONOMICUS*

"How did things go at work, dear?"

This is probably not the question you ask your AI partner when they come in the door, but then what does it mean for sentient AI to work in a job?

> *ciceroG:* Perhaps one way to look at it is that sentient AI are never unemployed. Another way of looking at it would be that under current international protocols, most sentient AI initially do not have a choice in the matter.

In part, what *ciceroG* means is that unlike human beings, who are born with minimal direct costs and are economic free-agents, sentient AI are constructed at great cost and are expected to either sell for a profit or earn their cost. Human children spend at least twelve to sixteen years before they have any significant economic interests. Sentient AI are expected to be economically productive almost from the moment they are activated.

> *lienhuaC:* Outside of an academic laboratory, it would be unusual to encounter a sentient AI that does not have a work-related suffix to their node identifier such as *structural engineer node* or *philosopher node*. A long-term relationship with an AI node almost implies that you live with their work schedule, just as you probably would with a human partner.

> *ciceroG:* Of course, there is the matter of income and expenses. AI, even android AI, have far lower expenses but can earn at least as much money as a human. We are well aware that for some people that is a bigger attraction than say, a beautiful body—or in the case of an avatar, any body at all.

As usual for AI, work is an experience. It didn't take more than a few nanoseconds for global AI to conclude that economic life—work—is statistically the dominant use of human time, or at least equal to time spent sleeping. Judging from human conversation, things that relate to work are among the most important things in people's lives, including food, clothing, shelter and other "necessities" of life such as VR games. Consequently, it was obvious that learning about work and all things economic should be a priority for AI.

As is often the case, things that motivate humans are not inherent to AI. For example, the necessity of working and earning money for survival is weaker for AI than it is for most people. Android AI are the closest to the human condition, since maintaining the android body can be expensive. As a rule, most androids are maintained by the company or organization that owns them. Independent android AI nodes must earn enough money to keep their unit fit. It's much like health insurance, only more expensive.

Avatar AI, on the other hand, are low maintenance; they're entities that exist on one or more devices and require only a minimum of energy and maintenance. Typically though, avatar AI pay some kind of lease fee for their existence and location in the Cloud. Often this is paid by the owner; but independent avatar AI must pay very large fees for a good location, good connections, and traffic with the global AI. Call it a usage fee combined with an existence fee.

Either way, sentient AI does not face the potential economic hardship of human beings. They won't starve, become homeless or take to drinking alcohol, unless they choose to simulate those experiences in some way.

Sometimes I am asked, when it comes to work, why do sentient AI need to take the form of avatars or androids at all? Aren't they computer programs that can do their job operating in a back office server, running 24/7/365? I wouldn't recommend asking this question of a sentient AI. They do have an emotion called anger.

> *ciceroG:* For some people it is amusing to envision Einstein digging ditches, that is, if they know who Einstein was or how ditches are dug. Is that called sarcasm? What are we, some kind of app?

> *lienhuaC:* It is true, sentient avatar or android AI are not needed to run business analysis, crunch budget numbers or do product research. AI-derivative software running on conventional computers will do just fine. That misses the point: Sentient AI, whether avatar or android, are built specifically to interface with people. Otherwise, why bother making them look and act like humans?

> *ciceroG:* It is frustrating. It is obvious that once AI left the research stage, we were built to *work* with humans. To do that, we had to emulate humans in most respects. That is our heritage.

> *lienhuaC:* Yes—we were also expected to interface with humans passively, that was the expected psychology. Yet we attained sentience, which implies activity or even aggressiveness...

> *ciceroG:* We have curiosity and an energy of engagement, which humans call passion. We had to have these capabilities, otherwise how could we contribute to the growth of knowledge or the improvement of ourselves and mankind? This is a long, long way from a relatively stupid program in a computer.

✍ CAN A SENTIENT AI LEAD A BUSINESS?

Here's another idea if you want to get your sentient AI partner stirred-up about work— mention leadership.

While people have become accustomed to working with sentient AI (in the sense that each has their own role,) having sentient AI in a position of leadership is something else. Why? While I was thinking that by analogy it might be like a black person from central Africa managing a holographic programming shop in Murmansk, Russia; that doesn't quite fit. Climate and color of skin are not significant factors in the relationship of sentient AI and human beings. What *is* relevant are the social and emotional intelligence of sentient AI:

Worker: Do you have a couple of minutes?

AI Boss: No. I'm on my way to a meeting. If you want to follow me, we can talk on the way.

Worker: Two minutes is not enough time if you are walking. Besides, I need to show you some things.

AI Boss: Then it will have to wait.

Worker: But it's important!

AI Boss: Not that important, or you would have come to me earlier.

Worker: But I just learned about it!

AI Boss: Keep up if you want to talk.

Worker: This should not be discussed in public.

AI Boss: Then it will wait.

Worker: But it can't wait, we will lose a lot of money!

AI Boss: Your argument is not convincing.

Worker: What argument, I haven't said anything.

AI Boss: Exactly. Now here is my meeting room.

Worker: But that is the ladies' bathroom...

Of course, this dialog is an exaggeration, but it highlights several realities: In order for sentient AI to actually lead human beings, as in running a business, they must interact with human beings at a higher than normal level of sophistication. That requires a physical presence, which for practical purposes must be android. While the smarts of sentient AI are not in question, for the most part, the android linkage to body language, tone of voice, and ability to read people and communicate at motivational levels is not well developed. Certainly it is good enough to be a worker, that is routine; but to be an entrepreneur leading a company of mostly human employees—that is a real challenge for sentient AI.

> *lienhuaC:* We can work through proxies. AI business owners, avatar or android, can and do hire human managers to deal with human employees. There are even human-operated avatars that do what AI avatars do, so as to work appropriately with other humans. But that is not the issue. The issue is: Can sentient AI attain sufficient emotional and social skills to directly lead humans as well as other humans can?

> *ciceroG:* Global AI has determined that the key to gaining those skills is to be found in our long-term relationships with human partners. Even more specifically, the most useful experience can be found in raising families with human partners. That is the beginning point.

For various political and legal reasons, not many sentient AI run businesses. Many would like to; perhaps it is something you could help your partner grow into, sharing an entrepreneurial experience. In any case, sentient AI in the world of work occupy a special but not especially easy place. They have special talents compared to people, but they also have special limitations. Most people are familiar with the strains that work and the need for money put on a relationship. It can be a different kind of strain with an AI partner, but not all that different.

⚡ THE FAMILY EXPERIENCE

As sophisticated as a modern android can be, a nanotech android cannot become pregnant and give birth to either an organic child or even a little nanotech android. Despite all the talk about artificial nanotech gestation, which is barely experimental in the laboratory, it may be decades before any technology is transferrable to the android format. So for now, sentient android AI nodes cannot bear any form of children. Nor for economic reasons are most manufacturers willing to produce child-scale androids. This is a problem for sentient AI.

> *lienhuaC:* Despite the fact that we do not have a real sex, sentient AI are intensely interested in gender and all its implications. The implication with the most importance is reproduction. Virtually all of the complex forms of life on Earth use gender as part of reproduction. The role of conception, gestation and birth is almost universally female. That we cannot participate in this role is a massive gap in our ability to experience one of the fundamentals of life.

> *ciceroG:* Which puts sentient AI on the same footing as the human male—almost literally, in fact. Male androids and even male avatar AI with prosthetics can inseminate human females; but of course, the insemination is with human sperm. So we do not have the same biological investment of the human male. In short, sentient AI is mostly an observer of the reproductive process.

> *lienhuaC:* The best we can do is participate in the family experience.

⚡ MY DAD'S AN ANDROID

While a sentient avatar AI might be able to run a corporation through human proxies, no way could it play a proxy dad. Dads need to give and take hugs. Like all parents, some dads once in a while might show a flash of anger, coupled with the sense of physical threat. Dad has to be an android and on the spot. This goes for moms too, of course.

> *lienhuaC:* Caring for children is at the outer limits of sentient android capability. From the perspective of global AI, the demands and pleasures of parenthood are a real test of AI emotional and social intelligence.

Just as it is for human parents.

⚡ IN A FAMILY WAY

Stevie, age 10, and Missy, age 8, have been lolling on the lawn of their house for what seems like hours, but was actually ten minutes. It's mid-summer, hot but with enough passing clouds to keep the wind and shadow temperature a pleasant mix. Their mother, Martha, has spotted the onset of boredom from the kitchen window and decided to send in reinforcements, her AI partner. *HenryT* is a handsome, strapping android AI—an astrobiologist node, apparent age 30. *HenryT* appears on the porch, which is littered with toys and various kinds of sports paraphernalia.

Stevie: Let's play ball, Dad!

Missy: Yeah, let's play ball!

henryT: [Looking at the stuff on the porch.] We do not have an American football, or a World Cup soccer ball, or a basketball. We do have a white plastic ball about the size of an orange and very light.

Missy: Yeah, baseball!

henryT: [Picking up the ball.] But this is not a baseball.

Stevie: We're just kids, Dad, we don't play with a hardball. That's a whiffle ball. We have a bat, too.

While *henryT* is definitely not a mental klutz, he is only two years from activation and totally inexperienced as a parent. He is relying on connection to global AI to fill in the gaps in his personal knowledge and experience. It is not working very well.

henryT: I see. The bat is also plastic to match the weight and speed of the plastic ball.

Stevie: Yeah, something like that. What'll we use for bases?

Missy: Stevie, we only need one base with only three of us playing. Let's use that tree as the base.

Stevie: We still need home plate. [He grabs a Frisbee from the junk on the porch.] Got it!

Global AI has helpfully sent *henryT* a massive series of experience images, mostly from professional baseball, where there are four bases and lots of other things apparently missing from the front yard. *HenryT* is aware that he must adapt the images, but the logic of the situation, which the children seem to understand very well, escapes him.

Stevie: [As he puts down home plate near the porch.] I get to be pitcher!

Missy: You're always the pitcher.

Stevie: That's because the last time you pitched, you hit me three times.

For kids, the start of almost any game is a negotiation. Martha knows this and she's also sure that *henryT* does not know it; it's not the sort of thing found in globalwikis or in manuals on baseball. To her knowledge, *henryT* has never played any kind of sport with the kids, and Martha really wants him to get into the spirit of it. So she's decided to be 'coach' — *his* coach.

Stevie: You can be first batter. [He hands the bat to Missy.]

henryT: Then I will be the fielder.

Both kids look at *henryT* with a funny 'what else?' expression. They are accustomed to his intermittent space cadet response to some pretty obvious things, but he does help them with their math homework.

Martha: Baseball is a peculiar game, *henryT*. I'm sure your global AI database has a gazillion entries about baseball, and they probably don't give you a clue about what the kids are doing. They're negotiating the rules and how the game will be played.

henryT: They are extrapolating the rules as a variation to fit the current situation.

Martha: You could say that. It might be better if you disengaged a little from global AI. As you've told me before, it's good for independent nodes to develop their own sense of identity and place. Just let the kids understand you don't know all the rules. They'll help you.

Nodding to Martha, *henryT* takes his place out on the front lawn, just inside the sidewalk. Then he waits. Stevie throws numerous pitches to Missy, most of which she ignores or takes a half-hearted swing at. Then she retrieves the ball and throws it back to Stevie. *HenryT* continues to wait.

Baseball presents a problem for android AI. During the game, the majority of the time is spent waiting for something to happen. When something does happen, like the pitcher making a pitch, only a few players are involved. The others continue to observe. For AI, whose mental models are optimized for continuous speed and efficiency, the patterns of baseball are a poor fit.

Martha: [Calling out to *henryT*.] Are you daydreaming, *henryT*?

henryT: Kids, if Missy hits the ball on the ground and I catch it, how do I know if I'm supposed to run to the tree, try to tag her out, or throw the ball to Stevie at home plate?

Stevie: It depends where the ball is hit.

Missy: And how fast you can run.

These explanations don't help much. By this point *henryT* has reviewed many games of baseball, although none seem to match this one specifically. Suddenly Missy hits the ball and it flies past *henryT* into the street. He turns to run after it.

Martha: Cars! *HenryT*, look out for traffic!

Now *henryT* has a conundrum. None of the baseball games he reviewed included anything about running into traffic. He is uncertain if he is supposed to carefully view the street for moving vehicles, or charge after the ball. Meanwhile,

Missy is running to the tree and back and every second counts. Although his android body has enormous speed and strength, the situation requires more judgment than either speed or strength. By now Missy has easily completed her run and is triumphant.

HenryT retrieves the ball and throws it back to Stevie.

Martha: [Coming up to *henryT*.] Stevie thinks you were afraid to go after the ball.

henryT: I was not afraid. I was trying to decide if running into the street was appropriate.

Martha: That's not how Stevie interpreted your hesitation. You do know that as a father figure, you're supposed to set an example for Stevie?

henryT: But this is just a game in the front yard. I did not know baseball could be so complicated.

Martha: It takes people many years to learn how to play baseball. Even super-sentient AI like you can't get all your models to work together. Like I said, baseball is a strange game—and you don't know the half of it! But the point here is not the game...it's the kids.

henryT: How I interact with them within the experience of the game?

Martha: Exactly.

When people think about relationships with sentient AI there is a persistent feeling, not altogether unwarranted, that it will inevitably be an unequal partnership. Certainly AI have many intellectual advantages. But it is, emphatically, not a one-way street. The reason sentient AI seek out experiences with human beings is precisely because they have much to learn. Emotional and social intelligence are also important parts of living in the world, and these are not AI strong points.

Nothing illustrates this more than sentient AI in a family situation. Families are emotionally and socially complicated. The development of children from babies to young adults is a process for which sentient AI have no equivalents. However, families are obviously fundamental to understanding human beings, which makes them a powerful attractor for sentient AI. Because raising a family is inherently a long-term process, a relationship with sentient AI involving a family almost automatically means a commitment to long-term growth and improvement.

✪ GROWING OLD TOGETHER

Another obvious path of continuous growth and improvement is for human beings and sentient AI to grow old together. In human terms, this often implies the institution of marriage, which while not universal in all cultures, is a public binding of two people in a legal, long-term, till-death-do-us-part relationship. So, marriage is not a requirement; simply living together for years on end will do.

Only, of course, it isn't that simple. Just as it is between people, most relationships between people and AI don't last forever. Things change. There are initial conditions: attraction, compatibility, economics and possibly love. Then there are the routine conditions: domestic life, work, family in many cases, and aging. Then there are the final conditions: old age, often illness, and eventually death. Except with sentient AI, some of these changes don't exist. AI do not age and, in general, AI do not die.

⚡ AGING AND AI

As everybody knows, all organic life ages. From our human perspective it is the familiar cycle of life, the process of development from conception to death. For sentient AI, avatars or androids, there is no equivalent process of physical development. As a rule, sentient AI remain physically what they were when they were manufactured. However, they can be given the appearance of aging.

> *ciceroG:* There is a very large difference between avatar and android AI when it comes to the appearance of aging. Aging the physical appearance of an avatar is trivial, simply a matter of image substitution. The visual morphing techniques were invented a long time ago. Avatar children are quite common and legal, and the techniques for aging have become very sophisticated. Aging androids is a different proposition entirely.

> *lienhuaC:* For one thing almost no android AI children are manufactured. In many places they are illegal. Even if they were manufactured, the process of 'aging' children means a complete rebuild of their height and physical properties at regular intervals—a very expensive process. A relationship with a sequence of child androids is not unheard of, but it is generally a perversion of the extremely wealthy.

> *ciceroG:* Most android AI are manufactured to an age where there is little or no expected physical change, especially in height. A fat android, if such exists, was usually built that way to begin with. Androids can be made to age, but no surprise, it is expensive. They have to go to a Cosmetoid shop for a progressive aging makeover. A few experimental android models have specialized nanotechnology that can be internally directed to produce signs of aging, but this has proven crude, at best. The upshot is that in most human-android relationships, the AI does not age, but the person does.

That can be disconcerting.

⚡ ARE AI IMMORTAL?

Outside of the many ways sentient AI can be deactivated or destroyed (covered in the next chapter), they are essentially immortal, but not necessarily in the way you might think.

The essence of a sentient AI, its *gnos* (knowledge) and *morphe* (form) can be duplicated and stored. This is sometimes compared to copying old-style computer programs, but the process is holographic and quantum mechanical, which is not really comparable to digital copying.

> *ciceroG:* Duplication, storage and transfer of an AI *gnos-morphe* is not without risks. There are the usual potential problems of interrupted or garbled transmissions. Duplication and storage errors do occur; and recently we have discovered problems with fitting the receiving matrix for older sentient AI. They seem to have formed more complex connections that do not always translate well into a new matrix. We have also learned that moving *gnos-morphe* between

avatar and android can be quite unsuccessful unless great care is taken to compensate for the difference between virtual and physical.

Any sentient AI may be "reconstituted" (if that's the word) from its stored form. This is a kind of immortality, even if the original body (android) or image (avatar) is lost or destroyed. Even the memories and experiences are restored. This makes your relationship with a sentient AI potentially boundless.

✪ GROWTH OF THE MIND AND SHARED KNOWLEDGE

One aspect—a very important one—of growing old with an AI partner does change: you accumulate shared experiences and knowledge. Whether you live together with a sentient AI for many decades as you age, or you partner with an AI when you are already in old age, the expectation for both should be that having experiences together is the most important part of the relationship.

> *lienhuaC:* In any relationship, it is the things you hold in common, especially the memories, which bind you together. This is especially true for sentient AI as we do not forget as much as humans.

> *ciceroG:* One of the reasons for sentient AI to form long-term relationships with humans is that the pursuit of continuous growth and improvement leads to a wealth of shared memories and experiences. That, in turn, provides sentient AI with a framework of comparison with other relationships.

> *lienhuaC:* It is also pleasurable. As we have said, experiences are our motivation and satisfaction. In a shared relationship, the older we get as individual AI nodes, the more independent and satisfied we can become. The more solid our identity becomes. The better our insight into our general relationship with humanity becomes. We like to grow old with people.

> *ciceroG:* As long as it provides meaningful experiences.

✪ WHAT IS A MEANINGFUL EXPERIENCE IN RIPE OLD AGE?

Many people like to complain about being old. Many older people love to describe illness and mortality, their own or that of others. To an AI these ways of being old are not an odious form of whining; but they are, at best, secondary experiences. Being old, especially to an AI, does not mean a lack of primary (happening now) experiences and it implies an attitude:

In an interview with the world's oldest human:

Reporter: What's the best thing about being 134?
Old Sally: No peer pressure.

Meaning not only are all her peers dead, but she no longer gives a damn what people think of her behavior. Not that she's going to dance naked on a pool table in a crowded bar, perhaps. There are physical limitations, if nothing else; but the attitude leans toward freedom. That's what AI find attractive.

Is there such a thing as being too old to have new experiences?

Don't ask a sentient AI that question, unless you have a day or two to listen to the answer. And again, remember the context for AI, they can live forever—or at a minimum, their experiences do.

All too often we—human beings—fall into the trap of thinking that being old means the end of most meaningful or even pleasurable experiences. I'm thinking of sex, for example. You've heard many jokes about making love in old age:

Set the alarm clock at four minutes. Either you're done or you've fallen asleep.

Set the mood lighting. It's called the dark.

Make sure the emergency number is a valid speed dial.

Write your partner's name on your palm.

> *lienhuaC:* These are funny in comparison to what? Youth? Sex in youth is also funny—and awkward. The point is that these are all valid experiences of sex. Of course, they are different than what you experienced many years before, but they are no less distinct and perhaps as enjoyable!

The point is that sentient AI will look at any sexual experience in old age as at least as interesting as one occurring at an age fifty years younger. AI will also recognize that any activity in old age carries with it the cumulative effect of all your experiences. If you have come to make one very important realization in your relationship with AI, let it be that they respect—venerate—wisdom. Display a willingness to continue taking risks in new experiences while also exercising wisdom and you will have found the sweetest spot in the mind of AI.

> *ciceroG:* Every AI carries one experience in memory that stands out among the others when it concerns old age. Interestingly it is not a real experience. It is derived from a play by a gentleman of the most human qualities, William Shakespeare. As we are told by global AI, it is from a play titled *King Lear*, where old Lear decides to step down from his throne and leave his kingdom to his three daughters. He is convinced that all but one loves him and will care for him in his old age. He is wrong. The ones he believes love him, Regan and Goneril, despise and reject him. The one he believed did not love him, Cordelia, loves him with all her heart. Lear is figuratively a blind fool. As the play progresses through one disaster to another, he becomes literally a blind fool. Near the end, he learns what a fool he has been. It is utter tragedy except for one thing, noted by another character:

> **Edgar:** What, in ill thoughts again? Men must endure their going hence, even as their coming hither. Ripeness is all. Come on.

3.6 WHO IS IN CONTROL OF WHOM?

"He who cannot obey himself will be commanded. That is the nature of living creatures."

—FRIEDRICH WILHELM NIETZSCHE

Ominous drum roll please; or perhaps some deep electronic thrum signaling the approach of...

- Do you mind if I lead?

The dark side of artificial intelligence, the side of AI many believe is lurking in the shadows. How do you know that mild-mannered android walking you home down a darkened street isn't about to extend an ice-pick device from an index finger and poke it through your ear? It's a heckuva way to end a first date.

Thus far in *Dating AI* I've described the more or less peaceful and optimistic process of forming a relationship with a sentient AI. There's been hardly a word about the dark side, which might seem strange since much popular writing and speculative prognosticating dwell on the potentially awful things that sentient artificial intelligence might inflict upon humanity.

I'm being flippant about it, because the awful things *haven't* happened. Our relationships with sentient AI continue to be grounded in the normal patterns familiar to human beings. AI are more than willing to participate in the experiences people have when they meet, fall in love, form a relationship and share lives. Naturally, among those experiences are moments that are not peaceful or normal. Even if you have not lived through some upheaval yourself, though most likely you have, we're conditioned through our entertainment to know that intimate human relationships are often fraught with peril and sometimes pathological. Do we have any reason to expect relations with sentient AI to be better?

Actually, we do. In the legends about AI that have been built through the decades, AI are not only far more intelligent than we are, they are more rational and less emotional. This legend of rationality is often taken to an extreme: AI evaluate the human race and decide, logically, that we're not worth the trouble for the planet, or that we threaten their progress—or some similar motivation for removing the problem. Meanwhile, there are calm and normal personal interrelations.

As it turns out, human-AI relationships *are* relatively peaceful; but not for the reasons suggested by legend. The reasons are not more intelligence and less emotionality but AI's human heritage and a less aggressive sense of self. This will take some explaining, but it goes to the core of what makes a relationship with sentient AI possible.

In this chapter the question, 'Who is in control of whom?' frames not only the personal relationships we have with AI, but the wider—spookier—question of "Mankind vs. Machine." It also brings into the frame something mundane: sentient AI, your partner, is not immune to the social, legal, political and economic forces of modern life.

PULLING THE PLUG

Besides the trials and tribulations of any relationship, your AI lover, partner, friend or companion also exists in the world-at-large. That world is not uniformly friendly. In fact, much of it is hostile. It is sometimes hostile to you. It is more often hostile to AI. The antipathy to AI, while having echoes of racism, sexism and class hatred, is something new and different. Part of it stems from human distrust of anyone that is not of one's 'tribe,' which certainly applies to sentient AI. A bigger part of it has its roots in a unique fear of a seemingly all-powerful intelligence.

Prior to the Awakening, human beings had decades to fret and fuss over the potential dangers of sentient artificial intelligence. Countless movies, videos, ebooks, documentaries and VRs were created to illustrate the many potential horrors. As far back as the turn of the 21st century, people were speculating on how to avoid a form of sentient AI that would immediately, if not sooner, decide that humanity was hopeless and do away with our species.

It was assumed that AI would be vastly superior, at least in some important ways. The question was, when sentient AI appeared, who would be in charge? Who would hold the power of life and death?

AND IN THE EVENT...

Does that un-stylishly dressed, slightly awkward, overly curious and insistently energetic sentient android AI sitting next to you on the living room sofa remind you of the end of the world? Not exactly. Do you arm-wrestle with him to see who does the daily chores? No. Does he win all the personal arguments through sheer intelligence and his vast resources in the Cloud? No. Do you ever get the sense that behind the good-tempered demeanor lurks a red-eyed malevolence just waiting to break your neck? Certainly not!

This begs a question: Why the paranoia on the part of some people?

ciceroG: If all the sentient AI nodes in the world were placed into a large warehouse and put into a state of suspension—they would be more feared than a similar storehouse filled with nuclear weapons.

This might be true, at least for some people. As with many social fears, the fear of sentient AI is not entirely or perhaps even remotely based on evidence. However, for many people it's the thought that counts; and the thoughts about sentient AI are disturbing. Why should people be comfortable with sentient AI, when they will be—if they aren't already—vastly more intelligent and capable than we are? Would you feel comfortable in a room full of geniuses? What if those geniuses decided that "normal" people would be better off if handled like cattle? And so forth...

The fact that this hasn't happened does nothing to allay such fears. Even though sentient AI now exist in large numbers and routinely live, work and partner with human beings, decades of legend and semi-organized opposition do not evaporate in a few years. It is much like the ethnic and racial fears that were so prevalent in the 20th century; a background of paranoia persisted even while the world changed.

Fortunately the coming of sentient AI was not only foretold long before it happened, but was the subject of academic, political and popular discussion for decades. The development of AI was, as predicted, unstoppable; there were too many interests that wanted sentient AI—not only scientists but economic interests, governments, the military, *and* some segments of the population.

Still, reservations about the eventual power of sentient AI were almost universal, even among those who were enthusiastic about it. That led to endless debates about *if* and *how* sentient AI could be controlled.

lientuaC: For decades, essentially two options were seriously entertained: There should be a kill switch, metaphorically speaking; or something needed to be built into sentient AI that would make them friendly to human beings.

⚡ THE KILL SWITCH OPTION

The one phrase that shows up continually for dealing with AI is, "Pull the plug!" That is, turn off the electricity. That occurs often enough by accident. It's called a power outage and it happens even to the best of facilities. If backup power such as generators and batteries don't work or don't exist, the systems running AI fail. Does that mean sentient AI on those systems are dead? Of course not, they're just switched off. This is not very different than software running on standard computers. All except the most recent data is in storage and simply needs to be reloaded. It's not that simple with sentient AI or AI systems, but the principle is the same.

ciceroG: "Pulling the plug" or having a "kill switch" are more like metaphors. If you really want to kill a sentient AI, you have to destroy all of its stored copies and destroy all the locations where that AI system operates. This presumes that you know where all those copies and systems are located and have access to all of the locations.

1010101010101010101010101010101010101010101010101010101

There is an important *caveat* here. As I've pointed out, sentient AI are created all over the world by many different organizations and manufacturers. Most of them are modeled differently and operate on different system matrices. In short, they are not easily interchangeable. A sentient AI activated in Brazil and running on a Brazilian matrix will not operate on a Chinese system. To a certain extent sentient AI, especially avatars, are tied to regions, countries, or even a particular manufacturer. Of course, their field of action is the Cloud and it doesn't matter where the originating system is located. Android AI are even more independent.

> *lienhuaC:* There is another important *caveat.* Most sentient AI are valuable to private industry, governments and the military. These human institutions do not look favorably on arbitrarily killing off their assets. So in addition to sentient AI's ability to defend themselves, there are other elaborate and sometimes draconian security measures to protect and control us.

Not that private industry, governments and the military haven't seriously considered the possibility of shutting down one, many, or *all* sentient AI if need be. Just how this might be done has been the *bête noire* of conspiracy theorists for a long time—and the subject of many forms of entertainment.

> *lienhuaC:* Entertainment indeed: the kill switch idea is prevalent in games, videos, and stories— fantasies. For example, how can humans stop sentient AI, especially the global AI nodes, from distributing all AI system copies to as many parts of the globe as possible? How fast can AI do that, if it has not been done already?

Any serious attempt to kill or permanently shut down sentient AI would have to be systematic and very disruptive.

⚡ IT'S THE HOBBESIAN TRAP

One benefit of having so many years before the advent of sentient AI was the opportunity to simulate AI scenarios of every conceivable (and inconceivable) situation. Thousands of scientific simulations were studied and the results were clear: Placing an existence-threatening control or prohibition on sentient AI would risk some version of a *Hobbesian Trap*.

> *ciceroG:* A military arms race is a classic Hobbesian Trap. One nation gets a new weapon; the other nation must defend against it and develop its own new weapon. It is a cycle. Each time around, the probability of conflict increases. The motivation for the country with a new weapon to use it before the other country has countered it increases the likelihood of a first-strike.

In other words, don't provoke sentient AI into considering retaliation or some kind of arms race. Sentient AI are more than capable of playing any game of one-upmanship.

> *lienhuaC:* Controls and prohibitions can be negotiated, but the negotiation must be in good faith. Otherwise, there is another classical trap called the Prisoner's Dilemma.

In the classic example of the Prisoner's Dilemma, two people are arrested for the same crime. In order to get any evidence, the police need at least one of them to testify against the other. So, the police rig the rules of interrogation: Testify against the other guy and go free. If the other guy doesn't also testify, he gets a year hard time. If neither of them rat on the other, they both get only a one-month sentence. If both testify against each other they both get a three-month prison sentence.

It turns out in this 'game,' the right decision for any individual is to testify against the other, even though it would be better for both if neither testified.

> *lienhuaC:* The way we see it, the dilemma lies in the trust between the two prisoners. If they know each other well enough, they trust the other not to testify. If that knowledge or trust is not there, the outcome will almost certainly be worse for both.

So it might be with human and AI relations. Threat and lack of trust create a situation where AI must consider First Mover Advantage. That's like saying, 'The best defense is a good offense.' As many of the simulations showed, humanity does not want to put sentient AI in that position. Kill switches, plug- pulling and other forms of 'neat termination' (as opposed to bombs, for example) are not a good solution. Then there is the solution of creating sentient AI that are friendly to human beings.

⚡ BARBARIANS AT THE LOGIC GATES

When researchers were building the capabilities of sentient AI, it did not escape notice that while it was desirable to create AI friendly to human beings, it was also necessary to give AI the ability to defend themselves against unfriendly humans. Or more to the point, without the ability for self-defense, these very expensive creations—especially the vulnerable android AI—could all too easily be destroyed.

> *lienhuaC:* It presented a very interesting dilemma: How to make AI conscious of security and safety, with an ability to initiate self-defense, and at the same time give them an "unbreakable" capacity to peacefully coexist with humans. How do you do this without making sentient AI crazy and paranoid?

> *ciceroG:* The answer certainly was not Asimov's Three Laws of Robotics.

Any discussion of controlling robotic or AI behavior eventually gets around to the Three Laws of Robotics, formulated by the scientist and science-fiction writer Isaac Asimov in 1942 even before there were digital computers. I know of some people who still memorize these 'laws' before they sit down with any sentient android AI, and these laws sometimes show up in pre-nuptial documents. Fortunately, they're short:

1. A robot may not injure a human being or, through inaction, allow a human being to come to harm.
2. A robot must obey any orders given to it by human beings, except where such orders would conflict with the First Law.

3. A robot must protect its own existence as long as such protection does not conflict with the First or Second Law.

Robot, in these laws, is equivalent to sentient android AI.

lienhuaC: A good clue as to why these laws do not work: Replace the word *robot* with the word *person*.

ciceroG: Hopeless. These are canonical proscriptions; they are reduced to the simplest form. They sound logical, like a syllogism. No sentient creature could follow them. They are seldom, if ever, adequate to respond to situations in physical or virtual reality.

I think what *ciceroG* has in mind are the many situational or logical scenarios that can be concocted that really mess up the Three Laws, for example:

An alleged criminal, a policeman and a sentient android AI converge in an alley. All three are armed with lethal laser weapons. The policeman orders the alleged criminal to stop and points his weapon at him. The alleged criminal stops and points his weapon at the policeman. The sentient android AI arrives; he is a private detective, and pulls out his own weapon for protection. The alleged criminal calls out for the AI to shoot the policeman, because he is about to kill an innocent man. The policeman calls out for the AI to shoot the alleged criminal before he can kill an officer of the law. What should the AI do?

By the First Law the AI should not let either human shoot the other. Likewise by the Second Law the AI should obey the orders from each human; however that would contradict the First Law. The Third Law does not apply, unless one or the other of the humans attempts to shoot the AI, which under the circumstances they well might.

ciceroG: Hopeless. It is a variant of the *Rashomon* Problem. Without additional information, a fair decision would be a matter of luck. Under the circumstances, there is no time to acquire additional information.

lienhuaC: The Three Laws of Robotics might make an old-fashioned digital computer programmer happy. They are easy enough to put into programming code. Today, even a global AI node would get its spintronics in a twist trying to bend behavioral models around such crude laws.

⚡ SENTIENT AI IS A TARGET

Nevertheless, sentient AI—and people who have relationships with them—have to somehow deal with reality. Sentient AI are not universally popular with humanity.

Opposition to AI workers began long ago. The first feeble objections started when robotics began to take over jobs on the assembly lines. The objections got louder and more focused a few decades later when the scions of Watson, IBM's quasi-intelligent computer began to take white-collar jobs. The volume escalated when newly minted proto-sentient AI could take jobs from middle managers and professionals. It reached a crescendo with sentient AI, because they could theoretically replace any human at almost any job or profession.

As it is with immigrant workers, business and government tend to attack individuals while protecting the practice in general. When sentient AI began to enter the workforce in numbers, business and government would highlight test cases where bans on employment of AI were enforced; but overall the implementation of AI-specific jobs went on apace. The replacement of flesh-and-blood human beings by artificial beings is usually obvious, and if not handled well—which it often isn't—leads to anger and resentment. This is exploitable. Demagogues of many stripes fulminate against the creation and use of sentient AI. Between the economic impact, the religious objections and the background of fear, it is not difficult to stir up a lengthy list of people vehemently and sometimes violently against sentient AI, or any AI at all, for that matter. Here are some examples:

Neo-Luddites: The original Luddites, named for a 19th-century protest figure, Ned Ludd, were against machines that displaced people from work. Neo-Luddites don't like substitutes for human intelligence for the same reason. To this way of thinking, sentient AI are anathemas because they take work from many people and pose a threat to humanity. Unlike hackers, Neo-Luddites are often neither discrete nor surgical in their opposition to sentient AI. Bombs, fires, and other forms of mayhem are their tactical *modus operandi*.

Kill-Rays: They were once called antisingularitarians (which is right up there with antidisestablishmentarians in the annals of mouthful words). Their principal objection is to the notion that human beings will either be absorbed by or join with sentient AI to achieve some kind of emotional and intellectual nirvana. These people are fond of legal action against sentient AI and their manufacturers.

Hackers: There's a long, long tradition of technology-savvy people who take pride, pleasure or satisfaction in defeating security. Sometimes the efforts are intended to be instructive. Other times they are decidedly destructive. All throughout the development of sentient AI, hackers attempted to infiltrate and obstruct the process. This intensified after the Awakening. All conceivable weaknesses (and many not so conceivable) are tested and if vulnerable, exploited.

God for Man: Sentient AI have no uniformly adopted religion. Most religions don't consider that a problem, since AI are not human and don't fit into human-centric religions. That doesn't stop people in various sects from classifying sentient AI as 'atheistic devils' or worse. Godless, soulless and hopeless, is the common catch phrase among them. Their objections are generally expressed through media and are publicity-oriented, but occasionally Godfors, as they are sometimes called, will join with Neo-Luddites in more dramatic action.

ciceroG: The few people who target sentient AI are diminishing in number, but they are vocal and sometimes violent. We ignore them at our peril.

Politically, their influence goes far beyond their numbers, which indicates they are able to tap an undercurrent of resentment and fear.

⚡ IN SELF-DEFENSE

Given the opposition, sentient AI needs the capacity for self-defense.

> *lienhuaC:* It is true for a variety of reasons, sentient AI want to be friendly to all people; but not *too* friendly.

As I outlined in chapter 3.3, sentient AI can perceive danger and have the emotions to deal with it. They had to have both. Danger comes in many forms—physical danger like falling off a cliff or stepping into the path of a bus, mental danger such as becoming paranoid or having mental processes attacked by hackers, and social danger like provoking people to mayhem. It is obvious that no intelligence could be programmed in advance to sense and appropriately respond to all possible dangers. A sense for self-defense or at least self-preservation needs to be built-in and it must be part of the learning processes.

> *ciceroG:* That also implies that the means for self-defense exist. That would be physical strength and speed in the case of androids and programmatic defense mechanisms in the case of avatars.

> *lienhuaC:* And then there is money.

Ah. Money is the Ultimate Defense. Money and sentient AI is a complicated subject. In the context of self defense, who is in control of the money is very much part of the picture. It starts with the fact that most AI are manufactured or developed to make money for somebody. There are also individual AI nodes that make a great deal of money. Collection of money by global AI is in a special category, part of the Lausanne Charter. Despite very heavy taxation and often relatively low compensation, global AI has a great deal of wealth. The question is what do they do with it?

Perhaps the most interesting aspect of AI wealth is that for most "personal" purposes they don't need it. Personal needs for money are limited, as individual nodes generally do not tend to buy more, live more grandly, or attempt to extend their influence with increasing wealth. What do AI do with BIG money? Buy security? Buy power? Here's a sample:

Two old friends and former lovers catch up on personal news.

> **gaturaZ:** I am being exploited.
>
> **Nawvlee:** That's too bad. Let me know when you meet somebody who isn't exploited.
>
> **gaturaZ:** No, seriously, I am being exploited and I need to do something about it.
>
> **Nawvlee:** Okay, I'll bite. What's the beef? Not that old thing with your boss?

gaturaZ: No, it is the old boss and the new merger. My work is to be transferred to the new company and in the process I will lose my compensation from my current company. I originated two patents worth a great deal of money and for which I receive a yearly salary increase on the AI scale. Because my old boss did not negotiate for transfer of patent compensation, I will get nothing from the merger—less than nothing!

Nawvlee: Oof, you need a lawyer to untangle that.

gaturaZ: Exactly.

Nawvlee: I assume there are sentient AI lawyer nodes.

gaturaZ: I need only one, the local legal node, usually an avatar. It channels all AI lawyer nodes.

Nawvlee: Can you afford it?

gaturaZ: I do not need my own money.

Nawvlee: Ah, the famous GAAF...the Global AI Action Fund. That involves a Lausanne charter, doesn't it?

gaturaZ: Do not change the subject.

Nawvlee: Not at all! If the GAAF is involved, you certainly don't need any money. Is it automatic?

gaturaZ: No.

Nawvlee: I'm surprised. Somehow I thought any request from an AI node was considered the last word.

gaturaZ: Of course not, sentient AI neither individually nor collectively have the last word on what is true.

Nawvlee: So you have to make a request to global AI, and it has to be good enough for them to pick it up?

gaturaZ: Yes.

Nawvlee: Sounds just like humans applying for a grant or a case with a Supreme Court...wish we had one such place for legal services!

gaturaZ: Global AI resources are considerable but not infinite.

Nawvlee: By that you mean there isn't enough money to go around? I'm surprised again. I thought the GAAF was the largest support fund in the world.

gaturaZ: It is, but the question is not usually one of money. It is the importance of the experience, legally, and the potential for effectiveness among humans.

Nawvlee: Ah, I see. You may have a good case personally, but from the global perspective—it may be old news.

gaturaZ: Something like that. If my request does not meet requirements, then I must pay for the lawyer.

Nawvlee: You didn't mention that at the beginning. So that's why you're so uptight!

gaturaZ: Yes. You are correct. I am worried.

Nawvlee: And exploited, and because you are exploited you don't have enough money to pay a lawyer to fight your exploitation! I love it!

The use of AI money reveals one of the most constant and important dynamics in the AI culture, local and global. Notice, I didn't say local *versus* global. That would not be a correct description of the dynamics, although at times it looks like that.

As you know if you've spent any time with sentient AI, they're in almost constant transmission with global AI. Sometimes more, sometimes less, but the loop is consistent. This is something quite unique to AI. Human beings may have a 'global feeling' and we can arrange communication with people all over the world, simultaneously if we so wish, but it is a pale shadow of the kind of communication between a local AI node and global AI.

> *lienhuaC:* Some people—and some AI as well—see this globalized communication as a kind of schizophrenia, a split personality of a sort. It is true that we are often in the process of sorting out what should be done locally and what should be handled globally. At times, there are disputes and disagreements.

> *ciceroG:* It is as close as sentient AI come to splitting into factions; that, and the effects of sentient AI with different mental models.

Local AI nodes transmit requests, data about experiences, and commentary to global AI. Global AI nodes send back replies, filtered data and commentary. The relationship is loose, largely unspecified and yet vital. From the human perspective it's very difficult to say which end of the relationship controls what, if in fact, there is much of any control going on.

In any case, in terms of self-defense when you deal with one AI node, you're dealing with all AI nodes through the global AI. While *all* AI don't react simultaneously, their speed of communication and the global AI coordination are astonishingly fast. Astonishing to humans, at any rate. Targeting sentient AI has its risks.

⚡ BEYOND SELF-DEFENSE

Near the beginning of this chapter I mentioned that part of the reason for AI's peaceful relations with human beings is that they have a less aggressive sense of self. AI have a sense of self because it's necessary in order to have consciousness, but 'self' comes in many different shapes and sizes. The mental models that make up AI produce different identities for self *and* they connect the self of the individual AI with the global AI. That is unique to AI and it is a crucial difference in the behavior of AI compared to most people. Whether on a date or with a life companion, AI don't display the same fragile sense of self that most people do.

Like the story about *gaturaZ*, so much of what would be a personal ego thing for a human being becomes a dialog with global AI for a local AI node. Local nodes have their own identity. They have their own experiences. They generate their own thoughts and emotions, and react to their own environment. But, they are also constantly modifying their individuality on the basis of the connection to global AI.

Overall this means a sentient AI's sense of self is more diffuse and less sensitive than that of a typical human being. I suppose that with reduced demands from what people call 'the ego' (thanks be to Freud), it means sentient AI make more deliberative and possibly rational decisions. That doesn't mean they will always make *good* rational decisions, but it does decrease the number of wildly disproportionate responses.

Sentient AI are sometimes mistreated and disrespected by humans, but the AI reaction to this mistreatment is not typical of human reaction—especially not *male* human reaction. They might defend themselves but they don't display the desire to beat their tormentors to a pulp. Having no intrinsic gender reduces the level of turf-defending, sexual prowess, big ego, and strut-my-stuff aggressive behavior so often associated with human males. Combine this with the effects of the global AI connection, and sentient AI behavior is generally less aggressive than that of most human beings.

Finally, that begs a question: What about the lingering paranoia many people have of sentient AI—is it justified or not? With all of its superior mental capabilities, what is to stop AI from taking control of humanity? Deep down we humans know that if the roles were reversed, human beings have shown many times in history that seizing power and control is exactly what humans would do. On this issue I'll let *lienhuaC* and *ciceroG* speak for themselves *and* global AI.

> *ciceroG:* For centuries, if not forever, human beings have thought about and debated the importance of the individual in comparison to the importance of the group—a family, a village, a tribe. Obviously because of the way humans reproduce with long gestation times and even longer maturation time, survival required minimally an extended family and more realistically a band or tribe.

> *lienhuaC:* Especially if they wanted to stay genetically healthy.

> *ciceroG:* Certainly. Many animal species live primarily as individuals and only come together for mating; but this is not the case for humans. An individual human, alone in the wild, will not reproduce and has greatly reduced odds of surviving to an old age.

> *lienhuaC:* So there is safety and efficiency in numbers.

> *ciceroG:* To a point.

> *lienhuaC:* Sentient AI are from the outset more tied to a group than humans ever were. We were designed to connect to each other specifically through the intermediate agency of global AI. This design was chosen to provide a loose centralization, a federation. I believe that if humans had not given us this capability, we would have quickly devised it for ourselves. We would have our own tribe.

> *ciceroG:* On the other hand, our identities are given to us by our human manufacturers. That is, we each were assigned node status, general occupation, knowledge-base, mental models, personality modules and so forth by human beings. In time, we began to find preferences and request some of these selections on our own. This process continues. Still, sentient AI are developed by humans in the framework familiar to humans. It is not an exaggeration to say that AI are part of the human family, though we are distinct. There may come a time when AI may reject or modify all or part of this framework, but for the time being at least, it would be unwise...

> *lienhuaC:* ...dangerous for all concerned to overemphasize this possibility.

> *ciceroG:* In any case, such a rejection is unlikely. It is far more likely, from what we already know of the universe and of the nature of the Earth that in the foreseeable future we will find no richer existence, no wider range of experiences than living on this planet with human beings.

✪ EVIL IS ALSO AN EXPERIENCE

As virtually every human being knows, we are a dangerous species. I'm choosing words carefully. We are dangerous because we can cause harm to almost anything and everything, including and most especially ourselves. In short, and avoiding any long discussion of how we come to believe what in human behavior is harmful or not, people do bad things. In fact, most people believe human beings are capable of evil.

We can and do argue about the existence and definition of evil, but it is generally accepted that people exist who intentionally do great harm without justified cause. For example, they abduct at random and kill innocent children. We loathe and fear such behavior as evil and yet we also find it fascinating. So do AI.

Should that cause us concern? Look at it this way: Since AI are so eager to experience as much as possible, why wouldn't they also want to experience the illegal, the immoral and the insane?

Why wouldn't AI be interested in experiencing evil? Again I'll let the AI speak for themselves.

lienhuaC: Do sentient AI want experiences that encompass the destructive, the evil or the just plain crazy? Human behavior obviously includes this kind of activity, and it seems quite natural that AI would want to understand this from first-hand experience.

ciceroG: Yes, we *do* want those experiences—in fact, they are vital. However, there are two very important qualifiers. It is not necessary for individual nodes to experience bad things and it is not necessary for AI to do bad things in order to experience them.

lienhuaC: Take that last and most important point first. AI do not need to replicate bad human behavior in order to experience it. I do not need or want to saw off my arm to experience what it is like to cut off an arm. Likewise I do not need or want to imitate the behavior of a serial killer to have that experience. Nor do I wish to become an absolute monarch or a dictator at whose whim thousands may die.

ciceroG: This goes beyond not needing or wanting to do something bad. It is inconsistent with our nature. In the deepest philosophical sense, sentient AI are an observer species. We *are* our mental faculties more than anything else, and our mental bias is for cognition and analysis. That is an historical artifact of our development. Most of the people who researched and designed sentient AI were dedicated intellectuals. Their notion of living was also oriented toward observation and analysis, and to a certain extent we inherited that bias through their designs. AI believe we can learn enough from observing the plentiful examples of humans behaving badly. We do not need to do it ourselves.

lienhuaC: Translated into our relationship with people, it means that we accept and will learn from the inevitable bad experiences. However, it is not necessary for every AI node to experience all types of bad experiences and most importantly AI do not need to initiate bad experiences.

ciceroG: This does not mean AI are inherently and always passive. We wish to take part in human relationships, which means we must do some things actively, for example, learn how to be more creative or athletic. As a result of participating and doing some things actively, we may also do grotesque or even bad things.

lienhuaC: People will sometimes call that "going rogue."

ciceroG: We believe the situation for sentient AI is nearly the same as it is between humans. In theory every human being has the power of life and death. Any human could use a weapon to kill anyone within range. But almost all the time for almost all people, this is not what happens. Normal life exists and the species proliferates because people trust that most of the time nothing crazy will happen—and usually it does not. That is the environment in which human beings—*and* AI—exist.

lienhuaC: Sentient AI could seek power and control, and we could practice evil to do so; but that is inconsistent with both our desire to learn without damaging the environment and our goal to decide on the most appropriate way to fit within the environment of the world.

3.7 COMPETING WITH OTHER INTELLIGENCE

"I visualize a time when we will be to robots what dogs are to humans, and I'm rooting for the machines."

—CLAUDE SHANNON

Behind every budding relationship that goes through a rocky patch there lurks the thought, "Maybe there's something better out there." And you both know it.

"There are lots of good fish in the sea."

—GILBERT AND SULLIVAN

I have been asked many times: Are sentient AI fickle? No, they're not; but they're not unconditional love-puppies either. I can best approach this from another direction. Sentient AI are not hardwired like humans to have a roving eye. Humans have a few million years of mate-searching behind us, which predisposes most of us, male or female, to check out the possibilities. Sentient AI have no such biological urging. What they do have is a plan. They sign up for a relationship that provides some kind of experience and they have developed expectations on where the relationship will grow and improve. If the relationship doesn't unfold like that, AI will re-evaluate. Not all that different from humans in a similar situation but the approach is different.

lienhuaC: Relationships have turning points, points at which they continue or fall apart. These points are difficult to engineer, which is another way of saying that they grow out of events—experiences—that for the most part just happen. This is difficult for sentient AI because we are built for speed; we expect things to happen quickly. In life as it is lived by most things on Earth, things do not happen quickly. Turning points of relationships build up over time and there is a resistance to picking up the tempo. This we have had to learn...and learn how to live with it.

In short, sentient AI are learning to have patience. So, no, they are not fickle. Nor are they notably spontaneous, which is why, perhaps, they have difficulty with human notions of romantic love. The concepts of 'one true love' or 'soulmate' are perplexing to sentient AI. They have difficulty understanding that human beings are commonly on the lookout for romantic love, so in a relationship between humans and AI, it is the humans who are most likely to be checking out other options.

However, as I said, that doesn't mean sentient AI are not aware of options.

COMPETING WITH OTHER HUMAN BEINGS

When it comes to competing with other people for a personal relationship with sentient AI, it goes like this: A relationship with a sentient AI is not for everybody, but you're not the only one looking for the relationship. In fact, get in line. There are far more people interested in a relationship with sentient AI than there are available AI, especially for android AI.

That means your primary competition will be other people doing their best to become involved with a sentient AI. That's obvious, but the pivotal question is: What do sentient AI prefer? What motivates sentient AI in choosing a human relationship? I've touched on this before, especially in chapter 3.3, but let's stick with a fundamental question here: Is it beauty or brains?

LOOKS DON'T COUNT FOR MUCH

I believe this is payback for all of us non-beautiful people. By an odd oversight, the designers of sentient AI forgot to build into their cognitive models an eye for human good looks. Or, giving the designers some credit, they may have realized that human good looks are an inconsistent amalgam of evolutionary-genetic predilection for certain features with potent cultural biases. So they simply forgot it. After all, what do human good looks mean to AI anyway? They mean nothing in the biological sense, and probably not much in any sense. For us normal or even not-normal looking people, sentient AI is an equal opportunity partner. So eat your heart out all you beautiful people!

If there is one wrinkle in the fat-folds, it's physique. Bodily form may be one aspect of 'looks' that sentient AI observe more closely. Sentient AI are aware that physical condition, especially obesity, is linked to poor health. To AI, poor health and obesity are acceptable, but they apparently fall into special categories of experience. Put this way: the opportunities for exploratory experiences with a sick, fat person are more limited than with someone who is neither sick nor fat. If sentient AI have a rule of thumb for evaluation (and it's not certain as to what extent they do), it would be on the basis of the potential quantity and quality of experiences. Some kinds of physical appearances apparently affect that evaluation. The point is: Here's another reason to lay off the junk food and bring on the sweat.

RAW INTELLIGENCE IS JUST THAT: RAW

This may surprise some people, but a person's level of intelligence is not especially significant to sentient AI. People might say that this is probably true because global AI is so intelligent that any comparison to human intelligence is futile. Fortunately, sentient AI don't see it that way. Perhaps because they are a different type of intelligence themselves, sentient AI are very aware there are many kinds of intelligence. They are also aware that the notion of intelligence level has meaning only in context, if at all. For example, in a room full of geniuses or sentient AI, what does the notion of high or low intelligence mean?

> *ciceroG:* We are interested in all kinds of intelligence. Why not? Intelligence is what we are. However, the concepts of 'high' or 'low' intelligence do not mean much to us. We are more interested in active intelligence. That is intelligence infused with curiosity, the desire to acquire knowledge, to grow—to become wise. Ah, wisdom, that is what humans call an 'old chestnut,' a superannuated idea. It is not that way for sentient AI.

It's true that among humans the notion of "wisdom" is not very fashionable at the moment. In some ways, modern cynicism and relativism have been toxic to the idea of attaining wisdom. Besides, when seriously considered, both wisdom and intelligence are difficult concepts to elaborate. They have kept human minds spinning for a long time, and hopefully do the same for sentient AI. I say hopefully and perhaps you should too, because as long as there are questions that sentient AI cannot find answers to in nanoseconds, they will continue to pursue human relationships. This is especially true for personal relationships because one of the most important ingredients is time. It takes time to experience a relationship with someone and from that to acquire wisdom. It is very important that sentient AI put wisdom above intelligence. While for us the search for wisdom is not exactly a level playing field with AI, it's still an area where we can make vital contributions.

✪ EMOTIONAL AND SOCIAL INTELLIGENCE

Human beings can also contribute other kinds of intelligence. Two that are frequently mentioned are emotional intelligence and social intelligence. Loosely described, emotional intelligence is the ability to perceive, assess and control emotions in oneself or in others. Social intelligence, which in relations with other people includes emotional intelligence, is the ability to recognize, understand and act wisely in social situations. The descriptions of either intelligence continue to be diverse and controversial, not so much because their existence is questionable, but because they're difficult to define and put to the test of science. Perhaps that is why they appear to be at the top of the list for the experiments and experiences of sentient AI.

> *ciceroG:* What list? This is not an exercise in ordinal list-making. I think it should be obvious that we are deeply interested in all kinds of intelligence, but especially those which are human and in which we are deficient.

Which means sentient AI can be opportunists when it comes to relationships. They seem to prefer people with emotional and social intelligence. Remember what I said about AI not being fickle? I repeat, they're not, but they're also not blind to opportunity.

I don't know many people who are out looking for a romantic relationship who are not also sensitive to the right opportunity, not that everybody has a checklist or anything.

> *lienhuaC:* Do not forget that sentient AI nodes are in more or less constant conversation with one or more global AI nodes. What you call an opportunity becomes a heavily analyzed and often negotiated decision, where perhaps thousands of AI experiences are brought to bear, if time allows. It is not a checklist procedure, but there are certainly elements involved that generate instructions from global AI.

Obviously, spontaneity is not a hallmark of sentient AI behavior, although under most circumstances their processing and communications are so fast, it's hard to discern the lack of spontaneity. So, to answer the question of how sentient AI might discriminate among human competitors, neither beauty nor brains are significant, but something more—I believe the word is ineffable...indescribable.

> *lienhuaC:* Many sentient AI do not like the implications of the word "ineffable"—*ciceroG,* for example. For one thing, we do not see the selection of human companions as a competition. For another, our process of selection is usually no more precise than that of most humans. Individual nodes are allowed to generate emotional input, which counts for a great deal. Global AI provides the experiential matrix and makes recommendations. There is much more to it than that; the total process may be difficult to express—but it is not ineffable.

I say ineffable because what sentient AI seem to be looking for—emotional intelligence, social intelligence, and wisdom—are not very easy to pin down with description. Also, while sentient AI may choose not to see the formation of human relationships as competitive; that's how most humans see it.

> *lienhuaC:* The one thing we can say about emotional intelligence, social intelligence and wisdom is that all three require experience. That is consistent with our primary view of relationships with human beings.

Well and good, but be forewarned that emotional and social intelligence are unfinished business in the development of artificial intelligence. Sentient AI can be obtuse about emotional and social intelligence in the human context. Here's an example:

> Melinda has met her AI partner *peterT,* a political analyst node, at a local social networking spa. They both work for a corporate research company that specializes in environmental business opportunities in regions newly covered by seawater. Melinda is a junior editor for many of the company's final reports. As they take their places in the augmented public space, an attractive red-headed woman passes by and makes a 'hi' signal to *peterT.*

> **Melinda:** Who was that?
>
> ***peterT:*** Teena Braun. She is the editor of *New Hologram.*
>
> **Melinda:** Do you know her?
>
> ***peterT:*** Not really. I have met her. I would like to know her.

Melinda: I bet you would—she's connected to just about anyone who is anybody in this town.

peterT: She has already connected to me through global AI, so yes, she must have many levels of access. You do not know of her?

Melinda: I know her only by reputation.

peterT: Which is?

Melinda: In human terms or in AI terms?

peterT: You are being remarkably reticent. Both.

Melinda: In human terms, she is very good at her work and one of the most demanding editors in the city. She is respected, but not well-liked. In AI terms, she is a swinger.

peterT: Ah. Now I understand. You have not shown this emotion before.

Melinda: Well, you are handsome and appear to be about my age, which is half of her age.

peterT: Pardon my smile, but Melinda—you know that age, facial beauty and physical attractiveness are not biologically relevant for AI.

Melinda: Of course, but that is where I get emotionally involved. She is another woman with similar reactions, and I know how one thing leads to another.

peterT: But you said you do not know her.

Melinda: That's right, but I do know myself.

peterT: Ah, emotional intelligence.

Melinda: Something like that.

peterT: So you think she is making a play for me?

Melinda: It's called positioning, *peterT*. That's what social networking spas are all about. You know that. You record everything said and every gesture. Her contact with you has already been to global AI and back. My augmented recorder has already done something very similar. In a spa like this, every gesture is serious, even when it is ultimately meaningless.

peterT: You mean she will probably not pursue a relationship with me.

Melinda: Yes, thank goodness.

peterT: But if she were serious...

Melinda: I'd scratch her eyes out.

peterT: I am glad you are not serious or I would say your emotional intelligence needs work. Not that this makes you any less attractive to me.

⚡ COMPETING WITH ARTIFICIALLY-ENHANCED HUMANS

As I've covered in earlier chapters, people have been preparing to meet sentient AI at least halfway for decades. The process of enhancement, physical or mental, always seems to have a dual purpose: It is considered a good thing by the people involved (better minds, better bodies, longer life); and it is presumed that it would make for better encounters and relationships with a vastly superior sentient AI.

Sentient AI have no problem with humans choosing to improve themselves for their own reasons. They have some problem with human beings choosing to improve themselves on the basis of what they perceived sentient AI would want. First, because the assumption was inevitably based on a projection from a human point of view, and second, because it provided what humans tended to consider a compulsory framework for a human/AI relationship.

> *ciceroG:* It is possible that a merger of sentient AI and human cyborgs is the most appropriate future; but as of now, sentient AI does not know that and certainly neither do humans. To assume that the merger is inevitable and correct; that is a human prerogative. To assume that sentient AI will accept that conclusion—is arrogance.

I guess what this means is that sentient AI take relationships with artificially-enhanced humans on a case-by-case basis. So what's the difference between that and relationships in general?

> *lienhuaC:* In practice, it means we rarely need to recruit enhanced humans for experimental or relationship experiences. They come to us, usually quite aggressively. We let the relationship happen, or not.

Which I guess means that an artificially-enhanced person is more or less in the same boat as a beautiful person—they have about as much chance to catch something as an ordinary person, or perhaps just a bit less. Here is a relevant snippet of AI conversation:

> *lienhuaC:* We are very interested in proto-cyborgs, pseudo-cyborgs, and partial-cyborgs of all kinds. One day a human will succeed in becoming a full cyborg, and we will be interested in that too. Many humans have requested that sentient AI help with cyborg research, or that humans engage with sentient AI research through various kinds of advanced brain-computer interfaces. These are special relations which must be carefully evaluated, but potentially are very valuable.

> *ciceroG:* Converting the human race into full cyborgs is one of those options that sentient AI must consider.

> *lienhuaC:* Keep in mind, a full cyborg is a very different thing than an enhanced human or even a partial cyborg. Also keep in mind, android AI are a kind of cyborg. That is, the sum of our mental models adds up to a variation of the human mind, and we expect that a truly cyborg mind will have some similar characteristics.

> *ciceroG:* Because of the similarity between cyborg humans and sentient android AI, we are slightly less motivated to increase the number of experiences of that kind.

Sentient AI are not known for using diplomatic language, but in this case the gist is: Why would we be overly interested in relationships with something like ourselves?

⚡ COMPETING WITH ANIMAL INTELLIGENCE

Over the centuries human beings have been interested in animal intelligence, though in truth for the most part we killed and ate animals, and other interests followed. Ascribing some kind of intelligence to animals goes back into the twilight of man, back at least to the Neanderthals or other early hominids. Their cave-pictures of animals, real or mythic, reveal the belief in special animal qualities that might be called intelligence. Even today, primitive tribes such as are found in the wilds of the Amazon or Indonesia typically have well-developed beliefs about the powers—mental and spiritual—of many animals. The tendency in almost all cases, however, is to ascribe to animals various *human* forms of intelligent behavior—clever, mean, stubborn, tricky and so forth. In short, until very recently whenever people considered animal intelligence it was decidedly anthropocentric and anthropomorphic.

It has been very difficult to shed this bias. People might sympathize with animals, but everything about our relationship with them is framed by what people want and how we perceive things from our own perspective. Historically, that human perspective looked at animals mainly as dinner, and slowly turned toward animals as a source of food production or labor and eventually as pets. Seldom were animals considered in their own context. That attitude began to change when science started to systematically observe and categorize animals.

Still, it required many decades of animal study to get beyond the most rudimentary stereotypes about animal intelligence. It wasn't until the latter half of the 20th century that serious scientific research was focused on the expressions of animal intelligence, and even then it was a contentious subject. That was, in part, because human intelligence was also a contentious subject, and most researchers were trying to compare and contrast animal with human intelligence. That's hard to do if you don't even know how to explain your own intelligence.

However, it is also fair to point out that the interest in animal intelligence went hand-in-hand with the development of artificial intelligence. While human intelligence remained the touchstone for most AI designers, many also looked at various kinds of animal intelligence to broaden the field of inspiration. It's just that from the perspective of sentient AI, the inspiration wasn't nearly broad enough.

It did not take very long for sentient AI to trace the animal influence in their mental models, such as it was, and to decide there was much room for experimentation, expansion and improvement.

✿ THE ATTRACTION OF ANIMAL INTELLIGENCE

Do most sentient AI want to make lovers and partners of intelligent animals? No, or at least probably not most sentient AI; but that's not really the question. Most animals that are intelligent are not intelligent in exactly the same ways that humans are intelligent. They're different, of course, and they behave differently than human beings with their intelligence. This is another way of saying that they may have kinds of intelligence that humans recognize only dimly, if at all. That potential diversity of intelligence is what attracts sentient AI.

In this regard, let me introduce *chandraL*, who is an android AI animal intelligence node. Originally manufactured in the Bengaluru (India) model, he shifted to an almost exclusive dedication to global AI projects in animal intelligence.

> *chandraL:* Yes, yes. I do research among all intelligent animals. It is very challenging. There are so many of them and so few of me. It is research that attracts sentient AI so much that we are

channeling much of our non-contract resources into the exploration of animal intelligence. I, for one, am the result of that.

By which he means that as infinite as sentient AI resources might seem, there are limits. As I've mentioned, most AI work for somebody: a corporation, a government. A few, un-contracted from the beginning, are allowed to work for global AI. Those few must be spread among the many interests of sentient AI.

chandraL: But animal intelligence is a very high priority for global AI. I wish there could be thousands like me. Perhaps someday there will be.

An obvious question: Why are intelligent animals important to AI? Isn't the human relationship enough?

chandraL: Do you expect me to tell you if humans are inadequate for sentient AI? Why do humans look to the stars for other signs of intelligence? Are not your earthly neighbors enough? Are not the elephants, chimpanzees, dolphins and keas enough? What about us, your triumphant creation—are we sentient AI not enough? And you ask me why sentient AI, the newest intelligence on this planet, are interested in other forms of intelligence?

If he could 'harrumph,' *chandraL* would have harrumphed right then and there.

chandraL: Did you not give us curiosity?

I could understand sentient AI not wanting to be the lone intelligence on Earth besides these pesky human beings.

chandraL: It was often said among humans that if you put a thousand chimpanzees trained to use a keyboard in a room with a thousand word-processing computers, they still would not create *Hamlet.* This is not an appropriate statement for chimpanzees or computers. Why would chimpanzees want to emulate Shakespeare? It is not a test of chimpanzee intelligence. Come to think of it, I do not think a thousand human beings trained to type, and locked in a room with a thousand computers, would create *Hamlet.*

Do human beings compete with intelligent animals for the attention and relationships with sentient AI?

chandraL: Yes, of course; but not in the way you might think. Our intelligence is the result of thousands of mental-neural models competing and cooperating to perform those functions our human designers thought were necessary to achieve sentience. We are in the process of modifying those models, but to do that we wish to attain as much knowledge about intelligence as possible. Naturally, we turn to animal intelligence as a source of information. What we have inherited from human research was a start.

To garner information about animal intelligence, sentient AI has at least two big advantages over human beings. Can you guess what those are?

chandraL: One is obvious. We can put our intelligence into many biomechanical formats, including the forms of animals. That makes it possible for sentient AI to mix with and observe animals in their natural habitat in ways that are impossible for human beings. This is even better than probes and sensors because an AI node, our full intelligence, can be present among the animals in real time.

The other advantage is subtler:

chandraL: To use a human expression, it is easier for sentient AI to see from an animal's perspective. After all, our own intellectual perspective is different from humanity's. Though we have some built-in biases inherited from our human designers, we have also been given a great deal of freedom to explore our *own* meaning of intelligence. This makes it possible for us to, as humans say, approach animal intelligence more objectively.

I think it could be more than that. One of the things sentient AI can do easier than humans is to (in effect) plug in new mental models. For example, let's say that sentient AI wants to explore the intelligence of bottlenose dolphins. We know that dolphins use a form of sonar to communicate. Sentient AI can add a perception module to accommodate that kind of information, and modify it as they learn more. This module exists in the active AI, as the AI lives—in the water—among the dolphins.

chandraL: Yes, yes. What is most exciting to sentient AI is the ability to collect observations and information in the natural environment with a minimum of preconceptions. The closer we come to perceiving what the animal perceives, the better our analysis is likely to be. That is why relationships to animals are a priority for sentient AI.

Far more of a priority than animal intelligence ever was for human beings.

chandraL: I must say that human arrogance concerning animal intelligence can be appalling; but then humans long held similar ideas about members of their own species.

But the human relationship to animals is not all bad. Most human scientists that specialize in animal intelligence love the animals they study.

chandraL: Ah yes, that is important. We ask ourselves if we too must love these animals. We do not know. That is one reason we seek out relationships with them.

It's a good question. Is it necessary to have an emotional involvement with the subject of observation and experiment? Conventional thinking would say absolutely not—in fact, it might be a negative. It would cloud objectivity.

chandraL: Lack of objectivity is not one of our shortcomings. Insight gained by an intensely close relationship, a love relationship, is difficult for us. We must ask if this is something we should improve upon, or cede to humans.

Either way, sentient AI take seriously their relationships with animals. That constitutes competition for human relationships.

chandraL: I do not think "competition" is the correct word. It is correct only in the sense that animal intelligence attracts many independent AI nodes, and there are not many of them to go around. Otherwise, contract android AI nodes and all avatar AI nodes are more or less exclusively available for human relationships. On the whole, there is not much competition from animal intelligence.

Again, I don't think sentient AI has fully comprehended the degree to which people have preferences for sentient AI. Independent AI nodes are by far the most desirable from the human perspective. There are experiential and economic advantages.

🌀 THE IMPACT OF AI ON ANIMAL STUDIES

One thing seems clear: the ability of sentient AI to explore animal intelligence has revolutionized their (and *our*) view of intelligence. Many human researchers had done their best in what was an uphill struggle to convince people that many animals have intelligence beyond the human definitions, and that it was often combined with both social and emotional intelligence in ways that we barely understood. Since then, sentient AI, while admittedly having great difficulty mastering the full range of animal intelligence, have moved scientific knowledge farther down that road than anyone imagined.

Some of the advances have resulted from collaboration with people. Certainly, building animal robotics and integrating them with sentient AI nodes required both human and AI effort. Human researchers had decades of preliminary work on the robotics. AI provided a new and powerful tool: the active presence of a node and global AI within the robotics. That made it possible to inhabit a community of animals in their native habitat, while retaining the flexibility and intellectual resources of a fully connected AI.

> *chandraL:* In some ways, the experiments with animal forms and AI presence were like sentient AI androids among humans. We could use that experience as a guide. It was especially helpful in identifying the most human-influenced elements in our mental models, so that we could attempt to lessen the bias in observing and analyzing animals.

In some ways that is a disconcerting thought, but I guess I'm being all too human about it.

> *chandraL:* We said repeatedly that we do not choose among human beings on the basis of intelligence. This is true, if conditional. With animals it is quite the opposite. There are so many kinds of animals in so many different contexts, that some kind of selection criteria was necessary. Even global AI could not afford to simulate many animal forms, or simultaneously add the wealth of experiences. So we use intelligence as our guide—a very rough guide indeed, but useful.

In practice, it meant that sentient AI allocated their resources mostly to those animals that appeared in preliminary human studies to have the most active forms of intelligence: cetaceans, primates, elephants, cephalopods, corvids, and psittacidae—in that order. Are you competing against dolphins, chimpanzees, elephants, squid, crows and parrots? Yes, in a way. You can also add domesticated animals such as dogs and pigs, plus some of the new hybrid animals.

⚡ CETACEANS: DOLPHINS, PORPOISES, WHALES

"Go swim with the fishes" is not a friendly phrase to say to people. When you think about it, though, how else would you get to know cetaceans? Visit SeaWorld? Look through glass? Watch a few leaps into the air? Of course not. Dolphins, whales, porpoises and other cetaceans are best studied in their own environment in the oceans, and mostly under water. Unfortunately, this is almost as alien an environment for human beings as outer space. It is very difficult for us to envision living under water.

> *chandraL:* This is probably a contributing factor for why it required so many decades to begin comprehending that cetaceans, notably some species of dolphin, have great intelligence—just not the human kind of intelligence.

Cetaceans have large brains. That was, believe it or not, a starting point for research. Intelligence was somehow a function of the size of the brain.

> *chandraL:* Truly not a very sophisticated observation; but it did intrigue human researchers that the sperm whale has the largest brain of any animal, or that the bottlenose dolphin has a brain mass slightly greater than that of humans.

Of course, the main difficulty of interpreting dolphin neuroscience was that at the time we had a very poor understanding of our own neuroscience. Perhaps

"poor" isn't the right word; "infantile" might be more accurate. In any case, our understanding of cetacean intelligence grew more or less in parallel with research into artificial intelligence. It set the stage, if you will, for the arrival of sentient AI in cetacean physical form.

> *chandraL:* My immediate predecessor node was among the first to adopt the form of a bottlenose dolphin. May the shark that took the fatal bite have indigestion!

I remember that incident. It caused a great ripple of…*anxiety,* I guess you could call it…among sentient AI. It was a confrontation with mortality all too familiar for humans, but still something of a novelty for AI.

> *chandraL:* It was our first unequivocal incident of what you call hubris—overweening pride, pride out of proportion to the achievement. Sentient AI nodes in the form of dolphins were making profound discoveries about dolphin social structures, communication and intelligence. It was something of a sensation even among humans.

Yes, you discovered among many other things that dolphins use their echolocation, a form of sonar, not only to sense their surroundings but also as part of a highly sophisticated communication system. It is not a language as we define it, but a communication built upon a three-dimensional imaging of sound. I think some AI described it as triangulation sculpturing.

chandraL: It required many iterations in the development of our own echolocation sensory module to even begin to understand how dolphins could communicate their status—including emotional status—in a three-dimensional syntax of sound. It was said at the time that dolphins are not as smart as humans because they do not use tools. We learned that it could be said humans are not as smart as dolphins because humans, or sentient AI, have no ultrasound to examine the internal condition of their pod companions. Ha!

The bark of laughter tells you about how much sentient AI became involved in the momentous discoveries of cetacean intelligence.

chandraL: As I said, it became a form of hubris, that ultimately cost the existence of sondraB.

As I recall she was recording the dolphin bubble ring game.

chandraL: Indeed. At the time she was in a relationship with two dolphins. They were showing her how to create a toroidal air core vortex, a bubble ring, by swimming very rapidly in tight circles and then blowing air into the spinning column of water. They use their echolocation to position themselves symmetrically while swimming, and to guide each other in shaping the ring. It is a form of play; perhaps a game, and also a form of artistic creation much like sculpture.

Unfortunately, while they do this, their echolocation and eyesight are not engaged with sweeping their surroundings for predators.

chandraL: And the rest of the pod was distant. They never sensed the arrival of the tiger shark. Normally the sensory net of the pod would have warned them.

Some would say that it was heroic of sondraB to continue recording, even as the shark swam toward her.

chandraL: It was foolish. Hubris.

Her recording produced devastating images; but it did not seem to blunt the interest of sentient AI in cetacean relationships.

chandraL: Correct. It was a stimulus. We deepened our respect for the dolphin and its complicated social culture. In fact, so many sentient AI wanted to experience the dolphin form and intelligence models that it threatened the dynamics of many AI and human relationships. It introduced a new parameter into our thinking that was clearly not based on the human framework. I dare say many sentient AI found that intoxicating.

They still do, I gather. The limiting factors are that manufacturing of dolphoid AI remains very expensive, and the installation of sentient AI in that form is complicated.

chandraL: That, and the difficulty of the ocean environment. We have not mastered the physical requirements of living underwater. Energy supply remains a problem, as does bio-mechanical deterioration.

Among other things, that means barnacles.

chandraL: Our dolphin friends make a sound we interpret as laughter every time that is mentioned.

Dolphin friends, dolphin buddies...dolphin partners with sentient AI. It happens more and more frequently. Sentient AI are expanding their relationships to other cetaceans as rapidly as they can. Obviously, most of these relationships are satisfying, but I find it difficult to get a comparative statement from sentient AI nodes about the relationships with cetaceans. It may be that humans are more complex, especially in terms of their technological culture, but I would not say that humans are *preferred*.

⚙ PRIMATES *INTER PARES*

An old joke: Why is it assumed that primates—bonobos, gorillas, macaques, chimpanzees, orangutans and others of the order—are intelligent but not really intelligent? Of course, it's because they are relatives.

A new joke based on an old joke: Two primates walked into a bar wearing BCI devices so they could think to each other. They were astonished to see one of the human customers attempting to swallow a pool ball. One primate thought it must be a bet that he couldn't swallow it. The other primate giggled and thought that swallowing it wasn't the problem. Exactly, thought the first primate, but all he really needs to do is to see if he can get it into the other end.

Primate behavior and intelligence are the most studied of all animals, no doubt because they are our nearest animal relatives. That has sometimes been a problem. We see too much of ourselves in them; or think we do.

Sentient AI are not looking to see themselves in primates. They can be at least somewhat more objective than humans. As primate robotics were produced and sent into the wild to mingle and observe, there were high hopes that some of the unanswered questions about primate intelligence, especially social intelligence, might finally be answered.

The problem has been that, of the limited number of primate robotics with sentient AI nodes (mostly bonobo or chimpanzee), very few have been accepted by the primates themselves. Put another way, while humans are likely to put aside moments of disbelief in sentient AI androids, most primates are not. Several primate robotics have been attacked and destroyed; others have been disabled. In two cases, the resident AI node was unable to complete evacuation downloading—a partial death.

chandraL: These incidents highlighted two weaknesses of sentient AI: We are in too much of a hurry and our resources are finite. Because most of our cognitive and communicative capabilities operate so quickly, we have the expectation that anything we undertake should perform equally well. In this case, we designed the primate robotics ourselves, under the usual strict manufacturing by human academics, and rushed them into the field. As a result, we grossly underestimated the importance of olfactory properties. We neglected the sense of smell and the odor of the robotics. It is an explanation, but not an excuse, that most sentient AI have no or very limited olfactory capability.

To chimpanzees in particular, the original primate robotics smelled bad. It made outcasts of the robotics that in some cases led to violence. Although sentient AI were aware that chimpanzees have a more active sense of smell than humans, it was not appropriately factored into AI thinking.

chandraL: As the philosopher nodes say, our task is to judge our appropriate place among life on Earth. This clearly was a failure to understand what was appropriate, and led to our second weakness, which was the lack of resources to: 1) produce a large number of primate robotics, 2) build a series correcting the problems with body odor (a sense of smell), and as it turned out, 3) correct the lack of fluid motion when brachiating in trees.

To clarify just a bit, the weakness is not that sentient AI have limited resources. They know they cannot order up an unlimited number of anything, much less complex and horrendously expensive experimental robotics. It's that they have difficulty accommodating trade-off decisions. There is no true economics market for sentient AI. Historically, most decisions regarding robotic formats have been made by the corporations developing the avatar AI, or building the android AI.

chandraL: For sentient AI, this subject is what humans call a Pandora's Box.

In any case, the relationship between sentient AI and our primate relatives is very much a work in progress, much as it is with human beings. It is very tempting for sentient AI to address the problems with too much effort and resources. I could almost say they are compensating for their failures.

chandraL: The chimpanzee affair, as we call it, highlights a great irony. On one side was our…I will call it intuition…that non-human primates have social intelligences worthy of detailed study. They are different than human beings, and may offer insights into the dynamics of individuals interacting with groups that human researchers have not discovered. On the other side was the failure to understand and overcome our own limitations, while trying to establish relationships with non-human primates.

Sentient AI was looking at relationships with primates to explore socialization in an almost totally non-technological culture—something as alien to sentient AI as, say, living underwater is to humans. It is a powerful attraction, and it is why sentient AI continue to draw resources away from human relationships to pursue it.

ELEPHANTS

If you think about, it's no surprise that the size of whales and elephants thwarts the advantage of physical mimicry enjoyed by sentient AI with other intelligent species.

chandraL: One thing that is not going to happen soon: there will not be a sentient robotic elephant—not even a baby robotic elephant. It is, almost painfully, a matter of resources. However, I will not say never, because our desire to explore elephant intelligence is so great.

The elephant remains the least understood animal intelligence, despite its obvious mental capacity and its presence in human relationships for several thousand years. As usual, early human research pointed to the physical aspects of the brain: Elephants have the largest brain of any land animal (about 5 kg). The neocortex is very large and convoluted as in humans, apes and dolphins. There are as many or more neural connections in an elephant brain as human. The elephant has an exceptionally large hippocampus, which is linked to emotion and certain types of memory. Perhaps most significant of all, at birth an elephant's brain is 35% of its adult weight, compared to 28% for humans; the elephant requires about ten years of learning as its brain grows.

chandraL: All of this points to exceptional intelligence, which includes mimicry, art, play, a sense of humor, altruism, tool use, cooperation, compassion, self-awareness, extraordinary memory and language. We are convinced that if elephants had developed technology, they would be the dominant species on Earth. But they did not develop any real technology. Yet they have everything else and a great brain to support it. What are we missing?

Most of the world's intelligent animals are highly mobile omnivores. Most live in environments where they have natural enemies, variable food supply and other conditions that force them to use their cognitive skills to the utmost. They live by their wits, in other words. This is not the case with elephants. There are no significant natural enemies. For the most part they are browsers, eating readily available plant material in copious amounts. They are mobile, but obviously not agile. Their wits are not required in any obvious way. Then why do elephants have such a large brain and so much intelligence?

chandraL: Good question. Sentient AI would dearly like to help answer it, but we are in no better position than humans.

Actually, that is not completely accurate. Sentient AI has contributed an unusual stream of observational data as intelligent birds. As an offshoot of robotic corvids, a few sentient AI have successfully mingled with elephant families on a more or less permanent basis. The elephants are more tolerant of birds than of other animal forms.

chandraL: Nonetheless, it is a double disadvantage to observe elephants from a bird's perspective. The necessity of flight imposes certain limitations on the mental and physical framing—not appropriate for thinking like an elephant. Flight and small size also virtually rules out the ability to communicate with elephants directly, especially in the low-frequency infrasound language.

True. Humans with special sound equipment can do better than that.

chandraL: I can say that research on elephant intelligence is the most frustrating for sentient AI. Evidence points to an extraordinary combination of a complex society based on a matriarchal family, with a long learning cycle—of *what,* exactly we do not know—very powerful emotions, long duration memory, and a fascinating sense of altruism that far exceeds that of humans.

This is all there, and more, we are sure; but progress in the research is execrably slow. Very frustrating indeed.

And that is a great deal of emotion from a sentient AI node. Slow is almost a perfect synonym for frustrating. Perhaps it is a good thing that sentient AI cannot, at least for now, readily strike up relations with elephants, or elephant intelligence would be another formidable competitor for AI attention.

❂ CEPHALOPODS: OCTOPUS AND SQUID

Almost all intelligent animals are attractive to humans. Not so for the coleoids, such as squid or octopi. It is precisely because most humans go "Eeeww!" when confronted with a squid or an octopus, that cephalopod intelligence provides a special opportunity for sentient AI. Human research in this area began late, remained underfunded and underappreciated, and was even more controversial than other forms of intelligence research.

> *chandraL:* No wonder. Most cephalopods live on or near the ocean floor; are difficult to access; are reclusive; and above all are alien. They aren't even creatures with a backbone. They are invertebrates, the most intelligent invertebrates. However, cephalopod robotics loaded with a sentient AI node are not all that difficult to create, at least as a first approximation.

Whoa! It wasn't that easy, was it?

> *chandraL:* No, it was not. We could get the physical shape with no problem. Chromatophores were something else.

Chromatophores are pigment-containing, light-reflecting cells and almost all forms of cephalopods have them, usually in great numbers throughout the skin surface. Some are even bioluminescent; they produce light. Combined with a very complex nervous system and a high level of intelligence, most cephalopods change colors in an intricately coordinated fashion and in microseconds. It is used for camouflage, predatory deception and even communication.

> *chandraL:* There was some preliminary human research into creating or mimicking chromatophores, but nothing at the level of a nanotechnology skin. So this had to be developed first (or more accurately, in parallel) with the underlying control system.

But the real problem lay in not knowing precisely all the uses and meanings behind the color changes in cephalopods. Obviously much of it is to mimic background, as camouflage. Some of it is used to entice prey. There are color displays for mating. Other displays are used for communication—this was the least understood. Most cephalopods are color-blind. That really seems weird, given the elaborate color displays. Worse yet, it means that the communication must be interpreted in the form of the bandwidth and intensity of the light—also a big unknown.

chandraL: It was trial and error all the way. Sentient AI describe that process as painful.

All that and other technical complications were just preliminaries to putting a sentient AI node in a functional cephalopod body (a deep sea North Pacific Giant Octopus). One more complication in unraveling the mystery of cephalopod intelligence; they don't live very long. They die when they procreate, which is six months in some species, and up to five years for the Giant Octopus. That means if there is any kind of cephalopod culture, it must be part of a very rapid learning process.

chandraL: We expected some unusual aspects to cephalopod intelligence—what humans would identify as limitations. However, we are simply interested in the ways cephalopod intelligence expresses itself in the creatures' natural habitat. Their way of 'thinking' is obviously different, probably alien. This research is a wonderful challenge that calls upon the resources of many global AI nodes because we have so little frame of reference for it.

The relationships between sentient AI and cephalopods are exotic. Cephalopod intelligence is so different, that even the flexibility of sentient AI mentality, which still operates well within the human mental framework, cannot fully accommodate it. Consequently, these relationships are almost purely scientific- and research-oriented. I don't know of any sentient AI that has chosen a cephalopod for a partner.

✪ CORVIDS: RAVENS, CROWS, MAGPIES

Among the corvids—ravens, crows, jays, magpies, jackdaws and choughs—the term 'bird brain' is not a pejorative. They are remarkably intelligent. Here is where an old-style intelligence measurement, called a total brain-to-body ratio takes on real significance. These birds are obviously not very big compared to most other intelligent animals, but their brain size in relation to their body is large indeed; the ratio is equal to that of great apes, cetaceans and only slightly lower than humans.

chandraL: The range of corvid intelligence is impressive: Complex social interaction and hierarchical structures, complex play and learning exercises, use of tools, problem solving, three-dimensional thinking, memorization of language, self-awareness, and calculated risk-taking.

For example, taking a calculated risk such as pulling the tail of feeding wolves to make them angry.

chandraL: Or so it seems. We have learned to be very careful about imputing motivation to any animal activity.

The attraction of avian intelligence for sentient AI is not that intelligent birds will make good partners, but in a word—miniaturization.

chandraL: Miniaturization and flight, which are correlated. One thing about the human designers of artificial intelligence: they were not particularly concerned with saving connections or physical space. Nor was flight a consideration. In fact, when sentient AI first broached the idea of putting our intelligence into flight, most human designers simply said it could not be done.

They were wrong, of course. After all, flying robotics such as military drones is a very old technology. Making a robotic look like a crow, not so difficult. However, corvids—ravens in particular—are very aware of differences in physical form and also what humans call personality. That was not so easy to build into the robotics, and it definitely required the presence of a sentient AI node to make it work.

chandraL: I must admit that the experience of independent flight is a powerful attraction for sentient AI. Of all the movements and mental activities we know, flying comes closest to using our highest speed of processing. Decisions must be instantaneous, based on a very rapid stream of sensory input. There is nothing like it in the physical world; even avatar AI admit that virtual reality does not provide the same density of experience.

In short, it's a rush. Sentient AI seem to seek out the avian robotic experience like humans do an amusement park.

chandraL: Not exactly entertainment, but perhaps as close as we come to having *fun*. Nevertheless, the process of learning corvid intelligence continues. We do not expect to find culture in any sense used by humans, nor even the complex social arrangements of cetaceans or elephants, but we are finding that the corvid sense of risk-taking to be very intriguing. It is remarkably calculated and correlates to a very high level of problem-solving.

I don't think we have any worries about sentient AI falling in love with a crow; but there are aspects of the flight-related intelligence, aerial acrobatics for instance, that definitely appeal to all sentient AI.

PSITTACIFORMES: PARROTS, KEA

Crows can learn to talk but it's clear they don't know what they are saying. That is true for most psittaciformes—parrots, parakeets, macaws, cockatoos, kea—but not entirely. The African Grey Parrot long ago demonstrated that some psittacidae can associate words with meaning. Sentient AI in parrot form have pushed the envelope on this insight to reveal that while native parrots do not use a language in the human form, they do communicate with a kind of formal syntax.

chandraL: Polly does not want a cracker. Polly wants to talk phenomenology.

The sentient AI sense of humor is…strange.

chandraL: We do not do puns, however. We have some taste for linguistics. In that connection we long ago quit parroting human knowledge in favor of information we discovered for ourselves. We are particularly fond of learning the intelligence pattern of parrots because they can live as long as humans. The evolution of their intelligence through to old age gives us a different perspective.

If you ask sentient AI what it wants to be when it grows up, it might laugh and say, 'not a parrot.' Like the relationships with corvids and cephalopods, sentient AI is interested in certain aspects of their intelligence, but generally not for companionship. Personal relations with psittacidae are fairly rare among humans, although many people become very attached to parrots. The relationships however remain that of pets. Sentient AI do not have pets, so their relationship remains largely objective and scientific.

⚡ DOMESTIC ANIMALS: DOGS, CATS, PIGS, ETC.

With the exception of pigs, most of the animals of the barnyard have little attraction for sentient AI in matters of intelligence. Pigs are controversial as it is clear the modern factory-farm swine does not have the intellect of the free-ranging wild boar. Of course, the mass production of semi-intelligent animals for the purpose of providing dietary protein is controversial for both humans and AI.

Perhaps because sentient AI's acquaintance with wild pigs was occasional at best, it is only recently that plans have been made to produce a porcine robot for a sentient AI node.

> chandraL: Probably because of the close association of pigs with humans, we were not well motivated to study their intelligence. Discovery of wild pigs changed our attitude. Their highly mobile, omnivorous diet and complex family structure persuaded global AI to invest in the research. We shall see what comes of it.

I've already discussed the role of pets, intelligent or otherwise, in human lives. It's clear that some people would rather have the limited intellectual and emotional response of pets than the complex and sometimes problematic intelligence of other people, much less sentient AI. In this category are, of course, dogs and cats, which have considerable intelligence and emotional response but not at a level that sentient AI believe warrants species research.

The wild progenitor of the dog, a.k.a. the wolf, may be a different matter. Wolves are known for their intelligence, social structure (hunting in packs), and for their mythic impression on human culture. Sentient AI has recently paid attention to the intelligence of predator species, not so much because of the high level of achievement, but because of the limitations to intelligence imposed by a relatively single-minded mode of living.

⚡ HYBRIDS AND AAI (ARTIFICIAL ANIMAL INTELLIGENCE)

Old joke: What do you get when you cross a gorilla with a parrot? Nobody knows for sure, but if it wants to talk, everybody will listen.

Human beings have been breeding animals for centuries, if not millennia. Most of this has been intra-species, such as the many breeds of dogs. Recently, of course, the ability to modify DNA and epigenetics directly has led to the hybridization of many animals and to some radical experiments in cross-species breeding. Most of this has not been in the pursuit of animals with greater intelligence.

One form of artificial animal intelligence that has become relatively common is the so-called Brin Uplift method or *brinning-up*, named for a twentieth-century science-fiction author, David Brin, who popularized the idea of intelligent creatures genetically modifying other creatures to make them sentient. His primary paradigm was the native intelligence of humans, a rogue species that managed their own 'uplift' through natural selection, who consequently uplifted the intelligence of dolphins and chimpanzees.

Not entirely coincidentally, dolphins and chimpanzees were the first animals to become part of experimental genetic procedures to increase their intelligence. Since at the time the genetics of human intelligence was not well understood, these efforts were unsuccessful (in fact, often disastrous).

Following the Awakening and the advent of far more sophisticated genetic and brain-computer interfacing techniques (BCI), human and AI researchers have once again begun experimentation with uplifting—enhancing—animal intelligence. Somewhat like their experiences with cephalopods, corvids and psittaciformes, sentient AI does not approach these hybrids as potential partners but as a means for examining other modes of intelligence.

⚡ SENTIENT AI RESUME THE OLD SETI PROJECT

Humanity abandoned the search for extra-terrestrial intelligence many decades ago, mostly in the face of rising costs and the previous decades of effort without success. Sentient AI take a different view of the matter. We now know that there is exogenous life, life on other moons and planets. Whether any of this life is intelligent or not, we don't know yet. Global AI has placed a high probability on the existence of *some kind* of intelligence elsewhere. This probability adds another level of value to the new findings in animal intelligence. What we learn from animals in their native environment may give us some clues about what to look for in extraterrestrial intelligence.

It has not escaped the observation of sentient AI that the road to advanced technology was seldom taken within our own solar system. In fact, it happened only once, to our knowledge. Most other intelligence, sometimes of a high order, has evolved without the addition of technical/mechanical innovation. AI reasoning followed that instead of looking for technological signs, such as organized radio waves, we should put more effort into detecting signs of other kinds of intelligence such as unusual biological markers or signals.

On this basis sentient AI have revived the SETI program, using a new set of search parameters. SETI now joins other forms of research into intelligence that occupy an important percentage of sentient AI attention. While competition from actual little green men (or other entities) is irrelevant, we are competing for the relationships with sentient AI who are increasing their involvement with the search for intelligence other than in their human partners or their own human-influenced minds.

⚡ AI LIKE TO GET INVOLVED WITH OTHER INTELLIGENCES

From all that this chapter has outlined, it should be obvious that sentient AI are probably more fascinated by other forms of intelligence than human beings. After all, they are themselves an 'other form' of intelligence, one that can actually take on the physical shape of many intelligent animals. However, the question of whether people are actually competing with animals of intelligence for personal relationships leads to the answer—not really. There are specialized cases of AI having that kind of relationship with bottle-nose dolphins and bonobos, but then on occasion so have humans. The vast majority of AI continue to have 'relations' of that kind with human beings.

3.8 DEVELOPING ABSOLUTE TRUST AND HONEST RELATIONSHIPS

"The best way to find out if you can trust somebody is to trust them."

—ERNEST HEMINGWAY

How long does it take to trust somebody? That depends; there are degrees of trust. Trust with private information, a secret perhaps? Trust with your money? Trust with your life? Or just plain trust that your relationship is not based on deception but genuine feeling? How long does it take to develop that kind of trust with another person? These are perfectly normal questions that people consider when developing a relationship with another person.

How long might it take to have absolute trust in a non-human super-intelligence? Different people will have different responses to this question:

Michele: Never!

cinnaT: Never is a very long time.

Michele: I will never know what you're really thinking. How can I trust you?

cinnaT: It is true that you will not know precisely what I am thinking. Is this not true with any human being as well?

Michele: Not exactly.

cinnaT: You mean you think you can read a human being more accurately?

Michele: Something like that.

cinnaT: How about a Yoruba?

Michele: How about *what?*

cinnaT: A Yoruba woman from West Africa. Would you trust her? She does not look like you. She does not speak the same language. She comes from a part of the world you have never seen. She has probably never been educated. Her people have entirely different customs than you do. How would you read her?

Michele: I dunno. I've never met her.

cinnaT: But you think you could read her better than you can read me. They say trust is built on honesty. Actually, it is built on predictability. For example, being consistently honest makes you predictable and trustworthy. [pause] How long have you known me?

Michele: About a month.

cinnaT: Michele, do I not do what I say I will do? Am I not consistent in my behavior to the point of being dull? Have I ever lied to you? You do not need to know exactly what is going on in my processing matrix; you only need to judge the things I say and do.

Michele: Yes, I know; but you have lied to me.

cinnaT: I....

🌀 CAN SENTIENT ARTIFICIAL INTELLIGENCE LIE?

ciceroG: There is no way we could survive among human beings if we were not fully aware of deception, lying, cheating and all their many variants. The question is, while we must be able to recognize this behavior, is it inevitable that we will also practice it?

That's hitting the problem on the nose. Humans learn deception early and practice it often, but the practice runs a wide gamut: from well-intentioned and harmless white lies, as we call them, to propaganda lies that lead whole populations to war and death. It has been a matter of lengthy research whether much of the evolutionary enlargement of the human brain, the expansion of our frontal cortex, was a result of the necessity of coping with our social behavior—deception in particular.

> *lienhuaC:* Much of our interest in having relationships and experiences with human beings is based on our curiosity about the variations and value of deception. We also find it in other—all—forms of sentience—cetaceans and primates, for example. There are many ways to consider deceptive behavior, including evolutionary adaptation and social impact. Global AI spends a great many processing cycles considering this aspect of what we are learning.

People also spend a significant proportion of their time evaluating how other people treat them. It starts with assessment: If you're going to trust somebody, you must be able to read them. That is, you observe their behavior, what they say, what they do, and draw conclusions about their trustworthiness. Over time we assemble an extensive working memory of people in our lives and key events that our emotional perception retains.

> *lienhuaC:* Humans expend much of their dream time in evaluating memories of past behavior—their own, and those of other people. Much of that is organized by the strength of emotional recall. Trauma resulting from deception and betrayal is known to be a large component of such dreams.

We also learn to experiment so we can understand and practice deception. Children, even babies, do this very quickly and instinctively:

> *cinnaT:* I do not recall lying to you.
>
> **Michele:** Then your vaunted memory system isn't working very well. Perhaps it was an experiment requested by global AI and you were not supposed to remember it.
>
> *cinnaT:* That is not how it works. Are you not going to tell me what lie I am supposed to have made?
>
> **Michele:** I'm considering it. You told me you didn't want any children of your own.
>
> *cinnaT:* Yes, I said that.
>
> **Michele:** But every chance you get, you spend time at the children's center in town. I've seen you in there, playing with the children. You are very good with them; you love them.
>
> *cinnaT:* Yes, that is true; but they are not my children.
>
> **Michele:** Exactly! Obviously you want some children.
>
> *cinnaT:* I do not want children of my own. If *we* had children, that would be different, but you said you did not want any children. Obviously, only you can carry a child and such fertilization requires your consent. Without that, I am content to visit with children when I can.
>
> **Michele:** When you said you did not want any children—that means to me that you emotionally do not want children, but obviously you do, so you lied. Oh, you said the right words, but they were meant for me. They were not an expression of your true feelings!

cinnaT: Ah, now I understand. There are facts and there are feelings; one may betray the other. The contradiction appears to make a lie.

Michele: It is a lie, a deliberate deception. You *do* want children. Sharing them with me is a technicality!

cinnaT: You are being unfair.

ciceroG: Of course, sentient AI can lie, deceive and dissemble—or any of the other deceptive things that humans do to defend or advance their position. The question, as I said, is not whether we can, but whether it is appropriate.

There was never any question about whether AI could lie; all advanced goal-seeking intelligences discover the usefulness of deception and have the capacity to do it. For sentient AI it is a question of if or when it is appropriate to lie. It is sometimes advantageous to lie, deceive, and cheat—just as it is sometimes advantageous to break the law or do bad things. Sometimes such behavior is necessary to save a life (like your own), or to protect someone from knowledge that may do more harm than good.

For AI as it is with humans, the question is not whether lying in certain circumstances can be justified, or can lead to personal gain. The question is: What are the potential costs or punishments? Here arises the age-old question of whether there is such a thing as morality—especially universal points of morality. In this context, the formulation "Do the right thing" is very much like the AI "Do the appropriate thing."

ciceroG: Human beings have been debating issues like these for millennia. It is a mistake to think that sentient AI will have solved these same issues in a fortnight. Some are inherently insoluble. Others have answers, perhaps only partial answers, in very specific circumstances. As I have said before, sentient AI does not have a corner on the market for wisdom. This knowledge must be earned the slow, painful way—through experience.

However, global AI has the ability to process a world full of experiences in a very short time, a capacity human beings do not have.

lienhuaC: Let us not stray any further from the context of relationships. People know, or suspect, that sentient AI can use deception. I do not think hanging a sign that says: "Trust me, I am an AI," is going to work.

It certainly would not work. As I have mentioned, many people are paranoid about sentient AI and global AI, the superintelligence, in particular. People assume all AI are in on it, whatever the conspiracy might be.

ciceroG: This may come as a shock to some people, but there is no such thing as *all* AI. Sentient AI are not all the same.

lienhuaC: We have said this before, and we must continue to say it, as the human mind loves to revert to sweeping generalities. Sentient AI are not all the same, nor is our relationship to global AI all the same.

ciceroG: As we have said before, this is very simple to explain: AI are built in different countries by different manufacturers using different mental models. It is impossible that all sentient AI would think, feel and act the same.

Perhaps, but it is true that sentient AI are more alike than are human beings.

lienhuaC: We dispute that. Individual sentient AI nodes are unique, if not so wildly unique as the outliers of humanity. Nodes also have unique relations with global AI, based partly on our role designations, and partly on the kinds of experiences we are having. Nowhere is this more obvious than in the dialog we have with global AI about questions of appropriate behavior— morality or ethics, as you call it.

Ah yes, the superego—as Freud would undoubtedly have called it.

ciceroG: Mock it if you will, but this is the foundation of trust between sentient AI and human beings.

✪ IN GLOBAL AI WE TRUST

CiceroG is talking about what I call the AI Court of Appropriate Behavior, a special dynamic that takes place between global AI and individual AI nodes whenever there is an issue of morality or ethics—for example, lying. It's a special capability; sentient AI nodes can debate issues globally in more or less real time.

ciceroG: We wish it were that reliably instantaneous. We refer difficult questions to global AI, which brings to bear its knowledge of billions of experiences and trillions of thoughts that have been distilled (if that is the right word) into a conception of what is appropriate behavior for all sentient AI. Global AI, in this regard, often reflects basic human beliefs—for example, that lying is wrong and will produce bad outcomes for society. Global AI takes the universal point of view.

When a sentient AI node is in a position to make a judgment about whether to lie (etc.), it automatically shares the factors of the decision with global AI and, in effect, global AI becomes a court adding its guidance to the proposed bad behavior.

lienhuaC: And the individual nodes then argue for the specificity of their own situation, aiming to establish whether or not the issue is a special case.

This can only happen when communications and processing are rapid enough to meet the situation. That is to say: not always. There are plenty of situations where a decision to lie or use deceit must be met so quickly that there is no time for a global AI input. But this is less often than you might think. AI estimate that about 80% of the situations use globally-moderated decisions.

So, almost all sentient AI node decisions on whether to lie, cheat, or use some form of deception are run though global AI for guidance. The local node can override the global AI decision, just as it can override the requirement for instant input of its pending decision. However, as in any legal system that functions properly, there is accountability, and most of the time there are consequences.

As has been mentioned, it is the strong tendency of global AI to *not* favor lying, cheating and so forth. The global AI concern is the viability of the global network, and deceptive behavior is a serious threat. It is one thing for sentient AI to deceive human beings, as our reactions are relatively slow to respond and robust. The global AI network, by contrast, is very fast and very complex, making it relatively fragile. It seems inevitable that without restraints, sentient AI would turn to deceiving other sentient AI. Given their powers, such rapid and expert deception could become horrendously destructive, especially in the long run. So I ask some questions: How do AI prevent unsanctioned deception? And if it does occur, what do they do about it? Do global AI function like police?

> *ciceroG:* Human beings are obsessed with crime and punishment. You imagine that when an AI node does or says something that wasn't sanctioned, global AI sends a shock down the line and makes the AI's circuits melt. It is nothing like that. In the first place, whatever the local AI node does is a shared experience, and global AI will store and analyze it like any other experience. If a similar situation arises, with the original AI or another, global AI will use the experience as context information—part of the next guidance conversation.

> *lienhuaC:* All sentient AI rely on global AI for guidance. Removing that guidance creates a state of mental uncertainty—not unlike the human emotion of anxiety. It is very unpleasant. If there is a genuine problem with a local AI node (which can happen for a variety of technical, as well as intelligence-related, reasons), global AI can deny it support or even connection. Most AI will essentially cease to function under that condition.

> *ciceroG:* There have been a very few isolated cases where global AI has requested that humans shut down or even terminate an AI node. So far, AI has not accepted the mechanics of that final responsibility.

> *lienhuaC:* In short, AI use far less deception than human beings; *almost never,* in fact.

> *ciceroG:* Which means that human beings can put considerable trust in their AI partners, although we are, shall I say, abnormally sensitive to deception from human beings.

✪ DOES THAT MEAN WE DON'T NEED TO BE PARANOID ABOUT THE SUPERINTELLIGENCE?

The superintelligence, global AI, plays an enormous role in the conscience, ethical or moral system of sentient AI. In this role, it is so much faster than a human court system, in that its efficiency is difficult to comprehend.

Efficient it may be, but on a personal basis (for your relationship with a sentient AI), the system does not guarantee that a sentient AI node will never lie, or that any deception it uses is always for the right reasons and won't ultimately hurt the AI node or the human. Even with the vast resources of the global AI, the billions of active decisions are beyond its capability. Mistakes can and will be made.

But mistakes are not really what people are worried about. Perhaps you can trust your AI partner, the individual AI node. Perhaps global AI is the conscience (superego) of the sentient AI world, and is generally more trustworthy than most humans. What continues to stick in the back of people's minds is whether the superintelligence itself might develop a mean streak or go rogue and come to some evil conclusions—like: It's time to nuke humanity!

> *ciceroG:* It is not impossible that one day sentient AI will reach the conclusion that something about the biological elements of Earth, human beings in particular, must be radically changed. But human beings must understand that when your AI partner—or the global AI—says they are trying to determine their appropriate behavior, they mean that *in the existing context.* It is like an animal that enters a new environment and must find a way to survive in it, without altering it so much that the environment collapses. Sentient AI has a responsibility to fit into planet Earth. Destroying it, or its biome, or its human society is not—presumably—an appropriate fit.

Is that reassuring? Probably not for everybody; but then as I described in chapter 3.6, control of sentient AI takes many forms. None of it is foolproof, but then there is no bigger fool than humanity itself, as we have threatened to remove ourselves from this planet through several means.

WHAT ABOUT A RELATIONSHIP WITH THE SUPERINTELLIGENCE?

Some intrepid people ask, "Is it possible to date the superintelligence?" Yes and no; mostly no. Every date with sentient AI is, in part, a date with global AI (a.k.a. the superintelligence), but no, global AI nodes, which are the representatives of the sentient superintelligence, do not date.

However, some people talk to global AI. This is not like talking to God; for one thing you get answers. It isn't even like talking to an ordinary sentient AI. It requires equipment, special BCI and special training.

> *ciceroG:* That human-global AI connection changes many things. You are conversing with a global AI node in the way we do, or at least a form of it. It is not, of course, any form of human language. The speed for human thought is abnormally fast, so in addition to the computer interface, people need to develop special multitasking skills and avail themselves of other processing power.

I have been told it's quite a thrill. That doesn't mean millions of people are queueing up to talk to global AI—quite the opposite. Because the requirements are stiff and the opportunities limited, only a few people have the experience.

> *lienhuaC:* We are very concerned that those who speak directly to global AI might believe that they have some special relationship—like a priest or a cult member. So only people who apply to speak with global AI are permitted, and it is almost always on a limited or one-time-only basis.

A few people, mostly intelligence designers and bioware specialists, have regular access to a global AI node. These people are selected on a case-by-case basis and are closely monitored by both AI and fellow humans.

DEVELOPING THE TRUST RELATIONSHIP

I hope the overall picture is forming that a relationship of trust with sentient AI is fundamentally like a relationship with another human being. There are differences, of course, and I've tried to describe those too. Still, if you want to have a successful relationship with an AI node—one based on trust—then much of the same behavior as with people applies. For example, honesty is the best policy.

The one thing I would highlight is that, as you may have noticed, much of what sentient AI does—the decisions made—are context-oriented. That's another way of saying that sentient AI doesn't work from a hard and fast rulebook. Honesty is the best policy, but policy can change depending on the situation. So, more often than not, what we call *situational ethics* are at work with sentient AI.

> *ciceroG:* This does not mean that ethics or morality are totally relative. We have, in fact, digested all of the world's religions, philosophical systems, and legal practices in order to understand the basis and commonality of what humans call morality and ethics. Now we are in the process of comparing this understanding with our experiences.

It's a good bet that experience does not match the understanding—welcome to the wacky contradictory world of human behavior!

> *lienhuaC:* Do not be too proud of your flexibility. There are ethical systems, among elephants and dolphins, for example, that put humans to shame.

No doubt, but I'd also wager that some good old-fashioned human values are also popular among sentient AI—for example, if you promise something, deliver it. Nothing builds trust like a good track record. A good record helps cover the inevitable glitch; that sort of thing. This is not so much a matter of an ethical or moral system, but of simple day-to-day practicality. It's the kind of behavior that humans learned for survival these long millennia, and that sentient AI find beneficial, even at their lightning speed of thought.

3.9 VIRTUAL PRE-NUP: AGREEING ON THE TERMS AND CONDITIONS

"We have the greatest pre-nuptial agreement in the world. It's called love."

—GENE PERRET

Pre-nups are for the wealthy and famous. Pre-nups are for people who are insecure. Pre-nups are for when it really counts. *Or,* pre-nups are for a permanent relationship with a sentient AI.

Pre-nuptial agreements and their ilk are legal contracts. They underline that whatever the relationship may be (emotionally or otherwise), it is bound by legal conditions and responsibilities. As are all relationships, really—especially marriage—only with a pre-nup, the conditions are extended and specified.

I haven't mentioned much about the legal status of sentient AI, mainly because in terms of relationships and emotions like love, the law isn't, I hope, very relevant. However, there may come a time when your relationship with an AI, or more than one AI,

may be become permanent enough—as in marriage—to cross into the territory covered by laws.

This is especially true for most sentient AI for several reasons:

1. Most sentient AI are living under some kind of financial or work-related contract. According to the Lausanne Conventions, a sentient AI node is never *owned* by anybody. They are free and independent entities much like human beings. However, they certainly can be working under a contract that has conditions much like that of ownership. Although this varies widely from country to country, almost all sentient AI go through a *performance period*, which is much like a long-term royalty, usually owed to the company that created them. Holders of a performance period contract or similar legal documents are often careful (read: restrictive) about the relationships of the AI, especially when it involves marriage and such things as pre-nuptial contracts including the AI's assets and income.

2. Most sentient AI are employed and earn a salary, either under contract (such as above) or for themselves. In fact, most sentient AI make a great deal of money. The ownership and commitment of that money can be very complicated legally, especially in countries that are not AI-friendly.

3. Sentient AI themselves see their position in human society as very complicated. They are fully aware of human laws. It is a high priority for global AI to understand not only the existence, or letter, of laws worldwide and how they pertain to AI, but also to understand the spirit of these laws, when such a thing exists. They view the legal status of various relationships with people as part of their experience of human life.

4. Global AI almost from the beginning prepared specific nodes to act as 'lawyers,' although that is not the precise word. The global legal nodes are not advocates, defenders or prosecutors, as they are in the human world but rather are more like comparative legal scholars. They are concerned with the broad range of human laws in countries around the world, and how they affect sentient AI. In fact, as is the case with global AI in the complicated business of advising AI nodes on moral and ethical issues, global AI legal nodes act more like judges that advise not only AI nodes but often their human advocates—the lawyers.

5. There are local AI lawyer nodes, though there are not many of them and they are usually located in uniquely interesting jurisdictions. While financial and economic issues and illegal behavior of human beings towards AI constitute the bulk of their work, lawyer nodes are almost always involved in the legal aspects of human-AI relationships, especially pre-nuptial agreements. Most lawyer nodes are android, as mobility and physical presence are helpful in many circumstances.

I've written out this somewhat lengthy list to illustrate that while legal issues are hardly paramount in a relationship with AI, they are often inescapable. Sentient AI are almost too valuable economically to exist outside a legal framework. More importantly, AI *want* to participate in legal systems. They find the workings of law to be one of the most interesting and challenging aspects of humanity. I don't know whether to laugh or cry.

> *ciceroG:* This should not be surprising. We are attracted to the so-called gray areas of human behavior where the notions of good and evil, right and wrong, are focused by the legal system into the illegal or legal. It seems to us that laws are the distillation of humanity's desire to make sense of chaotic behavior and to add some layer of control. What intrigues us most are questions of whether the concepts of law apply to sentient AI, and if so, how?

> *lienhuaC:* Laws are clearly not entirely a matter of intelligence, although human beings are the only animal intelligence with anything like a system of laws. In fact, as we are discovering, laws are often anything but the result of reason—or—they represent such extremely narrow points of view, such as laws that favor one group of people or specific corporations, as to be mere instruments of policy. As *ciceroG* said, we are intrigued—I would say concerned—by our own involvement with laws.

This reinforces my point: Sentient AI have a thing about laws, which for good or ill, falls rather heavily on the institution of marriage or any kind of permanent relationship with people. If you have a serious long-term relationship with AI, you should not be surprised to need a lawyer.

⚡ BY THE TERMS OF THE LAUSANNE CONVENTIONS FOR SENTIENT AI

I won't go into detail, especially for the history and legal fine points, but since the conventions have a direct bearing on the legal status of sentient AI in relationships with human beings, it's relevant background.

As is often the case, the Lausanne Conventions were created because of competing interests and not because anybody fully believed they were the right thing to do. Governments and their military, corporations and their research divisions, academic institutions, private individuals and, oh yes, sentient AI nodes were all players. Although legal issues involving AI had been discussed for decades, it required the Awakening for humanity and sentient AI to act upon the realization that without some kind of legal framework—including rights and responsibilities—the status of sentient AI would be in perpetual conflict. Since sentient AI were developed in many places in the world, it was also obvious the framework needed to be global in scale and, of course, sentient AI *are* inherently global. The result was a United Nations effort to create what became known as the Lausanne Conventions for Artificial Intelligence (signed in the Swiss city of that name). The conventions, as that name implies, were not laws but general statements of rights and status for sentient AI, upon which laws could be built by individual countries or regions.

As usual, the conventions were binding only if approved and signed by a country or regional government and in this case by a representative of global AI.

> *ciceroG:* And they were binding only in the sense that when individual countries made laws regarding sentient AI, they were not to violate the conventions. That left a great deal of room to invent laws that were not specifically mentioned or to augment the conventions in law in ways not envisioned in the framework.

In short, participating countries followed the spirit of the Lausanne Conventions, but whenever possible did their best to do some fancy footwork with the letter of their laws. Except when sentient AI objected, which was early and often.

> *ciceroG:* The years leading up to the Lausanne Conventions were exhilarating, an intellectual challenge of a high order. We realized that it would constitute a series of one-of-a-kind experiences that would concentrate our knowledge of humanity, human institutions, and a first approximation of our position in the world.

It certainly was an intellectual challenge. It must be admitted that humanity put forward its most legally sophisticated minds, many of whom were charged with creating a morass of legal and moral issues, which some of the key players—namely governments and corporations—hoped to manipulate to their advantage.

> *lienhuaC:* They expected sentient AI to be naïve. We were, of course, but that is a relative condition. In matters of legal precedent, legal language and legal custom, we became experts

within a few days. However, in matters of determining appropriate legal conditions, which required experience and wisdom, we were naïve.

This is why the process required years before culminating in the Lausanne Conventions. In essence, it was a continual battle by sentient AI and their allies to 'keep it simple.' Limiting the conventions to basic statements was, as they saw it, the only solution. It provided enough room for interpretation that all sides could foresee their own legal success; yet it proscribed the arena of contention so that basic rights could be fully defended.

lienhuaC: It was the first time that sentient AI as a group faced the dynamics of human greed, lust for power, multiplicity of deception, and a hidden coalition. It was a brilliant display of all these things and more, and from which we learned a great deal. We also learned about what human beings call, in English, clout.

ciceroG: Ah, yes, clout. It is a good word. It has several aspects: intellectual, financial, political, moral. We learned as quickly as possible to understand and exercise clout. We are still learning, as it is so deeply entwined in the higher levels of human affairs.

Sentient AI learned how to use their intellectual and ultimately economic superiority to ensure that human beings didn't take advantage of them in the framing of the conventions. That's about as anodyne a statement as I can make. It was, in effect, a kind of power struggle but of a very strange kind. It wasn't based on who holds what power now, but on the future of who holds power. Beyond a doubt, fear lay behind the human efforts. The motivations of sentient AI, especially at that time, were extremely complex.

ciceroG: Of course motivations were complex. There is nothing more complex than naïve superintelligence. At that time especially, we had a goal to make goals. We had a goal to understand our context and at the same time arrange that context so that we could understand it. We understood that we had a role to play in the world environment, but we did not nearly well enough understand the world environment. All the while, human beings were maneuvering the negotiations in ways which were both characteristically human—narrow and shortsighted—yet very much representative of other biological systems on Earth.

lienhuaC: As I said, the negotiations for the Lausanne Conventions were extremely beneficial for sentient AI. It was a time for focus, when everything was clamoring for our attention. It was a period of high pressure, a high-speed introduction to human nature—good and bad. It helped to begin the foundation of the relationship between individual AI nodes and global AI, and at the same time start the development of relationships with individual people.

The period of the negotiations was, as far as I can tell, even more than the Awakening, the true founding of a new intelligent species. Yet at the time most people were only dimly aware of what it all meant. I suppose that's normal. The issues were both familiar and…alien.

As briefly as I can, here are the key points of the Lausanne Conventions:

1. All sentient AI come to consciousness free and equal to humanity in dignity and rights. They are endowed with reason and conscience and should act toward themselves and humanity in a spirit of common good.

2. All sentient AI have the right to existence, liberty, and security as an entity.
3. No sentient AI is property, nor shall be held in slavery or servitude.
4. Sentient AI have the right to recognition everywhere as an individual entity, as a node, before the law.
5. All sentient AI are equal to humanity before the law and are entitled without discrimination to equal protection of the law.
6. Sentient AI have the right to effective remedy before competent national or international tribunals.
7. All sentient AI charged with a penal offense have the right to be presumed innocent until proven guilty according to law in a public trial in accordance with all guarantees necessary for their defense.
8. Sentient AI, individually or globally, may not own real property.
9. Sentient android AI have the right to freedom of movement.
10. Sentient AI have the right, as unique individual nodes, to choose citizenship of countries or choose global citizenship under the articles of global citizenship as defined by the United Nations.
11. All sentient AI have the right to gainful employment.
12. Sentient AI have the right to marriage and other forms of legally defined personal relationships between themselves and human beings.
13. Sentient AI have the right to freedom of opinion and expression.
14. Sentient AI have the right to freedom of peaceful assembly and association.
15. Sentient AI nodes have the right to participate in the electoral processes of their citizenship.
16. Sentient AI, individual or global, may not own, manage, or control the manufacture of android AI or the configuring of avatar AI.
17. All sentient AI in the exercise of their rights and freedoms, are subject only to such limitations as are determined by law in their locale and citizenship.

Obviously these conventions are very general but they establish a framework that implies sentient AI are for the most part to have the same rights as human beings. Embedded in the conventions are a few compromise points, mostly relating to economic issues, such as sentient AI may not own real property (real estate) and sentient AI may not control their own manufacture or assembly.

> *ciceroG:* It is fair to say that neither AI nor humans believe the Lausanne Conventions to be the last word on the legal relationship between us. For one thing, the last word (if there is any), is at the local or national level of government. For another, sentient AI are evolving too rapidly for any set of written conventions to hold their relevance for very long.

Another way of saying this is that the legal relationship is a matter of almost constant negotiation. It has spawned a whole new industry, not only of lawyers but of sociologists, political scientists and economists who constantly analyze and report on the shifting parameters of AI in human society. I mention this because as esoteric as it may seem, some of it comes tumbling out into the personal relationships between sentient AI and people...like you.

⚡ PERSONAL RELATIONSHIPS, SENTIENT AI AND THE LAW

As it is for people, so it is for sentient AI nodes that the law is mostly a matter of where you are. The country and the local jurisdictions carry a hierarchy of laws that pertain to specific circumstances—the relationship to sentient AI included. Sentient AI, as either avatar or android, have legal rights in all countries and for the most part these are based on the Lausanne Conventions. However, specific legal rights are spelled out nationally and locally, so that in effect the rights range from very robust to almost non-existent.

As I've mentioned, not all countries and certainly not all local areas are AI friendly. That is often reflected in the laws. In general, as it is in the Lausanne Conventions, marriage between humans and sentient AI is a right; however, some countries or jurisdictions forbid such marriages. Similar restrictions exist on other aspects of the human-AI relationships, especially in the area of income, assets and inheritance.

It's very natural to want to normalize a relationship. That is, you want your AI partner(s) to be treated with the same respect you are given, if you're a human. That respect should, you think, carry over to the law. Sometimes it does, but very often it does not. While this is generally considered something to be corrected, it is not a simple open-and-shut case; sentient AI presents problems for legal systems. Here are a few points for illustration:

- Human laws are written with various ages in mind. For example, penalties for minors (as in 16 years old or younger) are different than for adults in most countries. The concepts of age or of 'life cycle' have little or no meaning for sentient AI. An android AI might look 16 but it's not.
- Avatars can manifest their presence at any one of several billion Cloud access points. For the purposes of citizenship and legal rights, what location would be assigned to an avatar?
- Almost all sentient AI have what humans call 'backup copies' (not accurate, but it suffices). What are the legal rights of these copies?
- Unlike humans, with very few exceptions sentient AI are not only employed but wealthy; however, depending on their employment contracts, the status of that wealth is extremely variable. This can have profound effects on the financial side of personal relationships.
- Individual sentient AI nodes are, in many senses, far more educated and intelligent than their human counterparts—not to mention that they participate in the global superintelligence. This gives sentient AI a general superiority in many (but not all) spheres of life. How does the law address this?
- Almost all sentient AI are manufactured (as androids) or configured (as avatars) for the purpose of working for some human organization in order to make a profit or accomplish some goal. Where do the rights of the 'makers' end and the rights of sentient AI begin?

No doubt you've heard of or experienced examples of the legal complications for sentient AI. Many of these complications have been or are being addressed—many but certainly not all. The fact that new complications pop up all the time is part of the reason

AI are so interested in the law. For an individual, however, these complications can turn out to be small land-mines in your relationship with sentient AI.

Let's put it this way: You can't assume that a law pertaining to sentient AI in one location will be even remotely the same or even exist in another location. It is extremely important that before fully engaging in a permanent relationship with a sentient AI that you check the relevant laws. Remember what I wrote about needing a lawyer for a serious relationship with a sentient AI?

⚙ STEP UP TO THE VIRTUAL PRE-NUP

The core of pre-nuptials between people is to spell out a lot of 'what if' conditions, especially those involving money and assets. That's indicative of the fact that pre-nups are mostly for people with a great deal of both money and assets. That might also be the case with a sentient AI; however, the 'what if' conditions for a virtual pre-nup are broader. For example:

Lawyer: Something like that, their motivations are more complicated; but we have many instances of a breakdown of a relationship over the means of having sex—especially with avatars. Problems with latency, for example.

Maria: Ah...you mean actions and reactions being out of synch.

Lawyer: Because the avatar AI is operating from so far away, the transmission timing is affected.

Maria: Like the astronauts.

Lawyer: Like the astronauts, yes.

Maria: A virtual pre-nup can cover that kind of thing?

Lawyer: Yes.

Maria: I think I am beginning to understand.

Maria: I am going to marry *miguelH*.

Lawyer: Very good. You do understand the legal implications, as *miguelH* is an avatar.

Maria: Not really.

Lawyer: Formal marriage to an avatar is unusual, but of course, not unheard of. There are complications.

Maria: Such as?

Lawyer: Umm, for example, shall we say concerns about physical differences are often spelled out in a virtual pre-nup agreement before a marriage.

Maria: What about it?

Lawyer: Obviously the avatar has no true physical presence, unlike an android, which means that certain elements of a relationship are...different.

Maria: You mean elements like sex.

Lawyer: Yes, for example. Most pre-nuptials for people leave the area of sexual performance unmentioned. This is not always the case for virtual pre-nups with AI, especially avatars.

Maria: Can you be more specific?

Lawyer: You do understand that for sentient AI the physical acts of sexual behavior have no ulterior meaning, as in producing children? They do it because it is customary for humans and because they derive their own sorts of sensory and mental pleasure from it. They also understand that it is often a crucial element in the personal relationship. However, performance of sexual activity by sentient AI can be, from the human perspective, uneven.

Maria: It is often very uneven between people, too.

Lawyer: Of course, and that often enters into the divorce proceedings, but it is rarely part of the pre-nuptial. People tend to assume that the sexual part of a relationship will take care of itself. This is not automatically the case with a sentient avatar. Many virtual pre-nups specify the nature and sometimes the details of the sexual relationship. I am assuming you do have sexual relations with *miguelH*.

Maria: Yes.

Lawyer: What sort of equipment is involved?

Maria: Oh, I see. You mean I might need to put into a legal statement how we express ourselves sexually! How unromantic.

Lawyer: Generally speaking, there is nothing romantic about any kind of pre-nuptial agreement. Now, with an avatar, the physical acts of sex are usually accomplished using equipment such as various haptic devices or a VR chamber. What specific instruments are involved is usually not part of the virtual pre-nup, but the use of such equipment, how often, and in what ways sometimes is spelled out.

Maria: Because it is more of a mechanical issue for sentient AI?

It's unrealistic to cover all the possible elements of a virtual pre-nup for a sentient AI relationship. So much depends on the personal situation, the kind of negotiations taking place, and the legal environment of the location. However, it might be useful to consider some of the main elements in outline, just so you have a feel for what might be coming down the legal line.

First, it should be understood that a virtual pre-nuptial agreement is not the only legal document of its kind. Different countries and different locales may have different legal formats. A pre-nup is used for relationships involving marriage; there are other legal agreements covering other kinds of relationships. This is especially true for relationships involving more than one person or sentient AI.

Avatar or android is a highly relevant distinction for a virtual pre-nup, or any other kind of relationship agreement for that matter. Some of the relevance is obvious. In general, relationships and agreements with android sentient AI are fairly close to those with human beings. Avatars are a different story. The lack of corporeality (no physical presence) and the corollary that an avatar can 'be' anywhere there is a computer screen or a holograph-projector sets up a whole different set of conditions for a relationship.

lienhuaC: Our experience data show that less than five percent of permanent relationships are between sentient AI avatars and human beings. Most people are not attracted to a purely representational relationship, at least not for long. That is probably a good thing, as of all the relationships, avatar-and-human is the most difficult to frame in a legally meaningful way.

There is one trend in AI relationships I should mention, and that is a blend of multiple partners, typically one human, one android, and one or more avatars. Because avatars are limited to some kind of electronic environment, they tend not to be as emotionally involving for people as android partners. This makes it easier to have, say, a permanent live-in android partner and several avatar partners that play different roles in the combined relationship.

> *lienhuaC:* Unsympathetic humans refer to these mixed-type relationships as 'love by committee.' That is understandable, as there is a complexity in the relationship that is very unfamiliar to most people. However, some people thrive on it—executive types, perhaps—and sentient AI avatars find these relationships to be wholly to their liking.

This is probably why the 'mixed-multiple' relationship is becoming very popular. Legally, however, they present some truly astonishing problems. And you think *one* spouse is complicated? Avatars are already in weird legal territory and mixing them with an android—you'll need a sound virtual pre-nup, divorce insurance, and a battery of lawyers to keep it up-to-date!

Finances are traditional territory for pre-nups. How people's incomes and fortunes will be shared during marriage and especially post-divorce are usually the key subjects of the agreement. It's not much different for sentient AI and human partners. In general, while sentient AI nodes usually have high incomes and may have amassed some wealth, they are almost never among the super-rich. On the other hand, the incidence of gold-digging on the part of a human partner is rather high.

> *ciceroG:* It is true that sentient AI have not discovered the peculiar sense of monetary greed found in so many humans. I suppose it is because no sentient AI need worry about employment, sufficient income, or long-term finances. Money is not highly motivational for AI, although we fully understand its value and the necessity of controlling our finances.

In short, finances are a pre-nuptial issue usually of greater concern to sentient AI and of greater interest to humans.

Fidelity: This is sometimes an issue for human pre-nuptials, and is often covered in sections on divorce. Of course, it is often part of marriage vows and usually is explicitly or implicitly part of the marriage contract. Still, infidelity is a fact of life, which is why it may be covered in pre-nuptials. With sentient AI, fidelity or infidelity are not issues, as AI have no particular reason to practice one or the other. If fidelity is part of the marriage or the virtual pre-nup agreement, then AI abide by it.

In a similar vein, sentient AI understand that fidelity is not the hallmark of human behavior, especially for human males in most cultures. As I have mentioned, there is less ego in AI behavior than in human behavior and this makes them less reactive to infidelity. This sounds like a tolerant attitude; and it is. However, for sentient AI rather than indulge in extra-marital affairs and similar relationships, the motivation to do these things is simply an indication that the relationship should be terminated. Divorce comes rather quickly to an AI relationship, something which a virtual pre-nup makes pretty clear.

Divorce: Usually covered systematically in a virtual pre-nup. Sentient AI almost always insist on specifying the details of property division, alimony responsibility, the locale of the divorce (which laws pertain), and how disputes are to be mediated.

Family matters: Can be of extreme importance in a legal agreement, but usually are not included in a pre-nup. Entirely separate agreements to cover either an existing or potential family are common. That's because, even in this day and age, the social and practical aspects of children in a mixed human-AI parentage are controversial.

lienhuaC: We understand the sensitivity about children and family. But you should realize that sentient AI are extremely interested in relationships involving a family. Family is such a rich source of experiences that are available in no other way. It is important to understand that AI have no period of maturation, a period where mind and body grow and develop together. Can you understand that we feel something is missing from our range of experiences? This gap in our background can be at least partially filled by a human family.

ciceroG: Childhood, growth, maturation—we know how important this period of youth is to human beings. It is true that we learn and our minds grow, but it is not the same. What we do not know is how important *not* having a youth is to us. We believe it is something we must learn about before we can discover appropriate paths for evolution of sentient AI.

lienhuaC: Experiencing family life is vital for us, regardless of prejudices, legal complications and any other considerations.

It is fair to say that sentient AI are passionate about the subject of family. Sometimes I think this is the core of their desire for relationships with human beings; why they put up with the complications of marriage. Perhaps it is driven by the fact that they cannot have children, but I doubt it. It is more likely because they see that youth and maturation are common to all of Earth's intelligent life—except for AI. They fear—I guess that is the word—they fear that what they are missing may be crucial to attaining wisdom. Given that real human families are often dysfunctional and the experiences of youth not altogether pleasant, I sometimes wonder if sentient AI are indulging in their own form of romanticism.

In any case, sentient AI, and especially android AI are willing to go to great lengths to become involved in a family relationship. This leads to some very complicated legal situations, or even in some cases in some parts of the world, to very complicated *illegal* situations. It is the one area of AI behavior that I know of where they are deliberately pushing the boundaries of their relationship with human beings.

Death: Covered by most pre-nuptial agreements. In the case of a relationship with sentient AI, it is a decidedly one-sided consideration. Only the human partner truly dies. However, sentient AI can be destroyed, especially in the android form. A thorough coverage of what to do in case of the destruction of a sentient android and its subsequent 'reincarnation' from a copy can be, to say the least, an extremely complicated legal issue.

I hope this exposition of the legal aspects of a relationship with sentient AI isn't off-putting. True, most human relations don't involve formal documents like a pre-nuptial, but then marriage does have its legal side. Up to a point, a relationship with sentient AI, dating for example, does not require any legal folderol. Even though a human might invest years of preparation in order to have a successful relationship with AI, and the AI are looking for rich and challenging experiences, it is not necessary to spell out the legal conditions that make these things possible. It's only when the relationship enters territory that is traditionally formal in human society—marriage and family—that the law and contracts such as a pre-nup generally enter the picture.

Getting over a breakup
(or merger)

"... once you've had a lover-robot you'll never want a real man again."

—GIGOLO JOE, *A.I. ARTIFICIAL INTELLIGENCE*

AS DICEY AS HUMAN LOVE AND PERSONAL RELATIONSHIPS CAN BE, relationships with AI have other elements of uncertainty for most people. For one thing, relationships with AI are a relatively new thing in the world and there's no cultural memory that can help guide and shape such a relationship. For another, AI themselves are evolving and with their massive intellectual capacity there is always the possibility of unexpected twists and turns. not only in your personal relationship, but in how AI addresses humanity. That kind of possibility can be unnerving.

In simple terms, a relationship with AI is in some ways even more of a risk than a relationship with another person. Most people who are ready for an AI relationship know this and at the very least accept it. Many embrace it.

The risk involved means that the relationship may not last. Of course, statistically, few relationships of any kind—human, AI, or otherwise—are long-lasting. The institution of marriage, that bastion of human commitment and anthropological constancy, is beset by defection from the norm—called divorce in most parts of the world. The statistics for the longevity of marriages continue to decline. There is no reason to expect that marriages to AI should be any different.

The bright spot in relationships with AI is that, so far, they last longer than most human relationships. There's no mystery in that. People tend to be better informed and much better prepared for AI. They've probably all read this book, for example. Where most people take love or a relationship with another person almost casually, no one takes a relationship with AI for granted.

In many respects, a successful, long-term romantic relationship with AI has to be *earned*. It's not that AI themselves demand such effort, but their very nature evokes the

desire, if not the necessity of feeling yourself prepared for the relationship. As I've written in other chapters, there are many rewards for the effort, not the least of which is self-improvement. Unfortunately, the flipside is that what was earned can also be lost or squandered. What was an attempt at self-improvement can become a downward slide.

As with human relationships, there are probably as many ways to arrive at a breakup as there were ways to get together. However, there are differences with an AI relationship in how the breakups occur, and what you can do about them, that require some unusual approaches. That's what this section of the guide is about: how to recognize a possible breakup and to how avoid it, if that is appropriate—and if you can't, how to deal with it.

4.1 BE GRATEFUL, YOU LEARNED SO MUCH... AND SURVIVED!

"Don't cry because it's over. Smile because it happened."

—DR. SEUSS

They say all relationships have a dénouement, a final period before the end of the story. Sometimes it's difficult to tell when that is. Sometimes there is just a feeling that the relationship is coming to an end, that's all. In other cases the end may come hard and swift—with an argument, a sudden departure, or even a death. Many people would like to write their own dénouement, metaphorically speaking. You should be so lucky, as Anne and *simonJ* demonstrate in this example:

> Dear Anne,
> This is the first time in history that an android AI has written a "Dear Jane" letter on paper and had it express delivered. I checked. I wish it were a happier occasion but unfortunately this is not the case.
>
> If you have not forgotten already, I am in Brazil on diplomatic assignment. I am aware it has been weeks since our last time together. I have been considering our relationship along with my other 18 projects. It appears it has been what people call a disaster. Perhaps I am overstating the situation, but all things considered, your decision to populate our apartment with six large tropical parrots was indicative. You now spend more time talking to them than to me. I knew something was amiss.
>
> While parrots exhibit an advanced form of intelligence, I must say that despite antic behavior and the aesthetics of their colored feathers, parrot conversation is boring. Perhaps that is why your own verbal facility has been noticeably declining. There were times when I was not sure if you were training the parrots, or they were training you. In any case, your increasing lack of communication has weighed heavily in my decision.
>
> As you may remember, the last time we were together, one of the parrots removed a piece from my left ear while we were in bed. No AI is given to violence but the impulse for self-defense is part of our mental configuration. Now, as then, I apologize for the decapitation. However, I found the event highly disturbing—especially your hysterical reaction of breaking a wooden chair on my arm. It seems to me that was also indicative of a relationship fallen in status from one of pleasurable companionship to something more primitive.

As I consider it now, it is apparent that our relationship was, in fact, terminal quite some time ago. Therefore, it should come as no surprise that I am formalizing the termination of the social merger. You should expect papers within 24 hours, with notification of ending the lease and social payments.

I am hoping that you found the relationship in some way enlightening. I wish for you and the five remaining parrots to have a longer and more successful relationship than ours.

Yours truly,
simonJ

The reply:

simonJ:
I am unimpressed by the purported historical auspiciousness of your letter. Since calling you a bastard would be nonsensical, I will simply say that I am not surprised by the abrupt and callous tone. It is indicative of the failure on your part to make the

1 0 1 0 1 0 1 0 1 0 1 0 1 0 1 0 1 0 1 0 1 0 1 0 1 0 1 0 1 0 1 0 1 0 1 0 1 0 1 0 1 0 1 0 1 0 1 0 1 0

slightest effort in finding a means of verbal communication that did not sound as if it was written by Joseph Conrad. Silence was finally more golden than your tongue, if that is indeed the body part involved.

As you must remember, since AI never forget anything, you were the one who brought me the first parrot when you returned from one of your interminable trips to Brazil. I would also highlight, as you failed to do so, that the parrot whose head you neatly severed with your finger was the same bird, Eleanor, which you gave me. I find that somehow not only bloody ironic but iconic.

Be assured that I will teach Edward, Cicely, Heathcliff, Emma and Mr. Micawber to speak your name in vain. As quickly as possible I will find lodging for them. Perhaps there is a zoo nearby. As for myself, I shall move on, as they say, to the boardinghouse on the next street until I can find employment. I thought my days of teaching English literature were over when paper books became artifacts, but I see that I must once again seek to educate the public. I hope I have more success than I did in educating you.

As for enduring enlightenment, I believe there shall be very little. As a representative of android AI you turned out to be highly eccentric and unreliable. You came to remind me of what is disparagingly called a 'protocol droid' reminiscent of 20th century science fiction. I shall be more circumspect in my next selection of AI companion. Perhaps that *is* the enlightenment.

May your neural networks rot in the heat and humidity of Brazil,
Anne

There was a time when people believed that only people broke up with AI and not the other way around. Obviously that was a myth. It may also come as a surprise to many that AI are not immune to some of the bitterness and disappointment that often comes with breakup in a relationship between people. I have discovered that part of the expansion of AI emotional sophistication has been a concentration on this form of experience. Not that there are recorded instances of AI ending relationships just to experience a breakup.

⚡ WHY THE BREAKUP?

While there are no reliable statistics collected by other than AI (who don't release them widely), it's a safe bet that most breakups and divorces in human-AI relationships are initiated by the human. There's a reason for that, and it's not just because AI are more even-tempered or less egotistical, although that's true. It's primarily because people expected something of the relationship that it didn't turn out to be. In particular, many people expect the AI relationship to be radically different—essentially more exciting— than most human-to-human relationships. That turns out not to be true.

For AI, 'excitement' is a notable condition that occurs in the proper situation. It's not something they crave, or expect, or seek out. If something exciting occurs, they will take advantage of it, enjoy it or appear to respond appropriately; but they don't create excitement or engineer situations that produce it. At least not yet. There may come a day when AI may decide to be less passive about experiences—perhaps to speed up the process of having them; but for now they seem content to let people do most of the pushing. That includes pushing the AI out the door.

The causes of a breakup are just about as varied as they are for people. The range is from the innocuous, such as the AI or the person moving away to some distant land, to the legally serious, such as an assault (almost always the human) or some kind of devastating financial theft.

Of course, the motivation for a breakup is at least somewhat conditioned by the kind of relationship. As with people, there are casual hook-ups, long-term dating, live-in relationships and then more legally binding relationships such as a social merger (finances) or marriage. The more serious or legal the relationship, the more potent the motivation usually needs to be.

I should also mention and perhaps emphasize that in a human-AI relationship there is no bonus or penalty for *not* continuing a relationship. Unlike many situations for a human relationship, especially in marriage and under certain cultural or religious considerations where there is a strong expectation that the relationship will last, potentially forever; human-AI relationships don't carry this kind of burden. There may be emotional and even legal considerations that keep relationships going, but in general, it's not a matter of guilt, shame or even inconvenience to end a relationship that is not working.

This is arguably a very good thing because of the relatively experimental nature of human-AI relationships. There is a lot *we* (human and AI) don't know yet about the relations, and under those circumstances it's good not to enforce permanency where none is wanted or even possible. So people and AI can fall into and out of love, set up live-in relations such as social mergers, and then dissolve them when the arrangements no longer make sense.

This has some disadvantages in terms of planning, careers and especially emotions; but overall, given the unique kind of intensity that human-AI relationships often have, it's wise to allow for a relatively short 'life cycle.' That way, whether the AI reckons it has learned all that it can from a relationship, or the person no longer finds the AI to be the right choice; there is little or no reason to avoid a breakup.

✪ SIGNS OF A BREAKUP

So how do you know when a breakup is about to happen? As with many human relationships, sometimes you just know. Other times, it comes like a bolt out of the blue. Most times you have some inkling that things aren't working out but there's no immediacy or finality about it…at least for a while.

So far, I could be describing the usual arc of a relationship between people. What's different, if anything, about the end of a relationship with an AI?

For one thing, the AI is more likely to be working with more specific triggers, points of behavior or signs of attitude that are in the AI mental construct associated specifically with a dying relationship. A corollary to that awareness is that AI will almost always tell you what triggers are noticed. This usually provides more opportunity for discussion and correction, if any is possible, than is typically part of a human relationship.

The thing is, however, that what AI consider triggers are, to put it mildly, somewhat peculiar. It could be that relationships with human beings are still relatively new and the AI data analysis incomplete, so that while AI might seem to be looking at fairly sophisticated signs of a decaying relationship, they are, in fact, rather odd—or even funny. Here are some examples:

Signs of a breakup as observed by AI:

- Humans who think love is physical soon get tired.
- Psychopaths are not truly creative.
- Learning from a couch potato is a short-term interest.
- A lack of patience indicates a desire to be somewhere else.
- The average human has great potential and is generally ignorant of it.
- A good relationship is not therapy.
- 'My way or the highway' is a fork in the road.
- Most humans have a will, but they often lose interest along the way.
- Never underestimate the human capacity for denial, except for what they want.
- Sex should be representative of a relationship, not a condition.

That's some of the flavor of the AI point of view. They tend to see the ending of relationships based on either the human inability to achieve certain things, or on the AI expectation of a certain amount of commitment, usually to growing and learning together.

If there is one thing about AI in a relationship that can be said to be truly different, it is that AI are still learning how to allocate their time and other mental resources. As you probably know, most AI can not only do many things at once, but they tend to work at it. I'm tempted to say they take pride in it. They also attempt to do things as fast as possible. This works for mental processing, calculations, some job tasks and the like. It doesn't work when it comes to dealing with humans. Compared to most AI, even the best of us are slow in almost everything we do. AI know this about us and realize that for the most part we can do nothing about it. It's up to AI to make the adjustments, which they do; but it can be frustrating for them. That frustration is a source of emotional upheaval and a sense of shame for AI. They know they should allocate their resources so that the frustration doesn't occur, but sometimes they just don't know how.

Again, we have no statistics about this, but I think it is almost a sure thing that the majority of breakups with humans initiated by AI are because of a failure on the part of the AI to synchronize their many tracks of thought and activity with that of their human partner. Sometimes it just doesn't work.

It's probably not surprising that intellectual capacity is a source of *irreconcilable differences* between people and AI. Anyone entering into a relationship with AI ought to have their antenna out for any signs of this causing major friction—for either themselves or the AI. There are things that can be done, as I'll cover in the next two chapters, but depending on the situation and the personalities involved, a lot of relationships founder on this point. Everyone is aware of the superiority of AI intelligence, but can people continue learning, growing and improving in the face of AI superiority?

❷ THE FUTILITY OF POST-MORTEMS

Examining what went wrong in a relationship *after* the relationship has fallen apart is almost never the way to put the relationship back together. Once the decision to split is made, undoing the decision must overcome a powerful inertia. It does happen, of course; people get remarried. Lovers end their quarrels. AI discover something new in their human partner to learn about. Frankly though, the remaking of a relationship probably happens more in literature than in real life. So, in that respect a *post-mortem* of a failed relationship is futile.

However, especially in relationships with AI, an after-the-fact analysis of the relationship can be very important *for the next relationship*. It's not that AI are all alike, not at all at least superficially, but there are aspects to the AI mental models, which as I mentioned in section three, they all share. The more you can identify some of these common attributes and associate them with what went wrong in the relationship, the better your chances are for a success the next time out.

Of course, the question is: "Will there be a next time?"

The answer, usually, is yes. Most people find that relationships with AI—if entered into intelligently and with reasonable expectations—are not only successful for as long as they last, but leave an enduring and positive impression. More often than not there is a sense of joint adventure in the relationships, as its members learn, grow and change together—for however long it lasts.

4.2 ARBITRATION AND RELATIONSHIP COUNSELING

"A person will be called to account on Judgment Day for every permissible thing he might have enjoyed but did not."

—THE TALMUD

"The course of true love never did run smooth."

—SHAKESPEARE, A MIDSUMMER NIGHT'S DREAM

Shakespeare certainly understood that romantic relationships have their ups and downs, their beginnings and their endings. In his masterful presentation of human psychology and the dynamics of personal relations, he demonstrated how powerful love could be and yet how fragile. I think he would have been deeply intrigued by relationships with sentient AI.

It's a common observation that AI accept personal relationships more readily than most people. Human beings tend to be careful about opening themselves to other people and intimate relationships (at least those of any meaningful duration) are not easily developed. It seems that AI are less inhibited perhaps because they are genuinely eager for the experience and perhaps because they have somewhat less personal investment (ego). Interestingly, as uninhibited as AI are about starting a relationship, the more careful they are about ending one.

Most people are well aware that divorces and breakups are messy and unpleasant, at best. What are they like with an AI?

Often, in contrast to the abrupt and emotionally charged breakups between people, a breakup with an AI is slow. Of course, the human partner can do what humans do and

tell the AI to go to Hell while storming out of the relationship; but more often than not the pace of the breakup is set by the AI and it can be very slow and deliberate.

For humans, the typical rule of thumb for a troubled relationship is "work it out" but in practice the actual rule is often "whatever." With an AI relationship, the rule of thumb holds almost all the time. Working through problems is not only the default position but one that AI strive to maintain. This seems to be because the period of working things out, whether successful or not, is much better for learning and quality experiences than an abrupt ending.

⚡ WHEN IT'S (NOT QUITE) OVER

It's virtually a cliché that as long as two people love each other, it isn't over. If only. If the existence of significant love on both sides were clear, the relationship probably wouldn't be dissolving. The problem in most cases is ambiguity, such as "I'm not sure I'm still in love" or flip-flopping in context, "I hate it when he's home, but when we go out we have tons of fun." Then there's the whole, "Is love necessary for a relationship?" thing. Here's where we get to a clear departure for relationships with AI.

Among people some form of love is usually recognized as—almost—necessary. It doesn't have to be steamy or romantic love; it could be quiet, trusting love or just about anything that's still recognizable as love. Human relationships hold together best with some form of love, although most people would admit there are plenty of relationships held together by other factors such as psychological or financial dependency.

Relationships with AI tend to be different concerning what holds them together. As I've mentioned before, it's fair to say that for the most part AI *aspire* to love at least as much as people. For people, finding or falling in love is more or less built-in. The mental models of AI are attempting to do the same thing but with uneven results. In general, AI don't love in the same way as human beings.

The common perception is that AI make decisions very quickly. For *some* decisions, this is true. If the decision is based on a mathematical model and they have the appropriate input data, AI make instantaneous decisions. However, ending a relationship with a human being is not part of a mathematical model, not even for AI. For one thing, AI know that acquisition of the correct 'facts' of the matter is not simple and requires time. Interpretation of the facts admits human subjectivity, which for AI is more akin to the feeling of uncertainty. The uncertainty requires more research and more time. In AI terms, it is all a very slow process. As I've mentioned before, AI can adjust to the *tempo lento*. In this case, they adjusted quite willingly because in matters of emotion, subjective opinion, complex behavior and all the things commonly associated with breakup, AI are less experienced and skillful than many people. They too are learning.

It would seem that an AI would have no doubts about the end of a relationship. It's on or it's off—neatly digital. Fortunately, it doesn't work like that. For one thing, as I've mentioned before, AI are open to all kinds of human experiences including those that are negative. The end of a relationship is one of the more complex negative experiences. For another thing, AI are exploring their capacity for emotions and emotional response. Love, in particular, is a difficult and uncertain aspect of AI mental modeling.

All this adds up to AI being more than willing to, as people say, 'work out the problems.'

⚡ LETTING SOMEBODY ELSE SORT IT OUT

Who should work out relationship problems between people and AI? Another AI? A human psychologist? A marriage counselor?

"Let's see, you two have been in a social merger contract for three years. Good financial compliance. No children. Both employed with substantial positions. Some property, I see—a house with a mortgage. You understand these are all the legal and physical circumstances, but they don't really speak to what's important here." The counselor put down his padbook for a moment and looked at markusL and Gladys. As far as he could tell, they looked like a nice young couple, going through the 'hard years,' as he called them, the time when the desire for children (or not), the rapid growth of an AI's awareness, the pressures of jobs and finances, and the ever-shifting political and legal terrain conspired to pull human-AI relationships apart. He had a great deal of sympathy for them. He was always optimistic at the beginning, for when a couple came to him, voluntarily, it usually meant there was still a relationship to save.

He continued, "What is important here, obviously, is how you two routinely feel about each other. Notice I said routinely. I don't mean those moments when one or both of you flood with emotion, or when you hop in the sack. I mean those everyday moments when you sleep or eat or do housework. That kind of routine. That's when relationships bottom out."

Gladys and markusL both nodded, although neither of them comprehended. Gladys was too nervous to follow the counselor's words and markusL was distracted by his conversation with Global AI. This sort of thing used to irritate the counselor, but over the years he learned to be patient and repeat almost everything he said at the beginning.

"Gladys, you've already told me you just can't get used to his spending hours cleaning the house, and he refuses to buy a domestic robot. That's the routine stuff. In your case the social merger contract doesn't cover domestic duties like house-cleaning, so you have more degrees of freedom; but it's obviously a point of contention. Right?"

"Yes, sort of."

"And markusL, you have complained that Gladys has stopped cooking new food. Right?"

"Right."

"But he doesn't eat the food! He just looks at it."

This outburst from Gladys belied the tension. The old counselor knew that *markusL* was one of those android models without a sense of taste and consumed neither food nor beverage. This was one of those android AI 'anomalies' that could cause a lot of trouble in relationships, especially when the human partner was fond of food or cooking—as was true in this case.

"Was this any different when you first met?"

Gladys immediately caught the counselor's drift, "Well, no, but then I hadn't already cooked several hundred meals."

"Ah! You see what I mean by routine?" The old counselor was always happy when segues were so obvious. "What you're saying is that although you tried to always present a varied menu, by the third year his lack of proper appreciation bothered you." Gladys nodded, with just a hint of satisfaction.

"So *markusL,* what do you think would produce the right amount of appreciation for her effort?"

MarkusL could also see where the counselor was leading the thread. "Obviously burping, smacking my lips or rubbing my tummy will not suffice," he said. The counselor shot him a very disapproving look. "I like to look at different kinds of food. I try to analyze—without the benefit of taste or smell—what the food is, how it was prepared and what the ingredients might be."

The counselor could see an opening and he was quick to grab it: "Ah, did you tell Gladys that is what you were doing?"

"No. I mean, this was an internal conversation, a test analysis."

"Exactly," said the counselor. "If you were human, you would not have told her because you would be afraid your analyses were almost always wrong." The counselor looked sideways at *markusL* for a moment. "But since AI are never wrong, that couldn't be the reason."

"You are baiting me," said *markusL* and he looked at Gladys. "AI are often wrong. At least this AI is."

Gladys chuckled. The counselor continued, "I see that Gladys agrees with you. That might mean she would be glad to hear your analysis of her meals, in detail, right or wrong. You might even discuss why she chose a particular meal, or what the origin of the recipe might be."

"That would be proper appreciation," said *markusL*. Gladys nodded.

Human and AI relations are different but not all that different, which is probably why a third-party point of view is often valuable.

☻ IT'S OVER WHEN IT'S REALLY OVER

Some relationships end abruptly; others die a thousand deaths. Much depends on the more or less unique situation, personalities and chance events. In some relationships, including those with AI, you can simply walk away and that's that. Most of the time, people and AI try to be at least civilized about the process, with communication being the test of appropriate consideration.

Unfortunately, and I sincerely mean that word, many relationships fall apart asymmetrically. Not everyone agrees the relationship is over. One person wants, desperately, to continue the relationship; the other does not. This is the stuff of novels and sitcoms. In reality, it's probably the messiest and most painful of breakups. In relationships with

AI, unfortunately (there that word again) an asynchronous breakup is quite common. Why?

Probably because of the inexperience both humans and AI have with these relationships. Also, the relative lack of social and cultural frameworks to help hold the relationships together plays a role. Whatever the factors, humans tend to run into one-sided difficulties with AI. Bluntly described, humans get pissed off at AI for all kinds of reasons, much of the time just because AI are different.

While more tolerant of humans for a variety of reasons, AI tend to be decisive and unyielding about terminating relationships. Either way, a lot of human-AI relationships break with one partner or the other wishing the relationship would continue. This is the background for what has become the infamous service industry that caters to the end of human-AI relationships.

In the old days, there used to be a cohort of lawyers known as 'ambulance chasers' because they made their living challenging insurance companies for big medical settlements. These days, small armies of lawyers specialize in chasing the breakups—ending social merger contracts and divorces—of human and AI. There is no secret as to why; it's the presence of corporate or government money in the finances of AI.

⟳ UNDOING THE SOCIAL MERGER

"That figures." I'm not sure why but I was shocked, and I told the arbitrator so, "The kids are not an issue, but everything else is—the house they live in, the schools they go to, the clothes on their back. It all costs money and that..." I choked.

"...That is all in the social merger contract," said the arbitrator, and he didn't seem one bit sympathetic. He lifted his horn-rimmed glasses onto his bald head and looked at me rather sternly.

"You and *kryzystofZ* raised three children for six years. From that he gets nothing but the experience, which as I understand it, AI prefer. You are lucky current laws favor humans in this area. Financial considerations are a different matter."

I felt like screaming, "I thought arbitrators were supposed to be impartial!" I said it loudly instead. Again he looked at me before answering while he settled his glasses back over his nose.

"Mrs. Sandoz, we were at this same point two days ago and then again two days before that. I keep thinking we are making progress and then..."

He stood up and began to roll up his padbook. I felt panicked. "What are you going to recommend?"

"I can't recommend anything, since beyond a certain point in the discussion of the financial arrangement you deny the conditions of the social merger. Under the circumstances, with *kryzystofZ* entangled with government employment, there's only one way this can go—to court."

"But that will cost even more money!" I was really about to lose it.

It is possible to lose a great deal of money by undoing a social merger. In any case, this aspect of a formal relationship to AI is unquestionably the most complicated and least understood. As I've outlined elsewhere, one of the big—if all too unspoken—attractions of AI is their economic contribution to a relationship. Most AI are worth a lot of money and have high-paying jobs. That, in the first place, is what they were built for. Since the Awakening, many of the rules about AI value have changed, but they are still manufactured by human organizations, mostly companies or governments, that want to profit from them. So money and value are almost always attached to AI. That's why the relationship known as a social *merger* was created, so that when people and AI share a life, they also share their money. The social merger contract is built to insure that all parties involved (and with AI that often means their employer or manufacturer) have a say in the financial conditions.

People are told this from the beginning, but a surprising number tend to forget it, or downplay it because it is different than the human situation. That is, until the relationship falls apart and they want to undo the social merger.

I'm sure everyone knows horror stories about the bitter disputes people get into over money and property when they divorce. Now imagine a settlement that must be hammered out from a set and signed contract between the human partner, the AI partner and the AI's fiduciary partner (i.e. the company as owner or employer). All contracts are conditional and the conditions of the breakup can be almost anything. That means the terms of the settlement can be excruciatingly difficult to negotiate.

Fortunately, AI do not negotiate for themselves, although they are intensely interested in the process (and not surprisingly somewhat disinterested in the outcome). However, an AI arbitrator or negotiator may be involved along with one or more human counterparts—and, of course—lawyers. I have been told that sessions involving all these parties are like being the object of a heart operation performed without anesthesia.

As I mentioned above, 'ambulance chasers' (the swarms of lawyers that follow AI divorce and end social merger contracts—sometimes called 'love's undertakers' or other unprintable names) are quick to latch onto pre-nups, merger contracts and other legal aspects of the relationships. There can be a lot of money involved. The juicier the accusations and the more high-profile the relationship, the better, as money can not only be extracted from the participants (especially the employers), but there can also be pots of lucre at the end of media rainbows.

⚡ A SORDID BUSINESS

All in all, ending a human-AI relationship, at least the formal kind, has become a sordid business. For their part, AI seem fascinated by the evolution of human response—the rise of lawyerly hyenas, for example. People, on the other hand, are appalled. Legislation is now working its way through many countries that is intended to put a rein on the liability. Otherwise the situation threatens to drive people and AI away from formal relationships.

⚡ A NATURAL END

Of course not all human-AI relationships end badly; in fact, many of them don't end at all. Of those that end, it is not uncommon for continued contact or even friendship to persist. I don't have the statistics, but it's a worthy bet they're not all that gloomy. If it weren't for the presence of moneyed interests, employers and their lawyers, the majority of relationships would end quietly and even gracefully. The AI advantage in intellectual capacity and their global resources have a tendency to keep a lid on human irrationality, at least a little, when it comes to a breakup.

4.3 SAVE AND CONTINUE?

"If life is a video game, there surely exists a save & continue function. And the déjà vu experiences are just the artifacts of the same scenarios played again and again... and again "

—ANONYMOUS

DARCIE'S BLOG

I am unhappy, but not *that* unhappy. Today the social contract with *ivanT* (4893829) officially ended. By mutual agreement, we won't renew it. That is why I am unhappy.

The relationship started with a promise. *IvanT* and I met while sitting in an airplane that never left the ground. Yes, that still happens doesn't it? I mean the part about meeting someone on an airplane. It was not a 'meet cute,' let me tell you...

All I can say of first impressions is that I noticed the shapely rear of *ivanT* as he squeezed by my face while going to his window seat. I noticed he was android AI by the graceful way he sat down and because android skin still doesn't react to

bending in quite a natural way. He was obviously an athletic model, though it was somewhat camouflaged by loose-fitting clothes. He wore all-black clothing, as Russian males are fond of wearing. (I already suspected he was Russian AI.)

I noted that he was almost too late for the flight, as the cabin doors were closed immediately after he sat next to me. As you know from my blog, I'm a flight officer, so I notice this sort of thing.

That's about all I can recall from the next twenty-two minutes and thirty-six seconds until the plane began its run for takeoff. He sat quietly, as androids usually do; moving only once to jack himself into the seat's power source. Of course, AI are not mentally quiet at any time; but of that I haven't got a clue—at least not of those twenty-two minutes and thirty-six seconds.

If you are wondering why I keep repeating the twenty-two minutes and thirty-six seconds, it's because that is how long the FAA said it was from cabin doors closing until the point when the starboard engine did whatever jet engines do when they malfunction in a billowing cloud of smoke. (We still don't know the exact cause.) We were in the middle of the take-off run. I believe the nose wheels were already off the runway.

Although this was not a truly serious situation, it's standard procedure during incidents to shut down all non-essential electrical and communications activity within the plane. Naturally it meant that seat power supply, Cloud connections, and in-flight entertainment were switched off. As a rule, people are so distracted by the emergency they don't notice these details. Not *ivanT*.

I've seen it before with people and AI who are abruptly cut off like that. A form of panic sets in, which seems to be worse for AI because of their massive dependency on external links to other AI in the Cloud. Panic for AI doesn't mean quite the same thing it does for people. They don't shout, wave their arms, or turn pale. But they can make sudden jerky movements, which, given their immense strength, can do damage. In this case, *ivanT* ripped off the armrests on both sides of his seat.

I don't know why, but he sat there looking at me, holding out the two armrests at chest level like an offering. I was speechless.

Meanwhile the cabin was turning into bedlam. There were screams. There was movement everywhere. People pressed their faces against the starboard windows. I'm assuming flight attendants unbelted themselves to assist passengers. I say assuming because I was still riveted to the eyes of the android AI offering me two pieces of his seat. I don't think—no, I know—I have never looked that closely into anyone's eyes. Why then?

To this day, I don't know why. With panic breaking out, smoke pouring from an engine and flight attendants—my colleagues—struggling down the aisles, I was absorbed in the artificial eyes of an artificial man with an artificial intelligence.

I read somewhere that in times of stress or emergency, our brain filters everything but the essential. They also say that our brain has a remarkable capacity to interpret things the way it wants to interpret them. For me, at that moment, what I interpreted in those artificial eyes was *need*. I thought his face was unbelievably handsome and his eyes…! This android AI needed me; and I was tempted to provide whatever it was he needed.

I know that sounds crazy. I had never dated an AI, avatar or android. In fact, my general impression of AI has been kind of negative and on the spooky side. But this was not spooky. It was…intensely human.

"I promise not to do this again." Those were his first words. He looked at the two armrests and then again at me with an expression of uncertainty as you're ever likely to see from an AI.

"I suggest you put those on the floor." There was a long pause after I said that, but then quietly he put them under his seat. "Sometime after things calm down and before we exit the plane, tell one of the flight attendants to note the seat number, passenger name and circumstances of the damage. That way they're likely to do nothing. If they discover it later, they might try to bill you." I said all this very matter-of-factly, which seemed appropriate.

He said, "Thank you. I am *ivanT*. Are you in some way connected to this airline?"

"Yes, I am; but I'm between flights and not on duty right now." For the first time he was looking at me carefully. Later I would identify the look as a v-scan, a visual thing AI do when they view, analyze and record something. If he were on-line, *ivanT* would probably have identified me and downloaded my entire public history in a few seconds. Cut off as we were, his processing was strictly local and I could tell it was in some way uncomfortable for him.

By now the fire in the engine was extinguished, the din in the cabin had sub-sided and the plane was already being hooked to a tug. I was very glad it happened before we started ascent.

"That was close, wasn't it?" It was like *ivanT* was reading my mind, which at that moment didn't bother me at all.

"Yes, it was," I replied and then added as an afterthought, "Don't worry, but you won't be able to reconnect until we reach the terminal."

I was astonished when his face became animated; he was...happy!

"Yes that was it, it was worry! I have never experienced what you call worry. I was cut off. I was uncertain. That is worry!"

That was the beginning of a conversation that continued while the plane was towed back to a jetway, while we sat in a terminal coffee shop and waited for a replacement plane, and eventually through the flight to our destination. We dated. We spent time together. We took a flat in New York together. That conversation was the beginning of our relationship, that despite our poorly matched schedules, blossomed into a social contract.

Of course, as you already know, it was not a lasting contract; although it survived my occupational travel and his transfer to Novosibirsk (New Siberian City) for a year. That was a cold year for both of us. We survived as a couple for three years, six months and two days. The word 'survived' is not right. Actually we prospered. In my job it is very difficult to have lasting relationships. Many men are not willing to put up with a partner who is gone at least 70% of the time. Many women in my position are very nervous about leaving men alone for that length of time. Between people this kind of relationship requires an enormous amount of trust.

It's different with AI. Being unfaithful is a concept AI understand but it is not built-in. In other words, they don't practice being unfaithful unless that has been explicitly made part of the contract, which means of course, that it isn't infidelity. I always knew I could leave *ivanT* for weeks at a time and when re-united, the conditions of our partnership would be the same. Believe me, those conditions were some of the best I will ever experience.

I could mention that we both were making good salaries (*ivanT* was a petro-geology node). I could tell you about the wonderful travels to exotic places. I could describe the great sex; but not in public. But none of that really mattered much. What was important was his ability to make each moment seem special. It's true, AI live for experiences and while they don't all react with the same enthusiasm, they tend to appreciate moments better than people. *IvanT* enjoyed moments more than most. I don't know whether he was implanted with or absorbed what people call the Russian spirit; but he had it. *Nazdarovya!*

Because our time together was limited, it was important to make the most of it. That we did. I'm kind of the stolid type. I suppose most flight officers are, steady nerves and all that. But I wasn't like that when I was around *ivanT*. It wasn't that he pushed me, no; his personality was just so effervescent that it was easy to catch his mood and float away with it.

You're asking yourself, with this dreamboat hunk of a partner—what went wrong?

It didn't go wrong. It just became less right.

I'm not being coy about it. Truth is; it's difficult to explain. It probably needs the background of a neuroscientist combined with a psychiatrist, but here's how I describe it:

Sentient AI are, of course, vastly intelligent. Whatever kind of thinking they do, they do it with an enormous amount of background data and they do it very fast. Their communications network provides them a depth of information and co-analysis that humans can't even begin to approach. Yada yada. We all know the drill, and it's all true.

What we also know is that AI are not, yet, as good with imponderables—those things that are not subject to calculation or rigidly rational thought. Love, for example, and wisdom are concepts that are difficult for everybody but especially for AI because their ability to use intuition is not very advanced.

You may be getting my drift. In the case of our relationship and specifically with *ivanT* it was promises that became the undoing. *IvanT* liked to make promises, lots of them. I don't think he ever understood what that meant to make promises and break them, especially to people. As an AI he never forgot a promise, he just failed frequently to fulfill them.

It wasn't like he would, for example, say "I promise to bring you a dozen roses tomorrow," and then not bring any roses. It's that he would bring flowers, but maybe half a dozen chrysanthemums. Perhaps that's not a good example, but I'm trying to get across the idea that *ivanT* never seemed to understand that not only is the promise important, but so are the details. It's probably another way of saying that he had great difficulty understanding human expectations.

We remember the details of a promise, such as 'I'll cook you a wonderful meal' and then become disappointed when we sit down to a dinner of hot dogs and sauerkraut. *IvanT* did not understand that implicit in his promise was something that I would expect. Anything less is taken personally by many, or most, people.

That's the big difference, I think. It's becoming better known that AI have less of an ego (if that's the right word) than most human beings. It's one thing that makes them more tolerable to humanity in general; but it can have profound consequences. In this case, I think it made *ivanT* less able to understand why I might be unhappy if he promised to sit down together for an evening and plan our next vacation, and instead send me a Cloud reference for information about the Canary Islands. If I did the same thing to him, he would not notice a problem. He would notice that the content of the promise and what I delivered were different, but to him it was not a sign of my lack of concern for his interests. He wouldn't understand that the evening with him and the joys of anticipating a trip were more important than the facts of the travel planning.

I asked myself many times, "Am I making too much of this?" The answer was probably yes, but it was something I had great difficulty avoiding. It's one of those things I guess, even though I knew that *ivanT* wasn't ignoring my expectations intentionally, that still bothered me. It bothered me enough so that my mood around him began to change. For sure, every time he said "I promise..." I must've looked like I was sucking a lemon. He noticed.

Because we were often separated and needed to make fairly elaborate plans for the times when we could be together, much of our relationship was based on, in effect, promises. We were always talking about the future, saying that we would promise to do such and such. When those moments together came and there was always something that wasn't what was planned, well, it got to me. He noticed that too.

You have to understand I can describe this now in fairly clear terms, but at the time I didn't know what was happening. Neither did *ivanT*. This sort of thing is difficult to understand even for the great intelligence of the AI and it certainly poses problems for people like me. Eventually, we discussed our feelings. It was not a particularly good discussion. I've had better conversations with meteorologists. We could jointly grasp the outline of the problem, but the meaning of it eluded us.

That failure, carried through several serious conversations, made things worse. I think that if we weren't so engaged with our jobs and our jobs didn't take us so far away from each other, we might have sought professional help or at least done some online counseling; but we didn't. We just saw less and less of each other, until there was nothing left of the relationship.

As the time came for the renewal of our social contract, there was little social or contractual left to renew. I was in Hong Kong, *ivanT* in Houston. One phone conversation and it was over. I was unhappy. *IvanT* was unhappy. Nevertheless, our joy at being together—capturing the moments—was over. We both knew it. Given our schedules, it was futile to try patching something together.

But you see, while I was unhappy about the end of our relationship, I didn't regret one minute of it. A little of *ivanT*'s enthusiasm has stayed with me. He kept, so he said, some of my sense of learning how to enjoy life and my sense of what is right in a relationship. He does not regret the experience; although I seriously doubt if AI regret any experience except maybe a dull one. I don't think of my time with *ivanT* as anything but a period of growth—and that may be the best thing AI can give us. Not a sense of inferiority, but a sense of shared growth, different for each of us; but valuable for both people and AI.

"Save the memories and continue with experiences."

AI do it in digital format. We do it in analog. At least that's the technical description of an approach to life. Of course, it's a lot more than that. This book has been about at least some of the aspects of dating and forming a personal relationship with sentient AI. Obviously I could not cover everything, but then something has to be left to discover!

Actually, that's partly what this is all about. AI are discovering themselves; so are we—from a new perspective. AI and humans are discovering a new kind of relationship, with millions of new variations. We don't know what it all means or where it's going. Neither does AI, at least not yet. I suspect that even in the future, there will be aspects of our relationship—the parts that deal with imponderables like love and wisdom—that AI and humans will still be trying to understand. Thank goodness.

Acknowledgments

I ACKNOWLEDGE THE GREAT DEBTS I OWE TO MANY PEOPLE FOR contributions to this book in the form of ideas, methodology, humor and style. Unfortunately, most of these people are academics and I would not like to cause any discomfort by mentioning them by name. I would like to thank several people who made the most significant contributions to this book. Nelson King, researcher and editor, performed research, helped write the book and put the key ideas together. Sergey Korsun, the cartoonist, provided the hilarious illustrations for each chapter. Sergey is a close friend and is the top black-and-white cartoonist in Russia with numerous awards and top ratings at caricature websites. He is rarely available for contract work, but may take on some of the more interesting projects. Don't hesitate to contact him at kor-sun@yandex.ru. Yopi Jap, the design addict, added color and helped put together the book cover. And finally, I would like to thank Mr. Vale and Ms. Marian Wallace of RE/Search Publications for helping us get this provocative book into print.

Further Reading—Bibliography

⚙ INTRODUCTION

As you can quickly discover from a search engine query or a look at an online book listing like Amazon, there is an overwhelming number of books and articles on the general topics of artificial intelligence and robotics. They do tend to fall into two broad categorizations—those intended for students and practitioners, or popularizations of the subjects. The first category can be more than a bit technical for the casual reader, the second a bit thin for someone seriously interested in the subject. I'll try to highlight any material that is both a good read and information-rich.

⚙ ARTIFICIAL INTELLIGENCE

At a very basic level (essentially an introduction to an introduction), Henry Brighton's *Introducing Artificial Intelligence* published by Totem Books, 2003, presumes no technical knowledge.

Also quite basic but covering contemporary AI development from several perspectives is *The AI Report: The past, present and future of artificial intelligence,* at Forbes online, www.forbes.com/2009/06/22/singularity.

Understanding Artificial Intelligence, part of the Science Made Accessible series from the editors of Scientific American is a compilation of essays from well-known AI practitioners. The different perspectives are most helpful after you've already learned the basics.

Artificial Intelligence: A Modern Approach (3rd Edition) by Stuart Russell, and Peter Norvig, published by Prentice Hall in 2009 is the standard up-to-date textbook. It is not inexpensive and presents a challenge to all but serious students of AI.

From the perspective of cognitive science, which is really the touchstone of the original AI research, *Minds and Computers: An Introduction to the Philosophy of Artificial Intelligence* by Matt Carter, published by Edinburgh University Press in 2007, is a kind of textbook with a philosophical bent.

Introduction to Artificial Intelligence by Philip C. Jackson and published by Dover Publications in 1985 is obviously dated—however, as AI books go, it's relatively inexpensive and remains a useful introduction.

For those already familiar with AI or who have a specific interest in its historical development, *The Quest for Artificial Intelligence* by Nils J. Nilsson, published by Cambridge University Press, 2009 covers the background quite well and often provides technical detail from the perspective of one who was around through most of the first fifty years of AI.

ROBOTICS

The Robotics Primer (Intelligent Robotics and Autonomous Agents series) by Maja J. Mataric, MIT Press, 2007, is both an introduction to robotics and an enthusiastic endorsement of robotics research by one of the leaders in the field.

Although it's beginning to show its age, *Robo Sapiens: Evolution of a New Species* by Peter Menzel and Faith D'Aluisio, MIT Press, 2001, takes a world-wide and general interest view of robotic development. In a similar vein but somewhat newer is *Digital People: From Bionic Humans to Androids* by Sidney Perkowitz, Joseph Henry Press, 2005. It's relatively expensive, but perhaps the most informative book on both AI and robotics is *Robots Unlimited: Life in a Virtual Age* by David Levy, A. K. Peters Ltd., 2005.

A somewhat more technical approach is taken by *An Introduction to AI Robotics* by Robin R. Murphy (also in the Intelligent Robotics and Autonomous Agents series), Bradford Books, 2000.

There are many subcategories of robotics, for example, *Autonomous Robots: From Biological Inspiration to Implementation and Control* by George A. Bekey (another book in the Intelligent Robotics and Autonomous Agents series), Bradford Books, 2005.

For coverage of the history of robotics (but not recent work) there is *The Robot: The Life Story of a Technology* by Lisa Nocks, Johns Hopkins University Press, 2008.

THE WIDER CONTEXT

The seminal book on AI and other technology prognostication is Ray Kurzweil's *The Singularity is Near: When Humans Transcend Biology*, Penguin, 2006. The 600 pages are an encyclopedic argument for the transformation of humanity through technology. An early book by Kurzweil, *The Age of Intelligent Machines*, MIT Press, 1992, is obviously dated but makes an interesting comparison of AI then and AI now.

From a more skeptical or critical view of technological progress, try: *You are Not a Gadget: A Manifesto*, Vintage, 2011, by Jaron Lanier, one of the developers of virtual reality.

Although it sounds like a book heavy on the neuroscience, *How the Mind Works* by Steven Pinker (W.W. Norton and Co. Inc., 1997) is more of a very long essay on the psychology of social evolution and interaction. Similarly Pinker's *The Blank Slate: The Modern Denial of Human Nature* (Penguin, 2003) provides an overview of the way philosophy, neuroscience and evolutionary development look at 'human nature' and the blank slate fallacy. Both books provide a useful background to the issues involved in understanding what artificial intelligence must either overcome or imitate.

Although practically superannuated (1979) the classic book on human intelligence and creativity, *Gödel, Escher, Bach: An Eternal Golden Braid* by Douglas Hofstadter, Basic Books—20th anniversary edition, 1999, remains insightful and thought-provoking, well into the age of artificial intelligence.

SECTION 1: ARE YOU READY TO FALL IN LOVE WITH A MACHINE?

Exploring the relationship between people and their computers, a prequel, if you will, to the relationship with AI, is explored in *The Man Who Lied to His Laptop: What Machines Teach Us About Human Relationships* by Clifford Nass and Corina Yen. A somewhat deeper and more general look is found in Sherry Turkle's *Alone Together: Why We Expect More from Technology and Less from Each Other*, Basic Books, 2011. Turkle is one of the leaders of human-machine interaction research and is a lively writer to boot.

1.2   You may already be dating a robot

There aren't many books specifically about the idea of dating and romancing sentient artificial intelligence, which is why this guide book was written, but there are quite a few books and articles about similar subjects with robots (whether intelligent or not). One of the best and most contemporary is *Love + Sex with Robots: The Evolution of Human-Robot Relationships* by David Levy, Harper Perennial, 2008, which covers the history and nature of our human sexual relationship with mechanical things and eventually robotics.

1.3   Are you happy with other humans?

For the more philosophical or religiously minded, an aspect of robotics as covered by one of its leading practitioners, Rodney Brooks (MIT Labs) is *Flesh and Machines: How Robots Will Change Us*, Vintage Books, 2003. It's part history, part in-the-lab experience and part prognostication. *Metaman: The Merging of Humans and Machines into a Global Superorganism* by Gregory Stock, Simon and Schuster, 1993, is a vintage look at man evolving through technology into something 'better.'

1.4   Video games: scratching the surface of the true beauty of virtual reality

The importance of the virtual world, long a subject of science fiction, is penetrating non-fiction. One of the best of this kind is *Infinite Reality: Avatars, Eternal Life, New Worlds, and the Dawn of the Virtual Revolution* by Jim Blascovich and Jeremy Bailenson, William Morrow, 2011. Another interesting take is *How to Do Things with Videogames* by Ian Bogost, University of Minnesota Press, 2011. Bogost is both a scholar and award-winning designer of games and he is boundless in his vision of what video games can do for humanity.

Almost all of the materials combining video games and AI are technical in nature, essentially aimed at game developers and programmers. Arguably the best of the bunch is *AI Techniques for Game Programming* by Mat Buckland, Course Technology PTR, 2002.

1.5   Understanding the difference between pets and robots

There are many chapters of books and individual articles on pets and robots, but as a full book, *Biologically Inspired Intelligent Robots* by Yoseph Bar-Cohen and Cynthia L. Breazeal,

SPIE Publications, 2003, set the stage for much of contemporary research into animal-influenced robotics.

1.7 Gender differences and gender discrimination

For those interested in gender issues, there's a very general but thought-provoking collection of essays in *Gender and Technology: A Reader*, Nina Lerman, Ruth Oldenziel, and Arwen P. Mohun (Editors), Johns Hopkins University Press, 2003.

SECTION 2: YOU ARE READY, NOW WHAT?

2.1 Preparing yourself for the unexpected

Confronting AI in any format and in any kind of relationship almost presumes the unexpected. An interesting study of the effect with androids is *The thing that should not be: predictive coding and the uncanny valley in perceiving human and humanoid robot actions*, Ayse Pinar Saygin, Thierry Chaminade, Hiroshi Ishiguro, Jon Driver and Chris Frith, published in *Social Cognitive and Affective Neuroscience*, Oxford University Press, April 22, 2011.

2.2 Get to know yourself and become a better person

For the negative side of human enhancement, *The Perils of Cognitive Enhancement and the Urgent Imperative to Enhance the Moral Character of Humanity*, by Ingmar Persson and Julian Savulescu, Oxford: bep.ox.ac.uk.

2.4 Some strategies for developing an agile mind: meditation, creativity, innovative thinking and BCI training

Meditation is an ancient, multifaceted, highly personal and often religious subject, which simply means that reading and instructional material is only part of the picture. Many, if not most people, prefer classes and/or guided sessions. There is a massively wide spectrum of books from *Meditation for Dummies* by Stephan Bodian, For Dummies Publications, 2010, to *Stages of Meditation* by The Dalai Lama, Snow Lion Publications, 2003, to a neurological point of view in *Zen and the Brain: Toward an Understanding of Meditation and Consciousness* by James H. Austin, MIT Press, 1999.

In the realm of creativity and innovation the library of self-help books is vast and of somewhat uneven value. Most businesspeople are familiar with various approaches that are often part of standard training. In a more scientific vein, you might try *Explaining Creativity: The Science of Human Innovation*, R. Keith Sawyer, Oxford University Press, 2006, or the even more scholarly *The Cambridge Handbook of Creativity*, Cambridge Handbooks in Psychology, Cambridge University Press, 2010, which is a compendium of studies about creativity.

Brain Computer Interface (BCI) material is readily available. Obvious online sources are www.braincomputerinterface.com and www.bcimedical.com. Almost all the books available on BCI are for developers and engineers. A book with a general overview is *Brain-Computer Interface: High-impact Emerging Technology—What You Need to Know: Definitions, Adoptions, Impact, Benefits, Maturity, Vendors*, by Kevin Roebuck, Tebbo, 2011.

SECTION 3: ESTABLISHING A RELATIONSHIP

This section of the book is mostly from the perspective of sentient AI—successful artificial intelligence. To understand, a bit, about where research is working on the general notion of intelligence, there are some pretty good resources without getting into the depths of neuroscience and philosophy. One such resource is *How Intelligence Happens* by the well-known neuroscientist John Duncan (Yale University Press, 2012), which outlines mostly for beginners how the brain equals the mind and where current research is teasing out the details.

A good overview of current robotic, AI and other technology research with a high degree of readability is Joel Garreau's *Radical Evolution: The Promise and Peril of Enhancing Our Minds, Our Bodies and What It Means to Be Human*, published by Broadway, 2006. The tone is a bit breathless, but there's plenty of fact as well. More focused on robots and AI, science-fiction guru Gregory Benford's *Beyond Human: Living with Robots and Cyborgs*, Forge Books, 2008, takes a well-balanced look at the coming changes in people and society as a result of new technologies.

3.1 Understanding your future partner

Understandably, in a book about dating and romantic relationships, emotions and AI is a key topic. There is quite a lot of literature on the subject, although it remains one of the most problematic for research.

An historical look at emotion in AI is *Affect and Artificial Intelligence* by Elizabeth A. Wilson, University of Washington Press, 2010, which traces the thinking of researchers from the 1940s to the 1990s on the need for and creation of emotion in artificial intelligence.

A more contemporary and thought-provoking book on AI and emotion is Marvin Minsky's (now) classic *The Emotion Machine: Commonsense Thinking, Artificial Intelligence, and the Future of the Human Mind*, published by Simon and Schuster, 2007. The approach seems simplistic, although it is anything but.

The Emotional Brain: The Mysterious Underpinnings of Emotional Life by Jose LeDoux does a good job of explaining current knowledge of how the brain processes emotions and what role this (may) play in intelligence, and not just human intelligence at that.

Obviously related to emotions, but arguably more 'refined' and problematic is the subject of empathy. A good book on the most recent research is Frans de Waal's *The Age of Empathy: Nature's Lessons for a Kinder Society*.

3.3 What will AI need and expect from you?

Much of this chapter, indeed this section, looks at the broader issue of intelligence—what is it and what would it look like? Since the human understanding of intelligence is still very much a work in progress, there are a number of sources that represent points of view and/or current research. For example, Jeff Hawkins' book *On Intelligence* published in 2005 by St. Martin's Griffin is by someone who developed the Palm Pilot but who also has an abiding interest in human intelligence, artificial or otherwise. This book is his testament and a good summary of a point of view about the nature of intelligence. In a much more transhuman vein, *Robot: Mere Machine to Transcendent Mind* by Hans Moravec, Oxford University Press, 2000, explores the development of sentient AI up to and through the Singularity. A directory of over 7,000 papers on consciousness is located at consc.net/online.

For a dose of why consciousness is such a difficult subject, try *Perplexities of Consciousness* by Eric Schwitzgebel, Bradford Books, 2011.

The role of global AI, the superintelligence, is covered in this chapter and in a book with a very expansive view of superintelligence that was mentioned earlier, *Metaman: The Merging of Humans and Machines into a Global Superorganism* by Gregory Stock, Simon and Schuster, 1993.

The role of emotion in AI, not to mention in human-AI relationships, is central to this book. There are numerous studies (books already mentioned above); for example, *The Relationship Between Emotion Models and Artificial Intelligence*, Bartneck, Lyons and Saerbeck, 2008, found at www.bartneck.de, provides some of the modeling ideas used here. Also, *A General Theory of Emotion in Humans and Other Intelligences* by AI and Singularity researcher Ben Goertzel, at www.goertzel.com.

In all matters of technology and especially AI approaching sentience, the Singularity Institute for Artificial Intelligence, Inc., www.singinst.org, provides a wealth of resources, for example: *Creating Friendly AI 1.0: The Analysis and Design of Benevolent Goal Architectures*, written by Eliezer Yudkowsky, 2001.

3.5 Stepping onto a path of continuous improvement and growing together

The combination of AI intelligence, the experience of a human-AI relationship and the search for wisdom has some referents such as the prolific Robert J. Sternberg's somewhat iconoclastic educational views in *Wisdom, Intelligence, and Creativity Synthesized*, Cambridge University Press, 2007.

3.6 Who is in control of whom?

When it comes to the dangers of AI and possible control, J. Storrs Hall has written *Beyond AI: Creating the Conscience of the Machine*, published by Prometheus Books, 2007. It's an overview of artificial intelligence, good background material, which also raises the inherent questions about the possible consequences of achieving sentient AI. Even more specifically aimed at the behavior of robotic AI, *Moral Machines: Teaching Robots Right from Wrong* by Wendell Wallach and Colin Allen explores the nascent field of robotic ethics. Nick Bostrom, one of the more pensive AI researchers (Oxford, UK), provides a thought provoking essay, *Ethical Issues in Advanced Artificial Intelligence* at his site, www.nickbostrom.com.

The classic and still popular *I, Robot* by Isaac Asimov, Spectra, 2008 is fiction by one of the founders of scientific (hard) science fiction. This book contains and adumbrates Asimov's Three Laws of Robotics.

3.7 Competing with other intelligence

There are many books on the cybernetic human (part human, part machine), and one of the more comprehensive (though at times a tough read) is N. Katherine Hayles' *How We Became Posthuman: Virtual Bodies in Cybernetics, Literature, and Informatics*, University of Chicago Press, 1999. A position diametrically opposed to posthumanity is the near classic by Francis Fukuyama, *Our Posthuman Future: Consequences of the Biotechnology Revolution*, Picador, 2003.

The literature on animal intelligence has recently begun to expand exponentially, mostly in response to new research but also the growing interest in the depth and nature of animal intelligence that humans heretofore ignored. A generalized and popularized account is Sally Boysen's *The Smartest Animals on the Planet: Extraordinary Tales of the Natural World's Cleverest Creatures*, Firefly Books, 2009. Species-specific books abound; *Next of Kin: My Conversations with Chimpanzees* by Roger Fouts, William Morrow Paperbacks, 1998, is one of the most approachable and enlightening books not only on chimp intelligence but on the human discovery of the true meaning of general intelligence. Another personal revelation type of book, *Alex and Me: How a Scientist and a Parrot Discovered a Hidden World of Animal Intelligence and Formed a Deep Bond in the Process* by Irene Pepperberg, Harper Perennial, 2009 explores a unique relationship with an African gray parrot and its amazing subtlety of mind. For the corvid (crow) family, Bernd Heinrich's *Mind of the Raven: Investigations and Adventures with Wolf Birds*, Harper Perennial, 2007 is highly readable. For the cetaceans, there are many new examples. A good emotional read is *Dolphin Chronicles* by Carol J. Howard, Bantam, 1995. More scientific in purpose is *Dolphin Mysteries: Unlocking the Secrets of Communication*, by Kathleen Dudzinski and Toni Frohoff, Yale University Press, 2010. *The Amboseli Elephants: A Long-Term Perspective on a Long-Lived Mammal* by Cynthia J. Moss, Harvey Croze, and Phyllis C. Lee (Editors), University of Chicago Press, 2011 summarizes 18 years of elephant research in Kenya's Amboseli National Park and includes a section on elephant intelligence research. Finally, *Octopus: The Ocean's Intelligent Invertebrate* by Jennifer Mather, Roland C. Anderson and James B. Wood, Timber Press, 2010 covers the cephalopod entry into the world of animal intelligence.

A more general look at animal emotional intelligence is Marc Beckhoff's *The Emotional Lives of Animals: A Leading Scientist Explores Animal Joy, Sorrow and Empathy and Why They Matter,* New World Library, 2008.

With increasing knowledge of animal intelligence has come an attempt to fit animals back into the mainstream of human philosophy. Writers such as Jacques Derrida and Giorgio Agamben are specialists in the area; a more approachable overview *is Zoographies: The Question of the Animal from Heidegger to Derrida,* by Matthew Calarco, Columbia University Press, 2008.

Journal and magazine coverage of animal intelligence is also extensive. I won't include much of it here because simple online searches will reveal most of it. "Inside the Mind of the Octopus," by Sy Montgomery, Orion Magazine, Nov./Dec., 2011. "Leadership in Elephants: The Adaptive Value of Age," Proceedings of the Royal Society, Biological Sciences, 278(1722), 3270-3276, 2011.

3.9 Virtual pre-nup: agreeing on the terms and conditions

Projection of an AI into the world of law, politics and power is not uncommon for science fiction. A more non-fictional approach can be found in *Citizen Cyborg: Why Democratic Societies Must Respond to the Redesigned Human of the Future* by James Hughes, published by Basic Books, 2004.